COLLECTED WORKS OF ERASMUS

VOLUME 1

THE CORRESPONDENCE OF
ERASMUS

LETTERS 1 TO 141

1484 TO 1500

translated by R.A.B. Mynors and D.F.S. Thomson

annotated by Wallace K. Ferguson

University of Toronto Press

The research costs of the Collected Works of Erasmus
have been underwritten by a Killam Senior Research Scholarship
awarded by the Killam Program of the Canada Council.

© University of Toronto Press 1974
Toronto and Buffalo
Printed in Canada
ISBN cloth 0-8020-1981-1
ISBN paper 0-8020-6190-7
LC 72-97422

The Collected Works of Erasmus

The aim of the Collected Works of Erasmus
is to make available an accurate, readable English text
of Erasmus' correspondence and his
other principal writings. The edition is planned
and directed by an Editorial Board, an Executive Committee,
and an Advisory Committee.

Contents

Illustrations

Introduction

The correspondence of Erasmus constitutes a source of inestimable value, not only for the biography of the great humanist himself, but also for the intellectual and religious history of the northern Renaissance and the Reformation. Myron Gilmore has recently called it 'perhaps the greatest single source for the intellectual history of [Erasmus'] age.'[1] And Froude, in the preface to his *Life and Letters of Erasmus*, wrote with his customary enthusiasm: 'The best description of the state of Europe in the age immediately preceding the Reformation will be found in the correspondence of Erasmus himself. I can promise my own readers [he added] that if they will accept Erasmus as their guide in that tangled period, they will not wander far out of the way.'[2]

The volume of the correspondence is enormous,[3] and its cumulative effect fully justifies the claims that have been made for it. The letters are, however, very unevenly distributed throughout their author's mature life. Although Erasmus was an indefatigable letter-writer from his youth on, only about fifteen per cent of his surviving letters were written before the summer of 1514, at which time he was at least forty-five and possibly two or three years older. And of the letters addressed to him before that date those that remain form an even smaller proportion of the extant total. That even so many have survived is largely due to their having been included in manuscript collections from which they were eventually published.

So, until Erasmus was well into middle age, or according to sixteenth-

* * * * *

1 M.P. Gilmore *Humanists and Jurists* (Cambridge, Mass. 1963) 137

2 J.A. Froude *Life and Letters of Erasmus* (London 1894)

3 There are more than three thousand letters, of which some sixteen hundred were written by Erasmus, the remainder by a representative cross-section of educated European society.

century standards well beyond it, his correspondence presents a fragmentary and frequently exasperating source from which to reconstruct his career. The letters of this earlier period are nevertheless of exceptional value to his biographers. Not only are they the sole source for much of his life but, because of the preponderance of familiar letters filled with personal gossip, they cast a particularly revealing light on Erasmus' personality and character. It is this fact which gives to the first volume of Allen's edition of the *Epistolae*,[4] that containing the letters written before August 1514, its special character, and compensates for its relatively minor contribution to the intellectual history of the age. It is indeed so rich in biographical detail that, ungrateful though it may seem, one can only wish that Erasmus had saved more of his letters, that the exchange with his friends was less one-sided, and that there were not so many maddening gaps in the chronological sequence.

There are a surprisingly large number of letters surviving from the period of Erasmus' residence in the monastery at Steyn. By contrast, not much remains of his first two years in Paris, but the years 1497–1501, which include the greater part of his residence in Paris and his first visit to England, are once more fairly well filled. The next four years, however, are but sparsely represented, although this was an important period in the humanist's life when as a mature man he acquired the mastery of Greek which was so essential to his life's work. It is still more unfortunate that so little remains in the correspondence from his visit to Italy in 1506–9, a visit that we know from other sources left an indelible impression on the scholarly and peace-loving Dutch canon. There are only three of his letters extant for each of the years 1507 and 1508, and none at all for 1509. Not only the last six months of his stay in Italy, but also the first two years of his residence in England are, in fact, so far as the correspondence is concerned, a complete blank. From December 1508 to April 1511 not a single one of Erasmus' letters has survived.[5] After this hiatus the correspondence for the

* * * * *

4 P.S. Allen, H.M. Allen, and H.W. Garrod *Opus epistolarum Des. Erasmi Roterodami* 11 vols (Oxford 1906–47) plus index volume (Oxford 1958). Since Allen's numbering of the letters has been adopted in the present edition, letters are generally cited by Epistle number only, except where there is a reference to line numbers in letters not yet published in the Collected Works of Erasmus, in which case the reference will read Allen, plus Epistle and line number.

5 Cf J.K. Sowards 'The Two Lost Years of Erasmus' *Studies in the Renaissance* 9 (1962) 161–86.

remaining years of his sojourn in England is fairly constant, though still rather one-sided, most of it addressed to a small circle of friends and patrons in England and more often than not concerned with the trivia of daily life.

The return of Erasmus to the continent in the summer of 1514 seems to mark a definite change in the character of the correspondence, a change which reflects the beginning of a new phase in the career of Erasmus himself. After the years of study in the Netherlands and Italy and the quiet but productive years of labour in Cambridge and London, he was about to take his place as a dominant figure on the international scene. His reputation was already established by the publication of the *Enchiridion*, the *De copia*, his translations from Greek authors and, above all, by the *Adagia* and the *Praise of Folly*. He also had with him the manuscripts of the Greek New Testament with notes and a new translation and his great edition of the correspondence of St Jerome, as well as a number of other works, which would soon be published by Froben in Basel and would add still further to his reputation. His journey up the Rhine to Basel became a triumphal procession, and he was greeted everywhere by scholars who had read and admired his work. At the end of the trip he wrote to his English patron, Lord Mountjoy: 'Germany has received me with such honour that I am almost embarrassed.'[6] The enthusiasm of his reception seems, indeed, to have been a revelation to him. Living for the past five years in the quiet backwater of Cambridge and among his little circle of friends in London, he seems scarcely to have realized how famous he had become. The extent to which Erasmus now established contact with the broader world of serious European and especially German scholarship is reflected in the Deventer Letter-book, in which he had his servant pupils copy out letters in the years 1517–18.[7] This collection, which remained unpublished until its inclusion in the Leiden *Opera omnia*,[8] is of particular interest because of the unprecedented quantity of letters addressed to Erasmus, 168 in all, most of them written between the summer of 1514 and that of 1517. Some of them are from old and new friends in the Netherlands, France, and England, but a surprisingly large proportion are from new German and Swiss correspon-

* * * * *

6 Allen Ep 301:45

7 On the Deventer Letter-book of 1517–18, see Allen I 603–9.

8 J. Leclerc (ed) *Erasmi opera omnia* 10 vols (Leiden 1703–6), commonly cited as LB. The correspondence (LB III in 2 vols) contains 1,816 letters as against the 3,141 in Allen, many of the latter having come to light in manuscript collections scattered across Europe.

dents. Among these are such notable figures as Reuchlin, Ulrich von Hutten, Beatus Rhenanus, Zasius, Capito, Spalatinus, Pirckheimer, Zwingli, Oecolampadius, Froben, and the Amerbach brothers.

From this point on the volume and range of Erasmus' correspondence increase enormously, the letters dated after July 1514 filling ten of the eleven volumes of Allen's edition. The correspondence now includes letters to and from an endless assortment of scholars, printers, men of letters, school teachers, theologians, and religious leaders, not to mention princes and prelates, from every country in western Europe. The range and variety of subject matter treated in the letters are also greatly expanded. Alongside the running comment on personal affairs which still continues, the letters to a far greater degree than hitherto contain illuminating comments, sometimes developed into full-scale essays on classical, biblical, and patristic scholarship, on contemporary literary criticism, on the reform of education and theology through a combination of *bonae litterae* and the *philosophia Christi*, on the horrors of war, and on all the problems raised by the Lutheran Reformation. At a time when there were no learned journals in which scholars could have their articles published, letters, whether intended to be printed or merely to be circulated in manuscript, served much the same purpose. It was to a large extent through his correspondence with scholars, many of whom he had never met, that Erasmus gave unity and a common purpose to the movement of Christian humanism in the years before the decisive emergence of Martin Luther.

The years between 1514 and 1518 or 1519 mark the period of Erasmus' intellectual ascendance as the acknowledged prince of humanists and leader of all who hoped for a liberal reform of the church, theology, and popular piety. The correspondence constitutes our most revealing source for his activity during these hopeful years, as it does also for the troubled period that followed. No other body of material enables us to trace so clearly, step by step, the unfolding of Erasmus' reform program, his controversies with the conservative theologians following the publication of the Greek New Testament, and finally the gradual changes in his attitude toward Luther from his early attempts to protect the reformer to the ultimate irreparable breach. All of Erasmus' biographers have made use of the correspondence, but its riches could not be fully exploited until Allen's masterly edition made it available in convenient form, corrected many errors in chronology, elucidated obscure points, and added more than 1300 letters not included in the standard Leiden edition. Augustin Renaudet[9] was one

* * * * *

9 A. Renaudet *Erasme: sa pensée religieuse et son action d'après sa correspondance (1518–1521)* (Paris 1926) and *Etudes Erasmiennes (1521–1529)* (Paris 1939)

of the first to make full use of Allen's volumes as they appeared for the analysis of Erasmus' religious thought as it developed from 1518 to 1529, but every later study of this crucial period has been similarly enriched.

The last years of Erasmus' life, the years of voluntary exile in the little town of Freiburg in Breisgau, have been ignored unduly by almost all of his biographers. As Myron Gilmore has pointed out, 'they have concentrated on the earlier period when the "important" work was done and they pass over the years in which they consider that Erasmus was left behind by the stormy course of events and became a pathetic, hypochondriac, querulous old man.'[10] A careful examination of the correspondence of this period, especially the confidential letters exchanged between Erasmus and his trusted friend Bonifacius Amerbach,[11] will demonstrate the injustice of this attitude. Erasmus may no longer have occupied the centre of the European stage as he once did, but the volume of his correspondence did not fall off. It fills the last four volumes of Allen's edition. In 1529 Erasmus wrote that more than half his time was devoted to reading and writing letters.[12] He was still the foremost scholar of Europe, and many men whom he had never met, as well as his old friends, were eager to exchange letters with him. Erasmus answered as many as he could, though crippling arthritis forced him more and more to resort to dictating to his secretaries. Through these letters we can trace his untiring scholarly activity and the controversies that still plagued him, including a new one precipitated by the *Ciceronianus*. Above all, it was in the letters of these years that Erasmus defined most clearly his position in relation to both the old church, which for all its faults still claimed his allegiance, and the newer churches and sects with which he had now decisively broken.[13] In them and in the treatises written during the same years we can see stated once more the conception of religion as a matter of the spirit rather than of the letter which he had adumbrated in the *Enchiridion* in 1501 and had held to firmly through all the shifting climate of religious opinion in the intervening years.[14]

* * * * *

10 Gilmore *Humanists and Jurists* 117

11 See also A. Hartmann (ed) *Die Amerbachkorrespondenz* 5 vols (Basel 1943–8).

12 Allen Ep 1985:2–3

13 See especially K.H. Ulrich *Der späte Erasmus und die Reformation* (Münster 1961) and K. Schätti *Erasmus von Rotterdam und die Römische Kurie* (Basel and Stuttgart 1954).

14 On the consistency of Erasmus' religious thought throughout his life see M.M. Phillips *Erasmus and the Northern Renaissance* (London 1949) and R.H. Bainton 'The Continuity of Thought of Erasmus' in *American Council of Learned Societies Newsletter* XIX 5 (May 1968).

Erasmus always regarded his letters, of whatever kind, as a form of literature, and they were valued by his contemporaries for their style as much as for their content. Even today they possess for the student of Renaissance Latin literature an interest over and above their value as historical sources. The treatise *De conscribendis epistolis*, the first draft of which dates from his early days as a tutor in Paris,[15] demonstrates his concern with the problem of adjusting the style to fit the purpose, content, and recipient of each letter. The formal or stylistic aspect of his letters is not my concern in this introduction. Certain categories of his letters, however, are of such historical and biographical interest that they call for special attention here.

One such category is that composed of dedicatory prefaces cast, as was customary, in the mould of epistles addressed to the author's patrons. Taken together, these prefaces constitute one of our most valuable sources for the history of literary patronage during the century after the invention of printing had added a new dimension to the value of a dedication by giving it a far wider circulation than a manuscript could ever achieve. A sixteenth-century author might be given some compensation by the printer or publisher to whom he submitted his manuscript, but he could not hope to receive very much. No copyright law gave either author or publisher an exclusive interest in his work, and any book that gave promise of being sold profitably was usually reprinted again and again by other printers who had paid nothing for the privilege.[16] A writer who possessed neither inherited means nor lucrative benefices was therefore almost entirely dependent on patronage. This was an economic fact of which Erasmus was keenly aware, and since the dedication of a book was one of the recognized ways of attracting the attention of potential patrons or of expressing gratitude for past favours, he gave considerable thought to the choice of recipients. That his choice was influenced by the hope of securing a financial return seems more frequently the case in the years before he had achieved a reasonable degree of security. By that time, however, he had acquired many enemies in the ranks of the conservative theologians, and felt the need to have his works appear under the patronage of the highest authorities in church and state. The dedication of the New Testament to Leo x,[17] of the Paraphrases on the four Gospels to the four monarchs, Charles, Ferdinand, Henry, and Francis respectively,[18] of the Paraphrases on the Acts of the Apostles to

* * * * *

15 Cf Ep 71 introduction.

16 Cf P.S. Allen *Erasmus: Lectures and Wayfaring Sketches* (Oxford 1934) 133 ff.

17 Ep 384

18 Epp 1255, 1400, 1381, 1333

Clement VII,[19] and of those on the Epistles to various cardinals and other influential members of the hierarchy[20] was certainly motivated more by his desire to have these works appear under the most distinguished auspices than by the hope of a direct financial return.[21] At any rate, we have Erasmus' word for it that he never received a ducat from Leo x for the dedication of the New Testament, nor did the dedications of the Paraphrases bring him anything except the gift of 200 florins from Clement VII and 100 florins from Ferdinand.[22]

For books which, like his early educational treatises or translations from the Greek, needed no protection, Erasmus' dedications had a more business-like character. They were mostly either repayment for past favours or were frankly designed to elicit a gift in return. By attaching a patron's name to a book which in printed form would circulate widely, Erasmus felt that he was offering a substantial *quid* for a rather speculative *quo*.[23] The story, so often retold, of Erasmus' first meeting with Archbishop Warham to present to him his translation of Euripides' *Hecuba* and of Grocyn's comment that the reason the archbishop had given so small a gift in return was that he suspected it had already been dedicated to someone else[24] casts an interesting light on the ethics of dedication that were current at the time. If this was, as Grocyn hinted, a common practice, Erasmus at least cleared himself by dedicating not one but two translations to Warham in the printed edition of Euripides.[25]

* * * * *

19 Ep 1414

20 Epp 710, 916, 1043, 1062, 1112, 1171, 1179, 1181

21 The same motive probably accounted for other dedications when Erasmus felt the need for support from powerful patrons. See, for example, the dedication of the *Apologia adversus Sutorem* (Ep 1591) to Jean de Selva, sieur de Cormières in July 1525 when Erasmus was engaged in conflict with the Sorbonne.

22 Cf Allen I 42 ff.

23 It would be interesting to know what Erasmus actually received for his dedications, but the evidence in the correspondence is scattered and inconclusive. The article by Jean Hoyoux 'Les moyens d'existence d'Erasme' *Bibliothèque d'Humanisme et Renaissance* 5 (1944) 7–59, which attempts to deal with the problem, is so filled with errors and misunderstandings as to be quite useless.

24 Cf Allen 14–5; F.M. Nichols trans *The Epistles of Erasmus* (London 1901–18) I 393–4. H.W. Garrod's suggestion (*The Library* 5th series, 4, 1 [June 1949] 2) that in fact Erasmus had given both translations – or a first draft of them – to a patron of less importance seems to have slight foundation or is at least misleading. Cf Allen Ep 158:6n.

25 Epp 188, 198, 208

Despite his indignation at Grocyn's taunt, however, there is some evidence that in his early days Erasmus did not always feel that the dedication of a work in a manuscript first draft need prevent him from offering it to someone else when it had been reworked and expanded or from changing the dedication when it was finally published many years later.[26] Although his choice of recipients for his works may seem somewhat calculating to the modern scholar who can afford the luxury of dedicating his books to his wife, it was by no means invariably determined by considerations of patronage. Many of his books, indeed, were dedicated to friends of modest means who could offer no more than their friendship and occasional hospitality or personal services. Among his friends to be so honoured were Thomas More, not yet an officer of the crown, Beatus Rhenanus, and Pieter Gillis.[27] The dedication of edition after edition of the *Colloquia* to his godson, Johannes Erasmius Froben,[28] was a gesture of friendship to the family of the great Basel printer with whom Erasmus was closely associated for many years. And there could certainly be no other motive than friendship for his dedication in the last year of his life of the *De puritate ecclesiae* to Christoph Eschenfelder, the scholarly customs officer of Boppard on the Rhine, who had entertained him at dinner in 1518 and with whom he had continued to correspond at intervals in the intervening years.[29]

Important as the dedications are as evidence of Erasmus' relations with friends and patrons, many of them are still more noteworthy for their scholarly content, being in fact prefaces designed to introduce the accompanying work, to indicate its significance, or to justify the author's methods and point of view, very much as the prefaces of scholarly works do today. Some of them are developed into quite extensive critical essays. Such, for example, are the dedication of the *Hieronymi opera* to Archbishop Warham[30] and the dedication of Erasmus' edition of Valla's *Notes on the New Testament* to Christopher Fisher.[31] In addition there are some forty-three prefaces of this kind addressed simply 'To the Reader.'

Another category of letters, though not always so clearly distinguishable, consists of those that might be classed as *apologiae*. As Erasmus

* * * * *

26 Cf Epp 66, 71, 260 introductions.
27 Cf Epp 222, 312, 327.
28 Epp 1262, 1476
29 Ep 3086; cf Allen Epp 867:46–55 and 879 introduction.
30 Ep 396
31 Ep 182

became more famous he acquired along with a host of friends and admirers a growing number of enemies and critics. The *Praise of Folly* seems to have charmed most readers, including Leo x,[32] but many monks and conservative theologians were not amused. The *epistola apologetica* of May 1515 in which he replied to Martin van Dorp's criticism of the *Moria*[33] was but the first of many such defences. More serious and requiring more extensive replies were the criticisms called forth by Erasmus' publication of the Greek New Testament with notes and a new Latin translation in 1516. Of all his works none seems to have so enraged the conservative theologians, and their fury was further aggravated by the greatly expanded essay on the proper method of studying theology included in the second edition of 1519. Feeling their position threatened by the humanist's assertion that a knowledge of the languages in which the scriptures were originally written was an absolute prerequisite of the study of theology, theologians who had small Greek and less Hebrew closed their ranks in battle array against the champion of the new learning. And their attacks became increasingly virulent as they began to perceive a possible connection between the teaching and example of Erasmus and the heresies of Martin Luther. Always sensitive to criticism, Erasmus replied to his assailants in a series of *apologiae* or *defensiones*, the longer of which, even when cast in the form of a letter, are not included in the canon of the correspondence. They fill, together with replies to his Protestant critics, most of the last three volumes of the Leiden edition of the *Opera omnia*.[34] There are, however, a number of letters in the correspondence that could be included in the same classification, and comments on the controversies in which he was involved as well as appeals for support are a recurrent theme in Erasmus' letters from 1515 till the end of his life. His quick response to every criticism was inspired in part no doubt by personal pique and scholarly *amour propre*. There is certainly evidence of hurt feelings in his reply to Ulrich von Hutten's charge that he had deserted Luther through cowardice and indecision.[35] But to a far greater degree it was his conviction of the fundamental importance of his work that

* * * * *

32 Cf Ep 739.

33 Ep 337

34 LB IX and x. Erasmus' apologetic works have received less attention than they deserve; but see the recent study by Myron Gilmore: '*De modis disputandi*: the Apologetic Works of Erasmus' in J.G. Rowe and W.H. Stockdale (eds) *Florilegium Historiale* (Toronto 1971) 62–88.

35 See *Spongia adversus aspergines Hutteni* LB x 1631–72.

made him feel he must meet every attack with a rebuttal at length and in detail. Criticisms of the Greek text of the New Testament and of his annotations in particular could not be allowed to stand unanswered without imperilling his whole program for the revitalization of theology and popular piety. If the foundation of his scholarship and orthodoxy were undermined, he felt that the whole edifice of his life work would crumble.

The controversial letters, like the dedicatory prefaces and the scholarly essays that occur throughout the correspondence, are invaluable guides to the understanding of Erasmus' serious aims and achievements. But for clues to his personality and character and for the concrete details that enable us to envisage the circumstances of his daily life we must turn to the familiar letters. And here, as Dryden said of the *Canterbury Tales*, is God's plenty. Erasmus was a man who made, and kept, many friends and to them he wrote freely about his health (usually poor), about his financial straits (frequently acute), about his relations with his patrons (often disappointing), about the conditions of travel (generally deplorable), about the quality of the local wine (of which the less said the better). He wrote freely, too, about his successes and enthusiasms as well as about his moods of discouragement and frustration. Sometimes, indeed, he wrote too freely for the good of his reputation, thus providing his detractors with ammunition that could be used against him. As Allen notes, for many of the charges that have been brought against him 'Erasmus is the chief, indeed practically the only, witness against himself.'[36] He seems, indeed, to have been curiously indifferent to the impression his letters would make, provided it did not affect the success of his work. 'So [to quote Allen again] when his friends asked for more letters to publish, he gave them what he saw would amuse the public; without troubling to think that careful busybodies might lay sentence to sentence and piece up a calumny.'[37]

It has been Erasmus' peculiar misfortune that the opinion of almost all his biographers until recently has been coloured by their judgment of his position in relation to the great religious controversy of his age. Here for once Protestant and Catholic have seen eye to eye. Few could resist the insidious charm of his lighter works; still fewer could deny his brilliance as a scholar; but few could find any explanation for what they felt to be his equivocal position during the crisis of the Reformation other than some fatal defect of character. The Roman Catholic Ludwig von Pastor's dictum on Erasmus: 'a great scholar, but a weak character,'[38] reflects much the same

* * * * *

36 Allen *Erasmus* 22
37 Ibid 23
38 L. von Pastor *History of the Popes* VI (London 1908) 315

disparaging attitude as that of the Scots Presbyterian Lindsay: 'a great scholar, but a petty-minded man.'[39] Given such an initial bias, it is not surprising that the indiscretions contained in the familiar letters have been used to discredit him and to explain away his failure either, on the one hand, to adopt Luther's dogmatic faith which had wrecked the *concordia ecclesiae*, or, on the other, to cease his criticism of those aspects of his own church which still cried aloud for reform.

Erasmus has suffered, too, from a certain lack of historical imagination on the part of many of his biographers who have interpreted his letters in the light of nineteenth- or twentieth-century mores rather than of those of his own time. The *Farrago epistolarum* of 1519, which is the sole source for much of what seems to be to his discredit, was edited with his consent by his good friend Beatus Rhenanus and was published by Froben, the printer who not only was his loyal friend but also had a considerable financial interest in his reputation. Neither seemed to feel that there was anything in the letters that would be considered damaging. Certainly what have been called his 'begging letters' would have aroused no criticism. Patronage was a fact of literary life in the sixteenth century and soliciting it called for no apology. Let the scholar who has never solicited a fellowship or grant-in-aid cast the first stone.

Erasmus himself was somewhat uncertain about the wisdom of publishing his letters. He knew the value accorded by contemporary taste to elegantly written epistles, and from his early youth he made sporadic attempts to collect those which he felt were worth saving. Until he had reached middle age and was already famous, however, he seems to have been rather careless, or at least unsystematic, about preserving copies of his own letters, while he either did not bother to keep most of those written to him or thought them not worth publishing. In 1505 he announced to his old friend Franciscus Theodoricus his intention to publish a volume of epistles, and asked Franciscus to collect any of his letters that could be found, presumably in the neighbourhood of Steyn, especially those which he had written to Cornelis Gerard, Willem Hermans, and Servatius Rogerus.[40] It is apparently to the collection made in answer to this request that we owe the interesting group of letters from Erasmus' years in the monastery. The plan for publication, however, came to nothing, and the collection made by Franciscus remained in manuscript for a century longer.[41] Perhaps Eras-

* * * * *

39 T.M. Lindsay *History of the Reformation* (New York 1906) I 172
40 Cf Ep 186.
41 Cf Allen I 597f.

mus thought them to be less elegant than he had when he was young.

For whatever reason, Erasmus delayed publishing any of his letters, except the dedicatory epistles attached to various printed books, until 1515 when he inserted a much amplified version of four important letters in a miscellaneous volume which Froben had in the press.[42] Then in 1516 and 1517 two small selections from his correspondence were printed by Maartens at Louvain with prefaces by Pieter Gillis in which he took full responsibility for their publication and implied that he was acting without Erasmus' knowledge or consent.[43] This probably meant no more than the conventional modest disclaimer on Erasmus' part, and in fact he admitted to his friend Budé that he had at least connived at the publication.[44] The first major collection, the *Auctarium selectarum aliquot epistolarum Erasmi* (Basel: Froben, August 1518), with sixty-three new letters, was similarly published by his friend, Beatus Rhenanus, with a preface in which he said he had stolen them from Erasmus' library and published them after Erasmus had left Basel.[45] A still larger collection – 333 letters, including almost all those prior to 1514 published during Erasmus' lifetime – appeared from Froben's press in October 1519 under the title *Farrago nova epistolarum Erasmi*. This time there was no preface to maintain the fiction of literary theft, and there is no doubt that Erasmus had agreed to the publication. He evidently added some dates which, except for the more recent ones, were mostly wrong. He did not, however, oversee the printing, nor even the actual selection of the letters, which was left to the discretion of Beatus Rhenanus to whom Erasmus had sent sheaves of rough drafts.[46]

Finally in 1521 appeared the first overtly authorized edition, the *Epistolae ad diversos* (Basel: Froben, 31 August 1521) containing 617 letters, 446 reprinted from previous editions and 171 new. In his preface addressed to Beatus Rhenanus, Erasmus admitted revising the *Farrago* so as to soften some passages that might give offence, and then dwelt at length on his reluctance to publish any of his letters and the reasons why he had finally consented.

> Though as a young man [he wrote] and also at a riper age, I have written a great number of letters, I scarcely wrote any with a view to publi-

* * * * *

42 Epp 333, 334, 335, and 337
43 Reprinted in Allen II app XI, 601f; trans in Nichols I lxxxiv f
44 Allen Ep 531:524–30
45 Reprinted in Allen II app XI, 602f; trans in Nichols I lxxvi
46 Cf Ep 1206 and Allen *Erasmus* 19f.

cation. I practised my style, I beguiled my leisure; I made merry with my acquaintance, I indulged my humour, in fine, did scarcely anything in this way but amuse myself, expecting nothing less than that friends would copy out or preserve such trifling compositions.[47] But he had found manuscript volumes of his letters on sale at booksellers when he was in Rome and later in Germany. These he had burned. Finding this to be futile, for he 'had to do with a hydra,' he was finally forced to permit the publication of some selected and corrected letters, rather than have them appear in mangled form. Even so, he still regretted his decision since the hatred aroused by the conflict between the humanists and the conservative theologians and by the 'Lutheran tragedy' had made it likely that anything he wrote would be misconstrued. In the end he had been forced to give in to Froben's demand for a new edition[48] and, since he could not himself be in Basel, he besought Beatus to watch over the work so that its publication might do as little harm to his name as possible.

It was again his printer's demand for a new edition that persuaded Erasmus in 1529 to revise the letters already published and add more than 400 new ones. This edition, the *Opus epistolarum*, was the largest published during his lifetime, though smaller editions appeared nearly every year until his death. In the preface addressed 'to the Reader,'[49] he once more declared his indifference to his letters and his reluctance to publish them. Erasmus had always found the drudgery of working over old materials distasteful, and had generally left the editing of his letters to someone else. In this edition, however, he at least took the trouble to divide them into books for convenient reference and added an index. He also added a number of dates where they were missing, but he rejected the advice of his friends that he arrange the letters in chronological order. He gave no reason for this decision, but it was probably influenced, as Allen suggests, by a feeling that chronological arrangement was simply not worth the trouble since 'letters were to him elegant literature, not material for history.'[50]

Unfortunately more than half the dates added in the *Opus epistolarum*, like those in the earlier *Farrago*, are demonstrably wrong, and of those writ-

* * * * *

47 Ep 1206; trans in Nichols I lxxvi f
48 The *Farrago* had sold very rapidly. By the following February Erasmus heard from Basel that it was sold out and that a new edition was called for. Cf Allen Ep 1066:83–6.
49 Ep 2203; Nichols I lxxxiii f
50 Allen I 596

ten before 1505 the proportion is still higher. This should not surprise anyone familiar with the letters and other works in which Erasmus furnishes
autobiographical details. His memory for the dates connected with the
events of his life was always extremely unreliable, a fact that has caused his
biographers and editors infinite trouble. He should not, however, be
blamed too severely for this lack of accuracy. Men of his generation were
not so perpetually made conscious of the current *annus domini* as we are
today by seeing it in print wherever we turn. Nor was their memory of
autobiographical data so frequently renewed by the necessity of filling in
the forms demanded by governmental or academic bureaucracy. Erasmus
apparently kept no diary, and until he was in his late forties such letters
as he had preserved were mostly undated and so could not serve as reminders. In his early days, when he was writing from the monastery at Steyn
to friends who lived within walking distance, there had seemed to be no
reason for adding either place or date to his letters. Later, when writing to
his circle of friends in Paris, the Netherlands, or England, he apparently felt
it unnecessary to add, except to the most formal letters such as dedications,
more than place, day, and month, and frequently not even that. Even after
his return to the continent in 1514, when the circle of his correspondents
was greatly expanded, he continued for three or four years to date most of
his letters in this incomplete fashion. That this was common practice at the
time is shown by the number of letters from his correspondents copied into
the Deventer Letter-book which lack any subscription except place, day and
month.[51] Only when he had begun to think seriously of publishing his letters did he begin to date them *anno domini* with any regularity. For letters
written before about 1517 or 1518, then, where a year is appended in the
printed editions it was most probably added from memory by Erasmus or
by his editors, with results more confusing than otherwise.

The arrangement of the letters in chronological order was a necessary
first step toward making them a usable source for Erasmus' biographers.
And, indeed, no satisfactory life of Erasmus could possibly be written until
the chronological confusion in which Erasmus had left them had been to
some degree resolved. This task was first undertaken by Leclerc in the third
volume of his great edition of the *Opera omnia*. Unfortunately he did little
to rectify false dates, but accepted those assigned in previous editions
almost without question. Still, his work was an achievement of great value,
and with it Erasmus' biographers had to be content until the opening years

* * * * *

51 See note 7 above.

of the present century. The groundwork for a more satisfactory chronology was laid by F.M. Nichols in his *Epistles of Erasmus*, the first two volumes of which, published in 1901 and 1904, included besides translations and much critical commentary a chronological register of the letters from the beginning through 1517.[52] This was the period of the greatest confusion, for after that time Erasmus dated his letters with a fair degree of consistency. Then in 1906 came the first volume of Allen's masterly edition of the *Opus epistolarum* with others following at intervals until the editor's death in 1933, after which the remaining three volumes of the series were completed by his wife and Professor H.W. Garrod. Since its appearance the Allen edition has been universally accepted as the authoritative canon of Erasmus' correspondence.

W K F

* * * * *

52 A third volume, begun when Nichols was nearing eighty, carried the correspondence on to the end of 1518. It was published posthumously in 1918.

Editors' Note

It is obvious that without the foundation of Allen's edition the present translation would have been impossible. The translators and editors of the Collected Works of Erasmus hereby express their indebtedness to this remarkable and authoritative work. They have adopted Allen's ordering and numbering of the letters except in those rare instances where letters overlooked by Allen have been found since, and these have been included by the addition of a letter (eg 65A), without changing the general numerical pattern.[1] When, as is almost invariably the case, the editors have adopted Allen's dating of the letters, they have not felt it necessary to repeat his argument for his ascription of dates.[2] With the generous concurrence of the Clarendon Press, the editors have also made free use of the information contained in his introductions and notes to the letters, knowing that he of all men would have been pleased to have the results of his research used by other scholars. But while depending heavily on Allen, they have not simply copied. In many instances they have omitted detailed information that they felt to be superfluous for their readers; in others they have added information unavailable to Allen or explanatory notes on points which Allen, writing for another generation, took for granted. They have felt it unnecessary to repeat Allen's detailed bibliographical references, many of them now obsolete or referring to books not easily available, while at the same time they have added references to works published since the appearance

* * * * *

1 The four letters with biographical information situated by Allen at the beginning of volume 1 will be inserted in appropriate chronological order.
2 The date given at the head of each letter is that which is accepted by the editors. It may or may not agree with the date given in the text of the letter, but that date has been included in the translation to maintain consistency in the general policy of including everything of the texts in Allen.

of Allen's volumes where these seemed to be sufficiently important or to bear directly on a point at issue.

The editors' primary aim has been to provide in the introductions to the individual letters and in the notes on the text the information needed to make each letter intelligible and to place it in its proper context, to identify the persons and events mentioned in it, to note the sources of classical, biblical, or patristic quotations and, finally, through a system of cross-references to guide the reader to other relevant places in the correspondence. The notes dealing with technical problems of coinage and moneys of account are provided in this volume by John H. Munro. Biographical notes on correspondents are found in the introduction to the first letter each wrote or received. Biographical notes on people mentioned only in the letters are included in a footnote to the first place in the text where each name occurs. These biographical sketches attempt to do no more than identify the person and tell enough about him to make his place in the correspondence intelligible. Fuller biographical accounts will be reserved for the Biographical Register which is in active preparation.

In assessing the amount of information which should be supplied in introductions or footnotes, the editors bear in mind the assumption that many of their readers will not be Erasmian specialists, but will be scholars with a general interest in the sixteenth century or those who have a particular interest in one of the innumerable aspects of intellectual, literary, or religious life on which Erasmus' letters or those of his correspondents touch. It would be difficult indeed to find any aspect of sixteenth-century culture which would not fall into this category. At the same time the editors hope that their translation and their notes will be of service to specialists, if only by aiding them to cover ground more quickly. It is assumed, however, that such specialists would in any case consult Allen's text and notes on any point of particular interest to their research. Since the present edition follows Allen's numbering of the letters, cross-references can apply equally to either edition, except where the line numbers are also specified. In that case references to letters in this edition will be simply to epistle number and line (eg Ep 55:17). References to letters not yet published in CWE are cited with Allen epistle number and line (eg Allen Ep 301:45).

Finally, each volume of the correspondence will contain an index to the persons, places, and works mentioned in that volume. When the correspondence is completed, the reader will also be supplied with an index of topics, and of classical and scriptural references. The index for volume 1 was prepared by Eleanor Thomson.

The editors also wish to record here their personal gratitude to the

Killam Program of the Canada Council, the generous patron of this extensive undertaking, and to University of Toronto Press, whose editors have
shared so cheerfully the common burdens of our apprenticeship.

Translators' Note

We have translated Allen's text, with a proper sense of what we owe him; divergences, which are extremely rare, are recorded in the notes. For names of places we have used the modern vernacular form, except for those few which have an accepted English equivalent (Brussels, for instance); and we have attempted to find a vernacular form for the names of Erasmus' contemporaries except where this would have been obscure (we have retained Beatus Rhenanus, for instance, and not written Beat Bild). No solution of this problem is wholly satisfactory. Nor are we satisfied with our treatment of the opening and closing formulae of the letters. Except where the original survives, we cannot always be sure how a letter began and ended, and the forms then in current use ('to the most ornate theologian greeting') cannot be Englished without some discomfort. As we could not leave them out, we have done our best to render what we found in Allen.

As to the general sense: Erasmus' mind and his astounding command of Latin are such that the meaning is never in doubt, unless there is some underlying ignorance in our own minds of what he is trying to say. In historical, philosophical, technical matters we have been much helped by our annotators and by the other members of the Editorial Board. The mistakes which remain are ours. A special problem is raised by the expressions of approval and disapproval, of friendship and enmity which come so often in the letters. We know that Latin uses superlatives far more freely than English; we have had to guess the colouring of such phrases, and may not always have given just the right rendering. A further difficulty in the early letters was the artificial and elaborate nature of those which may be very largely exercises in style. The reader must be patient; it is not long before we get to the real thing.

The two translators have so divided their work that one has made a draft for each letter, on which the other has commented, and the agreed result has then been submitted to the Editorial Board. The drafts for the first two volumes (representing the first volume of Allen) are the work of DFST, but some responsibility for their final form must be shared by the Board.

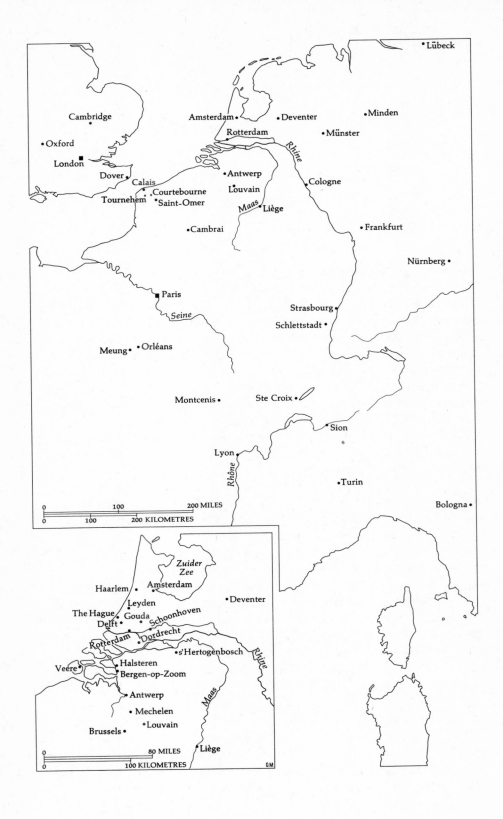

Lübeck

Cambridge

Oxford

London

Dover   Calais
Tournehem   Courtebourne
    Saint-Omer

Amsterdam   Deventer   Minden

Rotterdam   Münster

Rhine

Antwerp
Louvain

Maas   Liège   Cologne

Cambrai

Paris

Seine

Meung   Orléans

Frankfurt

Nürnberg

Strasbourg

Schlettstadt

Montcenis   Ste Croix

Sion

Lyon

Rhône

Turin

Bologna

0   100   200 MILES
0   100   200 KILOMETRES

Zuider
Zee

Haarlem   Amsterdam

Leyden   Deventer

The Hague   Gouda   Schoonhoven
Delft

Rotterdam   Dordrecht

Rhine

s'Hertogenbosch

Veere   Halsteren
    Bergen-op-Zoom

Maas

Antwerp

Mechelen

Brussels   Louvain

Liège

0   80 MILES
0   100 KILOMETRES

GM

THE CORRESPONDENCE OF ERASMUS

LETTERS 1 TO 141

1 / To Pieter Winckel   [Gouda, end of 1484]

Pieter Winckel was a master at the school attached to St John's church in Gouda where Erasmus received his first schooling. He was appointed by Erasmus' father, Gerard, principal guardian for his two sons. In the two most important sources for Erasmus' early life, the *Compendium vitae* (Allen I 47ff) and the letter to 'Grunnius,' August 1516 (Ep 447), Winckel and the other two guardians were charged with having mismanaged the legacy left for the boys' education. This letter, which indicates Erasmus' anxiety about the handling of their finances, was evidently written after the boys' departure from Deventer in the summer of 1484 and the death of their father shortly thereafter. It is possibly the letter referred to in Allen Ep 447:88ff as having been written by Erasmus in his fourteenth year (cf *De conscribendis epistolis* LB I 347E). For the events of Erasmus' early life, see Allen I 578ff; Mestwerdt 175ff; and Hyma *Youth of Erasmus*.

ERASMUS OF ROTTERDAM TO HIS FORMER GUARDIAN, MASTER PIETER WINCKEL
I am very much afraid that the end of this brief period may find our affairs not yet safely taken care of, though they should have been settled long since – belatedly even then. Therefore I think that all ingenuity, care and zeal should be devoted to seeing that our interests be not harmed. Perhaps you   5
will say that I am one of the kind who worry in case the sky should fall. This might be true enough if the capital were already there, waiting in our pockets. But your practical good sense will take special care to see that our property is accounted for. The books have still to be offered for sale, still to seek a buyer, still to catch a glimpse of a bidder. This is how far they are   10
from being sold. We have still to plant the very seed to make our bread; and meanwhile, as Ovid has it, 'time flies by on wingèd feet.' I absolutely fail to see what good can be done by delay in this business, while I see clearly what loss it may occasion. Besides, I hear that Christiaan has not yet returned the books in his possession. I beg you to overcome his procrastina-   15
tion by your insistence; if he holds back after a request it may be that a command will cause him to send them. Farewell.

        * * * * *

1:6 sky should fall] Cf *Adagia* I v 64.

9 books] Erasmus' father was a skilled copyist (cf Allen I 47f). Some of the books he had copied were apparently part of the legacy left to his sons.

12 Ovid] *Ars amatoria* 3.65

14 Christiaan] Allen suggests this may refer to Jan Christiaan, prior of the monastery of Steyn at this time.

2 / To Elisabeth, a nun   [Gouda? 1487?]

The identity of Elisabeth is uncertain. Allen suggests that she may have been one of the daughters of Berta de Heyen, a widow who had been kind to Erasmus and on whose death he wrote a funeral oration (LB VIII 551–60). This letter may have been written during the period of uncertainty and depression before he entered the monastery.

ERASMUS OF ROTTERDAM TO THE NUN, ELISABETH,
A VIRGIN CONSECRATED TO GOD

Dearest sister in Christ, your letter has been delivered to me. It is hard for me to express the pleasure it gave, for it offers the strongest possible evidence of your good will towards me, which I have always been at some pains   5
to earn. So my joy is great in the knowledge that there are still those who care for me even in my present misfortune, and who are sorry for it. I think it is all the more welcome since I am aware that it seldom comes the way of the unfortunate. When a man's circumstances are uniformly happy and prosperous there will be countless friends at hand to take pleasure in the   10
enjoyment of his friendship and to seek his company, but as soon as Fortune turns away her smile (for she has two faces) and begins to frown at a man he will at once see none remain of all his fair-weather friends. They flee as soon as Fortune does, and as her wheel revolves so their attitudes change. Surely this fact was wittily and cleverly expressed by the poet who   15
wrote:

> Erewhile with many a friend encompassèd
> When following breezes all my sails did fill:
> Now waves do swell, and clouds lower overhead,
> Shipwrecked am I, and lost, 'mid waters chill.   20

But I can see more clearly than the sun, as the saying goes, that you, dearest Elisabeth, are no member of that company, for in all the chaos of my affairs and the miseries of my condition I know that you both remain and have ever remained one who kept your affection for me undimmed. If then I can by no means rival you in devoted acts of friendship, still I need never be   25
outdone in the answering of your love and your letters. If you do not too much surpass me in your actions, I on my side shall not allow myself to lag behind in affectionate good will. If you disbelieve what I say, then test me, and I will do all I can to let you see how highly I esteem you. Ever my best wishes.   30

* * * * *

2:17–20 Erewhile ... chill.] Ovid *Epistulae ex Ponto* 2.3.25–8

3 / To Pieter Gerard   [Steyn? 1487?]

By 1487 Erasmus had entered the monastery of the Augustinian canons regular at Steyn near Gouda. The question of Erasmus' birth-date has not been settled, but he was almost certainly not more than twenty-one years old and possibly two or three years younger. His brother Pieter Gerard, three years older, was already a monk at Sion near Delft, the head of the congregation of which Steyn was a priory. Cf Allen I 576ff. Pieter appears under the name 'Antonius' in Ep 447, where Erasmus speaks bitterly of his betrayal in submitting to their guardians' pressure to enter a monastery, thereby undermining Erasmus' own resistance. See also Ep 1436. Erasmus, however, was still enquiring affectionately for news of him in 1498 (cf Epp 78 and 81). The derogatory description of his mental and moral qualities presented in Ep 447 is also contradicted by the present letter and by the fact that Willem Hermans described him as a 'courteous and most learned man' in an ode addressed to him in Hermans' *Silva odarum*, published in 1496 and edited by Erasmus (cf Ep 49 introduction, and Allen I 577). There is also evidence that Pieter was well regarded by his fellow monks at Sion (cf Allen III xxiii). In 1527 (Allen Ep 1900:23) Erasmus wrote that he had been able to bear his brother's death but could not bear that of Johannes Froben. But that was a rhetorical device.

ERASMUS OF ROTTERDAM TO MASTER PIETER, HIS BROTHER

Have you so completely rid yourself of all brotherly feeling, or has all thought of your Erasmus wholly fled your heart? I write letters and send them repeatedly, I demand news again and again, I keep asking your friends when they come from your direction, but they never have a hint of 5 a letter or any message: they merely say that you are well. Of course this is the most welcome news I could hear but you are no more dutiful thereby. As I perceive how obstinate you are, I believe it would be easier to get blood from a stone than coax a letter out of you! Where is your early good will towards me and the ardent brotherly affection which you once had for me? 10 Have you turned so quickly from a Micio into a Demea? Have you in fact grown cold to me? For what else am I to suppose? If – and I can scarcely contain my anger at the thought – you do not think our mutual love merits the little time spent on writing a letter, it must be that either I am of no importance in your eyes or else you have quite forgotten about me. If you wish 15

* * * * *

3:2–3 all thought ... heart] Cf Virgil *Aeneid* 2.595.

11 Micio ... Demea] Two of the *dramatis personae* in the *Adelphoe* of Terence, characterized respectively by mildness and harshness towards younger members of the family (sons, in the play)

to relieve me of this suspicion, if you care for your brother at all, if there is any vestige of fraternal spirit left in you, be sure to write to me at the earliest possible moment. If you do this, then, Pieter, I shall be glad some time soon to see you in health, and for my part will think nothing more desirable or precious than a letter from you. There is no other action by which you 20 could more surely convince me that you do in fact remember me and that your truly fraternal feeling for me, which long ago was attested by countless proofs, still remains unbroken. But, if I am now estranged from your affection not by any fault of my own, for well I know that none exists, but by the suspicion of a fault, then, I beg you, accept my apology even now and 25 resume your old feeling; put off Demea's character and put on Micio's again; and as you did not fail me at the hardest crisis of my life, so please now again lend me support in circumstances that are less harsh even if not exactly favourable. Since we are denied each other's actual presence, in no way can you give me closer support than by sending me very frequent let- 30 ters from your own hand. If you attend to this you will be doing me the most welcome favour.

If you desire to know what I am about, I love you intensely, as you deserve; your name is on my lips and in my heart; I think of you and dream of you and speak of you often with my friends, but with none more often, 35 more intimately or more pleasantly than with Servatius, our fellow-countryman. He is, believe me, a youth of beautiful disposition and very agreeable personality and a devoted student in those branches of learning which have given the greatest delight to us both from our boyhood onwards. This young man is very anxious to meet you, and if you make your 40 way here soon, as I hope you will, I am quite sure that you will not only think he deserves your friendship but readily prefer him to me, your very brother, for I well know both your warmheartedness and his goodness. Indeed, his nature makes everyone love him. This is why I earnestly ask you to lend him the small copy of Juvenal's satires which you possess. 45 Believe me, dear Pieter, you could not possibly invest a favour more wisely. His gratitude and his way of remembering such acts will impress you. Farewell, dearest brother.

4 / To Servatius Rogerus   [Steyn, c 1487]

Servatius Rogerus (d 1540) was a young monk whom Erasmus met shortly after his entry into Steyn. Hyma, *Youth of Erasmus* 56 and 172, argues rather uncon-

* * * * *

36 Servatius] See Ep 4 introduction.
45 Juvenal's satires] Possibly one of the books left by their father

vincingly that he and Erasmus may have been cousins. If so, Erasmus' brother
Pieter was unaware of the fact (cf Ep 3:36ff). The group of letters written to Servatius, as well as those to Franciscus and Sasbout, may be no more than exercises in epistolary composition, like the formulae in *De conscribendis epistolis*
(ASD I 2 157ff). Taken at their face value, though with considerable allowance
for rhetorical exaggeration, the nine letters to Servatius indicate that Erasmus
had become involved in an emotional attachment to his young friend, which
Servatius seems at first to have reciprocated, but then found irksome. He frequently failed to answer Erasmus' letters; but this is a common complaint that
Erasmus also directed against his brother and his other young friends. The
tone of these letters is paralleled closely by four early poems of Erasmus also
probably addressed to Servatius (cf Reedijk 143–52). See D.F.S. Thomson
'Erasmus as Poet in the Context of Northern Humanism' *De Gulden Passer* 47
(1969) 192ff, for a cogent argument that literary imitation is the motivating force
of these poems and that the letters conform in style and content to a well-
established tradition of monastic rhetorical letter-writing.

ERASMUS OF ROTTERDAM TO SERVATIUS OF ROTTERDAM
I should write to you more often if I were quite sure in advance that you
were not more apt to be wearied by reading my letters than I in writing
them. But your entire well-being is so dear to me that I would far rather
be tortured by your silence than cause you to become weary of my self-   5
indulgence. However, since friends are wont to find it more distressing
than anything else if they cannot meet, which you and I have only the rarest
opportunities to do, I could not avoid bidding this letter go to you in my
place. And I wish we might at long last enjoy such a stroke of fortune that
we might now cease having recourse to letters and be able to meet as often   10
as we wished. As things are, since we are denied this by fate (I cannot mention the fact without tears), am I to be entirely deprived of your company?
And if we cannot be together in person, which would of course be the most
pleasant thing possible, why should we not come together, if not as often
as might be, at least sometimes, by exchanging letters? As often as you look   15
upon these and read them over you can believe that you see and hear your
friend face to face.

    Ah, 'half of my soul,' what are you doing at this moment? Does all go

* * * * *

4:10 to meet as often] Although they lived in the same house, the regulations
apparently kept them from meeting frequently, perhaps seeing one another
only at chapel.
18 'half of my soul'] Horace *Odes* 1.3.8. This is a phrase that Erasmus uses very
frequently.

well with you? Does any vision of your most loving friend ever cross your
mind? For, since those who love are full of suspicion, I sometimes seem to   20
perceive vaguely that you are less mindful, not to say forgetful, of me. If
it were possible, I should have wished you might care for me as I do for
you and that you might feel the pangs of love for me as sharply as I am constantly racked by my yearning for you. Farewell.

5 / To Servatius Rogerus   [Steyn, c 1487]

ERASMUS OF ROTTERDAM TO HIS FRIEND SERVATIUS
Although I who seek to give you consolation am rather myself in need of
it, not only because there seems no kind of disaster left which I do not daily
encounter but also because for some time past I have endured no greater
or harsher misery than your particular troubles, still it is my very special   5
love for you, sweetest Servatius, that has caused me to forget my own pain
and to attempt to heal yours. Now, you tell me there is something that irks
you exceedingly, is causing you acute anguish, and, in brief, makes life disagreeable for you. Even though you say not a word, your countenance and
bearing make it clear that this is so; for what has become of your usually   10
delightfully gay expression and your former good looks and bright eye?
And what is the source of your present unhappy, downcast gaze, and of
this unwonted and protracted silence, and the sick man's symptoms on
your face? True it is, as the satirist says:
     The heart's despair, in suffering body pent,   15
     Ye may discern: and likewise happiness,
     For looks reveal man's joy and sorrow both.
Surely therefore, dear Servatius, you must be the victim of some disorder
which robs you of your former health. But what am I to do? Am I to offer
you consolation or be angry? I do not understand why you are concealing   20
your anguish from me as though we had never become acquainted. Are you
so subtle as to give no credit to the best of friends, no trust to the most trust-
worthy, or are you not aware that 'hidden fires but burn more fiercely'? Do
you then wish to carry the weight of your heart's troubles alone, to die by
your own will and destroy your best friend along with you? What a wicked   25
notion! What a cruel plan! Is this the common ground you share with
Menedemus in Terence – a tendency to punish yourself? Alas for me; what

* * * * *

5:15–17 The heart's despair ... both] Juvenal 9.18–20
23 'hidden fires ... fiercely'] Ovid *Metamorphoses* 4.64
27 Menedemus] Cf Terence *Heautontimorumenos* 81.

more can I do to please you, my soul? You surely know that you are dearer
to me than my life itself and that there is no task so difficult or unpleasant
that I would not undertake it gladly for your sake, and that in loyalty to you   30
none surpasses me; and, lastly, you know how keenly your suffering has
always made me suffer.

For the rest, my dear Servatius, what reason is there for you to withdraw
and conceal yourself so determinedly, like a snail? Indeed, I suspect, what
really is the case, that you have not yet become persuaded of my supreme   35
love for you. So I beg you, by all that is sweetest to you in life and by the
great love we share, if you care at all for your own health and if you wish
me to be preserved unto life, not to strive so much to conceal your feelings
but to 'confide to safe ears all that your heart contains.' For my part I will
help you in any way I can 'either with aid or counsel' but if I can do neither   40
of these things still it shall be my delight to rejoice and to weep, to live and
to die with you. Farewell, dear Servatius, and please look after your health.

6 / To Servatius Rogerus   [Steyn, c 1487]

ERASMUS TO HIS FRIEND SERVATIUS
What are you about, dear Servatius? I suspect that you must be occupied
in some great enterprise that prevents you from discharging the promise
you made to me. You agreed that you would send me a letter very soon, and
here is a huge interval within which you have not written a line or spoken
a word. What must I guess to be the reason? Surely, that you have been too   5
busy, or too idle. Indeed I suspect both of these are true at once: namely,
that you are engaged in a kind of leisure than which, it is agreed, there is
nothing less leisurely, nothing in fact busier. For every person who is at
leisure is caught up in love's longings, love being 'the sickness of an unoccupied soul.' So you will do something very pleasing and also useful to you   10
in many ways, if you interrupt your leisure and write to me as soon as you
possibly can. In any case, show more confidence in me and treat my opinion
of your behaviour with no less respect than your own. Thus you may talk
about everything with me just as with yourself, which will give me great
pleasure. Farewell.   15

* * * * *

39 'confide ... contains'] Horace *Odes* 1.27.17–18
40 'either with aid or counsel'] Cf part of a line from Terence *Heautontimorumenos* 86: 'aut consolando aut consilio aut re iuvero.' Erasmus,
dedicated to poetry, omits 'aut re.'
6:9–10 'the sickness of an unoccupied soul'] When the philosopher
Theophrastus was asked what love was, he replied, 'the affliction of a soul at
leisure'; Stobaeus *Florilegium* 64.29 (4.20.66).

7 / To Servatius Rogerus   [Steyn, c 1487]

ERASMUS OF ROTTERDAM TO SERVATIUS, HIS FRIEND

Considering that my affection for you is and always has been so deep, dearest Servatius, that I value you more than my very eyes and life and, in a
word, myself, what is it that makes you so hard-hearted that you not only
refuse to love him who loves you so well but do not even regard him with   5
esteem? Are you of so inhuman a disposition as to love those who hate you
and hate those who love you? Never was anyone so uncivilized or crimi-
nally minded or obstinate as not to entertain some kindly feeling towards
friends at least; is it that you and you alone cannot be moved by remon-
strances or swayed by entreaties or melted even by the tears of a loving   10
friend? Are you so savage as to be incapable of pity? I have tried upon you
all my appeals and prayers and tears, but you close up your heart and implac-
ably repel me with a harshness like that of the hardest rocks, all the more
so the more I continue to plead with you, so that I could with justice apply
to you the complaint that we find in Virgil: 'Nor wept o'erborne, nor pitied   15
love's distress.'

What am I to call it, dear Servatius – harshness or obstinacy or pride
or arrogance? Can your nature be like that of a young girl so that my tor-
ments yield you pleasure, and your comrade's pain gives you happiness,
his tears, laughter? How well might I reproach you in the words that appear   20
in Terence! 'O that I had an equal share and just division of love with you,
so that you might either feel this pain as I do, or I might care not what you
have done.' I ask you, what dreadful wickedness or crime or offence have
I committed against you to make you shun me thus and be so hostile to me?
Indeed I cannot see my sin, unless to love very deeply is itself what you   25
deem a sin. When you are so cruel to one who loves you, what, I ask, would
you be like to one who hated you? For you are ever on my lips and in my
heart; you are my one hope, the half of my soul, the consolation of my life.
When you are away nothing is pleasant to me, and when you are with me
nothing is unpleasant. If I see you happy I forget my own grief, while if any-   30
thing grievous happens to you I swear I suffer keener pain than you do
yourself. Is it by acting thus that I have earned such keen dislike at your
hands? But in fact, dear Servatius, I know well what reply you will make
to me, for it is the reply you often make. You will say 'What then do you
want to see happen; what do you require of me? Am I indeed showing dis-   35

* * * * *

7:15 Virgil] *Aeneid* 4.370
21 Terence] *Eunuchus* 91-4

A birdseye view of Gouda and surroundings, before 1550
map from Museum Het Catharina-Gasthuis, Gouda
Gouda ('Ter Gow') is in the centre with Steyn just to the left

like for you? What, I repeat, are you claiming?' If you put the question: I
am not asking for expensive presents for myself; only let your attitude to   40
me be the same as mine to you and you will forthwith make me happy. But
if your heart is so estranged from me that it cannot be swayed by any entreaty, then tell me so frankly. Why do you mock me? Why do you keep me
in uncertainty? Sometimes you pretend friendship, sometimes again its
opposite; and as you vacillate I suffer in mind the tortures of the damned.   45
So, my sweetest of comrades, if there be still any room in your heart for my
pleading, I beg and beseech of you one thing above all, to declare your feelings clearly to me and not destroy me any further with this cruelly tantaliz-
ing behaviour.

    But why do I pour forth these complaints in vain? For I know you will   50
not lend an ear to them. Why do I uselessly strive to plough the sand or wash
a brick; and why do I roll this stone any longer? If, then, you remain for
ever settled in your attitude, preferring to feel dislike rather than affection,
then dislike me as you will; I for my part shall never be able to cease loving
you. But I am resolved to do so with greater restraint in order to avoid tortur-   55
ing myself uselessly, since no solace comes from you. Farewell, my heart,
and, if there be any human kindness within you, vouchsafe an answering
love to him that loves you.

8 / To Servatius Rogerus   [Steyn, c 1487]

ERASMUS OF ROTTERDAM TO SERVATIUS, THE TRUEST OF FRIENDS
My dear Servatius, the fact that I see you are well gives me, too, very great
pleasure; for I cannot help delighting in your success and good fortune
since, though hardly a friend, you are still very dear to me. But one thing,
I must frankly say, causes me the most terrible distress: the fact that you   5
are buried in such long-continued forgetfulness of me, who am your friend.
I swear that the last handful of days in which I have lacked your company
have seemed longer than an entire year to me; they exhausted me with such
pain and racked me with such lamentations that I actually came to the point,
in my hatred of life's cruelty, where I more than once begged for death. In   10
the meantime, the wakeful hours were an annoyance, my sleep restless, all
my food tasteless, and the very study of literature, formerly my life's one

* * * * *

46 any room] Cf Virgil *Aeneid* 4.319.
51 plough the sand] *Adagia* I iv 51
51–2 wash a brick] *Adagia* I iv 48
52 roll this stone] *Adagia* II iv 40

consolation, became distasteful to me. So impossible is it, dear Servatius, that anything should suffice to wash away the cares of my spirit and cheer my heart when I am deprived of you, and you alone. In a word, the gloomy   15 look on my face, the paleness of my complexion, the somewhat depressed and downcast look – these things could easily have betrayed to you the inward struggles of my heart had you but observed them. But you, crueller than any tigress, can as easily dissemble all this as if you had no care for your friend's well-being at all. Ah, heartless spirit! Alas, unnatural man!   20 Even the fiercest beasts are responsive to the feeling of affection; they love in return those who love them, forgetting their savage instincts.

Indeed, there are countless examples of this phenomenon, but I shall select only one out of many. According to some writers, there was a certain young man who reared a serpent for which he had a considerable affection.   25 But when the serpent grew to full size the youth was frightened by the creature's wild nature and sheer bulk and threw it far away from him into the forest. Much later, it happened that the youth was ambushed by robbers as he crossed an unpeopled tract of land and cried out, perceiving that he must surely die. The serpent, awakened by the noise, recognized the voice   30 of one who had formerly fed it; straightway it rushed forth and rescued him from the savage hands of the robbers. So, then, if serpents and lions and dogs love those who love them, will you, Servatius, scorn one who is dying for love of you? Can that which moves the affections of wild beasts fail to move yours, who are a human being and young withal? Indeed, you would   35 have some reason to excuse yourself, if what I were asking of you were something arduous or difficult or wrong. But you yourself are surely aware what it is that I beg of you, inasmuch as it was not for the sake of reward or out of a desire for any favour that I have wooed you both unhappily and relentlessly. What is it then? Why, that you love him who loves you. What   40 is easier, more pleasant, or more suited to a generous heart, than this? I would repeat: only love me, and it is enough for me.

But I am not unaware how you are going to reproach me at this point, for it is surely the very reproach you usually make: 'What are you after; why do you trouble me? Does anyone avoid you or despise you or dislike you?'   45 Why, this is an honourable enough thing to say, dear Servatius, provided that your actions lent it credit. But, if you will kindly hear me without impatience, I shall answer it by revealing to you the occasion of my pain. You are destroying me with your pretences and dissemblings. Do you understand what I mean? And nothing is further from true friendship than   50

* * * * *

24 some writers] Cf Pliny *Naturalis historia* 8.17.61.

this. Shall I now rehearse to you the obligation of true love? First of all, that
friends must feel reciprocal good will; second, that neither should have secrets from the other; again, that each should be glad to help the other; that
each should participate in the other's joy and in his sorrow; that they should
think of themselves as sharing reciprocally all their thoughts, their plans,   55
and, in a word, their lives. These are the proofs of a true love. I beg you,
my dear Servatius, consider now whether none of these be lacking in you.
I, at least, think you do indeed lack some, but perhaps you yourself will not
agree. Still, it would not be strange if I, who am a human being, were in
error, especially in pleading my own case. If then the source of the fault lay   60
in me, and if there is anything in myself to offend you, why do you not candidly tell me so, as is the way of friends? I at least am entirely ready to right
that fault, whatever it may turn out to be. Why do you drive me to distrac-
tion by blowing hot and cold?

But why do I exert myself uselessly to mention these things – as though   65
you could be altered by these present letters when you could not by any
letters before, nay, not even by tears. Perhaps you will laugh at my talk of
tears; but laugh you would not, Servatius, if this mattered as much to you
as it does to me. Or perhaps it seems to you wrong or else absurd for me
to take this to heart. Well, I had reposed in you alone all my hope, all my   70
life, all the consolation of my heart, reserving nothing of me to myself; and,
alack for me, you on your part withdraw yourself so cruelly and avoid me
so determinedly – especially considering that you were not unaware of my
despondency which, if it has no one to 'recline and repose on' overwhelms
me with such bitter tears that I cannot face the prospect of living. I call God   75
and the genial light of Heaven to witness that each time I seem to see you
in my heart suddenly tears burst forth from my eyes. But it was not possible,
believe me, to write out even this letter without copious weeping, so much
does my heart refuse to contemplate our separation. My sweetest Servatius,
behold my troubled state, I beg you; and if you have a generous spirit   80
within you have pity upon me, even at the eleventh hour; nay, I would say,
upon yourself. But what am I doing? Am I returning once more to cajolery
and entreaties? I know you will not listen at all, much less act. You have
already been deaf for long enough; you have set your heart against me and
it is useless to assail it again. ' 'Tis hard; but patience easier makes to   85
bear/Whate'er cannot be righted.' But, as for this wound of mine, patience
brings no healing to it and lapse of time helps not at all. You alone are he

* * * * *

74 'recline and repose on'] Virgil *Aeneid* 12.59
85–6 'Tis hard ... righted.'] Horace *Odes* 1.24.19–20

who can bring healing, who can so easily turn sorrows into joys and mourning into laughter. So, my dearest Servatius, if I cannot acquire from you that
friendship which hereafter I would most heartily desire, I request that at   90
least the common intercourse of every day should exist between us. But,
if you think that I should be denied this also, there is no reason for me to
wish to live further. I ask you to inform me in a letter, as soon as possible,
what opinion you come to about these matters, and to do this sincerely, not
deceptively, as you were wont to do. Farewell, thou one hope of my life.   95

9 / To Servatius Rogerus   [Steyn, c 1487]

ERASMUS OF ROTTERDAM TO SERVATIUS, MOST CONGENIAL OF COMRADES
My sweetest Servatius, though your letter was such that I was unable to read
it without many tears, still it not only removed the distress of mind which
had already reduced me to an extremity of wretchedness, but even gave me
an amazing and unexpected degree of pleasure. But what has joy to do with   5
tears? For as I was reading your very sweet letter, the effective proof of your
love towards me which I long for, I wept as I rejoiced and in the same
measure rejoiced as I wept. Before, I shed tears of sadness all day long;
after that, the plentiful flow of moisture with which I continued to moisten
your letter took its source not from my heart's grief but from my astounding   10
love for you. Love, too, has, believe me, its proper tears and likewise its
proper joys. And indeed, dear Servatius, no one's heart could be so flinty-
hard that he would not be obliged to weep at such a letter as yours. How
sweet its language is and how pleasing its sentiments! Everything in it
smacks of affection and of a very special love. And as often as I read it, which   15
I do almost hourly, I think I am listening to the sweet tones of my Servatius'
voice and gazing at his most friendly face. Since we are seldom permitted
to talk face to face, your letter is my consolation; it brings me back to you
when I am absent, and joins me with my friend though he be away, so that
I am most fittingly to be described in the line of Virgil: 'By absent heart   20
the absent heard and seen.' Thus by your letter you have made me wealthier
and also happier than Alexander the Great was made by his many victories,
or Croesus by his riches.

But I beg you earnestly, O 'half of my soul,' by that extraordinary love
I bear to you, not to cast me again down into the pit of sorrows. Believe me,   25
your anger so much perturbs me that if I experience it again you will slay

* * * * *

9:20 Virgil] *Aeneid* 4.83
23 Croesus] Cf *Adagia* i vi 74.

me on the spot. I beseech you, have mercy on him who loves you; you know my character well enough and are not unacquainted with my nature. My heart is too tender to be able to endure so often a sport so cruel as this; and (for I must be frank) it is not a friend's part to hurt his friend, even in jest. 30 But if, as you say in your letter, it was I who first offended you by saying that you blew hot and cold, pretending one thing and then its opposite, then I beg you, dear Servatius, to reflect that if this was a harsh and bitter thing for you to hear it was so much the more bitter for me to endure at your hands daily. And what is more alien to true friendship than concealing any- 35 thing from a friend, especially that which it concerns him to know? To say sometimes nay and sometimes yea, to contradict one's utterance again and again: I ask you, is not this blowing hot and cold? Be as you please, I say, towards me, I only beg you not to deceive your most devoted friend by such tricks as these. However the matter stands speak out plainly, for nothing, 40 I think, is more irritating than coyness. But if in this one respect alone I can- not prevail upon you and if, as Virgil has it, 'Vain tears roll down unhappy cheeks,' then 'Pray I for death; Heaven's vault I loathe to see.' Farewell, my hope, my life's one consolation. Please see that I get a letter from you as soon as possible. 45

10 / To Franciscus Theodoricus [Steyn, c 1487]

Perhaps the Franciscus Theodoricus of Gouda who was at one time a monk at Sion, where he would have known Erasmus' brother (cf Ep 3 introduction). Since Steyn was a priory of the congregation of Sion, Franciscus may have been a resident of Steyn at this time. In that case Erasmus' letters were merely exercises or were occasioned by the fact that the rules prevented them from meeting frequently. A letter of Willem Hermans (Ep 35:138–9) seems to indicate that he was living at Steyn about 1494. Erasmus kept in touch with him in later years (cf Allen Epp 168:7 and 186). He heard of his death in July 1514 (cf Allen Ep 296:228).

ERASMUS OF ROTTERDAM TO FRANCISCUS THEODORICUS
The fact that you have devoted your mind to literature, and have thus begun to look to your own well-being, will bring not only great benefits to yourself but also inexpressible pleasure to me. But, in order to achieve your goal, since you are unacquainted as yet with the way thither, it is worth while 5 for you to attend to my advice and persuade yourself of the truth of some-

* * * * *

42 Virgil] *Aeneid* 4.449, 451

thing which I am going to urge for your sake as much as for my own. Your
well-being is, believe me, as important to me as it is to you, or as my own
well-being is to me. So please see that you govern your way of living according to my precepts; for, if you set out on that journey with no guide, you   10
may easily lose your way. Farewell.

11 / To Servatius Rogerus   [Steyn, c 1488]

ERASMUS TO HIS FRIEND SERVATIUS

Perhaps you wonder, my dear Servatius, what has caused me to send you
no letters for so long a period of time, and are suspecting that either my original intention has been lost sight of or my affection for you has dwindled
away. I should like you to believe that neither of these reasons has pre-   5
vented me; it was not desire that was lacking, but leisure; not will, but
opportunity. I would that my destiny permitted me the same degree of freedom as nature bestowed on me. You would then find that I was far readier
to teach than to listen. But you yourself can perceive the general chaos and
disorder, and I think you are not unaware just how much time is left to me   10
among the cares of my daily life. So I beg you to forgive my silence and,
to the best of your ability, strive towards manhood, and when happier days
dawn we'll take up the task again. Farewell, and continue in your love for
me.

12 / To Franciscus Theodoricus   [Steyn, c 1488]

ERASMUS OF ROTTERDAM TO HIS FRIEND FRANCISCUS

When you not merely urge me but beg and beseech me to write you some
kind of letter, this is, to tell the truth, dear Franciscus, a sign of your not
unfriendly feeling for me. But if the state of the times and of affairs and your
devotion answered the love I have for you in all ways, then I should not   5
allow myself even to be reminded, much less to be requested, in matters
of this kind. And on this score surely no one is so amenable or conscientious
as I. Believe me, I should like nothing better than to rival a good friend in
keeping up a steady flow of letters. As it is, since your good faith is (I shall
be a little censorious here) suspect in my eyes, and the general confusion   10
in affairs is such that one cannot safely trust even the most reliable people,
what do you think I should do? Am I to write or keep silence? Certainly the
latter would be safer, in my opinion, while the other I take to be the sign
of a kindlier disposition; so, though I am somewhat alarmed in case some
disadvantage should come of our acquaintance, still for the sake of the   15
unbroken love I bear towards you, and of our old friendship, I have decided

to humour your wishes. It is not seemly that any dislike or any quarrel
should arise between us, united as we are by the bond of brotherly affection. Further: when you adopt a kindlier attitude towards me, my letters
to you will be couched in kindlier terms as well. Farewell.   20

13 / To Servatius Rogerus   [Steyn, c 1488]

ERASMUS OF ROTTERDAM TO SERVATIUS,
THE FRIEND WHO IS SUPREME IN HIS AFFECTIONS

My dear Servatius, as there is nothing on earth more pleasant or sweeter
than loving and being loved, so there is, in my opinion, nothing more distressing or more miserable than loving without being loved in return; and   5
likewise, as there is nothing more worthy of humanity than to return the
love of him who loves us, so too there is nothing more inhuman, or closer
to the state of wild beasts than to shun, not to say dislike, one who loves
us. Perhaps you will already guess that I have drawn up this preamble so
that I may reconcile you to me again and repair afresh the interrupted good   10
will between us. But how can I expect to obtain from a voiceless letter a
result that no blandishments or appeals, poured out in your very presence,
nor even my tears could gain? I have left untried no means by which the
youthful heart could be affected, but you remain steadfastly of your former
mind, harder than adamant. What can I promise myself, unhappy man that   15
I am? What hope remains? Am I, like Sisyphus, once again with useless toil
to roll a stone uphill? No indeed. But what then? Am I to make up my mind
to live bereft of the companion I deserted? But life without a friend I think
no life but rather death; or, at least, a friendless life, if life it may be called,
is first of all unhappy and, secondly fit for beasts and not men. And I am,   20
if I may sing my own praises, so constituted that I think nothing in this life
to be preferable to friendship; nothing that should be sought for more
eagerly or preserved with greater care. But since, in Virgil's words, 'No toils
of ours shall ever serve to change thee,' I must do without friendship, the
very thing which of all things I most desire. ' 'Tis hard; but patience easier 25
makes to bear/Whate'er can not be righted.' And yet, dear Servatius,
though you have now forgotten, to put it rather mildly, your friend Erasmus, still he remembers and shall remember his friend Servatius 'so long
as he remembers himself, or the breath shall inhabit his frame.' Though you

* * * * *

13:23 Virgil] *Eclogues* 10.64
25-6 'Tis hard ... righted.'] Horace *Odes* 1.24.19–20
28-9 'so long ... frame'] Virgil *Aeneid* 4.336

may despise him, reject him, dislike him, still he will never be able not to   30
love, cherish, and esteem you.

Yesterday I would have met you in order to offer some consolation,
did I not know that my presence was so irksome to you; for I perceived the
change in your expression, your lowered gaze, your face's somewhat
gloomy hue, and your whole demeanour boding some grief to me. So I, too,   35
grieved, believe me, to no small degree when I saw my dearest companion
and 'the half of my soul' fordone with grief. For no unpleasant experience
ever assailed you, my dear Servatius, without torturing me much more
cruelly than yourself. And, unless I was mistaken, I was not altogether
unaware what was the source of your pain. I mean that person's shameless-   40
ness in hurling accusations against you without justification or right. But
I beg you, my soul, not to distress and torture yourself over a small matter.
I beg you to remember that we are human beings not gods, and are so constituted by nature as to undergo all the chances of fortune: 'And what man
hath not myriad cause of woe?' Pray remember that this is not your destiny   45
alone but the common destiny of mankind. Also, if you can think of
reasons, and indeed, as I judge, very slight ones, why you should grieve,
nevertheless there are many reasons, if you 'but recognized your blessings,'
for you to be glad, with much better cause.

So, that I may not delay you, if your friend's prayers have any force   50
in your eyes, if you mean ever to do anything for my sake, I ask and beg
only one thing of you: that you restrain yourself and prove your manhood
so that sadness may not subdue you for too long. Rather try by all means
to become such a man that you may triumph in your turn over those who
trample upon you, and in this you would already have succeeded if you had   55
obeyed my advice. But as things stand, since there is nothing that does not
encourage you to apply yourself to study, neither the subject nor the setting
nor the very season, it seems to me that you have incentives enough to cultivate letters. See that you shake off all the remnants of laziness and languor
that have plagued you hitherto. And, to fire you more keenly, you should   60
know that our friend Gualterus has managed this and is now completely
immersed in literary study, and regrets nothing so much as not having
begun this long since. Be ever cheerful, and I have nothing else to ask of

* * * * *

44–5 'And what ... woe?'] Ovid *Remedia amoris* 572
48 'recognized your blessings'] Virgil *Georgics* 2.458
61 Gualterus] Probably the 'Galterus' on whom Willem Hermans wrote two
epitaphs in his *Silva odarum* (cf Ep 33 introduction) lamenting his early death
and praising his devotion to learning

you. Since you are avoiding me, my friend Willem will help and console
you in all things, and I myself shall repeatedly urge him to do this assidu-   65
ously. Farewell.

14 / To Franciscus Theodoricus   [Steyn, c 1488]

ERASMUS OF ROTTERDAM TO HIS FRIEND FRANCISCUS
Since my affection for you is so great that no increase in it is possible, I have
not been able to avoid sending you letters from time to time, for I consider
that there is no more pleasant duty in friendship than such an exchange of
correspondence. Whenever I have looked at you carefully, dearest Francis-   5
cus, your expression has for some time seemed a little gloomy. This is an
omen of some bad thing; for generally the heart's inward pain is wont to
break out upon the countenance and the condition of the mind to be
reflected in the face as in a mirror. Thus I understand clearly that there must
be something that pains and racks you though I am not clear as to the cause.   10
Believe me, dear Franciscus, your pain does indeed bring pain to me too,
and there can be no room for rejoicing on my part when I see you fordone
with sadness. So I beg you earnestly to tell me what your trouble is. If I can
be of any service, I shall help you with deeds or at least with counsel. But
if it be from me that the cause of your pain arises, I shall see to it that the   15
remedy will likewise come from me and that right soon. I beg you, 'the half
of my soul,' not to torture yourself so dreadfully in a matter of no importance. Play the man; cast off all weakmindedness. In this way you will both
serve your own best interests and certainly bring cheerfulness and joy to
me, who am full of affection for you.   20

15 / To Servatius Rogerus   [Steyn, c 1488]

By this time Erasmus had begun to act as a mentor to Servatius and his other
young friends, inciting them to the study of good literature.

ERASMUS OF ROTTERDAM TO HIS MOST STAUNCH FRIEND SERVATIUS
My dear Servatius, I am more surprised every day at your silence, not to
say idleness, and I cannot admire you when with all the opportunities for
study so abundantly favourable, the only thing you lack is the will to work.
Oh yes, you say you are most grieved by your lack of experience – but what   5
do you expect? When the most famous men of antiquity had no hesitation

* * * * *

64 Willem] Hermans

in leaving their dear native land for a dreary place of exile and visiting lands
'warmed with another sun' and braving countless dangers on the stormy
sea and, in a word, enduring any amount of toil and expense for the sake
of a literary education, do you, you pillar of promise, think the gods will   10
get you all this while you are asleep? Have you never read a story that condemns your indolence: the story of the peasant who, it is said, once upon
a time saw that a wheel of his cart was stuck in the mud and could not be
pulled out by his oxen, so he did nothing himself, but called the high gods
to his aid. After he had prayed uselessly for a long time, Apollo pronounced   15
this prophecy from the clouds: 'If you wish the gods to help you, then you
must put your shoulder to the wheel.' In just the same way, my dear Servatius, if such a great love of letters possesses you, as you say it does, it
is your own help you need first of all. You need expect no god or man to
help you if you fail yourself, for Heaven sells everything to man at the price   20
of toil: 'May God give spirit; all else must thou provide.' And with what
pretext, pray, will you cover idleness in a place where there are so many
books and such a company of learned scholars at hand and eager, indeed,
to encourage you? What grounds for excusing yourself can you offer?

If then, my dear Servatius, you fulfil the one further condition that is   25
needful and desire, as you do if you have sense, to attain the end you long
for, then you simply must listen to my advice. First of all, it is of the greatest
importance that you be frank with me. Do you really think friends should
have any secrets from each other? Our favourite Horace describes the
Graces as 'ungirt,' and yet you bind yourself about with a kind of girdle   30
of pretence. Assuredly either you are making a mistake or the sage who said
'A friend is one soul in two bodies' was wrong. So I think it is worth your
while to be of one mind with me. Do not hesitate to ask, or feel ashamed
to admit there are things you do not know. Secondly, it will most of all speed
you on your way if you write to me more often than you are doing, and that,   35
too, not in your old style, taking little snippets of second-hand wisdom, or
even (which is worse) collecting phrases indiscriminately from Bernard
here and Claudian there and fitting them, or rather sewing them clumsily
on, to your own observations, exactly like a crow decking itself out in

* * * * *

15:8 'warmed ... sun'] Horace *Odes* 2.16.18
12 peasant] Cf Aesop fable 81 (the god is usually Hercules).
21 'May God ... provide.'] Ovid *Epistulae ex Ponto* 2.1.53
29 Horace] Cf *Odes* 1.30.5, 6.
31 sage] Pythagoras. Cf Cicero *De amicitia* 25, 92.
39 crow] Cf Horace *Epistles* 1.3.19.

peacock's feathers. That is not literary composition but mere scissors-   40
and-paste, and you must not suppose that I am so dull witted and stupid
as to be unable to make out what is your own and what is borrowed from
others. Rather, write down as well as you can, and I would rather you did
it spontaneously too, whatever comes into your head. Do not be ashamed
of any solecism you fall into: you will find that my purpose is to correct not   45
to sneer at you. How is a wound to be healed if it is not laid open? Why
try to conceal from men faults which they can detect in you better and more
certainly than you yourself can? Even supposing a fault has escaped us,
does it cease to be in you simply because its presence within you is not
recognized?   50

If, therefore, Servatius, dearest of my comrades, you have any regard,
I do not say for me, but for yourself; if you think at all of your own well-
being; then listen to my exhortations, shake off sluggishness, strip away
all faintheartedness; play the man and, at long last, even at the eleventh
hour, set your hand to the task. Why let today slip away in the hope of   55
tomorrow? Look, I beg you, and see how much time has already slipped
between your fingers, as the saying goes: already four years have gone by
and there you are stuck fast in the same slough; whereas if you had heeded
my warnings at the outset you would by this time have turned into one who
could not only rival me in literature but even school me in turn. However,   60
I do not think you should despair even now; time lost must be made up
by determined effort. You are still in good health, indeed in the spring of
your age, 'And the warm blood leaps high about the heart.' Before fleeting
youth departs, therefore, acquire for yourself now the means of enjoying
old age;   65

Now shape thy mind to last, and mould its beauty;
Only man's mind endures until his end.
How this is to be done, we shall consider later. Meanwhile it is for you to
see to it that I receive a letter from you as soon as possible to tell me of your
clear resolve. Or, if you think me unworthy of your friendship (I will not   70
contest this view), then only avoid me in such a way as not to by-pass your

* * * * *

44 comes into your head] *Adagia* I v 72
57 four years] If four years since his entry into the monastery is meant, this
letter should be dated later, but see Allen I 585.
58 same slough] Cf *Adagia* I iv 99.
63 'And the warm blood ... heart.'] Virgil *Georgics* 2.484
66–7 Now shape ... end.] Ovid *Ars amatoria* 2.119, 120

own well-being also: in that case, confide in Willem and tell him your plans;
he has your good at heart as truly as his own. Further, if you come to think
I can be of any service, you will find me as ready to do anything for you
as I am well disposed towards you. Farewell.   75

16 / To Sasbout   [Steyn, c 1488]

> This young man, if he can be identified with the Sasbout mentioned together
> with his wife in Allen Ep 296:229, was a layman, the only one among Erasmus'
> early correspondents.

ERASMUS OF ROTTERDAM TO HIS FRIEND SASBOUT
Though I should have preferred to receive a letter from you, still I was highly
delighted with the message you sent me to convey your feelings; for, as you
had said nothing during a long period, I was anxious in case you might have
put me out of your mind and quite forgotten our mutual tie of affection.   5
And I should gladly humour your wish had I been able to get any clear
meaning out of the messenger's words, which were to the effect that you
were extremely anxious I should give you some sort of 'little flowers'. Now,
you realize, if you have any sense, that flowerets are hardly in season, since
it is spring that produces them, and not winter's harsh weather. But this   10
was in jest! To speak seriously, however, I cannot see what 'little flowers'
you meant, unless it was perhaps the book in which I had painted a few
flowers when you and I were together; and which somehow or other came
back to me lately. In this very business it is hard to say what trouble your
negligence nearly caused me, for Hendrik, who brought it, said you had   15
asserted that I had sold it to you, and you yourself know how far from true
that is. So I naturally denied it vigorously, and convinced him that the facts
were not as he had supposed.
    But as for you, Sasbout, dearest comrade of mine, do be careful not
to devote yourself so completely to painting that you cease to care for litera- 20
ture. You are surely aware of what you promised to me when you were on

* * * * *

72 Willem] Hermans

16:7 messenger] A further indication that Sasbout was not a resident of the
monastery

15 Hendrik] This person has not been identified. The trouble caused by his
statement that Sasbout had said Erasmus had sold him a book may be
explained by the rule of the order forbidding the possession, and therefore
sale, of private property. Cf Nichols I 54 where, however, it is assumed that
Sasbout was a monk at Steyn.

the point of leaving me, and of the condition under which you took the
books of poetry away from me, namely that you would dedicate yourself
entirely to the love and pursuit of letters. If you take care to keep this promise, you will do something very pleasing for the sake of the love I bear   25
you and likely to be a source of great profit and pleasure to yourself. But
if you fail to do it, out of disregard for your own well-being, you will deeply
sadden me who am as pained by your misfortunes as by my own, and you
will be finished for ever. I could name to you, had I but the time within the
compass of a letter, very many persons, some of them from our own com-   30
munity, who have now at length discovered for themselves the fame conferred by letters and the disgrace incurred by ignorance of them, and are bitterly remorseful, when it is too late, because they see that the time of youth,
which is proper for the study of literature, has slipped away between their
fingers. So, my sweetest Sasbout, while your age is strong and fresh follow   35
the ant in garnering for yourself that which may delight and nourish your
old age: amass in youth what you would enjoy as an old man. And, in order
to increase your zest for this pursuit, it is worth your while at least to check
and restrain the immoderate desires of your time of life if you cannot
altogether suppress them, which is scarcely possible for a human being.   40
You know what I mean. Enough of all this. My earnest desire is to have a
letter from you, as soon as possible, to tell me how you are, what you are
doing, how you feel about these matters, what you want from me, and in
fact, anything else that it concerns me to know. Farewell, sweetest Sasbout:
I ask you, when you consider that you are lucky, to remember me, once your   45
bosom companion and now as affectionate as ever.

17 / To Cornelis Gerard   [Steyn, 1489?]

This letter is the first surviving of a series exchanged between Erasmus and
an apparently older friend with whom he could discuss literary and scholarly
matters on terms of equality. Cornelis Gerard of Gouda, also called Cornelius
Aurelius (a Latinization of Gouda; cf Ep 29:1n), was an Augustinian canon resident at this time in a monastery of the Windesheim congregation in the district
of Lopsen near Leiden. He was a kinsman, probably an uncle, of Willem Hermans (cf Epp 23:70 and 28:7) who was a childhood friend of Erasmus (cf Ep
33 introduction). Since he was also a native of Gouda where Erasmus had spent
part of his youth and may also have been an alumnus of the school at Deventer,
it seems likely that he had been acquainted with Erasmus before the beginning
of this correspondence. Elsewhere Erasmus alluded to Cornelis' character as
a boy (cf LB VIII 245E). In 1497 he went to Paris as a member of the commission
invited from the Windesheim chapter to reform the abbey of St Victor (cf Epp

73:7n and 78 introduction). He enjoyed a considerable literary reputation, having written besides the *Mariad* (cf Ep 40 introduction) a metrical version of the
Psalms. The Emperor Maximilian conferred on him the poet's laurel, probably
in 1508. He and Erasmus remained in touch for some ten years but drifted apart
after 1499. See P.C. Molhuysen *Cornelius Aurelius; Kort schets van zijn leven en
werken* (Leiden 1902) reprinted from NAKG ns II (1902–3) 1–15. Cf Allen I app
IV and Reedijk 49ff.

ERASMUS OF ROTTERDAM TO CORNELIS OF GOUDA, POET AND THEOLOGIAN
My very good friend Cornelis: though there is nothing of which I have less
doubt than your liking and affectionate esteem for me, still I can see this
more clearly from your recent letter which, though fairly long, was still too
short to gratify fully, though it did somewhat relieve, my yearning for you. 5
Supremely pleasant and welcome as was the whole-hearted devotion to me
expressed in your letter, still I felt a pang of especially acute grief at the
thought that the circumstances under which we live are such that I must
experience that devotion at a distance. If by any means it were possible,
I should myself prefer to have an opportunity of conversing with you face 10
to face and enjoying your company at close quarters, together with your
embraces and most chaste kisses. But since I cannot have what I wish for
I shall, like Micio in Terence, wish for what I can have; and, since what I
most longed for has not come my way, perhaps I may improve by my skill
the hand that fate has dealt me. 15
    Indeed, nothing on earth appears to me to contribute so much to this
end as your very delightful letter: whenever I read it, which I do as often
as I can, it brings before me so faithful and so lifelike a picture of my friend
that absence can claim to withhold for itself very little, indeed almost
nothing, of his physical presence. So, whenever I am distressed by the fact 20
that you are not with me, I at once take refuge in this letter of yours which
restores you to me though you are away and joins me to you in your
absence. It not only consoles me but also gives me vast pleasure, for it shows
both your marvellously graceful style and a great deal of 'Attic charm,' as
they call it, and also a special degree of personal good will which, while I 25
certainly have not earned it, is of a piece with your own civilized character.
Everything about that letter, indeed, has a ring of love and kindness, a
flavour of affection and of longing. What a propitious day it was, a day to
be marked with a pure-white stone, on which Fortune brought me to you
in friendship and you were added to my soul – and as no small part of it 30

* * * * *

17:13 Terence] Cf *Adelphoe* 738–41.

29 marked with a pure-white stone] The habit of marking days of good omen
with white stones is alluded to frequently in Latin poetry: cf *Adagia* I v 54.

either. In a word, I have been enabled not only to have a very good friend in you, but even to treat you as my property. Who would not approve and admire and deeply love such generous good will, such open-handed and ready generosity? I should be the most ungrateful man alive if I did not try my utmost to feel the highest degree of gratitude to one who pursues me   35
with such endless kindnesses, and also to repay these when I have a chance. But if you never need my help in any regard I shall still see to it that you are made aware that I am fully mindful of your favours, and that, though in deeds you far outdo me, at least in the heart's good will I never fail you. For believe me, dear Cornelis, I preserve towards you, and always shall, the   40
same devoted affection as Euryalus is reputed to have shown to Nisus, Pylades to Orestes, Theseus to Pirithous, and Pythias to Damon; the same warmth of friendship with which the youthful Jonathan embraced the youthful David. Further, whatever I may consider as bearing upon the protection of your good report and reputation, that will I keep so attentively   45
at heart that nobody shall ever take more pains over his own self-
preservation than I shall over your honour and good name. But, if there is anything further you may wish me to do, nothing will be more pleasant or prized than a request for help from you, since nothing stands higher in my eyes, or ever will, than the gratification of your wishes in every way. Ac-   50
cordingly I beg you to consider as wholly at your disposal whatever you think I can provide by devotion or labour.

That you have been so kind to our friend Willem is, I must say, some-
thing that gives me the greatest pleasure and is entirely worthy of your unparalleled courtesy, for in my opinion he deserves not only your esteem   55
but also, in the fullest measure, your love: partly because of the exception-
ally distinguished scholarship he commands, for a young man, and partly because of the intense affection which he has chosen to bestow on you.

Farewell, my sweetest Cornelis, and continue to love me deeply, as you do. I earnestly request you to give my greetings to Pieter, who, as you   60
say, is very fond of me, and of whom I also am very fond.

18 / To Cornelis Gerard   [Steyn, 1489?]

ERASMUS OF ROTTERDAM TO THE LEARNED POET AND THEOLOGIAN CORNELIS
Best of friends, I can easily see that you have a very high regard for me when you heap letter upon letter, all full of love and good will. You call them non-

* * * * *

53 Willem] Hermans cf Ep 33 introduction).
60 Pieter] Allen identifies him with the Pieter in the convent of Marienpoel near Leiden to whom Hermans sent greeting via Cornelis in the Gouda MS 1323.

sense, but I call them a remarkable manifestation of the exceptional wisdom
and scholarship you possess, as well as reliable evidence of your truly   5
benevolent attitude towards me. Indeed, dear Cornelis, if you write nonsense so elegantly, what, I ask, will happen when you try seriously? Or have
you learnt to adapt yourself to the occasion and to the characters of men,
producing complicated and highly finished works for perceptive readers
and hasty effusions for shallow wits?   10

Enough of jesting. You write that you can safely confide to me all of
your own works that you possess, inasmuch as you have long been convinced of my faithful friendship, as you put it, devotion, goodwill, and
absence of jealousy. It is kind of you to think of me in this way and I shall
do my best to see that your high opinion of myself is not betrayed. If you   15
cannot trust mere assurances, try me out: if you do, you will assuredly find
that you will never lack due support from me whenever you need it. And
when you say that I am easily able to wipe away your diffidence and by my
own skill, as you put it, make my daily bread from your store, I would,
to be frank, suspect you of laughing at my simplicity were it not that I have 20
so many proofs of your good will. So I can well believe that if you have an
inflated opinion of me, who am nothing, it comes rather from an excess of
friendly spirit than from deliberate choice. But, in order to prevent you from
alleging that I am obstinately unresponsive to you in the kind offices of
friendship, I promise you my help in matters of this sort, on the strict condi- 25
tion that you shall give me your own help in return. Farewell, and keep me
in mind.

19 / From Cornelis Gerard   [Lopsen, May 1489?]

CORNELIS OF GOUDA TO ERASMUS, A MAN OF CONSUMMATE SCHOLARSHIP
After keeping at him and pressing him with many requests, although he
had long evaded the issue lest he reveal his ignorance, I bound our friend
Martin by a vow of mutual friendship to let me have some of your poems,
for which he was to ask you. As a result there came into my hands a poem   5

* * * * *

19:4 Martin] Probably a lay brother who acted as a messenger

5 poem] The poem 'against the barbarians,' which Cornelis recast with some
emendations in the form of a dialogue, was published by a mutual friend,
Reyner Snoy, in his edition of the *Herasmi silva carminum* (1513) with the title
*Apologia Herasmi et Cornelii sub dyalogo lamentabili assumpta aduersus barbaros
qui veterum eloquentiam contemnunt et doctam Poesim derident*. It was published
from a different MS in LB VIII 567, with 35 lines added by Cornelis. Critical
edition in Reedijk, 161ff; cf *Opuscula* 8ff.

lamenting the neglect of the art of poetry. I cannot easily tell you how
cheered and pleased I was when I received, examined, and read this poem.
But though I cannot altogether refrain from praising you, please remember
to preserve your modesty entire; if this does not fail you, it will make the
flower which you now exhibit in bud blossom liberally into fruit upon the   10
tree. But, to avoid tarnishing your distinguished character with my foolish
compliments, let it suffice me to say that I ardently hope to have a bond of
brotherhood with you, a single enthusiasm for common pursuits, and, in
short, a single basis for enduring affection.

In order, however, that you may become more fully aware of the high   15
value I set on your talent, I have made an effort to divide up your poem,
which deserves all due commendation, into a dialogue between us, however rough-shaped; and so I have produced an apologetic dialogue, as the
title prefixed to this little work, in which we share, may easily show. I hope
you will not be offended, because I have in places changed your verses to   20
the extent of a very few words and towards the end have turned them into
a different metre. I should like it to be clear that this was done with the most
careful consideration and under a kind of sweet presumption of mutual
affection between us. For, in order to make the poem, composed in your
elegant style, give still greater pleasure to all and sundry, I took pains to   25
see that it could be recited aloud with pleasant effects of sound if one wished
to do so, and, in order to achieve this more readily without impediment,
I carefully excised all hiatus of vowels. Will you very kindly excuse me for
placing my incapable hands on your crop of flowers – and even consider
me a good friend for the very reason that I have made out of your poem a   30
book in which each of us has a share?

Finally, since my esteem for you is so profound, I earnestly beg you
to give your attention also to my book *De morte* and send it back at the earliest convenient moment, improved by your judicious revising hand.
Never let any envious rivalry such as a certain person has attempted to   35
engineer, subsist between us, but though we may at times have to give way
to each other's judgment let us still remain united by a single bond of affection. Farewell, and return my love.

* * * * *

33 *De morte*] 'On Death.' *De improvisa morte et proposito melioris vitae ad Cel-
sum* published by P.C. Molhuysen from Gouda MS 1323, f 33, in NAKG 4 (1907)
72

20 / To Cornelis Gerard   [Steyn, 15 May 1489?]

ERASMUS OF ROTTERDAM TO CORNELIS OF GOUDA,
A MAN OF CONSUMMATE SCHOLARSHIP

My dearest Cornelis: your book was unexpectedly delivered to me by Master Jan, your good friend and mine, when I had quite given up hope of it. I do not think I could easily express how delighted I was to learn from your 5 own pen that it was finished, for this meant that I had received at your hands more than I could ever have hoped for. Yet when I sent Martin to you, intending that he should bring back to me anything at all of either your letters or poems, he remarked when he saw me again that you had a fixed intention of asking me to be the first to break the ice, as the saying goes, 10 and that you would return the compliment as soon as possible. He added that you already had some work or other in progress, which you had decided to dedicate by name to me; so that I was in the process of getting ready the poem which you tell me has at length flown to reach you, taking the lead in the matter not because I was superior to others in age or literary 15 attainments but as your most loving friend of all. And I cannot say how surprised I am at its failure to reach you earlier; for I gave it to him with the utmost care and with the most forceful insistence possible that if he ever meant to gratify me at all he was to be careful to do as I wished in this business which I intended to treat as most important, and deliver it promptly. 20

And indeed I would not wish you to suspect me of being prompted in this by foolish arrogance or motives of jealousy, for I see in my poems a source not of reputation but rather of embarrassment. All the more, then, should you be confident, as you will be in any case, that I did it in order to charm a song out of you by my foolish things, just as Pan's rustic reed 25 used to wake Apollo's lyre. For he said nothing else would make you write. But I hear from your letter that he cheated me of my wish and you of your earnest desire by keeping it to himself and pretending that he had delivered it, perhaps to cover up his own incompetence. If I had managed to find out about his shilly-shallying I should have insisted on his delivering it to you, 30 or alternatively returning it to me so that I might entrust it to someone else's charge; but he was marvellously cunning at concealing his shifts, for upon

* * * * *

3 your book] The *De morte* (cf Ep 19:33n).
4 Jan] Cf Epp 21:31 and 23:115. Allen suggests this perhaps refers to Jan Christiaan, fifth prior of Steyn (cf Ep 1:14n).
10 'break the ice'] *Adagia* III v 95
28 pretending] Reading 'simulauitque'

my questioning him on his return about what passed between you he fab-
ricated a long and plausible story giving an account by chapter and verse
of all that you said or did.

35

Such was the impression his words made upon me that, under the
misleading influence of all this rhetoric, I began to entertain serious
apprehensions that my unpolished verses might have given offence to your
refined ears and that you might have understood them otherwise than I
intended in composing them. Thereafter, when I saw a long time pass with
no poems or letters from you, I felt that this confirmed my previous guess:
that is, that you were provoked by my foolish pieces and did not consider
them worthy of an answering contribution of your own. But I am delighted
that what happened was utterly different from what I had thought. I am very
pleased that my poem has reached you and that it quite clearly has not only
caused no offence, despite my justifiable fears, but has even occasioned a
substantial increase in your good will towards me; for you have condes-
cended not only to seal my poem with your approval but also to exhibit your
esteem for it by blending it with your own brilliant lines. Your most friendly
action in so doing, dearest Cornelis, is proportionate not to my deserts, but
to the unrivalled and generous kindness with which you habitually admire
other men's talents, however rudimentary these may be, and prefer them
to your own; or else to that abundance of affection towards me which makes
you see charms even where there are none, for blind love is a stranger to
good judgment. And my embarrassment at receiving so much undeserved
praise from you was outweighed by pleasure at being not only liked, but
loved, by a scholar of such eminence.

40

45

50

55

For my part, sweetest Cornelis, believe me when I say that there is
nothing in the world I could long for more ardently than that the love I have
always felt in special degree, and deservedly so, for you should be returned
by you in kind. For this reason I am glad to echo your remark and make
it my own: 'Suffice it to say that my supreme desire is to join with you in
a single bond of brotherhood, a single devotion to the literary pursuits we
share, and lastly a single foundation of enduring affection.' And as, in a
charming proof of your good will towards me, you have put together a
single Apologetic out of your verses and mine, so, admitting the possibility
that we may find anything divided between friends, may the hearts of both
be linked by a single bond of mutual love to the end that, just as your verses
have been woven into the fabric of my poem and mine into yours, so your
spirit may ever dwell in me and mine in you; and if we be sundered by distance and cannot meet each other in person as often as we wish, still we
shall so far enjoy mental intercourse, exchange of letters, and attention to
mutual obligations, that we shall seem never to be apart.

60

65

70

Lorenzo Valla, translation of Demosthenes' *Pro Ctesiphonte*
The preface, showing a portrait of Valla in the initial
Illuminated MS, Ferrarese school, 1475–82
Biblioteca Apostolica Vaticana, cod. Urb. lat. 337, f 1

As you also remark, whatever is redolent of envy or of rivalry – even, I would add, of unfriendly suspiciousness – must be totally absent from our 75 relationship. And may God forgive (for I would not curse one of our brethren) the person who has, in time past, contrived some such impediment between us. How, indeed, could I feel envy of you, and not rather congratulate you sincerely, and think myself lucky in the fact that in my loving good will towards you I consider whatever rank and renown I see you gain 80 as accruing entirely to my profit? It is a true as well as an ancient saying that friends have all things in common. Surely, again, you do not imagine me to be so uncivilized as not to be able calmly to tolerate an occasional difference of opinion between us, and to deem it my duty forthwith to attack, maul, and savage whatever fails to fit my own notions? I acknowledge that 85 there does exist a category of persons who hold that anything they are ignorant of, or do not agree with, deserves immediate condemnation, but I should not like you to include me among them. Of course I am well aware that Augustine and Jerome, who were both eminent literary scholars and famous saints, were at variance, and even actively disagreed, in their 90 opinions; and it is not only between these two that I believe this to have occurred, as witness a host of others, including Aristotle, Plato, Chrysippus, Epicurus, and Zeno, whose opinions were individual and usually different from one another's. Yet there is no reason to suspect that on this account any rivalry or jealousy arose among them. I have my own guides 95 to follow; if you perchance have others, I shall lose no sleep over the fact. My authorities in poetry are Virgil, Horace, Ovid, Juvenal, Statius, Martial, Claudian, Persius, Lucan, Tibullus, and Propertius; in prose, Cicero, Quintilian, Sallust, and Terence. Again, in the niceties of style I rely on Lorenzo Valla above all. He has no equal for intelligence and good memory. I must 100 admit it: I should not dare to make use of any phrase not employed by these authors, while, if you would include any others, I shall by no means hold it against you. But enough of this.

As for your request to me for careful revision of your little work *De morte*, I must tell you that I have long since read it and also the history of 105

* * * * *

82 friends have all things in common] *Adagia* I i 1

100 Valla] Lorenzo Valla (1406–57) was the most acute critical philologist of the first half of the fifteenth century. His *Elegantiae* (cf Ep 23:108n) and his *Adnotationes in Novum Testamentum* (cf Ep 182) exercised a profound influence on Erasmus. Valla's name is written here and in Epp 23:77 and 24:29 as 'Vallensi' (of Valla). Elsewhere Erasmus used the more common form.

104 your request] Cf Ep 19:32ff.

the War of Utrecht and the tale of St Nicholas, as told by you with marvellous charm of style and an abundance of gems of wisdom; but all of them,
dear Cornelis, seemed far too meritorious for the application of my doltish
correcting hand, and I do not think I have any knowledge which you lack.
Yet you will tell me that in a lengthy work even the finest scholars are   110
plagued by errors which they cannot fully clear up, whether through carelessness or pressure of work; and you will reproach me with these words
of your own:
 Though perfect art the bard command,
 Plain faults escape his hurrying hand.   115
But, my dearest Cornelis, whatever fault has eluded your Argus-like vigi-
lance could not possibly be detected by my poor eyesight. Yet now, as I suspect, you are about to confront me with the popular saying that two eyes
are better than one. By this, I confess, you have completely barred me in
advance from excusing myself; and so, most beloved brother, since this is   120
what you are resolved on and have determined to do, I would rather indulge
your wishes in the matter, far beyond my capacity as it is, than impair your
affection for me. But you ought also to know that your little work *De morte*
has long since ceased to be in my possession, since I have given it back to
Martin, who had brought it to me. You will therefore need to arrange for   125
its return to me as soon as possible; and I shall take pains to note with care
any fault I find in it, though I expect to find none, and shall still submit
whatever I revise to your keen judgment for a second revision. Farewell,
sweetest Cornelis, and continue to love me as you do. Steyn, 15 May

21 / From Cornelis Gerard   [Lopsen, May 1489?]

CORNELIS OF GOUDA TO ERASMUS OF ROTTERDAM, POET,
ORATOR, DIVINE, AND CONSUMMATE SCHOLAR
My dear Erasmus: even though nothing could have pleased me more than
the evidence of an attitude in you that obligingly held out so fair a prospect of friendship and trust, still I am overwhelmed with a kind of shame   5
at my own baseness, inasmuch as you have covered me with undeserved
praise. Your sentiments and written tributes are so lofty and generous that
you almost seem to have sought to arouse my friends' envy of me. But, since

* * * * *

106 War of Utrecht] The civil war in Holland and Utrecht between an anti-
Burgundian and a pro-Burgundian party, known respectively as the Hooks
and the Cods, raged 1477–92 (cf P.J. Blok *History of the People of the Netherlands*
II (New York 1970) 192f *et passim*). The suffering it caused was particularly
severe in the neighbourhood of Gouda (cf Hyma *Youth of Erasmus* 26f).

the church does not invariably condemn an error arising from goodness,
when you, out of mistaken affection, protract my praises unjustifiably, I   10
would rather that they did not blame you; otherwise they must, in con-
demning your mistake in regard to me inevitably be proved to condemn
also Peter's anger, when he refused to accept the passion of Our Lord.
Further, I would that all men should recognize that you are as incapable of
flattery as I of being angered by abuse or charmed by undeserved praise.   15
But perhaps in writing this I am preparing a fresh snare of malice for my
friends' use: they may say that it is worse to voice my own praise than it
would have been to accept it from the lips of another. For this reason I shall
illustrate in a tale of action what I have said in words, so as to satisfy fully
my envious rivals; since I believe that as a result they may forego their   20
insane rage, and be forced to love your praise of me and my love for you.
Let all who are willing give ear, and let unbelievers scoff.

Once, then, when that friend of ours had given me many accounts of
your industry, I formed a desire to strike up a friendship with you and to
compensate for the distance between us by the exchange of frequent letters.   25
That was when I first gave him, as a hostage, the tale of St Nicholas, which
I had composed in rough-and-ready verses; but I insisted that he should
first carefully inspect your poems (this I admit) and, if he thought it appropriate, should go on to present my trivial works to you as well. For I was
anxious, having heard of your reputation some time since from our friend   30
Jan; anxious, I repeat, in case I should be outdone by your incomparable
genius, and be obliged to face the disgraceful acknowledgment of my own
presumption in thrusting my trash into your refined ears. If, however, he
observed that your march was on a higher plane altogether, as I confidently
expected at the time, and have now, with extreme pleasure, found to be so,   35
then he was to keep concealed in his possession the ill-favoured beast I had
placed in his charge. So he proceeded from delusion to raving and, when
at length he came back to me, hinted that you had indeed read my poems,
but after reading them made a sour face and, assuming a supercilious look,
made fun of them and savaged them, to use his own words, tearing them   40
to pieces from every direction. When I had given a decent hearing to these
slanderous statements, I remained unperturbed, as God is my witness,
merely thinking that I had received a well-deserved scolding for my follies;
while I decided to give them up for ever from that moment to avoid black-
guarding a friend and new brother, if my self-control gave way, or stirring   45

* * * * *

21:23 friend] Martin: cf Ep 19:4n.
31 Jan] Cf Ep 20:4n.

old sparks of trouble to life. My object in saying this is to make all my friends acknowledge that, as I was in no way filled with arrogance because you praised me, so too I was not at all angered by your disparaging remarks, as I supposed them to be.

But, passing over the hostile criticisms of malicious persons, let me 50 briefly tell you what my reaction to your compliments has been. My view, sweetest Erasmus, is that your object in showering your praise upon me was to banish my slothfulness and lack of spirit, to spur me to run with you in the race of literary composition, so that you could have made something at least resembling yourself out of a raw tyro. The kind of praise that only 55 benefits one's friend, and has no admixture of flattery, is truly to be commended. As Julius Caesar testifies, the desire to be praised and the fear of disgrace rouse men to heroism, and it is in the search for praise that a man properly forms himself by the character and pursuits that earn it. What shall I say of those supremely eminent men whom posterity honours because in 60 their desire for praise they willingly offered to undergo any danger as much for the sake of their integrity as for the liberation of their country? I would be creating a false impression if I did not adduce a single example from ancient times, and so, to omit mention of the Fabii and Fabricii and the Scipios and Camilli and all the leading heroes of Rome, I shall instance Han- 65 nibal alone, who, when he was little more than a boy, since 'Juno gave him this spirit, wearying the heart with hope of glory,' dreamed of

Destroying th' Aegat isles, his forbears' shame,
And sinking treaties in the Sicil main.

Therefore we ought to admit that it is both fitting and helpful to apply the 70 spurs of praise upon occasion in order to arouse the indifferent and the slack, to impel them vigorously to perform virtuous deeds of every kind, and to pursue the honourable arts – by laudatory blows, if I may thus express it. In conclusion let me say that you cannot possibly be held guilty in the eyes of the envious, inasmuch as you have driven a friend to self- 75 improvement by means of your praises; so they must keep silence, and allow you and me to make progress through mutual compliment, while they continue to injure themselves in their malice. Farewell; and be diligent to serve God zealously through good works.

* * * * *

57 Caesar] Cf *De bello Gallico* 7.80.
66-9 'Juno ... main'] Silius Italicus 1.63 and 1.61–2

22 / To Cornelis Gerard   [Steyn, June 1489?]

ERASMUS OF ROTTERDAM TO THAT MOST ELOQUENT OF MEN, CORNELIS
My sweet Cornelis, I am eternally grateful to you for your kindness, for I see
you are so attached to me that you have taken great care to furnish me with
a dart, as you put it, to transfix those who scoff at me. This is also a clear
proof of your unrivalled affection for me. But (oh, the shame of it!) wherever   5
there is a discussion about poetry here, the weapons used in debate are
those not of rational argument but of slander and backbiting. If men listened to reason as they should, then scarcely anything would be easier than
to persuade them. Where they condemn immoral themes dressed in a brilliant style, I too condemn this; where they blame immoderate devotion to   10
poetry, I too refuse to commend it. But does it follow that we shall have to
censure for indecency everything that is wittily expressed or poetic? You
at least, accustomed as you are to reading the poets' works, are clearly aware
how much the honeyed flow of poetry abounds not only in elegance of style
but in gravity of thought and in knowledge of all things. Where there are   15
so many shining virtues, am I to be offended by a few flaws? But those
worthies are only drawing a cloak over their own lack of culture, with the
result that they seem to despise what they despair of achieving. If they
looked carefully at Jerome's letters, they would see at least that lack of culture is not holiness, nor cleverness impiety.   20

    As for your inciting me to read through these letters, I am most grate-
ful. But I have long ago not only read them, but copied out all of them with
my own hands: and, although in them we can find the greatest possible
number of darts to repel the barbarians' assaults more easily than mentioning them, as they say, still it would be enough to cite the single example   25
furnished and polished so carefully for us on the page where, discussing
the husks of the prodigal son, he adduces the illustration of the Captive
Woman. But, my dear Cornelis, let us lay aside our weapons, and refrain
from beating the air in vain. I have long thought that it will be the most

* * * * *

22:15 Where there are ...] Cf Horace *Ars poetica* 351-2.

19 Jerome's letters] The reference is to St Jerome's *Epistles* 27 and 53. The second passage is referred to in the *Antibarbari* (ASD I 1 103:12–15).

27–8 Captive Woman] Jerome *Epistles* 21:13. The same figure is used in the
Antibarbari (ASD I 1 112:18–19) the extracts being taken from Jerome
Epistles 70.

glorious kind of victory we can win, if we pass by their barkings of Scylla   30
with deaf ears, not trying to take their fortress by storm but despising them,
in the words of your own witty verses:

> Envious churl, wouldst gird at me?
> Eat thy heart out with jealousy!
> Great men I'd rather seek to please;   35
> Do noble steeds attend to fleas?

23 / To Cornelis Gerard   [Steyn, June 1489?]

ERASMUS OF ROTTERDAM TO CORNELIS OF GOUDA
Since I think I have already given a sufficient answer to your letter, I should
like to send you something inspired by the intense affection I bear you, to
which you may reply in turn. Indeed, dear Cornelis, for some inexplicable
reason I do not become wearied by continuous letter-writing, in the normal   5
way, but am rather filled with an ardent desire to go on with it: the more
I write, the more I wish to write. By this means I have the illusion of circum-
venting the fact of our separation, and of rejoicing in your sweet presence
as I converse with you in person. And I think I am not too far deluded in
doing so; for, if we believe the testimony of Turpilius, to send and receive   10
letters is the sole means of uniting absent friends. One can find no more
pleasant or familiar kind of intercourse, among those who are separated,
than an exchange of letters in which the correspondents draw a picture of
themselves for each other, while each of them places at least his mind and
feelings, if not his physical presence, at the other's disposal. It was by such   15
means that the two famous Fathers of the church, Jerome and Augustine,
prevented as they were by enormous temporal and spatial distances from
being together and enjoying each other's embrace as they would have
wished, still managed never to lack each other's presence; and each was
ever aware of the other's feelings of good will. Let us accordingly, my sweet   20
Cornelis, be careful to ensure that frequently something of yours is on the
wing to me or something of mine to you. This will enable us to compensate
for separation and to fulfil the duties of a perfect affection. Let us ever be

* * * * *

32 verses] The following verses are quoted from the *Apologia Herasmi et
Cornelii*, Reedijk 162, lines 181–4 (cf Ep 19:5n).
23:10 Turpilius] The Roman comic poet (fragment 213, quoted by Jerome
Epistles 8:1)

competitors in this most pleasant kind of friendly rivalry, in which I will
not mind being outrun by you, while to be defeated by you will give me   25
the greatest possible pleasure. For, however hard you work at it, you will
never be able to send me enough letters to satisfy my longing for you, much
less turn it into distaste; while you will not very easily become tired of my
company if you really possess the affection for me which your letter pro-
fesses – and of this I make no doubt. To speak in plainer terms, if in fact   30
your attitude to me is of this kind, you will take the same pleasure in my
writings as I do in yours.

 As for me, I find it almost impossible to express how much pleasure
your *Apologeticus* and also your letter brought me; yet I should be glad to
record the fact were I not apprehensive that my statement might appear to   35
proceed from a wish to flatter, rather than from the heart, for I know, dear
Cornelis, how averse your modest nature is to receiving praise. However,
leaving all else aside, suffice it to say that you could not have sent me a more
welcome present than this, since from boyhood I have loved literature, and
still love it, so much that it seems to me rightly to be preferred even to all   40
the treasures of Arabia, and I would not give it up in exchange for Croesus'
entire fortune, however great. And in proportion to the intensity of my love
for literature is the delight I take in the pursuits of literary men. So, my dear
Cornelis, if you love me, as you surely do, pray let me always have some
share in your own studies. Besides this, I should like you to be sure to send   45
me some productions of other men in your circle who have some acquaintance with the art of poetry, so that I may take special pleasure in them and
publish, in this place also, the praises of those eminent men.

 Now, you mentioned in your poem a certain Girolamo, who spent,
you say, twenty-five years in the practice of poetry, both in Italy and in   50

* * * * *

24 in which I ...] The translation follows the reading in Allen's text; but a
better sense would be given if we supposed Erasmus to have written 'mihi
a te' (line 22) through haste, where he meant 'tibi a me.' Taking the latter reading, we should translate: 'in which you will not mind being outrun by me,
while ...'

34 *Apologeticus*] Cf Ep 19:5n.

49 Girolamo] Girolamo Balbi (c 1460–1535?), a Venetian humanist who taught
at Paris 1484–91. He was made much of by the small humanist circles there.
In 1486 or 1487 he published a volume of *Epigrammata* containing some funeral
poems. He also gained considerable notoriety, from his quarrels with Fausto
Andrelini and other scholars, which finally forced him to leave Paris. Cf
Renaudet *Préréforme* 121–4; and P.S. Allen 'Hieronymus Balbus in Paris' EHR
27 (1902) 416–28.

Paris. You have taken care to subjoin, in a note, a funeral poem written by
him, but this is too short to allow us to see his talents clearly, and so I shall
be obliged to you if you will send me some lengthier and more cogent evidence of his ability. And I am most surprised that you describe him as the
only writer who follows the tracks of antiquity; for, not to mention yourself,   55
it seems to me that I see countless well-schooled writers of the present day
who approach quite closely the ancient ideal of eloquence. I think
immediately of Rodolphus Agricola, the former teacher of my own teacher
Alexander. He was a man not only exceptionally highly educated in all the
liberal arts, but extremely proficient in oratory and poetic theory, and   60
moreover as well acquainted with Greek as with Latin. To him may be
added Alexander himself, a worthy pupil of so great a master; so elegantly
did he reproduce the style of the ancients that one might easily mistake the
authorship of a poem by him if the book's title page were missing; and he,
too, is not quite devoid of Greek. Then again, it would be difficult to express   65
how much Westphalia owes to the masterly skill of Antonius Gang and his
friend Friedrich Morman, both of whom, in my opinion, deserve the eternal
remembrance of posterity. Also, there is Bartholomaeus of Cologne, who
I think should by no means be denied his place among men of letters. And

* * * * *

58 Agricola] Rodolphus Agricola (Rudolf Huusman or Huisman) (1433–98),
the celebrated Frisian humanist, was one of the pioneers of the 'new learning'
in the north. In the words of Erasmus, 'he first brought with him from Italy
some gleam of a better literature' (Nichols I 20). On a return trip from Italy
in 1474 he met Hegius at Emmerich and introduced him to the study of Greek.
Erasmus frequently referred to him as Hegius' teacher and always spoke of
him with great reverence (cf *Adagia* I iv 39; and Allen Ep 311:25–7). On his place
in the history of northern humanism, see L.W. Spitz *The Religious Renaissance
of the German Humanists* (Cambridge, Mass 1963) 20–40.

59 Alexander] Alexander Hegius was rector of the school at Deventer from
1483–98 and greatly improved the standard of classical education there.
Although Erasmus left Deventer in 1484, he frequently referred to Hegius with
gratitude as his teacher. Cf Erasmus *Compendium vitae* (Allen I 48; and Ep 19f).
On Hegius at Deventer, see Hyma *Youth of Erasmus* 105ff and *The Christian
Renaissance* (New York 1924) 125ff.

66 Antonius Gang] Erasmus' text may be corrupt; see the note by Allen, who
suggests the reading 'Langen,' ie, Rodolf von Langen, whose identity Erasmus confused with that of Antonius Liber.

67 Morman] Friedrich Morman of Emden was one of the Brethren of the Common Life who taught for some years in the school at Münster in Westphalia.
Agricola in his letters praised Morman's lyric poetry.

68 Bartholomaeus] Bartholomäus Zehender of Cologne (1460–c 1514) was a
pupil of Hegius and later a teacher at Deventer, Münster, and Minden.

I should certainly not leave unmentioned the name of our own Willem of   70
Gouda, your kinsman, were he not so closely bound to me by friendship
and literary studies: I should prefer to hear his praises sung by you, in case
I should be thought to be deluded by affection. Every one has been, and
is, a child of the present generation, and of our own Germany too. If you
are interested in their poems, I shall see that copies reach you as soon as   75
possible. And to pass to Italians, could anyone be a more devoted follower
of the ancient style than Lorenzo Valla, or Filelfo? Or can Aeneas Silvius,
Agostino Dati, Guarino, Poggio, and Gasparino be rivalled for eloquence?
And nobody disputes that all these writers have survived almost to our own
day.   80
    But, my dear Cornelis, the change in the fortunes of literature seems
to me to be just that which has occurred in the other functions of craftsmen
– those, I mean, that are called mechanical. For the poems of nearly all the
bards bear witness that in the earliest ages there flourished craftsmen of vast
renown. As to later times, if you examine reliefs or paintings or sculptures   85
or buildings or indeed works of art of any sort more than two or three
hundred years old, you will, I think, be astonished and laugh at the artists'
extreme crudity; but in our age, again, the diligence of craftsmen has once
more achieved every effect of art. In just the same way it is generally agreed

* * * * *

70 Willem] Willem Hermans. Cf Ep 33 introduction.

77 Filelfo] Francesco Filelfo of Tolentino (1398–1481) was an accomplished
scholar in Greek, which he studied in Constantinople, as well as in Latin. He
taught at Florence 1429–34, but, having taken sides against the Medici, was
forced to leave after the fall of the Albizzi. From 1439 till just before his death
in 1481 he was at Milan in the service of the Visconti and Sforza dukes. His
vanity, avarice, virulent attacks on rivals, and excessive flattery of patrons did
much to give the humanists of his generation a bad name. Cf Rossi 37–43.

77 Silvius] Enea Silvio Piccolomini had made a great reputation as a humanist
before his election as Pope Pius II.

78 Dati] Agostino Dati of Siena (1420–78)

78 Guarino] Guarino de' Guarini of Verona (1370–1460) was the most famous
pedagogue of the fifteenth century; his school at Ferrara was considered a
model of humanist education. Cf G. Saitta L'educazione dell' umanesimo in
Italia (Venice 1928) 91–104.

78 Poggio] Poggio Bracciolini (1380–1459) was one of the most distinguished
Florentine humanists of the first half of the fifteenth century. He discovered
many previously unknown classical MSS and wrote extensively in a fine classical style; cf E. Walser Poggius Florentinus: Leben und Werke (Leipzig 1914).

78 Gasparino] Gasparino Barzizza of Bergamo (c 1370–1431) lectured on
rhetoric at Padua 1407–21 and also maintained a private school in his home.

that in ancient times, while the pursuit of all the arts was flourishing, that   90
of eloquence flourished with particular distinction, but afterwards, in the
obstinate growth of barbarism, so completely disappeared that not a trace
of it remained to be seen. This was when the most uneducated of mankind,
who had never learned, began to teach that of which they were ignorant
– to teach, I repeat, and for a large fee, how to know nothing, making their   95
pupils into greater fools than they were when they took them in, or rather
reducing them to a condition where they failed to know even themselves.
This was the period when men turned their backs on the precepts of the
Ancients and had recourse to new-fangled rules, framed by ineptitude:
modes of signifying, long-winded explications, and countless fancies   100
added to absurd rules of grammar. When, with infinite toil, they had got
all this by heart they had reached such a peak of literary skill and eloquence
that they were incapable of delivering a single discourse in good Latin. In
fact, as far as I can see, if this uncivilized race of human beings had carried
to its end the process it began, it would have turned our art into I know   105
not what new kind of jargon; but at that point both our good Lorenzo Valla,
and Filelfo with admirable scholarly application rescued it from death when
it had all but expired. Valla's books, known under the title of *Elegantiae*,
will inform you how zealously he fought to refute the foolish notions of the
barbarians and to bring back into use the regular practices of authors of   110
prose and verse, long since buried and forgotten. But if, as indeed I suspect,
you have already read these books, there is no need for me to persuade you.
If, however, you have not done so, I urge you, and indeed earnestly desire
you, to begin to read them through; you will never regret the effort. If you
wish to search for copies, be sure to pester Jan for them; he is a very good   115
friend of yours.

* * * * *

108 *Elegantiae*] The *Elegantiarum latinae linguae libri vi* (1444) of Lorenzo Valla
was a landmark in the history of Renaissance philology, setting a new standard of classical Latinity. It was printed frequently from 1471 onward. At about
the time of this letter or a little earlier Erasmus wrote an 'epitome' of the
Elegantiae at the request of a schoolmaster to whom he had recommended it
as the best source from which to teach Latin. Later in Paris he wrote a fuller
paraphrase, which he continued to lend to friends (cf Epp 80:26ff, 81:42, 123:2,
124:29ff, 156, 168). In 1529 the earlier version was published without Erasmus' knowledge by Gymnich in Cologne and quickly reprinted by Etienne
in Paris. Erasmus then revised the work and published it with Emmeus in
Freiburg in March 1531 (cf Allen Epp 2260:63ff, 2412, and 2416). The work soon
became popular and ran through over fifty editions in the next twenty years.
It is in LB I 1069ff.

115 Jan] Jan Christiaan, fifth prior of Steyn (cf Ep 20:4n).

Enough of this. Your letter adds that you gathered from the heading
I wrote in Greek letters that my ode was addressed to 'Cornelis,' but, since
the compliments there paid to you did not square with your opinion of
yourself, you ask me to inform you, if there is someone else whose praise   120
I was trumpeting, who he may be, so that such a great talent may not be
hidden any longer. But – to answer one joke with another – for my part, while
I suspected from the frequent repetition of my own name that your letter
was addressed to me, yet since I cannot find in myself the skill that would
justify compliments like these, I urgently request you to make me better   125
acquainted with the person, whoever he is, whose praises you have sung;
and, when you have produced your second Erasmus, then I shall point out
the second Cornelis I had in mind. So far, I have been joking in your own
way; but, to be serious, I have no doubt that your letter was meant for me,
and want you to be equally sure that my ode was addressed to you. But as   130
you, in your unequalled modesty, assert that those compliments of mine
are undeserved, though I think them far inferior to your deserts, so too I
cannot doubt that those you pay my undeserving self are caused by love's
blindness, and you would have added to them also had you not feared I
might be overtaken by the balmy breezes of vanity. I, too, would certainly   135
add to your praises, did I not realize your intense dislike of being praised.
Farewell, distinguished Father. Willem's letter will reveal to you his feelings about you. I earnestly beg you to give my greetings to those in your
circle who love both you and me – and again, farewell.

24 / From Cornelis Gerard   [Lopsen, 1489?]

CORNELIS OF GOUDA TO THE CONSUMMATE SCHOLAR, ERASMUS
Your lavish kindness, dear Erasmus, reveals itself on all hands, and it has
placed me under strong obligation to you by a service that will not be forgotten. For you have consented to what I long ago requested and shall always
continue eagerly to demand – such is your unequalled good will and innate   5
amiability. You did it of your own free will too, and even did more than
I requested. You say in your letter – and I cannot believe that you wrote without meaning it – that nothing has given you more pleasure than the fact that
you and I are joined in our studies and compensate for our separation by
frequent correspondence. All this, dear Erasmus, raises my love for you to   10
a high pitch and I shall converse with you unfailingly and often by means
of letters; and rightly too, since not only is it, as Cicero testifies, an act of

* * * * *

24:12 Cicero] *Epistolae ad familiares* 1.10

insolence to make an indifferent reply, but it is arrogant to refuse to make
any reply at all. Consequently I am both gratified and happy that you are
seeking my help and that you, who are extremely gifted and truly eminent,   15
do not despise even my unskilled and inexpert self. How noble your nature
is and how endearingly generous in affection! What a vast amount of sheer
love and kindness you reveal! For you were not content to express these sentiments in words alone, but you must also strive to make the fact good, more
forcibly and more clearly still, in the practice of classical study. Accordingly,   20
you put before me as examples those two church Fathers – Jerome and
Augustine, who were most perfect in learning and life and who, being
unable to enjoy each other's company as much as they wished, yet became
so bound together through harmony of minds and similarity of interests
that each was well aware of the other's spirit and good will.   25

Your kindness was increased by your desire not only to spur me to correspondence by citing the example of those saintly authors but also to give
me a teacher to follow in improving my style. The fact that you accordingly
beg me so earnestly to read through Lorenzo Valla brought me both amusement and profit. I do not know what has so blinded your eyes (this I now   30
say in jest) that you recommend for my imitation the writer against whom,
as is well known, many men of considerable learning have joined hands,
as the saying goes, and sworn to do battle. Surely you have not forgotten
the broadsides fired against him by Poggio, a person of no small skill in
eloquence? Do you think it will be a good thing to entrust your friend to   35
one in the study of whose works he cannot persist without getting himself
disliked? We are surrounded by a pack of yelping critics who say positively,
and with emphasis, that one ought not to read an author who, as they put
it, cannot look beyond fussing over a jot or a tittle. Poggio attacks Valla in
a quatrain that goes like this: 40

Now Valla's gone, the shades to seek,
PLUTO's afraid Rome's tongue to speak:
Celestial courts he might have sat in –
But JOVE's afraid he'd scorn his Latin!

So you must consider whether it was right for you to entrust me to one who   45
is condemned by the whole world as a scandalous and vindictive person.

But this was only comic relief. To continue: how much benefit I have
gained from Valla's books, which I read on your recommendation, you can
very easily detect by your own judgment, even in the informal style I am

* * * * *

34 Poggio] See Ep 23:78n. For the exchange of polemics between Poggio and
Valla which became a literary *cause célèbre* in 1452–3, see Rossi 89f.
41–4 Now ... Latin!] These lines are not in Poggio's printed works.

writing now, if I may say so without seeming immodest. Lastly, I could not   50
easily express my gratitude to you for pointing out your own teachers to
me, for you thereby reveal a pure kindness without any trace of jealousy,
and you are pleased, as so few men are, to share with me the secret tricks
of your trade. Farewell.

25 / From Cornelis Gerard   [Lopsen, July 1489?]

CORNELIS OF GOUDA TO THE CONSUMMATE SCHOLAR, ERASMUS OF ROTTERDAM
My dearest Erasmus: in your letter you said that you were most surprised
that I named only Girolamo Balbi, now residing in Paris, as one who, better
than all others, follows the footsteps of antiquity in his poems because it
appears to you that you observe countless writers of the present day who   5
fit the ancient ideal of eloquence well enough both in prose and poetry. And
in treating individual instances you give me a pleasant surprise, as you
clearly show that even our native Germany has produced not a few who are
most adept in prose and poetry alike. I agree with what you say, and it gives
me great delight; yet you do not compel me to abandon my view. However,   10
to convince you that what I said about Girolamo without arrogance was also
said with good reason, it seems to me worth while to illustrate what I have,
in principle, propounded.
    Well then: to go back a little, in order better to understand the matter
– we are aware that Greek *poesis* is called *fictio* in Latin. Let us keep this   15
translation in mind. Now, the ancients taught that every poem contains two
essential elements: external form and content. The term 'external form' is
applied to what the literal sense conveys to the reader at first sight, while
'content' is what the author of the poem wished to be understood under
cover of the metaphor. It follows that the name of poet, or at least of expert   20
in poetry, should be accorded to one who composes a harmonious 'fiction'
in terms of either content or external form or both. If, in the critic's view,
this has not been achieved, then a judgment is made, not that a poet has
composed a poem but that a writer of verse has composed verses. Assuming
this to be a reasonable inference, I return to the instance of Girolamo, in   25
the belief that he is not unfairly to be rated more highly than these men you
speak of who are still alive in the flesh – I omit the dead. At the present time
I can find none save him, among those I have read, who has fully absorbed
the similes and characteristic devices of the poets. And, with the exception
of those vestiges of the poets which seem to consist mainly in the choice   30
of adjectives, he harmonizes his sounds so aptly within the strict limits of

* * * * *

25:3 Balbi] Cf Ep 23:49 and n.

the poetic art that he very fittingly personifies for us a second Ovid, both
in the charm of his poetry and in the frivolity of his mind, though I will
not praise the latter aspect. This can ultimately be tested upon its proper
ground in his own poems, of which I possess very few.   35

And, in case anyone reproaches me with the vice of frivolity for my
observation that the poet conceals the truth under fable and metaphor, let
me, since the opportunity arises, quote the opinion of the ancients on this
point. I will not say the poets, since none of them states his view explicitly,
but the old philosophers and legislators invented fables for the public good. 40
If you ask why, let Strabo himself answer you in his own words. 'Since,'
he says, 'no account of philosophy can be presented to the common herd,
and it cannot easily be adapted to religious formulas and faiths, man needed
the fear of divine powers; now, this cannot be engendered without the use
of fictitious tales and wonders, and consequently the entire theology of   45
early ages was characterized by the thunderbolt, aegis, trident, blazing
torches, staff of Bacchus, serpents' hair, barking of Cerberus, and weapons
of the gods.' Virgil too was making use of this pattern when, in order the
more forcibly to impress on the unschooled multitude the opinion of Pythagoras who held that a snake is engendered from a dead man's backbone,   50
he recounted in his poem how a serpent crept forth from Anchises' tomb.

But enough of this. Be assured that all your poems dazzle me to such
an extent that I have already made up my mind to dedicate my own poor
efforts to Deucalion, if you do not take pains to give me relief from the
benumbed state in which the excessive brilliance of your poems has now   55
left me. Farewell.

26 / To Cornelis Gerard   [Steyn, July 1489?]

ERASMUS TO HIS FRIEND CORNELIS; WRITTEN AS A BOY
First of all, my dear Cornelis, I should like you to rest assured that I regard
you in a spirit of perfect friendship; and I not only trust, but have already

* * * * *

41 Strabo] *Geographia* 1.2.8

51 serpent ... from Anchises' tomb] Virgil *Aeneid* 5.84ff

54 to Deucalion] That is, to destruction by water (see the account of the flood,
for example in Ovid *Metamorphoses* 1).

26:1 as a boy] These words ('scripsit puer'), which appear also in the
address of Ep 29, were in neither case part of the original MS nor of the first
printed edition in which the letters occur, the *Farrago epistolarum* of 1519. They
were added in the *Epistolae ad diversos* of 1521. By that time Erasmus had forgotten how old he was when he wrote the letters, or wished to appear to have
been younger. These two letters are the only ones from Erasmus' monastic
days to have been printed during his lifetime.

fully established by countless proofs that you so regard me. So if in my letters you come upon a rather flattering phrase, you are to assign it not to the   5
wiles of a Gnatho but to true affection while, if for the sake of defending
my views or for any other reason I have said something with excessive frank-
ness, you must not suppose that my love for you has declined, much less
died altogether. I wish to say these things, not because I see that you and
I now disagree in any respect, but in order to safeguard our mutual good   10
will should anything of the kind occur in the future. For I interpret your
remarks about our Valla in such a way as to suppose that you penned them
not as a sincere expression of opinion but with some ulterior motive, either
in order to exercise your literary talents on a paradox or to furnish me with
something to write about; that is, just as Glaucon in Plato by reviling justice   15
incites Socrates to undertake its defence, so you would draw me on to
defend Valla by rehearsing the disgraceful slanders, the drunken ravings
against a first-rate scholar, of perfect fools who have graduated in barbarism. This indeed can be easily inferred from the evidence; for you admit
that you not only studied Valla but imitated him, and even if you denied   20
this fact it would be proclaimed aloud by your elegance of language and
style. Anyone then who, loving his own incompetence as a pig loves the
mud, thinks it may bring him fame and distinction if, ignorant as he is of
all worthy concerns, he assails the most learned of men with ill-will, hatred,
and abuse, may speedily, if he is willing, discover how very foolish he is.   25
    To begin with, it is proper to assess everyone in terms of his own good
qualities, not of other men's judgments; what we must observe is not the
value set on him by rumour, which is the most deceptive thing in the world,
but how he actually behaves. Otherwise it will happen to every man that
from time to time he suddenly becomes someone else and completely   30
denies his own character. I am thought educated by some, barbarous by
others; good by some, bad by others; rather boastful by some, rather modest by others; finally to one man I appear handsome, to another ugly. Shall
I not outdo in changeability the most Protean character possible, shall I not,
in fact, become some kind of monster, if I have to be whatever the crowd   35
takes a fancy to make of me? On the contrary, just as all that wins enthusiastic popular approval ought to be regarded with suspicion, so the violent dislike of the mob is a first step to a justified reputation for excellence. It will

* * * * *

6 Gnatho] A 'parasite' in Terence's *Eunuchus* (251–3), whom Cicero (*De amicitia*, for example) helped to make proverbial for flattery. See also below, lines 62ff.
15 Glaucon] Cf Plato *Republic* II.357–66.
16 defence] See the more fully developed defence of Valla in Ep 182.
22–3 pig loves the mud] Cf *Adagia* IV iii 62.

even happen on occasion that I become now white, now black in the same
person's judgment. Stesichorus depicted Helen as ugly; but presently,   40
when he had been blinded, he represented her as the fairest of women,
though nothing in the meantime had altered Helen's looks for better or for
worse. Those, therefore, who object that Valla's reputation is regarded with
extreme disapproval by most men are proving nothing; for this trouble is
one to which excellence has always been vulnerable. Yes, many dislike   45
Lorenzo: but who are these? Why, the very men who dislike polite literature
itself!

Someone may say at this point: 'While we ought to pay no attention
to the petty talk of the crowd, how was Valla regarded by Poggio – a man
of some taste and learning?' Poggio, it is true, was hostile to him, and Pog-   50
gio alone; and it was Poggio's nature to prefer to be regarded as most
learned rather than to acquire more learning. I should myself accept his
inclusion among scholars, with the reservation that he is not entirely remote from association with barbarous men, being naturally fluent rather
than erudite and possessing a greater capacity for loquacity than eloquence.   55
Lastly, if Poggio censures Lorenzo, it is obviously because he is an unpleasant man and a personal enemy of Lorenzo's. This was the spirit in which
Sallust and Asinius criticized Cicero, Caligula criticized Virgil and Livy,
and Rufinus criticized Jerome. It is also a simple matter to explain how
Lorenzo stirred up so much unpopularity for himself; for it was a clever   60
remark of Sosia's in Terence's play, that 'Flattery earns friends, while the
truth engenders hatred.' On the other side, that well-known parasite
Gnatho, who had made it his rule to agree with everyone, to say no if anyone else did, praise if anyone else did, and then again say the opposite if
he had a mind to – how easily he won everyone's good opinion, so that he   65
not unreasonably thought that that way of making a living was the most

* * * * *

49 Poggio] Cf Ep 24:34ff and n.

57–8 This was the spirit ...] The names that follow are well known examples
of authors whose greatness is universally acknowledged and who were
attacked by critics moved by personal spite, which nullified the effect of the
criticism. The historian Sallust and Gaius Asinius Gallus (d AD 33) both published attacks on Cicero. Sallust's survive (they are in fact spurious); Gallus'
are mentioned in Pliny *Epistles* 7.4.3 and Aulus Gellius *Noctes Atticae* 17.1.
The emperor Caligula thought of eliminating the works of Virgil and Livy
from all libraries (cf Suetonius *Caligula* 34.2). The attack of Rufinus provoked
an *Apologia* from St Jerome to which Erasmus frequently refers.

61 Sosia] Cf Terence *Andria* 68, *Adagia* II ix 53.

63 Gnatho] See line 6n.

rewarding of all. Very different was the nature of Demea when, without any previous acquaintance with civilized life, he tried to befriend the truth and made himself no friends at all as a result – to such an extent that even his children deserted him, and his life was thenceforth bereft and solitary, so bitter and unacceptable is truth to most people. Therefore, if our good Lorenzo had elected to pass over in silence, rather than reveal, the ignorance of the barbarians, he would now be considered charming and agreeable; but as it is, since he caused the removal of the whitewash from the ill-deserved reputations of some to prevent them from seeming to be that which they were not, all men are ready to sink their angry teeth into him.

But as concerns even the behaviour of scholars on occasion, has anyone ever lived in Athens, or in Italy, the conqueror of Athens, who was so well informed that nothing escaped him? And just as we are all by our very nature prone to error, so also we are much more ready to err if there are authorities to afford a precedent for doing so – especially if these have to recommend them the prestige of a distinguished reputation. And it is the way of the uneducated to ignore whatever authors have said well, just as the cock in Aesop's fables ignored the jewel he had found, whereas they carefully cull, for the purpose of defending their own mistakes, any mistake those authors make. For this reason it was necessary not to conceal the slips made by even the greatest of men. And whom can we entirely acquit of error, if Cicero be guilty of a sin against elegance in his Latinity? Nay, if Poggio had chosen frankly to confess and amend his faults, rather than peevishly defend them (and he would have so chosen, had he been willing to behave like a man of intelligence), far from thinking Lorenzo deserved attack he would certainly have judged him to be worthy of honour and gratitude for his good advice.

Hard-pressed by these arguments, some take refuge in the following as a kind of last resort: 'Granted that he was right to blame famous men,' they say, 'still he did it with an excessive degree of sharpness.' Personally, I fail to see what he said against them that was too sharp, unless perhaps they are prepared to describe as highly distinguished the very men I consider to be outstanding as ringleaders of barbarism, namely Papias, Uguc-

* * * * *

67 Demea] Cf Terence *Adelphoe* 855ff.

84 Aesop's fables] Cf Phaedrus *Fables* 3.12.

99 Papias] An eleventh-century Lombard, author of a glossary in general use in the Middle Ages, printed in Milan in 1476

99 Uguccio] Uguccio of Pisa was a bishop of Ferrara and canonist who died in 1210. His *Liber derivationum* was an enlargement of Papias' glossary.

cio of Pisa, Eberhard, the *Catholicon*, John of Garland, Isidore, and others   100
not even worth mentioning: or, alternatively, unless they place upon 'say
with sharpness' exactly the same meaning as upon 'blame.' But let us grant
that he was too sharp: does the fact that he spoke the truth sharply make
him guilty of an untruth? Is the sharpness you mention so distasteful to us
that, for dislike of it, we must vilify so many things both necessary and   105
worth knowing? Are we to insist on showing no forgiveness to one who
has helped us in so many ways? A man who gives a dinner is excused if
one dish among many delights appears slightly burned or not properly seasoned. If, with the enemy at the city's gates and the citizens at their last gasp
of extremity and despairing of safety, someone unexpectedly presents him-   110
self to repel the foe at the peril of his life and restore freedom to his countrymen, then surely all men vie in awarding him fame and favour. Is it going
to make us loathe him if he is somewhat intemperate in drinking, and is
such a slight fault likely to wipe out the remembrance of his great service?
And, in the same way, is anyone so small-minded, so pinched at heart by   115
the narrowest sort of ill-will, as not to accord generous praise and the warmest possible affection to Valla, who bestowed such intense industry, application, and exertion in combating the follies of the barbarians and rescuing
literature from extinction when it was all but buried, in restoring Italy to
her ancient literary glory, and even in conferring a benefit on scholars by   120
obliging them to express themselves more carefully in future?

This, then, dear Cornelis, is a man to whom you may safely entrust
yourself, unless you are afraid of being mauled by the fellow's dangerous
teeth; and you may do so, if not without the unpopularity which always
tends to wait upon great and glorious achievements, yet, in my opinion,   125
with the greatest profit and honour. While you are doing this, and I do earnestly beg that you do it more and more; you will find that not a little polish

* * * * *

100 Eberhard] Eberhard of Béthune, called Graecista, was a twelfth-century
grammarian, author of a Latin grammar in verse entitled *Graecismus* which
explained Latin words derived from the Greek. It was printed in Paris by
P. Levet, 4 January 1488.

100 *Catholicon*] A Latin grammar and dictionary composed c 1286 by Giovanni
Balbi, a Genoese Dominican, and printed in Mainz in 1460.

100 John of Garland] John of Garland (c 1180–c 1258), an Englishman who
taught in Paris; his *Dictionnarius, Compendium grammaticae*, and *Accentuarium*
were standard works.

100 Isidore] Isidore of Seville (c 560–636) was one of the most important trans-
mitters of antique learning to the Middle Ages. His *Etymologiae* was a widely
used encyclopaedia.

is added to your compositions – unless of course you are writing them for
Dutchmen alone! Farewell.

[1490]

27 / To Cornelis Gerard   [Steyn, July 1489?]

ERASMUS OF ROTTERDAM TO THE LEARNED CORNELIS OF GOUDA

In spite of the very great utility, and to some extent the attractiveness, of
the kind of prose that deals with struggle and conflict, I must confess, dear
Cornelis, that I take much more pleasure in what is called the familiar kind;
for while the latter is gentle and peaceable, the former is somewhat too   5
agitated, and whereas the latter is cheerful and friendly, the former frequently verges on ill-will. For, if one proceeds to form judgments about
famous or at least well-known men, no matter what the tendency of one's
remarks may be, since everybody has his own opinion there will always
be some who take offence and resent it and attack you. But I do not wish,   10
dear Cornelis, to seem too independent, much less obstinate and supercilious, if I forget to reply to your letter; so I shall give you in a few words my
views about Girolamo Balbi.

First of all, I do not consider myself at all qualified to express an opinion on the poems written by men of letters. Just as nobody is able to judge   15
rightly about sculpture and painting and so forth unless he himself is a fully
qualified artist in the same field, similarly how is anyone to judge whether
poems are well made or not, if he has but a slight acquaintance, or none
at all, with the art of poetry? Next, I should like you to observe how closely
our views agree. You say in your letter that *poesis* means 'fiction,' in Latin, 20
and that nobody deserves the name of poet unless he veils and conceals
some deeper meaning beneath a kind of exotic display of words; and your
conclusion is that out of this whole class it is Girolamo Balbi who has best
deserved to be given pride of place. But does one who has earned the name
of poet automatically deserve to be called an accomplished poet – as if the   25
word poet had not been applied even to the victims of Virgil's witty line:
'Let him who shuns not Bavius admire your lines, O Maevius.'

The difference between a poet and a skilful poet is the same as that
between a painting and a work of art; and just as a painting must be
endowed with many qualities if it is rightly to be called beautiful – for exam- 30
ple, pleasing colours and dexterous use of contrasting tones, good propor-

* * * * *

27:11 too independent] Reading 'minus' for 'nimis'
13 Balbi] Cf Ep 23:49n.
26 Virgil] *Eclogues* 3.90

tions, technical application, and attention on the part of the artist, so also in writing poetry a great many points have to be watched if the result is to be creditable. Of the first importance are these: a lively power of invent- ing themes, clever arrangement, harmony of style, a retentive memory. We   35 must add to them the brilliant effect created by rhetorical devices. We have further to take great care to ensure that there is no confusion in the figures of speech and that we are not too long-winded or excessively obscure. Lastly, we must erase much and revise still more before we regard what we have written as ready for publication. But why should I attempt to include   40 the whole world in a small map, as it were – to embrace the entire science of rhetoric and its rules within the compass of a short letter? Why should I endeavour to teach Minerva, as the saying goes, or carry wood into a for- est? You know your Cicero, your Quintilian, your Horace, your Geoffrey of Vinsauf, and you are certainly not unaware of the abundance of excellent   45 advice on the art of poetry which they contain; whoever keeps their advice faithfully is bound to fulfil to perfection his function as a poet. But I do not really think that the glory of great poetry consists in epithets or a charming style, for it can be observed that the first of these is somewhat rare in Ter- ence and in Horace, while the second is scarcely to be found in Persius,   50 Sidonius, and various other highly sophisticated writers. There is the fact, besides, that while Ovid and Tibullus are certainly much more suave than our favourite Virgil, nevertheless they do not by any means automatically rob him of his supremacy. And so, my dear Cornelis, while you have cer- tainly proved that your friend Girolamo is a poet, you have not yet achieved   55 your whole purpose. But even if we grant that he is foremost of all, have I really done your Girolamo an injustice if, when you extolled him as the only poet to follow the footsteps of the ancients, I rejoined that this was no solitary feat but one he performed in company with a great many others, whereby I neither set anyone else above him, nor him below anyone else?   60

All this, dear Cornelis, was my contribution to the battle of the gladiators, as it were, or rather of the wrestlers in the training-schools; or rather, it was but my jesting. But 'now put we sport aside, and serious themes indite.' When I study the poems of your Girolamo, no, our Girolamo, it gives me inexpressible pleasure to find such distinguished and   65

* * * * *

43 teach Minerva] *Adagia* i 1.40
43–4 wood into a forest] *Adagia* i vii 57
44–5 Geoffrey of Vinsauf] Or Geoffrey de Vino Salvo. An Englishman who is thought to have written the *Poetria nova* c 1210
63–4 'now ... indite.'] Horace *Satires* 1.1.27

lively reminders of the ancient style of eloquence surviving today; and to
find their author wholly worthy to be loved, cherished, and read by all men
who are fond of letters. All the same, I am not sure that I should venture
to set him above all contemporary authors; partly because it is easy to write
epigrams prettily, partly because of the 'songs that challenge the victor's   70
crown' on either hand. But you will greatly oblige me by lending me
Girolamo's other poems as well, or those of any others you have. I am most
grateful to you for your great and generous acts of kindness, and shall continue to be so as long as I live. Farewell.

27A / To Cornelis Gerard   [Steyn, 1489?]

A fragment from the Gouda MS 1323. A facsimile is published in Allen I
between 116 and 117. See Allen I app IX.

ERASMUS TO HIS FRIEND CORNELIS
Both for the sake of our friendship, dear Cornelis, and because of your
unequalled scholarship, I speak highly in my work, as it deserves, of all that
comes from you; so please take care that you do not allow anything not quite
finished or quite well considered to see the light of day. Certainly whatever   5
you write deserves to be preserved for posterity, but please make sure that
all of it accords with your talents, your reputation, and your learning. For
although ...

28 / To Cornelis Gerard   [Steyn, 1489?]

ERASMUS OF ROTTERDAM TO THE POET AND THEOLOGIAN CORNELIS
My dearest Cornelis: your letters capture my spirit with a peculiar joy and
fire me with intense longing for your presence. You say in your letter that
you have heard that I had written a narrative poem in honour of St Bavo;
this was a false report, brought to you by deceitful rumour, for it was not   5
myself but my second self who wrote the poem, your most affectionate kinsman Willem. Between him and me such a warm friendship has sprung up
that one might say we are one soul in two bodies. But, since you kindly
remind me of this, I have decided for the future to write nothing which does
not breathe the atmosphere either of praise of holy men or of holiness   10
itself. Yet if any of the poems I am sending to you seems more self-indulgent

* * * * *

70–1 'songs ... crown'] Juvenal 11.181

28:4 St Bavo] This refers to Willem Hermans' Ode 12 'In laudem diui Bavonis
Haerlemensis oppidi presidis,' from his *Silva odarum* (cf Ep 49 introduction).

than is proper you will readily forgive this in consideration of the time of
life at which I wrote them; for, apart from the lyric ode which I was writing
when your letter arrived, and the funeral speech which as a new production
I thought I ought to send you in order that you may have evidence of my   15
capacities in prose also, and that one solitary satire, all the rest of the poems
were written by me when I was a youth and virtually still a layman.

I had nothing more at hand to give to you, for whatever I had left was
wrested from me by a friend of mine, and taken partly to Alexander Hegius
the schoolmaster, my former teacher, and to Bartholomaeus of Cologne, a   20
man of unique learning and a great lover of poetry, whose poems I have;
and partly to Utrecht. But I have taken care to send you a copy of the letter
which I once sent on request to Master Engelbert, who is distinguished by
the sanctity of his life, hoping that by your mediation I may perhaps deserve
thereby to receive at his hands something in return, which has eluded me   25
thus far. I do not for this reason hold such an eminent man under suspicion
on the grounds of superciliousness or arrogance, but I do view with suspicion the prattling tongues of my friends which have most maliciously be-
smirched my good name in his hearing. Therefore, it must devolve upon
your kindness, dear Cornelis, to make me acceptable once more in the eyes   30
of him with whom you carry the greatest weight. Such an action would be
consistent with your generous nature and also win my deep gratitude.
Farewell, and
                    with faithful heart
Let love responsive keep us, though apart.   35

* * * * *

13 lyric ode] Allen suggests a possible reference to the Sapphic verses on St
Michael mentioned in the *Catalogus lucubrationum*, Allen I 3 line 31.

14 funeral speech] Probably the *Oratio funebris in funere Bertae de Heyen*, LB
VIII 551

16 satire] Probably one of the satires in elegiacs published by Reyner Snoy
in *Herasmi Roterodami silua carminum* (Gouda 1513); critical edition in *Opuscula*
14ff and Reedijk 207ff

19 Hegius] Cf Ep 23:59n.

20 Bartholomaeus] Zehender (cf Ep 23:68n).

22 Utrecht] Probably some verses designed to win favour with David of Burgundy, bishop of Utrecht, who became his patron and ordained him priest,
22 April 1492. Cf LB X 1573A, Nichols I 85, and Allen I 588.

23 Engelbert] Engelbert Schut of Leiden was a schoolmaster and apparently
of sufficient means to make him a potential patron. See M. Van Rijn 'Engelbert
van Leiden' NAKG ns 20 (1927) 289ff; and Reedijk's introduction to Erasmus'
poem addressed to Engelbert at about this time and possibly the 'letter' referred to here (Reedijk 156ff; cf *Opuscula* 4f).

34–5 with ... apart] Tibullus 1.6.75, 76

29 / To Cornelis Gerard   [Steyn, 1489]

ERASMUS OF ROTTERDAM TO CORNELIS OF GOUDA, WRITTEN AS A BOY
'Such enmity's twixt me and thee / As lamb and wolf by Fate's decree.' Come
now, please either resume good relations with my friend Lorenzo Valla, or,
take it from me, I declare open war on you. 'Why this sudden upset?' you
ask. As if you had forgotten those disgraceful, unforgivable insults you   5
uttered about him when you were staying here with us recently. I shudder
to recall the effrontery of it! To think you dare to give the name of 'croaking
crow' to the most eloquent of men, whom one might quite justifiably call
the marrow of persuasion, and describe him as no orator, but a pettifogging
critic. Were he alive to day, you'd certainly pay for that! And you would   10
find that you were up against somebody who was anything but toothless;
indeed, it would be made clear to you that the animal you had provoked
was a horned species. He would use every known weapon, including all
the arrows of invective, against you, and you would receive no kinder treatment at his hands than the unfortunate Poggio did. But you are not afraid   15
of a man long since in his grave, and are only too conscious that dead men
don't bite. Oh, you hero: ranting at one who cannot answer you! It is quite
safe to say, or do, whatever you please against him: but, in case you are
inclined to gloat prematurely, it is not quite as safe as all that.

In me you see the avenger of Valla's wrongs; I have undertaken to de-   20
fend his scholarship, the most distinguished I know. Never shall I allow that
scholarship to be attacked or destroyed with impunity because of anyone's
insolence, or ill-will for that matter. This is why I have instructed the present letter to go to you as my emissary and to demand satisfaction from you.
Be careful how you treat it for you have the choice of either satisfying my   25
delegation or, preparing for war. Do not, however, cherish the thought that
you will get away with a crime like this by relying on my indulgence. Certainly, I am somewhat remiss in dealing with wrongs against myself; but
as for the defence of my literary friends, you may, if you wish, find out

* * * * *

29:1 Cornelis of Gouda] The address here is in the unusual form of 'Cornelius
Aurotinus.' Normally Erasmus addressed his friend as 'Cornelius Goudanus'
or 'Gaudanus.' Cornelis was also known, especially in later life, as 'Cornelius
Aurelius,' a fanciful Latinization of Gouda, from the Dutch 'goud,' meaning
'gold' (cf Ep 17 introduction). The cognomen 'Aurotinus' used here was
similarly derived.

2 'Such ... decree.'] Horace *Epodes* 4.1, 2

16–17 dead men don't bite] *Adagia* III vi 41

24 emissary] Erasmus uses (as he does elsewhere) the Roman idea of 'fetiales,'
two priests who went as plenipotentiaries to demand satisfaction from
another state, with powers to declare war instantly if it was not granted.

how aggressive and how determined I am. I permit you, if you so desire, 30
to call to your colours that Engelbert of yours, who, you tell me, is so drunk
upon the waters of poetic inspiration that he exudes verses at every pore,
together with any others like him; and it is easy enough anywhere to find
a stock of such people. But you are not to suppose that I shall fail to find
my troops, too, since the wrong you have done affects not only me but all 35
friends of good literature. In hurting Valla, you have hurt all educated men.

   For my part, dear Cornelis, I dislike nothing so much as civil war, and
to it I would prefer any kind of peace at all, even the most unjust. So if you
too prefer peace to war you will find me well disposed enough so long as
you accept my terms; of these there are three in particular which my delega- 40
tion will offer you, and they are not particularly hard ones, so that you can
complain neither of their number nor of their unfairness. Now pay attention and listen. First you are to atone by praise for your wicked slanders,
by referring to Valla as 'the marrow of persuasion' and the Attic muse
instead of a 'croaking crow'; secondly, you are to learn Valla's *Elegantiae* so 45
thoroughly that you become as familiar with them as with your own toes
and fingers; lastly, you are to place at my disposal the books, of which you
have a large collection, over which you have thus far brooded like a dragon
over the Hesperides.

   Are you laughing, and do you think I speak in jest? Laugh as much 50
as you like, then, but do not imagine that I have been joking in all that I
have said, for I would not wish that remark about sending me books to be
taken as a joke. Furthermore, do not think it does you credit to use the
tongue's darts to attack Valla, whom nobody but a barbarian can dislike;
for you yourself are the most faithful devotee of literary culture. Farewell. 55

   1489

30 / To Cornelis Gerard   [Steyn, 1489?]

ERASMUS OF ROTTERDAM TO HIS FRIEND CORNELIS
As Cicero wrote, there are two things above all that usually enervate our
minds: leisure and solitude, and I have no lack of either of them. It is true
that my kind of life requires solitude, but the chief reason for my leisure
is that I observe literature, which once won benefits and fame for its 5

* * * * *
31 Engelbert] The tone of this reference to Engelbert is quite different from
that in Ep 28:23. Reedijk suggests that Erasmus' overtures may have been met
with a rebuff (Reedijk 157f). Years later in the *De conscribendis epistolis* (ASD I
2 231) Erasmus wrote that Engelbert's model epistles taught boys nothing but
how to write ineptly.
48 dragon] Cf *Adagia* IV iii 16.
30:2 Cicero] *De officiis* 3.1.1

devotees, causing loss and disrepute among the men of today, since things have come to a pass where the more educated a person is the more he is pursued by misfortune and derision. Accordingly, my dear Cornelis, I saw no reason to spend my life idly in the study of literature, with the result that I have long since completely given up its pursuit. To these considera- 10 tions was added the unsatisfactory state of my health, a factor which as a rule not only reduces mental energy but even destroys it.

At the same time, since no object in my life means as much to me as gratifying, obeying, and obliging you, and of course I owe you this in the highest measure for the sake of the extraordinary generosity with which 15 you have treated me, I have resumed this occupation for your sake and have finished, as diligently as I could, that oration of yours for which you had

* * * * *

17 oration] The *Antibarbari*, which Erasmus had begun about this time or earlier. In 1520 he wrote that he had begun it when he had not yet reached his twentieth year, that is, before October 1488 at the latest (Allen Ep 1110:20). In the *Vita divi Hieronymi* (1516) he also referred to it as having been written when he was a youth less than twenty years old (*Opuscula* 176, line 1135). Later, probably in 1494 when he was in the service of the bishop of Cambrai, he revised it and cast it in dialogue form in two books (cf Ep 371, Allen I App. v). It was later planned in four books, of which only the first survives. On his arrival in Paris he showed what he had done to Gaguin, who approved it with the slight criticism that the preface was too long (Ep 46). He also showed the first two books to Colet, who was favourably impressed (cf Allen Ep 1110:29f). In Italy he expanded the first book with a view to publication and amended the second (ibid 38f, and Allen I 34). When passing through Ferrara in December 1508 he deposited them with other papers, including the *De copia* (cf Ep 260) and *De ratione studii* (cf Ep 66), with Richard Pace (cf Ep 211). Eras- mus returned to England the following year and had no opportunity to recover the papers. Pace, on leaving Ferrara, then entrusted them to William Thale, who sold what he could and gave away others, including the *De copia*, which he gave to Sixtinus (cf Ep 244). In 1517 Erasmus was apparently considering rewriting the *Antibarbari* with More as one of the interlocutors, but had not yet recovered the MS from Pace (cf Allen Ep 706:32n). Later he found a copy of book I in Louvain and after revising it sent it to Froben, who published it in May 1520 (Ep 1110). The remaining books were never published, though Erasmus was still trying to get book II from Pace in June 1521 (Ep 1210:18). An earlier draft, dated 1519, is to be found in the town library at Gouda. It was at one time in the library of the Brethren of the Common Life in Gouda and may have been copied by one of the brethren. Allen called attention to its exis- tence in 1924; see Allen V xx (this page, however, is missing in some copies of Allen v). This draft, which he asserts to be based on the original version completed before 1495, was published by Albert Hyma, together with the printed edition, in 1930 in his *Youth of Erasmus* 239–331. For discussion of the history and contents of the *Antibarbari*, see ibid 182–204, and R. Pfeiffer 'Die Wandlungen der *Antibarbari*' in his *Ausgewählte Schriften* (Munich 1960) 188–207. Critical edition in ASD I 1 1–138.

asked me. I have taken pains, moreover, to add careful notes on the divisions of oratory, and similarly the form and appropriate rhetorical treatment of each, so that you gain your wish, and men of letters applaud my 20
interest in the matter, while the unschooled look on with hostility and those who vaunt their superficial knowledge blush for shame. As for men of moderate talents, they actually benefit in some degree. These, dear Cornelis, are types of mankind you will meet everywhere. Men who are truly educated cannot but view literature with approval and affection; but those who are 25
incompetent at each and every art think all of them should be condemned and attacked and harried; they allow no praise of anything of which they are ignorant and no dispraise of anything they know. How clever of them! They belittle whatever they do not possess, to avoid the reputation of lacking a single element of greatness. In their opinion Cicero himself is a bar- 30
barian, while Eberhard is an expert. Why? For the sole reason, plainly, that they are familiar with the one and know nothing about the other.

Now, it matters not a straw to me if these people look askance at my little oration, or malign it, or even explode about it. Indeed, I shall consider it a distinction not to win the approval of such as these for, being incapable 35
of holding their tongues, they will demonstrate to all the world their ignorance and absurdity. There are also some to be found who, resembling Thraso in Terence, though incompetent in every art, with rash confidence, or confident rashness, claim to be qualified in all of them. You cannot confront them with a subject at which they are not past masters; they declaim 40
and debate and poetize prettily; they have a pretty command of grammar and of music and what not else: 'Well do they nothing; yet they do all prettily.' If this class of men ever have the leisure to read my little oration they will discover, unambiguously, I believe, that it requires no small skill to speak or write in a good Latin style; and if they have any sense of shame 45
they will cease to profess their proficiency in those arts which they have never learnt. But, if they are so thirsty for fame that they would pursue it at all costs, let them strive rather to master those activities by which it is possible for them to win undying fame, or else they may be marked as men of deceit not of destiny. For ill-gained fame is but short-lived, whereas true 50
fame puts down roots and shines more widely and more brightly each day. When people of only moderate ability read the speeches or poems of gifted

* * * * *

38 Thraso] The braggart soldier in the *Eunuchus* of Terence
42–3 'Well do they ... prettily.'] Martial 2.7.7
50–1 For ill-gained fame ... day.] Cf Cicero *Philippics* 2.27.65; also *De officiis* 2.12.43.

writers, they feel strong emotion and are carried along perforce wherever
the argument leads but without knowing what it is that has moved them.
Such persons will in part at least be able to find out, by using my work, what   55
it is that gives them such great pleasure. My final hope is that even you,
sweetest Cornelis, will gain from my studies something either of profit or
at least of enjoyment; if, however, you gain nothing of the kind I shall still
have done my duty as a most devoted friend. Farewell, and continue to love
me as you do.

60

31 / To a friend

[Steyn, 1489?]

Allen has found no clue to the identity of the person addressed, beyond the
fact that he was a married man and had shown Erasmus some kindness. This
Erasmus acknowledges by the gift of a MS of Terence written with his own
hand.

ERASMUS OF ROTTERDAM TO HIS FRIEND
Whenever the thought of your many very great kindnesses, and indeed
your extremely generous attitude, comes into my mind, I always blame the
circumstances, pinching, grudging, and unfair as I call them, that prevent
me from returning in kind the lavish affection you have shown me. Person-   5
ally I consider as the most annoying and depressing of all the troubles that
have from boyhood beset me, whether of God's command or by the
influence of my birth-star, that I am innately disposed to prefer giving to
receiving, or at least returning thanks for favours with interest, to the circumstances which require me to accept benefits from anyone but permit   10
payment to none. And what could be more galling to any man of an honourable and generous nature? When Aeschines, who in youth was gifted but
indigent, saw his fellow pupils making presents to their teacher Socrates,
each according to his ability, he began to be conscious of his straitened
means purely and simply because he had not the wherewithal even to sug-   15
gest the depth of his gratitude. Nevertheless his talents found a way of providing what fortune had denied to him for the present he gave his teacher
was himself, and by his modesty and wise address he made the gift most
acceptable to Socrates. But in proportion as I am poorer than Aeschines,
inasmuch as I have not now even that to dispose of, please accept in lieu   20
of the token of gratitude you deserve the assurance that the heart of your
Erasmus is filled with thankfulness, remembrance, and affection and ever

* * * * *

31:12 Aeschines] Cf Diogenes Laertius 2.5.34.

wishes his friend everything that is good. And all this I know to be acceptable to men of generous disposition, even without a material gift, whereas
the latter, given without the feelings I have mentioned, never gave pleasure   25
to any but the basest of men. In the event I can promise you, in ample
measure, all the customary verbal and written expressions of gratitude.

At the same time I beg you to accept as a pledge and souvenir of our
friendship the accompanying book which I have written out with my own
hand; I have in fact taken more pains over correcting it than writing it.   30
Please bestow on this my little gift, or souvenir if so you prefer it to be
called, the same affection as you have shown me. I shall finally be sure you
have given it such affection when you show that you have studied it diligently and when I hear that it is always on your person and in your hands
and on your lap. I consider as lovers of books, not those who keep their   35
books hidden in their store-chests and never handle them, but those who,
by nightly as well as daily use, thumb them, batter them, wear them out,
who fill up all the margins with annotations of many kinds, and who prefer
the marks of a fault they have erased to a neat copy full of faults. And I think
that, as with other authors, this ought to be a common practice when read-   40
ing Terence, the author of this book, for anyone who wishes to acquire
a proper command of the Roman idiom, not the half-Latin–half-French
which is approximately what our schoolmasters and their Alexander teach.
The style of his comedies is wonderfully pure, choice, and elegant, with
very little roughness, considering that he is a comic writer of such early   45
date. There is also a polished and witty charm; and without charm all prose
style, however elaborate, is crude. So you will be able to learn from him,
if from anyone, how those ancient writers of Latin actually spoke, who nowadays are made to stammer even worse than ourselves; and this is why I
am of the opinion that you ought not merely to read him again and again,   50
but even learn him by heart.

Be on your guard against paying any attention at all to the prattling
of those ignorant and indeed malevolent dwarfs who, once they realize that
they have grown old over most incompetent authorities (the *Florista*,

* * * * *

28 pledge] Cf Virgil *Aeneid* 5.538.

43 Alexander] Alexandre de Ville-Dieu, author of a mediaeval grammar in
verse: *Doctrinale puerorum*

49 stammer] Because of the corrupt state of contemporary texts, alluded to by
Erasmus in his remarks on correction in the preceding paragraph

54 *Florista*] Allen suggests Ludolph of Luchow (c 1317), author of *Flores artis
grammatice alias Florista*, printed by Quentell at Cologne in 1505.

Eberhard Graecista and Uguccio of Pisa) and have never been able to make   55
their way out of the maze of ignorance, for all their turning about, offer
themselves one sole and sufficient consolation for their own foolishness: to
entice all their juniors into the same web of error. They say it is sinful for
a Christian to study the plays of Terence. Why so, I ask? 'Because,' they say,
'these plays contain nothing but lechery and immoral love-affairs between   60
young people, which cannot but corrupt the reader's mind.' He who is
already corrupt will easily be corrupted by anything. ('Unless the vessel be
clean, 'twill sour whatsoever you put there.') And are we to believe that
these pedants, who are blinder than moles where other subjects, even the
most important, are concerned, turn lynx-eyed when it comes to lechery,   65
if such there be? No, these fools, these goats, who grasp only at wickedness
since wickedness alone is native to them, for they are at once ignorant and
malicious, fail to perceive how much moral goodness exists in Terence's
plays, how much implicit exhortation to shape one's life, and how much
charm there is in their epigrams; nor do they understand that this kind of   70
literature is entirely suitable – nay, was invented – for the purpose of showing up men's vices. For what are comedies but the artful slave, the love-
crazed youth, the suave and wanton harlot, the cross-grained, peevish,
avaricious old man? These characters are depicted for us in plays, just as
in a painting, so that we may first see what is seemly or unseemly in human 75
behaviour and then distribute affection or rebuke accordingly. In the
Eunuchus one may study the alteration in Phaedria's character through love,
like a most dire disease, from great sobriety to such utter folly that he
becomes unrecognizable, which is a superb example for inculcating the lesson that love is a most unhappy and anxious business, treacherous and   80
quite full of the most discreditable sort of madness. To flatterers, that
obnoxious species, you may counsel examination of their very type,
Gnatho, the founder of their profession. As for those who complacently
blow their own trumpet, whom we observe to include most of the ignorant
men of wealth, they should look at their brother Thraso, and understand   85
at last how absurd their boasting makes them look.
   But, if God wills, at least, you shall read about these matters at greater
length when I publish the work I have written on literature. For the present

* * * * *

55 Eberhard] Cf Ep 26:100n.
55 Uguccio] Cf Ep 26:99n.
62–3 'Unless ... there.'] Horace *Epodes* 1.2.54
88 on literature] The *Antibarbari*, the tone of which is very similar to that of
this letter

it should be enough to refer to the comedies of Terence. I am convinced that
these, read in the proper way, not only have no tendency to subvert men's   90
morals but even afford great assistance in reforming them, and beyond any
doubt are essential for learning good Latin: or are we rather to be told to
look for this to the *Catholicon*, Uguccio, Eberhard, and Papias, and others
still more foolish? Really it would be surprising if, with such men as authorities, anyone ever said anything in good Latin, since they themselves   95
spoke barbarously at all times. Anyone who may desire to stammer can
cleave to works like these, but he who wishes to speak must choose Terence,
whom Cicero and Quintilian and Jerome and Augustine and Ambrose
learned in youth and frequented in old age; whom, lastly, no one but a barbarian has ever failed to love.   100

But enough of all this. I have received your longed-for letter; it was,
quite seriously, more correct in style than I had expected, and gave me
immense pleasure, both by its wit and by the affection which it displays.
I love and dream of you, and am extremely excited at the agreeable prospect
of seeing you. My greetings to your excellent wife, and to you.   105

32 / To Jacob Canter   [Steyn, end of 1489]

Jacob Canter was the third son of Jan Canter (not Antonius as in line 19), of
a family famous for its learning. In a letter of 1521 Erasmus coupled the Canters
with Agricola and Langen as Frisians who had long since embraced good letters (Allen Ep 1237:11). Jacob's father and mother were both well educated, and
the children were taught to speak Latin from their earliest childhood. Latin
was said to be the only language used in the household, even by the serving
maid. Jacob was at this time teaching at Antwerp and also working as editor
for the printer Gerard Leeuw. Erasmus may have hoped that his letter might
be included in some later edition.

ERASMUS OF ROTTERDAM TO THAT EXCELLENT SCHOLAR, JACOB CANTER
Most learned sir: I have long desired eagerly to write to you, but have
hitherto been prevented by lack of messengers, or at any rate suitable messengers, particularly since I was not quite sure where my letter would find
you. Now that I have found one who I think will not lack either care in con-   5
veying the letter, or determination in seeing that it arrives, or good manners
when he meets you, and from whom you may be able to learn all that I have

* * * * *

93 *Catholicon* ... Papias] See the same list of Erasmus' *bêtes noires* in Ep 26:99ff.

in mind even without the aid of a letter, I could not refrain from giving him
a letter to take with him since he was going in your direction. Indeed I envy
my letter's luck somewhat – for it has a chance to visit you, while I do not.   10
    'But,' you will say, 'what makes you so anxious to see me?' Why, the
very great love I bear you. Perhaps you will ask what the source of this is,
since not only have I never had any dealings with you but I have never so
much as set eyes on you. An absurd argument, as though you yourself had
ever seen your own face! But, and more to the point, I am acquainted with   15
your good character, and your talents are known to me; and even if you were
not distinguished in these respects, still your father's reputation would
draw attention to you; for is there anyone in whose ears there has not
resounded the famous name of Antonius, a man distinguished equally for
scholarship and moral integrity in a way that belongs to the learned age of   20
Cicero rather than to our own? Your family's fine reputation is common talk
on all sides, whereby it is said that when you were of extremely tender years
you drank in Latin with your mother's milk, while over the spinning it was
not the gossip of elderly dames, such as women usually enjoy, that was listened to, but gems of wisdom, worthy of an educated person's attention.   25
Yours was a father who was quite worthy of such a family; while you, his
family, were in turn worthy of such a father as he. Is there anyone, dear
Jacob, however obscure, who can doubt that it was as the result of such an
upbringing as this, beginning too at the very cradle, as the saying goes, that
you grew into a highly educated man? And is there anywhere on earth   30
where your goodness of heart is not noised abroad? When a soil so fertile
was cultivated with such diligence, is it not understandable if the harvest
that repaid the husbandman's toil proved so profitable?
    However, in case you think that I am merely speculating, though
speculation is no part of my character, it was in the first place a printer   35
named Gerard Leeuw, a very clever fellow, who told me your whole story.
For as he was departing from us I escorted him to the bank of the IJssel
which he had to cross, and it was then that he told me a great deal about
you, while I listened eagerly. This circumstance greatly increased my affec-

* * * * *

23 mother's milk] Cf Adagia I vii 54.
29 very cradle] Cf Adagia I vii 53.
36 Leeuw] Gerard Leeuw was a native of Gouda. He was a printer there
1477–84 and in Antwerp 1484–93. He was evidently paying a visit to his native
town when Erasmus met him.

tion for you, and I lost no time in arranging for a copy of the lady Proba's   40
poem to be brought to me, since I had heard that it was your work. When
I began to study it, and at the same time discovered that Proba was indeed
the author, it did not greatly attract me. However, your letter and prologues
gave me such pleasure that though I read them over and over I was unable
to exhaust my enjoyment; for I swear they display so much of the ancient   45
style of eloquence and learning that, were it not that your family had already
brought universal renown upon Friesland, nobody could believe that you
were born either in a barbarous district or in these modern times. Since,
then, I am sure, dear Jacob, that you are not only a man of the utmost distinction in Letters but a staunch supporter of that art, I decided to ask you,   50
first to return my love (which, while it is a most pleasant thing for any men
at all, is doubly so as between fellow students of literature), and in the second place to ask you to continue, as you are doing, to deserve well of literature in its sadly depressed condition, and to strive to discredit the appalling
barbarism which now prevails almost from pole to pole; and lastly to join   55
me in a correspondence by which we can compensate for our separation,
since we cannot live together. If you indulge me in these desires, you will
both please me greatly and act in a manner that befits your reputation. I cannot now write more, and do not think I need do so, for the bearer of this
letter will tell you everything in person; he is my companion in study, as   60
in all else. Farewell, and pray return my affection.

33 / From Willem Hermans   [Steyn, 1493?]

This is the first surviving letter in the correspondence between Erasmus and
one of the most intimate friends of his youth. Willem Hermans of Gouda
(1466?-1510) was a kinsman of Cornelis Gerard, about the same age as Erasmus,
and like him had been a pupil of Hegius at Deventer and had become a monk
in the monastery of Steyn. He is introduced as one of the interlocutors in the

* * * * *

40–1 Proba's poem] The *Probe coniugis Adelphi cento Virgilii* ... (Gerard Leeuw:
Antwerp, 12 September 1489) was a *cento* or patchwork of verses from Virgil
strung together to make a poem celebrating the Christian religion. It was composed by a fourth-century Roman, Proba, wife of the Prefect Clodius
Adelphius. Proof of its popularity is the fact that it was included among the
books listed in the statutes of St Paul's School as recommended for junior
classes (Lupton *Colet* 279). The Leeuw edition was edited by Jacob Canter with
a preface deploring the absence of Virgil from the schools and a concluding
letter (cf Nichols 1 77f).

Antibarbari (cf Ep 30:17n), where he is represented as paying a visit to Erasmus. Later Erasmus arranged the publication in Paris of a collection of Hermans' poems, the *Silva odarum* (cf Ep 49 introduction).

The present letter was probably written shortly after Erasmus left Steyn to take service with Hendrik van Bergen, bishop of Cambrai (cf Ep 49 introduction), who needed a skilled Latin secretary in expectation of his going to Rome to receive a cardinal's hat (cf *Compendium vitae* Allen I 50). Erasmus had apparently kept his intended departure secret until it was definitely arranged, which would mean securing permission from the bishop of Utrecht to leave the monastery. Hermans had evidently been invited to join him on his journey from Utrecht by way of Gouda to the family seat of the bishop of Cambrai at Bergen-op-Zoom.

WILLEM OF GOUDA TO HIS FRIEND, THE CONSUMMATE SCHOLAR ERASMUS

I wish I had been allowed to accompany you on your journey; it would have given me great pleasure and perhaps given you some also, while to both of us it would have been most useful. Indeed, after I received your messen- 5
ger I began to urge, beg, and finally pray the prior to allow me to go, and after the messenger's departure and his refusal, I upbraided him bitterly for his great unkindness. But what can one do? That is the way he is. It would be intolerable, were it not that it was rather a kind of fear, awkward and ungenerous indeed, that underlay the action, rather than any ill-will. Still, I find very tedious the sort of person who is anxious where there is 10
no need for anxiety, and where there is has no trace of any misgiving. Once I was outside the city, I waited at least an hour for you to arrive, sitting by the wagons as you bade me; but when you did not come, I began to reproach you silently in my heart with angry thoughts; though I could quite readily guess that you were detained against your will, still I could not but be indig- 15
nant that you allowed yourself to be delayed. I am looking after your affairs here as our friendship requires, and as you have a right to expect. Theodoricus will be serviceable to you; he possesses a measure of sophistication, he will compliment you in the proper season, and will not be useless to your domestic economy – he is a first-class cook. If finally you find him 20
a burden or a nuisance you can easily throw him out, for he comes to join you against his will.

When you bid me be of good cheer, because you will not be away for ever, I take pleasure in your encouraging words which cannot but proceed

* * * * *

33:18 Theodoricus] Perhaps Franciscus Theodoricus (cf Ep 10 introduction).

from love. All the same, I wish you to be aware of my views on this matter,   25
and I think I will go back a little. I have not yet got over my amazement that
you not only did not consult anyone about your departure, but never even
told me what you yourself had resolved upon, even though it would have
been a sign of your own good sense if you had taken advice, and the latter
course would have shown your good will towards me. In the event, you do   30
not give the appearance of having acted either like a prudent man or like
a friend; but in fact your affection towards me is abundantly revealed by
your kindnesses, while your wisdom is proclaimed not only by your quite
unique scholarship but by other accomplishments also. For these reasons
I am of the opinion that you concealed your plans in order that I might not   35
hinder them, as I should have done, had I known what was to happen. My
dear Erasmus, I am inexpressibly anxious to see you back here (whom else
would I more gladly choose to live with?), but only on condition that such
a return was in your own interest, and, equally, that it was on honourable
terms. No one knows better than I what difficulties you escaped from, since   40
I am tossed on the same stormy waves at this very moment. I swear I often
congratulate you and think you fortunate in having swum to safety.

I have nothing to report about my own affairs. I am well, as I am sure
you will be glad to hear. I have, however, decided that I ought not to do
anything precipitately, but imitate the patient cunning of Ulysses. I have   45
come to a point in my career where I have to do this if I wish to provide
for my well-being. But come, you must not grieve for my sake; I myself have
so strengthened and steeled my heart that I have come with no difficulty
to despise the power of Fortune. I hold that the wise man stands in need
of nothing; as Horace says,   50

Being the Muses' friend, I will bestow
Sadness and fears on wanton winds, to blow
Over the Cretan sea,

even though I am crushed, and long shall be crushed, beneath a tyrant's
reign. I am sustained by the example set by great men; I keep in my mind's   55
eye the unjust imprisonment of Socrates, best of men, and the harsh slavery
endured by the great Plato himself. I live wholly for literature, and by this
means, thanks to philosophy, not only am free from annoyance but can even
laugh at it. As for you, how goes it with you there? Is it well enough? Is
it all to your liking? Are you able to do as you wish? Farewell.   60

* * * * *

45 precipitately] Cf Allen Ep 83:38, where the word is recalled.
50 Horace] *Odes* 1.30.1–3

34 / From Willem Hermans   [Steyn, end of 1493?]

WILLEM OF GOUDA TO ERASMUS,
A CONSUMMATELY LEARNED POET AND THEOLOGIAN

I have received your letter; it told me what I knew but I was hardly able to
learn from it what I wanted to know. What I had asked, and was wondering,
was whether your move would be good for both of us. The person you men-   5
tion deserves to be avoided, if he resembles your description of him. I am
glad I did not agree out of hand, but referred the decision to you, though
even when that Protean figure was with us his tricks made me smell a rat.
I recognized that he was a monster, but what can one do? It is a wise saying
that if you go to sea with the Devil you must make the crossing with him.   10

About the matter mentioned in my previous letter: I should like to
have your advice; are you in favour or against? I am in rather a hurry to find
out, because I fear that something is being decided at your end which is
not in the interest of both of us, and also so that you may know my opinion
when you take whatever action seems expedient.   15

I am reading through Lorenzo Valla's Thucydides; it is a little difficult,
partly because I have too little acquaintance with Greece, partly because the
style runs on tersely and rapidly in the manner of Sallust. This is in no way
Valla's fault: his style is correct, finished, elegant, carefully following the
precepts of his own *Elegantiae*; he has got in every possible kind of refine-   20
ment. And he undertook this responsibility at the command of Pope
Nicholas v, a supreme promoter of the Latin tongue.

As for you, what are you doing, reading and writing where you are?
Send me some of your writings here so that I may have something by my
friend Erasmus. I have sent you all of your poems that I could scrape   25
together, and also such of my own as I decided to include. When I have time

* * * * *

34:3 your letter] A letter of Erasmus to Hermans which has been lost seems
to have been concerned with some plan of action which involved Hermans,
possibly a suggestion that he should leave the monastery and take some kind
of service or go to Paris. That Hermans was unhappy in the monastery, but
was unwilling to do anything hastily, is suggested by Ep 33:40ff.

8 Protean figure] Cf *Adagia* II ii 74.

16 Thucydides] Valla's translation of Thucydides was published in Venice
c 1485.

20 *Elegantiae*] Hermans may have derived his enthusiasm for this work from
Erasmus (cf Ep 23:108n).

22 Nicholas v] The humanist pope, elected in 1447, who founded the Vatican
Library and encouraged the translation of many Greek works

I shall answer again, at greater length, the letter to which I have hastily
scribbled this reply. Would you please date your letters in future? Farewell.
I send best greetings to Batt, who is your friend and mine.

35 / From Willem Hermans to Jacob Batt   [Steyn, beginning of 1494?]

Jacob Batt (1464?-1502) was a native of Bergen and was at this time secretary
to the town council. He had studied in Paris and fully shared the enthusiasm
of Erasmus and his friends for classical literature. Erasmus had met him in Bergen and had praised his character and learning so highly that Hermans was
eager to make his acquaintance. Batt was made the principal speaker in the
first book of the *Antibarbari*, being at that time nearly thirty years old (cf ASD
I 1 88). His friendship with Erasmus remained constant till his death in 1502.
About 1496 he entered the service of Anna van Borssele, vrouwe van Veere,
in Tournehem castle (cf Ep 80 introduction) as the tutor of her young son
Adolph (cf Ep 93 introduction) and used his position to solicit her somewhat
uncertain patronage for Erasmus.

WILLEM OF GOUDA TO HIS FRIEND JACOB BATT
Distinguished sir: Though I had no tie of domestic intimacy or of any other
close association with you and we did not even know each other, still I
longed exceedingly to write to you for the sake of inaugurating a friendship
that has not existed hitherto. My affection for you is such that it is hard to   5
express, and harder still to credit. I do not think I am acting impulsively
in conceiving so ardent an affection for you whom I have never seen, inasmuch as that great man, with his wonderful qualities (I mean my Erasmus,
or rather our Erasmus, for he is yours too) esteems you so highly. Again
and again, both in our talk together and in letters when he is absent, he   10
has praised you in such friendly terms and with such eloquence that he
must surely be very fond of you. And anyone whom Erasmus loves, I must
inevitably love also, for I respect him so highly that I consider as deserving
of all affection anyone whom he has deemed worthy of his own. His good
opinion of you is not a figment, for, to mention but a few of the admirable   15
qualities you possess, your eminence in scholarship stands high in my
sight, wins my warm devotion, and gives me intense pleasure. Indeed, if
this were all, it would alone suffice to bind me to you, being as I am one
who must love men of letters, especially in this age when such men are
scarce indeed, if they exist at all.   20

* * * * *

29 Batt] Ep 35 indicates that Hermans had not yet met Batt.

Any who look for scholars at the present day will seem to be fishing
in upland coverts or hunting game in the sea. On many occasions, my dear
Batt (for I have a fancy to speak familiarly and tell you my troubles as to an
intimate friend), I have not only been pained but have even groaned aloud
at the long cessation of activity (I wish it were not more appropriate to say   25
'death') in the noblest of arts. The entire human race (allow this brief digres-
sion, I beg you, and let me indulge my wrath); the entire human race, I
repeat, is following aims that are unworthy of it. Some, the majority, attend
to the accumulation of wealth, and 'grow old in zeal for possessions,' wan-
dering through countries and crossing seas in the pursuit. 'The merchant,   30
tireless, runs to furthest Ind'; and thinks happiness belongs only to him
whose coffers are well lined. But what kind of happiness, I ask, is this to
which men so noisily hurry? They accumulate money with great toil and
danger to life; anxiously and fearfully they guard what they have
accumulated; they lament its loss, and never enjoy what they have gained,   35
always hungering for what they are to gain in future. Yet fathers continually urge their sons to this ignoble pursuit, encouraging them and eternally
intoning the poet's words:
       My countrymen, first money must you seek:
       Virtue may follow later;   40
and
       Each man hath credit by
       The measure of his store.
     On the other hand we may see some men so fired with a lust for public
honours that they think these to be the chief end in life. For the sake of them   45
they are willing to sacrifice everything and are not ashamed to do violence
to personal ties, the most sacred thing in human life, and to waste themselves and all they have in pursuit of their ambition. As a rule, through
either the envy of their rivals or their own arrogance, they suffer punishment by beggary or exile or death; this is the price they pay for that transitory   50
bauble, public office. Holland has recently suffered this plague in over-full
measure on the outbreak of that devastating war, when everyone wanted
to be the master.

       * * * * *

35:22 hunting game in the sea] Cf *Adagia* I iv 74.
29 'grow old ... possessions'] Horace *Epistles* 1.7.85
30–1 'The merchant ... Ind'] Horace *Epistles* 1.1.45
39–40 My ... later.] Horace *Epistles* 1.1.53–4
42–3 Each ... store.] Juvenal 3.143–4
52 war] Cf Ep 20:106n.

But what shall I now say of those who, without regard to decency or
virtue, wallow in bestial self-indulgence? Such men, if men they are and   55
not rather cattle, as the poets say, spend all day in enjoying frivolities as
if we were born for play and amusement, attending to dance and song,
holding out wool for spinning-girls among their spindles and baskets like
Sardanapalus, and even themselves sometimes spinning, along with the
girls. One may see them grow pale and waste away with their amours,   60
dragging themselves along, as the saying goes, enslaved like Hercules to
a mistress, the most importunate and demanding tyrant of all. One may see
them roam the streets even by night, prostrate themselves, and weep on
the threshold of a false and hard-hearted girl. One may see them sometimes,
forgetting their loves, devote themselves to drinking-bouts by night and   65
by day, and sit endlessly in taverns, so that, as Plato says of some people,
never do they see the sun either rise or set. This is the kind of life in which
well-born and, what is worse, well-educated young men throw away their
money and health and even their lives. And how many men can one find
who love the liberal branches of learning and think the humanities are not   70
undeserving of just a little labour? Hardly one in a thousand, I believe. Yet
these arts are of the utmost use if usefulness be your guide, for they give
rise to the satisfactions of virtue and these are the real riches. For anyone
who prefers fame, such arts confer an everlasting fame which is better than
any military triumph. Moreover the pleasure they give is also unparalleled: 75
the more you drink of them, the more you thirst, whereas bodily pleasures
are usually accompanied by disgust and contain far more harm and remorse
than useful or agreeable qualities. I pass over for the present the fact that
whereas virtue is increased by the liberal arts, the passion for office and
wealth and pleasure is often accompanied by great crimes. How wise the   80
Romans were indeed! Though they were indefatigable in expanding the
empire they owned, they still devoted themselves with extraordinary diligence to the cultivation of letters, realizing at least that literature is a glory
in success and a refuge in adversity.

But why am I complaining so loudly over the present dearth of stu-   85
dents, when one should rather complain of the lack of teachers? All the
schools resound with nothing but sheer barbarism; the Latin authors are
nowhere read; Papias howls in the lecture-room with Uguccio, Eberhard, the

* * * * *

88–9 Papias ... Graecista] Hermans is here echoing Erasmus' customary list
of bad authors (cf Epp 26:99ff and 31:93). That he was not personally familiar
with all of them is shown by his separating Eberhard and Graecista, as though
they were two persons (cf Ep 26:100n).

Catholicon, Graecista and the *Brachiloquus,* who are not only most arrogant
but rival each other for the prize of ignorance; they teach everything and   90
know nothing. These are the leaders of the barbarians who have completely
vanquished the language of Rome. They are the chief cause of the deplorable demise of Letters. They have indeed earned the loathing of the whole
human race. They deserve to be sewn in a sack and sunk in the Tiber with
their books. Ah, my dear Batt, if only Letters might some day return to life   95
once more! You can see how much hope there is. Those fools refuse to part
with the barbarity upon which they were once nourished; on the contrary
they foster it and welcome it, partly from a sense of fairness since they assert
that nothing is right but what has won their favour, partly out of malice,
whereby   100

> They think it shame, a younger man t' obey,
> And what in childhood they did firmly learn,
> In old age to confess they must abandon.

But let me make an end, finally, of this complaining strain, which
would deservedly have aroused irritation in your eyes for its length were   105
it not that you, as a man of learning, shared it with me, and return to you.
It is not surprising, dear Jacob, that Willem has a strong personal affection
for you since he is aware that you have by diligence succeeded in achieving
a state where, though born in the most barbarous region, you might well
be taken for a native Roman. For you have mastered not only the Roman   110
tongue, though this itself might seem much, but also the knowledge of many
arts, characteristic of the nation, and, more wonderful than either of these,
true eloquence. Yet there are other reasons, too, why I should find no less
cause for devotion to you. You have the most attractive character: full of
kindness, amiability, wit, and the modesty which suits a scholar so well.   115
You are generous in praise of men of letters and second to none in cherishing them. Besides this you have such affection for me, and such
enthusiasm, that, unless I were the most ungrateful of men, I should never
dare not to love you or, rather, to answer your own love with all my heart.
I am not unaware of the value you set on me and on my writings; I do not   120
forget that you were the cause why there are men in your circle who know

* * * * *

89 *Brachiloquus*] Reading *Brachiloquus* for the *Graxiloquus* of the original; the
x conceals a Greek *ch.* (It seems quite possible that the same book might be
known indifferently as *Brachiloquus* or *Brachilogus.* Cf Allen Ep 698:5n, where
Allen records the gift to the abbey of Kampen in 1499 of a vocabulary entitled
Braxilogus.)

99 nothing ... favour] Cf Horace *Epodes* 2.1.83

101–3 They ... abandon] Horace *Epodes* 2.84–5

and love Willem and praise him and long to set eyes on him. I am enormously grateful to you for such kindness and shall be so as long as I live, and
I would that I might return it some day. Yet I shall earnestly strive to make
you as well known here as you have made me there. And today Holland   125
contains not a few men who love, admire, and praise you, and wish to see
you, and congratulate me on having your friendship. Thus, most distinguished sir (for I would not wish to weary so busy a person as you are
with a letter of too great a length), I think I should say just this to you, not
indeed for the sake of winning your friendship, for I knew you were   130
devoted to me already, but in order to strengthen your affection and, as it
were, spur the willing horse, and at the same time so that through your recognition of my love there might arise between us a friendship of the better
kind that will last for ever. If this should come to pass, I shall be the happiest
of men. I for my part will see to it that not only this generation but all time   135
to come shall know of my affection for you. Farewell, my dearest Batt, and
continue to love my friend Erasmus and me as you do now.

My friends Servatius and Franciscus and all my friends, who are as
much yours as mine, send you their greetings.

36 / From Willem Hermans to Cornelis Gerard   [Steyn, beginning of 1494?]

WILLEM OF GOUDA TO HIS FRIEND CORNELIS

In compliance with your desire, I am sending you Thucydides, intending
shortly to send you George of Trebizond; I feared that both together might
make too heavy a load for the messenger. I keep reading your poems, dear
Cornelis, and, as always, I admire the richness of your talent. But it is   5
absurd of you to have decided that I am to be your censor, your Aristarchus,
as it were. Yet I will say just one thing: that it seems to me you stand in
need of more restraint. If you did not pursue copiousness as much as eloquence, you would rival, not only me, for you can easily beat me with one
hand tied behind your back, but Erasmus himself. I would recommend you   10
to pay attention to purity of style. How much credit I give you, how unceasingly I praise you, is something I would rather that you learned from others.

You enquire of me what I think you should do. Here, to be candid,

* * * * *

132 spur the willing horse] Cf *Adagia* I ii 47.
36:3 Trebizond] George of Trebizond (1396–1484) came from Crete to Venice
in 1417 and became one of the most famous of the Greek exiles. He translated
Plato's *Laws* and many of the Greek Fathers. He also wrote the *De rhetoricis
praeceptionibus* (cf Ep 122:4).
6 Aristarchus] The famous editor of Homer, founder of Homeric criticism

I think your overriding principle must be to grasp the chance offered to you
which you are not sure will recur. The saying has it that opportunity comes   15
each man's way but once in his life; he who sees it coming holds it, whereas
if you let it go past you, you will pursue it in vain, for
    Occasion's forehead hath long hair;
    Behind, the head is smooth and bare.
So much for my opinion. I am in the grip of an enormous longing to come   20
and visit you. My greetings to Thomas, who is a fine fellow and your very
good friend. Farewell.

37 / To Cornelis Gerard   [Halsteren, spring 1494?]

An outbreak of plague while he was in the service of the bishop of Cambrai
in Bergen or possibly Brussels had forced Erasmus to seek a country retreat
at Halsteren near Bergen, where he spent his leisure revising the *Antibarbari*.
Cf Ep 30:17n and Allen I app v.

ERASMUS TO THAT EXCELLENT SCHOLAR, CORNELIS OF GOUDA
I am delighted that you have at last begun to remember your dear friends:
for when you were prattling about nothing save fields and finances you had
no time for us. What curse could I, then, most suitably call down upon those
who made you an administrator? Why, that they should become adminis-   5
trators themselves! My sweetest Cornelis, now that you have as it were
reached harbour from the high seas, or have been blown there by some
wind or other, you should eagerly return to the studies you have interrupted. After this interval the Muses will be more congenial to you, and you
to them, than if there had been no gap.   10
    If you ask me what I am up to, I have in hand at present a work on
literature which I have been threatening for a very long time to write and
have been attending to during my retreat in the country, though I do not
very well know how it is going. I intend, at any rate, to finish this work
in two books. The first book will be almost entirely concerned with refuting 15

* * * * *

18–19 Occasion's forehead ... bear.] Cato *Disticha* 2.26
21 Thomas] Allen does not identify this person.
37:5 administrator] Cornelis had been for some time steward of the monastery of Hemsdonck, and the administrative duties attached to the office had
apparently forced him to abandon his literary activity temporarily. His
appointment as prior of Hemsdonck at about this time would, Erasmus
hoped, free him to return to his studies. This may be the chance Hermans was
urging him to seize in Ep 36:13ff.

the absurdities perpetrated by the barbarians, while in the second I am
going to depict you talking about the glory of letters with some scholarly
friends of your own sort. So, since the credit will be shared among us, it
is proper that the toil of preparation should be shared between us also.
Accordingly, please be sure to send me, and be kind enough to share with   20
me for our friendship's sake, anything you have read (what have you not
read?) which you may think relevant to this subject – that is to say, any arguments for or against the study of letters. Farewell.

38 / From Willem Hermans to Johannes   [Steyn, 1494]

The person to whom this letter was addressed was the tutor of the young Philip
the Handsome, Duke of Burgundy, son of the Emperor Maximilian I and Mary
of Burgundy, but is otherwise unidentified. From the reference to Batt, it
appears that the letter was probably written after Hermans had visited Erasmus at Halsteren and had met Batt there.

TO MASTER JOHANNES, THE LEARNED TUTOR OF DUKE PHILIP,
FROM WILLEM OF GOUDA
When your name was mentioned in the course of a friendly conversation
I had with Jacob Batt (who is most dear to me for the sake of his very great
learning and the special affection he bears me), Batt told me that he had read   5
my poem to you. While I took this opportunity to ask him about your
character, your scholarship, your talents, he began, learned sir, to praise
and extol you, so that I could easily see how he himself admired you. As
for me, he so fired me with enthusiasm that now I cannot help entertaining
a warm affection for you. In this he himself earnestly encouraged me, and   10
endeavoured to persuade me to write to you as soon as possible in order
to win your love, saying that nothing would give you greater pleasure. And
indeed I was by no means loath to do what he urged, for there is nothing
I covet more than a scholar's friendship; but I must admit that I had some
diffidence about writing, partly because I was completely unacquainted   15
with you and partly for lack of anything to say. Also I entertained a certain
fear, not a groundless fear, but one I had to take seriously, I believe. I was
extremely apprehensive that, if I should send you a letter without any
reason, my action might be attributed not to affection (the real cause) but

* * * * *

38:6 poem] Perhaps the fourth ode in Hermans' *Silva odarum*, which expresses his desire for Batt's company

to flattery or personal ambition. Though these are faults to which I think   20
my nature and my principles are totally alien, still I could not avoid being
afraid that someone might come to suspect them, either because of human
malevolence or because of your own high position which, to my immense
pleasure, is such that you can manifestly help anyone you choose to help,
either with money or with counsel. In the end love conquered both diffi-   25
dence and fear. I am writing without anything to say except that I love you,
and am eager to have your love.

But in order not to appear to confine myself to this alone, and for the
sake of prolonging the conversation with you as I delight to do, I will add
something more, although that something, too, arises entirely from affec-   30
tion. Dear Johannes, I congratulate you with great pleasure on the fact that
Duke Philip employs you as his tutor in liberal studies, a fact which, as I
hope and trust, will be of great advantage to you and bring you much distinction. I congratulate our duke also, inasmuch as he has found one who
can instruct him in the true method instead of the crass barbarism that is   35
taught almost everywhere. They say the duke is of a gentle temper and loves
literature, which so eminently becomes a man of birth. As God is my witness, I rejoice not only for your sake, because you will receive a great deal
of credit if he makes good progress, but for all our sakes inasmuch as we
hope that if he acquires a literary education he will conduct all his enter-   40
prises with wisdom and moderation. The cultivation of letters engenders
mildness in the disposition and from letters he will learn what to require
both of himself and of others: how he ought to conduct himself in prosperity
and in adversity, in peace and in war, towards his fellow citizens and
towards his foes. It is the opinion of that most excellent philosopher, Plato,   45
that the state will prosper if either philosophers become kings, or kings
apply themselves to the study of philosophy; this was a wise observation
of Plato's, one of many. Its truth is illustrated by the Roman state, which
flourished at a time when it contained men educated in letters, and when
sunset fell on these it fell upon Rome also. As a youth he should from time   50
to time be gently admonished and encouraged more and more to conceive
an affection for letters; he should be told how splendid a thing it is for a
prince to be well schooled and how shameful if one of so eminent a rank
should not be wiser than others and distinguish himself in learning, considering how distinguished he is in birth. It will do good also to explain   55
to him the pleasure afforded by the arts, a pleasure the magnitude of which

* * * * *

45 Plato] Cf *Republic* 499.

is attested by all the Romans and especially by that exceptional scholar, King Juba, who used to remark that literature meant more to him than his realm itself and if he had to lose one of the two he would prefer to be stripped of his kingdom. I am not unaware how great our prince's distrac- 60 tions are and how very little time he can afford for study, when on the one hand he is preoccupied with the laws and the affairs of so many peoples, and on the other hand his enemies are taking the field against him. Still, while it is true that Roman generals took books with them even on active service, they had time while they were in camp to write literature as well 65 as read it. As for most of us, what we chiefly lack is not so much the opportunity as the will. He will find it particularly useful to read Terence, for this author is at one and the same time a mirror of human behaviour, as it were, and also indispensable for acquiring good Latinity. He should also browse through Livy, partly for the sake of his light and pleasant prose style and 70 also because of the story he tells which offers many inspiring examples of heroism and also a guide to military practice. Then again, take Cicero's work *De officiis*, which in my opinion deserves all praise and should not merely be read repeatedly, but carried everywhere as one's constant companion; if the prince adheres to its advice he will be the best and most pros- 75 perous of men and gain everlasting glory for himself, with peace and quiet for us, his subjects.

But it is foolishly outspoken and, I am afraid, even insolent of me to write to you after this fashion; your own decision what to do will be far sounder, and so I now cease to play the sow teaching Minerva and to carry 80 wood into the forest, as the proverbs say. My one plea is that there should henceforth be friendship between us, for it has ever been to me a source of pleasure and happiness to enjoy the friendship of learned and venerable men. In your own vicinity you have Erasmus, the very greatest scholar of our age: but it is better to say no more, for fear I may seem to be deluded 85 by affection. I myself have lived on very close terms with him while this was possible, and it is one of my life's greatest vexations that I cannot now enjoy his company. He has been taken into the service of the bishop of Cambrai, who is well disposed towards literature. If you care to cultivate the friendship of one so learned, loyal, upright, and agreeable as he, you will, 90 believe me, gain great satisfaction.

I should commend our friend Batt to you, did I not believe him to stand

* * * * *

58 Juba] Juba ii, the learned king of Numidia in the second half of the first century BC

81 as the proverbs say] Cf *Adagia* i 1 40 and i vii 57.

sufficiently high in your esteem for his own sake. Farewell; and since I love
you, pray do not dislike me.

39 / To Willem Hermans   [Brussels? 1494?]

This letter evidently answers letters and a poem complaining of Erasmus'
silence. The latter part of the letter (lines 138ff) suggest that it was written during a period of depression because of the abandonment by the bishop of Cambrai of his proposed visit to Rome, on which Erasmus had hoped to accompany
him.

ERASMUS OF ROTTERDAM TO WILLEM OF GOUDA

It may be, my dear Willem, that by this time you feel considerable surprise
at my indolent failure to answer those heaps upon heaps of letters you have
sent me. As for yourself, you follow verse with prose and then again prose
with verse, seeking by sheer persistence to extract something from me and   5
thus to break my silence. Shall I so far forget our acquaintance, and my old
habit of pestering you with a superabundance of letters, as to send no reply
at all? Yes: I do believe that the bird of ill omen, which (you tell me) perched
on your roof, has chanted over you some spell of awful suspicion. She is
to be sure a bearer of evil tidings of whom our Virgil writes: 10
    While on the roof the owl, with mourning wail,
    Doth oft lament, and gloomy strains prolong.
But tell me, Willem, for I am in a joking mood, are you giving your time
to omens or to philosophy? Previously I thought it was the latter, but my
observation seems to indicate the former. Come, tell me what god or mys-   15
terious power of nature it was which endowed that bird of yours with such
extraordinary wisdom that, hoarsely muttering from its sacred breast, it can
reveal things unknown even to you? Aye, perhaps, if I may speak in
Pythagorean terms, the soul that dwells within that breast is Cato's; or at
least the bird has come to you from the abodes of the gods, to herald some   20
dire mischance and ensure that you are apprised of the will of Heaven, for
such is the burden of your verse: 'That ill dost oft announce.'
    I am intensely surprised that Juno's Iris, whose role it is to announce
all lamentable and untoward events, failed to glide down to you, in order

* * * * *

39:10 Virgil] *Aeneid* 4.462–3
23 Juno's Iris] Messenger of the gods; see especially Virgil *Aeneid* 4.693f.
24 glide down] *delapsa*, the verb used by Virgil in describing the descent of
Juno herself, *Aeneid* 7.620.

to bring you such heavy tidings as these: but possibly the queen of the gods   25
had sent her to take a message somewhere else at that moment. Why then
were the owl's services required? She was called, came up quickly, got her
orders, traversed Heaven's wide path, and alighted upon your roof where,
in a voice of doom, she duly informed you of the dreadful event whereof
you had not known. And when I ask you the riddle of the omen, you, not   30
without shame, suppose that my love for you is dead. What a helpful soothsayer! And what a witty explanation! Believe me, Willem, as far as I can see,
I think this is what happened: while your soothsayer was looking too attentively at the appearance of sun, moon, stars, and the other phenomena of
the sky, she forgot what Juno had enjoined on her; so what was she to do?   35
She cudgelled her fertile brains, since of them she had plenty; she worked
out a new message and brought it to you; and, all too trusting, you were
taken in by it. For really the former good will, which arose from my affection
for you and which you have interpreted as dead, has not only not died, it
has not even cooled or weakened. On the contrary, it grows stronger day   40
by day, and day by day receives some increase and gathers strength from
time, strength which will never give way before fate's vicissitudes or the
schemes of any rivals. Though they may divide us in the flesh, prevent us
from meeting, forbid us to communicate, one thing they will never achieve
is to alienate my heart from yours. And, to use Virgil's expression: 45
    While boars shall roam the mountain tops, and fish the rivers cleave,
    And thyme remain the bees' repast, and crickets sip the dew –
    And while the clear stars of the ancient sky
    Roll on, and Ocean with his waves enfolds
    The earth's vast orb; reluctant am not I,   50
    Nor shall be, to remember friend so dear.
But come now: is it not really you who seem to have blotted our mutual
friendship in being led by such specious indications to suppose that it was
dead? I am afraid you may be censured for censuring it as a feigned friendship for, says Seneca, any friendship that is capable of coming to an end   55
never was a true friendship at all. Had you not believed that my love for
you was feigned, you would not have doubted that it was eternal, and there
you are, demonstrating its extinction from an inference, and a very fragile
one: believing, just because my letters do not come to you thick and fast,

* * * * *

45 Virgil] *Eclogues* 5.76, 77
48 And while] Seneca *Oedipus* 504, 505
51 to remember] Cf Virgil *Aeneid* 4.335.
55 Seneca] In the (spurious) *Liber de moribus* (cf *Adagia* II i 72, IV v 26).

that I have forgotten all about you. Is this the degree of importance you   60
attribute to my silence?

Well then, I shall proceed to acquit myself of the charge with which
you are anxious to smite me. I shall throw your own weapon back at you
and despatch you with your own sword. Did I not long since, when you
were quite somnolent, attack you so relentlessly with letters that you   65
reached the point of irritation? You begged me not to worry you more than
usual because you had begun to concentrate on some little oration. Now,
you did not merely fail to answer those letters; you hardly spared the little
time required for reading them; you found tedious, not to say distasteful,
even such brief converse with me as this. But you are perhaps about to   70
accuse me of falsehood, inasmuch as you have, on frequent occasions, written to me. This I do not deny. I did indeed finally extort from you by my
importunity a number of little notes, not deserving the name of letters, as
distinguished for brevity as they were for scarcity; full of flatteries as bad
as Filelfo's, disordered in style, heavier than the dust, and speciously dis-   75
playing the measureless good will of your heart towards me. And, what I
found hardest of all to endure, you quite failed to suit your action to my
wishes when in those letters you indulged in certain rather frivolous jokes
and turns of wit. Now, it was not right to conclude, because in my letters
to you I had written sometimes in a more or less jesting vein, that I was   80
therefore joking throughout. The comic and the serious ought each to have
been dealt with on its own level whereas you kept joking on both levels.
Besides this, in attempting to answer my jokes in kind, you forgot the dictum of our favourite Seneca, 'Let not your wit be barbed,' and similarly,
'One should not give offence to a friend, even in jest.' Do you understand   85
my meaning? So, if you indict me for having rested my pen for a short while,
how much more justly shall I in my turn condemn you on the same charge
for writing abusively after a long silence. I think I have now cleared myself;
I have thrown back at you the weapon you aimed at me; I have despatched
you with your own blade. But it is possible that you will not yet admit this;   90
accordingly, I shall proceed to employ another weapon, of greater efficacy.

You pretend you were so little able to endure my silence that it quite
disheartened you; but when you learned that I was writing to you in haste,
you attacked it when it was on the point of arrival and criticized it adversely
before you saw it. This I should call soothsaying rather than critical judg-   95
ment, unless you are proposing, perhaps, to appraise this letter in terms
of some poems which I once put into circulation and which you find charge-

* * * * *

75 Filelfo] Cf Ep 23:77n.

able with obscurity. I myself will admit that it is a primary responsibility
of both prose writer and poet to see that his style should be not only erudite
but also clear and engaging, as Horace bears witness: 100
>   Verse that is beautiful doth not suffice;
>   It must be charming too, and where it wills
>   Must move the feelings of the listener.
And I am most surprised that, whereas when I read you my own poems you
have always praised most highly their gay, engaging clarity, you should   105
now have changed your mind, or else your tongue, and are censuring them
for obscurity and dullness, though I am unable to say whether you do this
in jest or in earnest. If you are joking, please tell me so; if you speak sincerely
I should be obliged if you will tell me precisely who are the people who
find them hard to understand. If they are rude and barbarous, you must   110
indict along with me both Cicero and Virgil and all the poets together, since
men of that kind quite fail to understand them. But if they are men of learning like yourself, then I acknowledge the fault. For that very reason, however, I beg you to send me frequent letters, in order that I may imitate the
Ciceronian clarity manifested in them and learn how to avoid being   115
obscure. Besides, while it is mere loyalty to a friend to correct him if he
makes a mistake, it is unnatural to jeer at him; yet you show yourself ready
to carp at my letter rather than correct it. But have you not deserved by such
conduct never to set eyes on a letter from me? Of course you have. Yet I shall
present to you, for destructive criticism, this letter and no more. In case you   120
notice anything that requires revision or excision, I ask you earnestly to correct your friend in a friendly manner, and I shall not only take no offence
but shall owe you an eternal debt of gratitude, considering that I have
received a very great favour. If, however, you are disposed to hurt your
friend, then, Willem, it is an unequal contest. For while you are deeply   125
immersed at present in studying Cicero's artistry, I have been deprived of
any opportunity to study at all:
>   You read all the latest books, and in such elegant copies!
>   Scarcely do I have a chance, tattered old pages to scan;
>   Heavenly poems emerge from your small study;   130
– while I have lost through cruel misfortune all the vitality my brain used
to command:
>   For toil, long borne, has all my talent crushed,
>   And naught remains of strength I once possessed.

* * * * *

100 Horace] *Ars poetica* 99, 100
130 Heavenly ... study] Juvenal 7.28
133–4 For toil ... possessed.] Ovid *Tristia* 5.12.31–2

But if there is no way of escaping this formidable contest, please tell me so   135
in advance, in order that the letters I shall send you may not be exposed,
unguarded, to its dangers.

Thus far I have spoken in jest; now let me speak seriously and sincerely. I am quite astonished, Willem, that you are so surprised at my silence, as though you had never read that wise man's saying, 'Like music   140
in the house of mourning is a tale told out of season.' Do the kindly arts
of humane study suit this most unhappy time? Surely, as the poet says,
'Songs are the work of joy, and peace of mind require.' And where now,
pray, are happiness and heart's-ease? The world is full of bitterness and
uproar and no matter where I look I can see only gloomy and savage sights: 145
'On all sides grief abounds,' and 'death in many a shape.' If I were to go on
to enumerate all of these severally, I should appear to be composing a
tragedy rather than a letter. And do you bid me, thronged about as I am
with all these harsh noises, attend at leisure to the Muse's task? Rather it
is for you, under the watchful eye of lucky stars, to go on, while you can,   150
to confer immortality on a subject distinguished for virtue. It is for you to
publish some notable work which future generations may rehearse.
Nothing is fit for me but to weep and wail; and through these distresses
my brain has already so lost its edge and my heart has so wasted away that
I have come to take no joy at all in my former studies. I find no pleasure   155
in the poets' Pierian charm, and the Muses who were once my only love,
repel me now. Yet I confess that when Servatius, your good friend and mine
too, brought me your little speech, polished as it was and in every way
redolent of Cicero but forgetful of me, I began for a short while to breathe
freely again, like one aroused from a deep sleep. And so, chiding myself   160
for my indolence, I forced myself to write something. Indeed I would reply
separately, and in order, to each sentiment contained in your letter, were
it not that I am forced to stop, having come to the end of my paper.

You ask for my views about Johannes' letter; in a few words, here they

* * * * *

140–1 'Like ... season.'] *Ecclesiasticus* 22:6
143 'Songs ... require'] Ovid *Tristia* 5.12.3, 4
146 'On all sides ... abounds'] A quotation from Hermans' ode 3 from his *Silva odarum* on the civil war in Holland (cf Ep 20:106n).
146 'death in many a shape'] Virgil *Aeneid* 2.369
156 once my only love] 'quondam unica cura' (cf Erasmus' *Carmen bucolicum*, Reedijk 136, line 4).
157 Servatius] Erasmus' old friend at Steyn (cf Ep 4 introduction) had evidently paid him a recent visit.
164 Johannes' letter] Possibly an answer to Ep 38

Cornelis Gerard *Mariad* c 1494
manuscript page
Athenaeum Stadsbibliotheek, Deventer

are. The letter seems to me to suggest St Bernard rather than Cicero.   165
Nevertheless, I admired in it, first the arrangement of the language, which
was not inelegant, and secondly the old head on young shoulders. For the
rest: for lack of space, I cannot give you my opinion about Cornelis, who
is my very good friend; and in any case a manifest fact contains its own evidence. But I do ask you earnestly to admonish, urge and beg him to devote   170
himself to literary work and to go on to publish the precepts of a forgotten
art of eloquence. For he is capable of this; all his circumstances are favourable, even though Heaven gives us everything only at the price of hard
work. Farewell, dear Willem, and continue to love me as you do.

40 / To Cornelis Gerard   [Brussels? 1494?]

This fragment of a letter occurs at the end of Cornelis' preface to the first ten
books of his poem, *Mariad,* addressed to Jacobus Faber (cf Ep 174 introduction)
which exists in MS in the Athenaeum Library at Deventer. His appointment
as prior of Hemsdonck had apparently afforded him the leisure and Erasmus'
urgings had given him the impetus to resume work on his poem (cf Epp 37:
5n and 39:170ff).

ERASMUS TO CORNELIS GERARD
You are so modest, dear Cornelis, that I am already prone to imagine that
you are a little put out when I mention your good qualities. But, even if you
feel some annoyance, I shall still be unable ever to refrain from singing your
praises. Further, I ask you earnestly, for I have a mind to be quite shameless   5
and I am absolutely second to none in my affection for you, to be good
enough to dedicate by name to me that distinguished work of yours, the
Mariad of immortal fame, which you have in hand at present. For my part,
I have resolved to cherish, protect, and adorn that same work, not as I do
my own, for it seems to me that I am somewhat neglectful in that respect,   10
but as aggressively as anyone ever protects his works. Please just send it
to me for copying out, as you agreed to do in my presence when we were
reading it. Farewell.

41 / To Franciscus Theodoricus   [Brussels? 1494?]

Erasmus' apology for not writing to his old friend in the monastery (cf Ep 10
introduction) parallels that to Hermans in Ep 39.

* * * * *

168 Cornelis] This might refer to the change in the position of Cornelis Gerard
since his appointment as prior of Hemsdonck (cf Ep 37:5n).

ERASMUS OF ROTTERDAM TO HIS FRIEND FRANCISCUS
Though I have long been quite sure of your affection for me, still I am made
more aware of it day by day through the very pleasant letters you sent me
by messenger lately. Accordingly it will afford me inexpressible pleasure
if you can arrange to write to me frequently. The fact that hitherto you have
received answers from me less often than you had expected should not, I
beg, give rise to suspicion on your part that I am negligent. I ask you to recognize that this was the result, not of thoughtlessness, but of endless dis-
tractions which prevented me from writing. Later, when I can get free of
business, I intend to bombard you with such frequent letters that you will
begin to put more urgency into asking when I mean to stop than you ever
before put into your requests for a letter. Farewell; give my greeting to your
friends, whom I consider to be mine as well as yours.

42 / To Jacob Batt   [Brussels or Mechelen? 1495?]

This letter contains the first suggestion of Erasmus' plan to leave the bishop
of Cambrai, who no longer needed him and had become less friendly, and go
to Paris to study. Cf *Compendium vitae* Allen I 50:100ff. For the success of this
plan he relied heavily on Batt's influence with the bishop's family in Bergen.

ERASMUS OF ROTTERDAM TO THE EMINENTLY LEARNED JACOB BATT,
TOWN CLERK OF BERGEN
I am delighted that my letters have reached you, for I was a little anxious
in case the boatman, a rather irresponsible fellow, might have been careless
in carrying out my instructions. As for your letter, it was so welcome and
so long awaited that I opened and read it the very moment it was delivered
to me at the boat. Thereupon I was torn between two emotions: at first
glance I began to be a little annoyed with you for sending such a short note,
since my appetite for my dear Batt is such that I would wish you to write
not letters but books. Subsequently, as I read on with flying eye, as they
say, and discovered that you had caught a most persistent fever, I trembled
all over and began to concentrate on the letter and reread it, with rather
more attention. When I found that my letter had made you better I was at
once relieved of my anguish, or fear, and I read the rest in a more cheerful
frame of mind.

My sweetest Batt, I leave the whole affair to your discretion. All the
same, I enjoin you earnestly not to prejudice my interests through
unseasonable ambition. Take care in the first place to think of your Erasmus. Thereafter, I shall duly marshal in my turn all that my attention or my
recommendation or my writings can do to advance you. I am glad the letter

pleased my lord of Bergen though I did not write it merely to give pleasure but to cause him to fall in with my wish. You never mentioned what hope of this there was. I have begged you as ardently as I could, and now once more I beg, beseech, and pray you, dear Batt, to pay special attention to a matter which I have much at heart. So read my letters carefully, understand-   25
ing that I have put nothing in them thoughtlessly, even if I express myself badly. Farewell.

43 / From Robert Gaguin   [Paris, September 1495?]

By this time Erasmus had arrived in Paris with the expressed intention of securing a doctor's degree in theology (cf Ep 48:27ff). He enrolled in the collège de Montaigu, which was then under the stern rule of its reforming Flemish principal, Jan Standonck (cf Ep 73:11n). He stayed less than a year, finding the living conditions intolerable and the intellectual atmosphere uncongenial. Cf M. Godet 'La congrégation de Montaigu 1490–1580' in *Bibliothèque de l'Ecole des hautes études* 198 (1912); Mestwerdt 283ff. Years later in the colloquy *Ichthyophagia* he presented a bitter condemnation of conditions in the college (cf Thompson *Colloquies* 'A Fish Diet' 351–3).

Meanwhile Erasmus was eager to gain entry to the circle of Parisian human-ists and to that end dispatched a letter of greeting with more than the custom-ary flattery to the aging Robert Gaguin (1433–1501), the most distinguished and influential of the French humanists. Gaguin was general of the Trinitarian order and had frequently served as dean of the faculty of canon law and as a royal ambassador. Combining deep religious feeling with enthusiasm for clas-sical literature, Gaguin commanded universal respect by his character as much as by his numerous literary works. No one in Paris could have been a more valuable friend for an aspiring young scholar like Erasmus. Cf Renaudet *Préréforme* 114 *et passim*; and F. Simone 'Roberto Gaguin ed il suo cenacolo umanistico' *Aevum, Rassegna di scienze storiche, linguistiche e filologiche* 13 (1939) 410–76.

ROBERT GAGUIN TO ERASMUS

You write to me at great length, Erasmus, with the particular purpose of earning my good graces by some kindness, and for this reason you employ a kind of prelude, as if you were going to have difficulty in gaining from me what you seem to be looking for. So, too, you take it upon yourself to   5

* * * * *

42:21 lord of Bergen] Either Jan, fifth lord of Glimes and Bergen (d 7 September 1494), the bishop's father, or Jan, sixth lord (d 1532), the bishop's brother

furnish an excessive quantity of compliments, by way of recommendation. Whether you are justified in uttering these about me must be for you to judge; you do it, as I am well aware, not so much to inform me what I lack, as what I possess. For, just because a man is his own closest neighbour and best friend, he never pays proper attention to himself. I do confess that I 10 have made diligent search for letters and learning without acquiring them, resembling a rather unwise purchaser who wanders through the fair and looks at a great deal of merchandise but, through lack of money, takes none of it home. As for these rough-hewn works of mine which you claim to have read with pleasure, I think of them as resembling the premature fruits, 15 picked when not yet ripe, which one sees being carried to market and which are given as a first course to persons afflicted with poor health, for the relief of queasy stomachs: they do indeed stimulate the appetite but they afford little nourishment.

But even if this be true, I would not prevent others from judging me 20 as they wish. What grieves me is that you poured the lavish vein of elo-quence which you possess into the narrow channel of compliments to me; exalting me, a mere novice and still learning, to the level of Scipio's integrity and of Nestor's famed eloquence. Would you like me to say frankly what I feel, Erasmus? The craft of oratory gathers a wealth of material for its elo- 25 quence from every quarter, and cannot easily be confined within its proper limits, being always exuberant and profuse by nature. Still, as Horace says,

There does exist a Mean in all that is,

And, in the end, appointed bounds are set.

For this reason, Erasmus, I would wish that you had been more restrained 30 in penning encomiums upon me, and had eschewed extravagance; not because praise makes me blush, but because, whenever undeserved plau-dits are awarded by a speaker they are put down to flattery or falsehood. I shall therefore write frankly. So far as I can tell by your letter and your lyric poems, I judge you to be a scholar: and for this reason I look forward to your 35 friendship as much as you to mine. Attachment to similar pursuits is the bond of love and charity. If in addition to this I have picked up any educa-tion, any tincture of learning, as you think I have, then I freely declare that your affection shall have access to my heart and my love, as wide open as

* * * * *

43:9 his own closest neighbour] Cf Terence *Andria* 636.

27 Horace] *Satires* 1.1.106

34–5 lyric poems] Including probably the poem *Ad Gaguinum nondum visum carmen hendecasyllabum*. It was printed in the *De casa natalitia Iesu* (cf Ep 47 introduction). It is in Reedijk 239f.

the doors of my house are to my friends. Take away all the pretence that lies   40
in flattering words and come with unveiled face; keep for yourself the free
exercise of your judgment in loving me if you think fit, or, if otherwise, in
setting me aside. Farewell.

44 / From Robert Gaguin   Paris, 24 September [1495?]

Erasmus had apparently taken the hint regarding undue flattery in Ep 43 and
had written a second letter in a more sober tone to which Gaguin now replies.

ROBERT GAGUIN TO ERASMUS
Your letter, Erasmus, assuaged my grief for as long as it took me to read
it, since it is as admirable for its arrangement of words as it is distinguished
by the nobility of its sentiments. This is the style that suits a cleric best, not
the frivolous style that uses language to flatter and aims only to score paltry   5
hits and is seasoned yet tasteless, and sickly-sweet yet without charm,
so that when one has made one's way through some lengthy work of this
kind one draws from it no vital sustenance at all. This fault is often committed by poets who are not content with a single tale to fit each place but
heap theme upon theme until one tires of them. And it has hitherto been   10
a fault also of lawyers; they are not satisfied with one or two laws, but must
have a mightily long document overflowing with them. But you, Erasmus,
are in my opinion acting sagely in practising a style worthy of your cloth;
so pray go on seeking to imitate those moral and sober writers by whose
wisdom you may train your mind and shape your character.   15
    I do not write this with the intention of teaching you, for you are fit
to be the teacher of others. I only wish to show what hope of glory lies in
the journey you yourself have undertaken. For I have come to believe of you
that you combine piety with integrity of character, and do not in any respect
hide behind a façade of flattery or of falsehood. Although I mentioned these   20
things in a previous letter to you, my purpose there was only to censure
those who dishonestly curry favour. I despise such men's Gnathonical
tricks more than I do the low type of Thersites, for they assume whatever
expression they choose and practise deceit under the guise of friendship,
while your Thersites proclaims himself to be such as he is, living in the   25

* * * * *

44:6 seasoned] Reading 'sapidum' for 'aridum'
22 Gnathonical] Coined after Gnatho, the 'parasite' in Terence's *Eunuchus* (cf
Ep 26:6n).
25 Thersites] Homer *Iliad* 2.212

Robert Gaguin
André Thevet *Les vrais pourtraits et vies des hommes illustres*
Paris 1584, leaf 530
Houghton Library, Harvard University

squalid way he does. I swear that there is no class of mankind I dislike more than flatterers, for nearly all other vices are plain to see, whereas flattery alone conceals its tricks for a long time so that it may practise them upon you when you are off your guard. For this reason I have always been suspicious when a flatterer gives me more deference than I am worth, for there is an Italian proverb to the effect that if any man pays you unusual honour, either he has deceived you, or he is trying to do so.

But let us leave these crimes to those who commit them. If you have discovered anything from Fausto Andrelini's book on celestial soothsaying which would make this a lucky time for you to resort to me, then hasten to come. I shall be delighted to see him, for he is an old friend; and to see you, too, because I am anxious to make of you a new one. Farewell.
Paris, 24 September

45 / To Robert Gaguin   [Paris, beginning of October 1495]

A complimentary letter inserted to fill an unnumbered blank leaf at the end of Gaguin's history of France, *De origine et gestis Francorum compendium* (Paris: P. Le Dru, 30 September 1495). Although he had just made Gaguin's acquaintance, Erasmus was able to seize this opportunity to demonstrate his literary skill to a wide audience, writing hastily since the opportunity did not occur until the book was completed, including the dated colophon (cf Allen's introduction to Ep 43).

GREETINGS FROM ERASMUS OF ROTTERDAM TO THE CONSUMMATE SCHOLAR, ROBERT GAGUIN

Inasmuch as you, Robert Gaguin, the principal ornament of the university of France, have resolved to publish in immortal prose an account of the achievements of the kings and princes of the French nation, which heretofore lay well-nigh buried in darkness for lack of a fitting historian, I cannot fail to lend your undertaking my warm approval. For you have taken up, or rather have laid upon your shoulders, a task which I regard as highly honourable: one that not only will occasion immense pleasure to all lovers of Latin literature but will, especially, bring to your own country dignity and prestige and what I may call triumphal splendour and which, finally, is entirely worthy of your scholarship, literary skill, and patriotism. I should

* * * * *

34 Fausto Andrelini] One of Erasmus' first friends in Paris (cf Ep 84 introduction). The reference is to Andrelini's poem *De influentia Syderum et querela Parrhisiensis pauimenti*, published, with a dedication to Guillaume Budé, by G. Marchand (Paris, 10 May 1496).

find it hard to believe that anything but a lofty patriotism could have
induced you to undertake the task, since you have never been influenced
in the slightest degree by thoughts of gain or personal glory, whereas you   15
share with the great heroes of history the high value you set on patriotism.
Doubtless you were grieved at the fact, which I myself sometimes ponder
with surprise, that the courage of the French receives such grudging acknowledgment at the hands of fame, and that a nation which in distant days
often emulated the feats of Italians and nowadays has surpassed them must,   20
for want of a chronicler, fall so far behind Italy in reputation and renown.
The Italians may excuse me for holding an opinion which Francesco Filelfo,
an Italian born, thought it no shame to express. There is a letter from him
to King Charles, the grandfather, I think, of the present king, in which, to
the many compliments he pays the realm of France, he adds the frank   25
admission that although the Romans had indeed once won for themselves
the greatest by far of all empires by practising the arts of war and peace,
and also had challenged the Greeks as vigorously in intellectual matters as
they had earlier done in warfare, this ancient imperial glory had fallen into
decay through internal dissension and vice. The French realm, on the other   30
hand, has increased so greatly, by the wise rule of its kings, the loyalty of
its princes, and the peaceable conduct of its populace, that it can now easily
claim comparison with any other domain in Christendom whether in
wealth or extent or magnitude of achievement or the fame of its sovereigns.
Among these it is recognized that there have been many who were dis-   35
tinguished not merely for bravery, but for piety also; this is why the Christian council of this realm has clearly reserved to itself the role of chief and
sole defender of the faith against the armed aggression of the Turk.

Yet it was plain that the majesty of that mighty realm still lacked one
thing; Italy, equal or inferior in other ways to France, surpassed her in the   40
persons of Livy and Sallust. As the poet Horace has sagely remarked, it cannot but be that the fine deeds of kings and captains, be they never so splendid, must to some extent be lost, or eclipsed through time, if their praises
be not sung in literature, the sole repository of past events, by an historian
who is a master of style; and their renown will be impressed on posterity   45
in proportion as the genius of their chronicler is itself impressive. Such
then, most eloquent Gaguin, is the supremely important task you, like a
second Scipio, have undertaken with everyone's heartfelt approval, as

* * * * *

45:22 Filelfo] Cf Ep 23:77n. His letter was addressed to Charles VII. Only the
sense is given here.
41 Horace] Cf *Odes* 4.9.25–8.

though the Fates had reserved it expressly for you: a task that is hard
indeed, and toilsome, yet altogether worthy of you. If you ask me why I   50
think so, it is for two reasons among many others. We habitually look for
two qualities in an historian of repute, namely honesty and scholarship; for
an unscrupulous author sometimes deprives even a true account of cre-
dence, while a sense of responsibility in the historian often adds a certain
credibility to the facts themselves, because of his personal authority.   55
Similarly, while lack of skill on the writer's part, assuming that he can win
his reader's confidence (and even this is beyond the powers of the incompetent writer), may reduce to dullness facts in themselves brilliant, and reduce
their significance and change them for the worse, so too the gifts of a clever
writer may cast light upon what is dark, and give importance even to the   60
trivial fact, shedding what one might call a light of glory upon famous
events. And since you possess both honesty and scholarship in unequalled
measure, surely no one could have been better adapted to the task you have
chosen; or rather the task itself fitted no one better than you, inasmuch as
you were capable both of carrying conviction by your unrivalled conscienti-   65
ousness and of embellishing the subject with a distinguished style.
       But at this point, most courteous Gaguin, I could easily believe that
you are a little annoyed with your Erasmus for venturing to pay you even
the smallest of compliments; for it is no secret to me how retiring and modest, not to say over-modest, your natural disposition is, when you are, as   70
a rule, much more put out even by a friendly little speech in your honour
than anyone else would be by an insult. But do please, I beg you, indulge
my affection for you to the extent of allowing your friend to mention what
everyone is shouting from the housetops, for who is there among your
friends that is not thoroughly convinced of the amazing rectitude and inno-   75
cence and sobriety of your life and character and where on earth are these
things not common gossip? Not the least suspicion of vanity could ever fall
upon the spoken words of Gaguin, much less upon his writings. Besides,
everybody is aware that the French kings have always held you, and rightly
so, in high esteem, for they very frequently employed your services in great   80
affairs of state and you were repeatedly summoned to participate in the
king's secret councils and often charged with embassies in the king's name
– to the Italian states among others; so it is easy for men to conclude that
you are the only person to have both read attentively the old accounts of
French exploits and made careful researches into those of more recent date.   85
What am I to say, moreover, about your learning? As the saying goes, it
speaks quite adequately for itself. There is abundant witness to it in the
famous university of this city of Paris; for you were the first to adorn its
studies, flourishing as they were already in other ways, with the resources

of Latin letters, augmenting them with the lovely addition of eloquence, the   90
only art they appeared still to lack. Italy herself bears witness to it; she has
on many occasions, while you discoursed upon important topics in a very
impressive style, listened to you with an admiration that even perhaps had
its rueful side, inasmuch as she saw that on your account she must share
with France the crown of eloquence, the only crown that had hitherto been   95
hers alone, as Apollonius remarked of Cicero. Further witness is borne by
the best writers of our time, who vie with one another in proclaiming and
praising in unison the quality of your genius: in all of them there is hardly
a page that does not bear the name of Gaguin. Finally, distinguished sir,
your own books, in all their wealth of learning bear witness: books which   100
are now spread abroad through the whole world, and are everywhere read
and re-read by students with the utmost pleasure. Though in all of them,
poetry and prose alike, you give complete satisfaction to the ears not only
of scholars but of connoisseurs, yet it is in the branch you have made your
own – history, I mean (if you will allow the cobbler to go beyond his last   105
for a moment) – that you clearly exhibit an astonishing, and in a sense
unique, mastery of the craft; whereas in other kinds of writing you appear
to surpass all the rest, in history it seems you surpass yourself. There is in
these books such complete purity of diction, together with the elegance of
a Sallust, the good taste of a Livy, the highest degree of clarity, the most   110
engaging variety, and extraordinary skill in observing counsels, plans, seasons, convenience, propriety, and other things of the kind, which demonstrate a historian's ability. There is such liveliness in the narrative that one
seems to see the event occurring rather than to read an account of it, nor
is there any lack of a kind of agreeable brevity which in books of history   115
is as uncommon as it is pleasing to the reader. For, great heavens, what an
enormous quantity of material you have so perfectly compressed into such
a small volume, with the result that you are comprehensively brief and also
briefly comprehensive.

Surely, then, the whole world will agree that French history is well   120
served in being given such a spokesman as you. When Alexander the Great
came to Achilles' tomb, he said: 'How fortunate wert thou, O Achilles, in
the chance that brought thee the great poet Homer to pronounce thine
encomium!' Similarly, who will not think France most fortunate in securing
in Robert Gaguin the best voice to proclaim her glories? And what finer,   125

* * * * *

96 as Apollonius remarked of Cicero] Cf Plutarch *Cicero* 4.
105 cobbler] Cf *Adagia* I vi 16.
122–4 'How fortunate ... encomium!'] Cicero *Pro Archia* 10.24

more splendid, or more divine role could the gods' good will have brought you? None, surely; and, most learned sir, assuredly you could have given no more cogent proof of your exemplary patriotism than this. Even though your country was previously much in your debt because you had been the first to enrich it with the treasures of Latinity, yet you have now so bound   130
her to yourself with this priceless additional gift that she can never match it with her gratitude, however thankful she may be. Can statues or inscriptions or monuments ever equal the magnitude of your service to her? Our early forbears used to pay godlike honours to those of their countrymen who had either won imperial power or increased the boundaries of the com-   135
monwealth or otherwise deserved well of their fatherland: they honoured them with inscriptions graven on bronze; they presented them with golden statues. Yet it is a much nobler act to spread the fame of one's ancestors from the rising to the setting sun than to extend the boundaries of one's territory, and it is a lesser achievement to protect a city's stone walls and buildings   140
from an enemy's torches than to rescue the fame of truly good kings and citizens from envious oblivion, as Horace calls it, and so from perishing. It seems to me a considerably fine thing to promote, enrich, and adorn one's native land with the best literature than to dress it up with spoils, trophies, waxen effigies, and memorials of that kind; for no tablets or   145
effigies of wax or coins or statues or pyramids either indicate royal fame more clearly or preserve it more faithfully than the literary works of an eloquent author. In time to come the praise of the French nation, concealed hitherto as if narrow walls enclosed it, shall flash out like lightning and, with a Frenchman to recite it indeed, but, as is more seemly, with a Roman   150
trumpet to accompany the chant, shall thrill the ears of all regions of the earth. It shall be read and sung and made famous in every country and city and school and, thanks to Gaguin, can never perish; rather shall it continue to increase as time goes on. Therefore shouldst thou, O France, embrace the everlasting memorial of thy glory, love, cherish, and honour Robert   155
Gaguin, thine own son and the champion of thine immortality. For ourselves, reverend sir, and all such as are devoted to the higher studies, we and they shall never fail to love you, knowing that it is through you that increase has been given to that which they held to be supreme among the treasure of literature, namely, history. Farewell, thou who art literature's   160
bright star and my own.

* * * * *

142 Horace] Cf *Odes* 4.9.33, 34 Erasmus substitutes 'invidis oblivionibus' for Horace's 'lividas obliviones.'

46 / From Robert Gaguin   [Paris, 7 October? 1495]

Erasmus had evidently shown the first book or two of the *Antibarbari* (cf Ep
30:17n) to Gaguin and had asked for the elder scholar's criticism. Hyma asserts
that on this occasion Gaguin advised him not to publish since it would create
much hostility which Erasmus could not afford, and that as a result the work
remained in MS till much later (*Youth of Erasmus* 184). No such advice, however,
appears in this letter or elsewhere in the Correspondence.

ROBERT GAGUIN TO ERASMUS, CANON OF THE ORDER OF ST AUGUSTINE
You have undertaken, Erasmus, to conduct a war against a contemptible
sort of man, who unceasingly denigrates the humanities: a war not so much
difficult as distasteful for no one can by any warlike devices overcome those
whose ignorance only makes them more stubborn in defeat. It would be   5
impossible to bring against them any heavier artillery than their own
admission that only those authors who combine wisdom with eloquence
enjoy a reputation among the educated, and that, as the very dullest of them
can by no means deny, even the tellers of legendary tales and writers on
almost useless subjects are forgotten with the passing of time, but still enjoy   10
a ripening old age and are read with wonder and delight, whereas those
whose utterance is but an old woman's hesitant stammer are remembered
for a short time only. When from time to time they themselves remember
this, they borrow highlights from the authors they deride and, fitting as it
were purple patches to their own work, seek by this means to gain a reputa-   15
tion for literary style. And strangest of all is the fact that, although among
sacred authors they award the highest praise to those who had the power
of expressing their thoughts with polished and easy fluency, they censure
in someone else what they admire and commend in these. Why do they
think it reprehensible to excel in that very thing by which it is considered   20
praiseworthy to outdo all other writers in the same field? If it is reason that
separates man from inanimate nature, why should we not labour to be
foremost in that activity wherein one man may surpass another without
doing him any wrong? The difference between a dumb man and one who
lisps is no greater than that between the lisper and a lucid speaker or   25
between a merely lucid and an eloquent stylist.

    Now although I myself simply hold the impudence of these people in
contempt, nevertheless I do not disapprove of the campaign you have
launched against them. They should be assailed with every kind of weapon;
you have accumulated these with discretion and can shoot them skilfully   30
and brandish them most fiercely, and it would be superfluous for me to give

you any advice on their use and wrong of me to seek to take anything away from or add anything to a work you have already finished. You outline your scheme most succinctly, clearly classify the divisions of your subject-matter, and conduct the argument with great skill. Your arrangement is well   35
planned, you adorn your theme attractively, and you have something of Carneades' vigour in controversy. Please do not take one observation amiss from a friend: your preface is too long-drawn-out, and it may be that fault will be found with the leading role given to Batt on the ground that his monologue is somewhat too protracted, for a speech that goes on too long   40
is boring but when the discussion is relieved by a change of speaker the hearer is both refreshed and entertained. I should not like you to take only my advice upon this point. Look at those who make use of dialogue: they seldom employ continuous speeches, but often use brief clauses and phrases. Among the Greeks the celebrated Plato will serve as a leading   45
instance; among the Latin writers, Cicero and some others of later date. But I will seem to you a ridiculous masseur if I trouble myself about the blemishes on the skin of fair Venus! You are quite capable of erasing whatever is superfluous and adding anything that may be lacking.

As for the glorious achievements of the French in the very recent past,   50
they would require a long letter, or rather, indeed, an enormous treatise, for there is general agreement that, during the year, King Charles, soon after crossing the Alps, marched through Liguria and the Insubrian territory, and Tuscany and Latium as well, and led an expedition against Campania and Naples, put to flight King Alfonso and recovered the entire district.   55
And that when he had triumphed over his enemies and thereafter arranged matters to his own satisfaction, the Venetians, allied with Lodovico of Milan and many Italian princelings, faced the victorious Charles with their army as he was marching back to France, believing that they could cut off his retreat although he had offered them no provocation. But the event   60
failed to turn out as they expected. At Fornovo an attacking force of the

* * * * *

46:37 Carneades] Academic philosopher, 2nd century BC; for his 'vigour' see Cicero *De oratore* 3.9.71.

39 Batt] A speech by Batt in defence of good learning occupies the greater part of book I, although it is not an unbroken monologue.

48 blemishes] Reading 'naevos' for 'nervos'

57 Lodovico] Lodovico Sforza, called Il Moro, Duke of Milan

enemy, thirty thousand strong in close formation, was repulsed and routed
with the loss of four thousand men, whereas Charles' own force suffered
much lighter losses. In this fashion he withdrew to Asti with his army
intact, having discomfited the enemy. At present he remains at Turin with   65
an augmented force, ready to take the offensive. In case you desire a fuller
account of these events, I enclose a letter on the subject of this victory, written by one who witnessed the battle. Farewell.

47 / To Hector Boece   Near Paris, 8 November [1495]

The preface to Erasmus' *Carmen de casa natalitia Iesu* (Ant. Denidel, January
1496?), a volume containing several poems including complimentary verses to
Gaguin and Fausto Andrelini. See text and critical comment in Reedijk 224-43.
    Hector Boece was a Scot who was studying in Paris and resident with Eras-
mus at Montaigu. He apparently left Paris while Erasmus was still at Montaigu
to take a post at the newly founded university of Aberdeen as principal of
King's College. Some thirty-two years later he wrote to Erasmus reminding
him of their association at Montaigu and requesting a list of his works (Ep
1996). Erasmus replied (15 March 1530) with the requested *Index omnium lucubrationum*, his last such catalogue (Ep 2283).

ERASMUS OF ROTTERDAM TO HECTOR BOECE,
GREAT SCHOLAR AND GREAT FRIEND
What is the meaning of all those scolding letters from you? What, pray, has
made you so relentless? You keep writing again and again, threatening and
abusing me, in fact declaring open war upon me if I do not send you a copy   5
of my poems. Please consider how unfair it is of you to insist upon having
something which I do not even own myself. I swear to you most solemnly
that for a long time now I have not been engaged in the pursuit of poetry
and if I wrote trivial verse as a boy, I left it in my native land. I did not even
venture to import my barbarous Muses, with their uncouth foreign accent,   10
into this famous university of Paris, for I was aware that it contained a great
many persons who were exquisitely gifted in every branch of letters. Yet
you believe none of these things and think I am being poetical even in
asserting this! Confound it, who has put it into your head that Erasmus was
a poet? This expression, by which you keep describing me in your letters   15
from time to time, is in bad odour nowadays through the foolish ignorance
of many of its practitioners, although it once implied reverence and honour.
So please be good enough to refrain from using it to address me in future.
At the same time, my dear Hector, I must give a somewhat fuller and franker

explanation in order that you may not weary yourself, and bore me, by   20
penning the same request again and again.

   First of all, I am not such a fool as to wish to be esteemed by anyone
at more than my true value. Now, although in boyhood 'more than all else,
the Muses brought me joy,' still I did not work diligently enough at this kind
of literary activity to make it possible for anything to issue from my study   25
'worthy of Apollo and the cedar.' Being satisfied, accordingly, to 'sing to
the Muses and myself alone,' I preferred the obscurity attendant upon
failure to publish to exposing my lack of skill by incompetent writing. It
is for those who, in Horace's words, 'dread not the critic's penetrating
glance,' and who with Cicero, are not reluctant to have everyone read their   30
entire works, to relish having their poems recited on every stage and at
every street-corner. As for me, anything I do write is written for the people
of Sicily and Tarentum, as Lucilius says of himself. At this point you will
ask, 'How is it that you are less venturesome than this or that group of
writers, who are below you in both technical training and style?' To which,   35
if you wish, you may add, with the satirist, 'Taught or untaught, we versify
at large,' and, as a burden to this, you can hum another satirist's strain:
   'Tis foolish kindness, when you meet a bard at every turn,
      To spare the page you write upon; for paper's made to burn.
My own habit, dear Hector, is to shun, rather than imitate, such men's inept   40
fluency or lust for writing, as it might be called. Those 'infant prodigies,'
to use Quintilian's name for them, rush into writing the moment they have
read a poet or two and run their fingers over Apollo's pipe so as to make
some kind of shrill sound, their very first. In their foolish self-satisfaction
they admire, love, and cherish whatever they have thus produced, as fondly   45
as a she-ape does her ugly brood. For, if one may admit the truth, our

* * * * *

47:23-4 'more than ... joy'] Virgil Georgics 2.475

26 'worthy of Apollo and the cedar'] Persius 1.42. 'Cedar' implying cedar-oil
(as a preservative for books). Cf Adagia IV i 54.

26-7 'sing ... alone'] The phrase is taken from Jerome Ep 50:2; cf Adagia III
v 80.

29 Horace] Ars poetica 364

33 Lucilius] Cf Cicero De finibus 1.3.7.

36 the satirist] Horace Epistles 2.1.117

38-9 'Tis foolish ... burn.] Juvenal 1.17, 18

42 Quintilian] Cf Institutiones oratoriae 1.3.3.

present age produces a great many creatures like Marsyas or Pan who do
not hesitate to challenge even Apollo himself at a moment's notice, as they
say. And those fellows do indeed find admirers worthy of the performer;
they find their appropriate Midases, whose gross ears they may charm with   50
their savage verse and, assuming that the critics will be beguiled, look forward hopefully to enjoying a reputation like Virgil's. For myself, 'I canvass
not the People's fickle vote' and, since I fail to satisfy my own judgment,
I find no pleasure in the approval of men of little competence, some of whom
admire nothing save what they have themselves achieved, or could achieve,   55
while others on the contrary admire only what they do not understand. This
one is captivated by the grotesque and pretentious: 'sonorous nonsense,'
as Horace puts it; while another makes obeisance before out-of-date language borrowed from the darkest ages, 'and "hervest-beryng erthe"
astounded reads.' Still another takes delight in the piling-up of words and   60
equates eloquence with talkativeness. Others deny any claim to a poem
unless it be crammed with a thousand fables. As for real quality, those who
respect it are few indeed, for few indeed can even discern it. If I remember
aright, it was embarrassing to the painter Apelles to have his works
criticized by the mighty monarch, Alexander; if so, is not a trained scholar   65
likely to be embarrassed when he faces the criticism of any cobbler or
ploughman? There is also that persistent phenomenon of envious ill-will,
which as a rule is only too ready to assail everything that is truly excellent.
Why should I for no reason call forth the hisses of this serpent against me?
This is a contest which those may enter who are led into writing poetry at   70
their bellies' dictation, or at any rate are so strongly allured by the siren-
song of praise and glory that they prefer even notoriety in Herostratus'
manner to a life without fame. But I myself would not purchase glory at the
price of personal enmity.

You will say, 'Now, what is the point of all this?' This: that, being too   75
unskilful to give satisfaction to the ears of those who are skilled, if any such
there be, and yet too skilful perhaps, or at any rate too well bred, to stoop
to wrangling with busybodies such as these, I made up my mind to dedicate

* * * * *

47 Marsyas] A satyr who issued a challenge to Apollo and was flayed alive
on being defeated

48 at a moment's notice] *Adagia* III vi 45

50 Midases] Cf Ep 104:49n.

52–3 'I canvass ... vote'] Horace *Epistles* 1.19.37

58 Horace] *Ars poetica* 322

59–60 'and ... reads'] Martial 11.90.5

72 Herostratus] In order to draw attention to himself Herostratus set fire to
the temple of Artemis (Diana) at Ephesus in 356 BC.

whatever I might write to Harpocrates, rather than Apollo. All the same, in order to avoid appearing as a Demea in relation to one who is linked to me by a tie of exceptional good will, I have, like Micio, allowed myself to be won over (for who could resist a Hector?), and by deviating slightly from my usual custom I have sent you a couple of my poems, which I threw off on holiday, when we were walking by a country stream. In these you must not look for the happy rightness of a Virgil or the exalted strain of a Lucan or the fluency of an Ovid or the learned appeal of Baptista Mantuanus, for, though I admire all these qualities, when I come to compose I somehow favour the direct, spare style of Horace. If you admire real quality rather than pretentiousness, I hope you will not on every count despise my poems. But there, I nearly forgot the demand I most wanted to express: if you have any affection for your Erasmus, please give no advertisement whatever to his trifling compositions. Farewell.

Written in haste in the country, 8 November

48 / To Nicolaas Werner   Paris, 13 September [1496]

After a few months residence at Montaigu, Erasmus fell ill, a result, as he later said, of the bad eggs and the insanitary condition of his room (cf *Compendium vitae* Allen I 50:104f). To recover his health he left Paris and returned to the bishop of Cambrai at Bergen. Later in the summer he visited his friends in the monastery of Steyn, who encouraged him to return to Paris (cf ibid, lines 106–8).

Nicolaas Werner was one of his most sympathetic friends at Steyn, an older man who later became prior. He evidently encouraged Erasmus in his desire to leave the monastery (cf Allen Ep 296:165–9). Erasmus wrote to him frequently and with affection till his death in 1504.

ERASMUS OF ROTTERDAM TO THE REVEREND FATHER, NICOLAAS WERNER
I hope and trust that you and the community are well: for myself, thanks be to Heaven, I am in excellent health. If anyone was hitherto unaware of the high value I set upon holy writ, I have now made this clear in my actions.

* * * * *

79 to Harpocrates] ie to silence. Cf *Adagia* IV i 52.
80–1 Demea ... Micio] Leading characters in the *Adelphoe* of Terence; cf Ep 3:11n.
86 Baptista Mantuanus] Battista Spagnuoli of Mantua (1448–1516) was a Carmelite friar, a prolific writer of verse who was much admired in his own day (cf Ep 49:112ff). His collected works were published by Bade in 1513 in three folio volumes.

Perhaps that was rather a vain thing to say, yet it does not become me to   5
keep anything secret from my most beloved Father. Lately I happened to
meet some Englishmen, all of them nobles and men of influence. To their
company was added, most recently, a certain priest, a very wealthy young
man who had just declined the bishopric he was offered because he was
aware of his own deficiency in liberal education. He is none the less to be   10
recalled to a bishopric by the king within a year though, besides any emolu-
ments he might have as a bishop, he possesses an annual income of more
than two thousand *écus*. When this youth heard about my literary activities
he began to show me extraordinary signs of affectionate devotion, attention, and respect, for he had stayed for a while in my household. He offered   15
me a hundred *écus* if I should agree to be his tutor for a year, together with
a benefice within a few months' time, and also a loan of three hundred *écus*
if they should be required for keeping up my position until they could be
repaid from the benefice. Had I agreed to accept, I should have put all the
English in this city under obligation to me (they are all of the highest rank), 20
and all England through them. I spurned this glittering reward and still
more glittering prospect, and I spurned their entreaties and the tears that
accompanied them. I tell you the truth without exaggeration: the English
now understand that the wealth of all England means nothing to me. And
it was not heedlessly that I declined, and am still declining, such offers; it 25
is because I have no desire to be diverted from religious studies by any
monetary inducement. I did not come to Paris to teach, or to make piles of
money, but to learn; and indeed my intention, God willing, is to seek my
doctorate in theology.

The bishop of Cambrai is being extremely kind to me. His promises   30
are generous though, to be quite frank, he does not send generous remit-
tances. My good Father, I send you my greetings, and earnestly entreat you
to pray to God for me. I shall do likewise for you.

From my library in Paris, 13 September

* * * * *

48:8 priest] Allen suggests this may have been James Stewart, second son of
James III of Scotland and brother of James IV, as most nearly fitting the circumstances of the young priest. He was about twenty-one at this time and was
shortly after made archbishop of St Andrews. He may previously have
declined the see of Argyll, which was vacant 1493–7. Erasmus does not say that
the young priest was himself English. Allen further notes that he can find no
English bishopric vacant at this time and filled by a young man.

13, 16, 17 two thousand *écus*], a hundred *écus*], three hundred *écus*] *Ecus à la
couronne* or *écus au soleil*. See the Glossary and Appendix A on gold coinage.

49 / To Hendrik van Bergen   Paris, 7 November 1496

This letter was printed at the end of Willem Hermans' *Silva odarum* (G. Marchand: Paris, 20 January 1497), which Erasmus edited and saw through the press. During his visit to Steyn in the summer of 1496 he had spent some time with Hermans and had persuaded him to entrust some of his poems to him for publication. The elaborate fiction about Hermans' unwillingness to publish is no more than the conventional affectation of modesty expected of a young poet. The volume contains eighteen poems by Hermans which furnish valuable information about the friends and circumstances of his youth. There is also one poem by Erasmus: *Ad Robertum Gaguinum carmen de suis fatis*, probably written during his illness in the spring of 1496. See Reedijk 243–5.

Hendrik van Bergen (d 1502), bishop of Cambrai, has already been mentioned several times. He was the second son of Jan, fifth Lord of Glimes and Bergen-op-Zoom (cf Ep 42:21n). He was made chancellor of the Order of the Golden Fleece in 1493, a position which made him the senior ecclesiastic at the Burgundian court.

DESIDERIUS ERASMUS, A CANON OF THE ORDER OF ST AUGUSTINE, TO THE MOST
REVEREND FATHER IN CHRIST, HENDRIK, BISHOP OF CAMBRAI, GREETINGS
Have you ever seen a thief so brazen as I? You ask what sort of opening this is? I am sure your distinguished lordship's natural kindness will excuse my effrontery. I knew that you were endowed with a combination of qualities   5
that was as unusual as it was admirable: that you held the highest rank while you maintained the easiest and friendliest of attitudes, and combined with such supreme affability the greatest dignity; nevertheless I chose for the moment to hold in view your kindness rather than your eminence and, if I may be permitted the expression, to jest for a while with your   10
beatitude. Am I not then the height of brazenness? Did Terence's Phormio himself ever scheme quite like this? It seemed an insufficiently bold exploit to purloin another's property against the will of its owner; I had to go on to disclose, indeed advertise, my own theft, and to you, moreover, which is more shameless than anything possibly could be. I stood in no awe, either   15
of your censure or of any ordinances or laws, not even of the notoriously strict ruling delivered by Quintus Scaevola: 'If anything be given to a per-

* * * * *

49:11 Phormio] The title-role in a comedy by Terence
17 Scaevola] Cf Aulus Gellius *Noctes Atticae* 7.15.2. Quintus Mucius Scaevola (consul 95 BC) was not only a statesman but a famous jurist, author of a standard work on the 'ius civile.'

Jan and Hendrik van Bergen with their patron saints
artist unknown
Gemeentemuseum, Bergen op Zoom

son for safe keeping, and he makes use of it or, being given it for use in a particular way, applies it to another use, he is guilty of theft.' Is there any kind of subterfuge that will enable me at least to slip out of this imbroglio? Will not everyone think my deed deserves the punishment of the sack? But at least I would that your serene lordship might concede me one privilege, that of stating my case in a few words. When you hear my story in due order, you will not only acquit me but, like a second Apollo, greet with laughter and approval the theft committed by your Mercury.

In Willem Hermans, of Gouda, I have always uniquely found, 'from the tender nails,' as the Greeks say, onwards, a most delightful friend, a very Patroclus or Pirithous, in literary studies as in everything else. He is the first and chief hope of our own Holland, which was formerly a waste of weeds, yielding nothing but brambles, thistles, and other wild growths, but now has belatedly begun bearing certain crops in the Italian mode. For very many reasons, he has elected to consecrate the first fruits of this harvest to you. I stayed with him for some days recently in order to restore my health; at one point in the course of our usual friendly and pleasant exchanges, he produced some odes upon which he had practised his pen in early youth. No doubt his purpose was to put an end to them as a result of my criticism; for, said he with his usual modesty and wit, those odes seemed to him the kind whose faults not even a thousand erasures could remove (but one grand erasure might!) and he thought them fit not for Apollo but only for Vulcan or Neptune. With equal gaiety he added that those offspring of his had long been unwelcome in their father's eyes, like misbegotten and hence degenerate children, bound to come to no good, and he remarked, 'Paternal feeling forbids me to do this deliberately for myself; you must be the Harpagus.' At the same time he handed them to me in order that I should expose them to death without the slightest inkling of what the sequel was to be. Taking my cue from the mention of Harpagus and finding delightful precedents in Cyrus, and afterwards in Moses and

* * * * *

21 the punishment of the sack] To be sewn in a sack and thrown into the Tiber was the Roman punishment for parricide (ie murder of a near relative); cf *Adagia* IV ix 18.

24 Apollo] Cf Horace *Odes* 1.10.9–12.

26–7 'from ... nails'] ie from early youth; *Adagia* I vii 52

28 Patroclus or Pirithous] Friends of Achilles and Theseus respectively

40 Vulcan or Neptune] Meaning, of course, destruction by fire or by water

44 Harpagus] A member of the household of Astyages, king of Media, to whom the king gave his infant son with orders to kill him; the child survived to become the great king Cyrus (Herodotus 1.108–22). Moses, Oedipus, and Romulus were all exposed as children, and lived.

Oedipus and Romulus, I decided, with affectionate treachery, that I ought
to bring up in secret the children whom he, in his strictness, and in defiance
of right feeling, had abandoned. I was buoyed up, you see, by the hope that   50
the offspring thus despaired of by its parent might flourish and in time
might inherit its kingdom even against its father's will.

   Consequently I returned to Paris, taking my prize away with me,
while I pretended that it had been destroyed. Here in Paris I had no wish
to keep my peculation exclusively to myself and so allowed myself to betray   55
it to a number of close friends: at first very few, to be sure, but subsequently
the affair leaked out to quite a few people, as these things will. Briefly, the
final result was that they marched on me in a body and vigorously demanded that I should abandon my grudging concealment of the earliest
work of so promising a writer, and that I should instead obligingly give all   60
those eager young scholars what they were seeking. Sometimes they incidentally used a threatening tone, hinting that it would be better for me to
do it with a good rather than a bad grace. To me at least, my distinguished
lord, the talents of this eminently scholarly and modest young man have
ever been a source of admiration; and I felt sure that from such gifts as his   65
we might always expect outstanding rather than average, much less
inferior, results. However, I did not place entire confidence in my own
unsupported judgment for fear I might be deluded and blinded to some
extent by my affection for a very close friend. Once Robert Gaguin, whom
France justifiably celebrates as the supreme parent, doyen, and prince of   70
her literature, had expressed warm approval of my Willem's poems and
spontaneously urged me to publish them, I readily fell in with his verdict,
for I cannot but think that both the character and the scholarly judgment
of that great man exact absolute deference. And I am not wholly unaware
that Willem will take issue fiercely with me, after Demea's manner too: 'O   75
heaven and earth and Neptune's ocean wide ...' So I must look for letters
full of a thousand insults. He will shout 'wretch!' and 'traitor,' and eventually, I believe, he will hale me to court. What counter claim can I invent?
And what forensic refinements can I employ to defend myself? I should
need a Cicero, but I apprehend that even he might prove inadequate. Still,   80

                 * * * * *

69 Gaguin] On his return to Paris in September 1496 Erasmus showed Hermans' poems to Gaguin and persuaded him to write a letter to Hermans, in
answer to one which Erasmus had brought with him, to serve as a preface to
the *Silva odarum*. The approval of Gaguin would guarantee a favourable reception for Hermans' poems among the Parisian literati.
75–6 'O heaven ... wide ...'] Terence *Adelphoe* 790

I will follow the example of Micio, who is not the worst of advocates for a brazen culprit: I will urge that it is illegal to bring a charge of theft against me, since, as Pythagoras has truly remarked, friends have all things in common. Alternatively, I shall with greater candour acknowledge, as Chaerea does in Terence, that I sinned from affection, not dislike.   85

Whatever his reaction may be, I myself was unwilling to let my theft in all its deep-dyed wickedness meet the public gaze and so, my most generous lord, I desire that it might be published under your sponsorship: partly because I have decided to dedicate all my studies to you, my unrivalled patron, partly because I could easily foretell that these poems would earn   90 your lordship's kind approval, inasmuch as they plainly embraced in union two things, both of which I know you have much at heart, distinguished learning and an exceptionally high moral tone, qualities which, when they are combined, are as peerless in beauty and perfection as their combination itself is rare. For in most cases we respect men's morals, but what we find   95 to be missing is learning, without which virtue appears somehow defective. On the other hand, it usually happens that men endowed with intellectual gifts are either cursed with a foolish liking for vain display or else, worse still, disposed to vice and indifferent to the goodness and simplicity which belong to the Christian faith. For this reason I tend to be privately   100 indignant from time to time with the poets of modern times (even Christian poets) because in choosing models they prefer to set before themselves Catullus, Tibullus, Propertius, and Ovid, rather than St Ambrose or Paulinus of Nola or Prudentius or Iuvencus or Moses or David or Solomon, as though their Christianity were forced and not spontaneous.   105

However, I shall check myself before I go too far, especially in regard to my former 'darlings,' as people call them to discredit me. I am myself happy to be of my friend Gaguin's opinion in thinking that even ecclesiastical subjects can be treated brilliantly in vernacular works provided the style is pure. And I would not reprehend anyone for applying Egyptian trim-   110 mings, but I am against the appropriation of Egypt in its entirety. In this

* * * * *

81 Micio] See Ep 47:80–1n.

83 Pythagoras] Cf *Adagia* I i 1.

85 Terence] Cf *Eunuchus* 877, 878.

104 Paulinus of Nola] Correcting Allen's text, which reads Paulum Nolanum.

110–11 Egyptian trimmings] 'Spoiling the Egyptians' is a Biblical phrase (*Exodus* 3:22); for its present sense of using pagan literature to give grace to Christian writing, see especially Augustine *De doctrina christiana* 2.40.60–1, *Confessions* 7.9. (15); a similar idea underlies Jerome *Epistles* 70.

regard the celebrated Baptista Mantuanus performed a model service in my
opinion. As he happened to have Mantua for his native land, like Virgil,
so too he came close enough to Virgil in learning, and seems to me to deserve
the title of the Christian Virgil just as much as Lactantius deserves that of   115
the Christian Cicero which Agricola used to give him. And, if my prophetic
sense does not deceive me, there will surely come a time when Baptista will
fall but a little below his fellow countryman in fame and renown, as soon
as the passage of years draws aside envy's veil. Fortunate indeed is the Carmelite Order to have in him a source of pride and a challenge to all others.   120
Yet even so I would not venture to compare to Baptista, now in his old age,
the still youthful Willem, though these preliminary exercises in poetry
induce me to hope most ardently that Steyn may eventually contain within
its meadows that which Mantua, already twice blest, cannot afford to
despise. For if an author's premature children are so gifted, what may he   125
not promise in those that are to be timely born? As it is with a number of
creatures, so it is with minds: their first offspring usually tend to weakness.
If Willem's weaklings are as lively as this, what are his mature and established products to be like? And the barbarous country from which he
comes, its dearth of instructors, and the total want of respect in which   130
studies are held among us, all help to crown the miracle. I would therefore
earnestly desire any peevish criticasters who may come upon these poems
to be advised beforehand to have regard for their author's age, country, and
upbringing, and not to assess his talent in the light of these preliminary
products but rather through the richness of the vegetation to infer the soil's   135
fertility. Further, if they come across any unpolished passages, they should
remember that Willem did not write these poems so much as throw them
off by way of recreation. If anything in them seems extravagant, they should
reflect that an over-productive mind is better than one that offers little, for
it is easier to prune excess than to fill up exiguity. If, moreover, any senti-   140
ments they contain appear too freely expressed or too immature, they
should be willing to recall the reply of Accius, who in youth once read to
Pacuvius, himself a tragedian, and already well advanced in age, at his
request a tragedy entitled *Atreus*. When Pacuvius said that he approved of
it all, but that some parts of it appeared a little unripe and bitter, Accius   145

* * * * *

112 Baptista Mantuanus] Cf Ep 47:86n.

115 Lactantius] A Christian writer who flourished c 300

116 Agricola] Cf Ep 23:58n.

145–8 Accius ...] Aulus Gellius, *Noctes Atticae* 13.2 Accius and Pacuvius
were tragic poets of the 2nd century BC.

answered, 'I admit it, but am not really repentant, for they say that minds are like apples: those which are unripe and bitter to begin with become mellow and agreeable later.' As for the freedom with which my friend Willem handles this kind of poem, in which hardly anyone has distinguished himself since Horace, I personally find it acceptable, partly because it is a proof 150 of fertile inventiveness to be able to deploy such resources when faced with the narrow restrictions imposed by the lyric metres, partly because I observe that Quintilian disliked those who never venture out to sea for fear of storms and, as he himself has it, keep one hand always pinned within the cloak. It is Quintilian too who commends the odes of Horace and pro- 155 nounces them almost the only ones worth reading, because they sometimes 'rise majestically,' and are 'happily audacious.'

But I have made this letter too long. I would but request the reader to blame me, not Willem, for anything that may offend him in these odes. And, my lord Bishop, if I may once again address you, if you should adopt 160 into your own family these more than orphaned children, exposed as they were to death, which I now commit to your care, then you will act in a manner worthy of your former kindness. If they have you for guardian, they will feel no need of a parent. I forbear to say more; for here they come in person, dressed as well as I can manage. Farewell, and pray accept my 165 humble duty.

Paris, 7 November 1496

50 / To Nicolaas Werner   [Paris, January 1497]

ERASMUS OF ROTTERDAM TO THE REVEREND FATHER, NICOLAAS WERNER
Greetings, venerable Father. I wrote previously to your reverence, but believe the messenger did not deliver my letter. I hope you are well, as I am. Lately I fell into a quartan fever, but have recovered health and strength, not by a physician's help (though I had recourse to one) but by 5 the aid of Ste Geneviève alone, the famous virgin, whose bones, preserved

* * * * *

153 Quintilian] *Institutiones oratoriae* 12.10.21; cf *Adagia* II x 31.

155 Quintilian] *Institutiones oratoriae* 10.1.96

50:6 Ste Geneviève] Many years later Erasmus fulfilled a vow made at this time by writing a poem in praise of Ste Geneviève and in thanksgiving for his recovery from a quartan fever: *Erasmi Diuae Genouefae praesidio a quartana febre liberati carmen* (Freiburg: Jo. Emmeus, 1532); cf Reedijk 350–5. In this poem the physician who treated him without result is identified as Wilhelm Cop (cf Ep 124:18n).

by the canons regular, daily radiate miracles and are revered: nothing is
more worthy of her, or has done me more good.

I am afraid the rains will have drowned the fields and all else where
you are. Here in Paris it rained without stopping for almost three months.   10
The Seine left its bed and poured out upon the fields and the middle of the
city. The shrine of Ste Geneviève was brought from its usual place of keeping
to Notre Dame. The bishop and the whole university went forth to meet
it in solemn procession, led by the canons regular, then the abbot, and all
his monks walking barefoot. Four bearers, completely stripped, bore the   15
shrine. Now the sky is perfectly clear.

I am prevented by the pressure of business from writing more. I ask
your reverence to look after and to favour Willem, who is a part of my soul.
His name is honoured and revered in this university, and deservedly, for
he is worthy of the admiration and affection of the whole world, though   20
among his associates his exceptional learning brings him nothing but envy.
He cannot but become a man of note. Let any who please, sneer; but no
one will be able to hinder him. Farewell.

51 / To Hendrik van Bergen   Paris [January, 1497]

Evidently sent with a copy of Hermans' *Silva odarum,* which had just been
published.

ERASMUS TO THE REVEREND FATHER, HENDRIK VAN BERGEN,
BISHOP OF CAMBRAI
My lord Bishop: It was my desire to make a close friend's talents as widely
known as possible, for they deserve to be immortalized, and I thought in
the end this might best be achieved if your distinguished name were like   5
a torch to add lustre to his new work. It was not that I judged this kind of
service to be suitable to, or eminently worthy of, your exalted rank, but I
thought that your prestige might lend some recommendation and authority
to a fledgling author. My intention, as it seems to me, has amply succeeded,
for my friend Willem is now read, seized upon, and kept by all the students   10
of this university, with an almost unbelievable enthusiasm, while all the

* * * * *

12 shrine] It was customary to carry the shrine of Ste Geneviève, patron saint
of Paris, in solemn procession to Notre Dame when the city was threatened
with disaster. This was done when the Seine overflowed on 12 January 1497;
cf M. Félibien *Histoire de la ville de Paris* II (1755) 892.
14 abbot] Philippe Cousin, abbot of Ste Geneviève
18 Willem] Hermans

colleges and public lecture-halls resound with his name. If I perceive that
you are not offended by being asked to do this service, I am happy enough;
but if I also win favour thereby, I am positively exultant. My gift, you see,
is another man's work, for I have not been able to produce anything of my   15
own, being so busied with my studies in theology, and having followed
Jerome's advice, learning what I would teach. All the same, you may presently look for some fruits of my studies which I shall dedicate to you. As
for me, a sickness has quite worn me out, and my body and my coffers are
both in a sadly depleted state; meat must mend the former, money the latter.   20
Pray act as you are accustomed to do, and farewell.

    Paris [1498]

52 / To Jan Mombaer   Paris, 4 February [1497]

Jan Mombaer (Latinized as Mauburnus) of Brussels (d 1501) was an Augustinian canon of a monastery of the reformed Windesheim congregation near
Zwolle. Here he wrote *Rosetum exercitiorum spiritualium*, printed in 1491 and
following years, a guide to meditation which may have influenced Loyola's
Spiritual Exercises. At the suggestion of Jan Standonck (cf Ep 73:11n) he was
brought to Paris in September 1496 as leader of a group invited to introduce
reforms in the monastery of St Severinus at Château-Landon near Fontaine-
bleau. About 1498 he was also induced to undertake the reform of the abbey
of Livry near Paris, of which he became abbot in April 1501. Through him Erasmus must have kept in touch with the movement for reform in the spirit of
the Devotio moderna led by Standonck even after he himself had left Montaigu. Cf Renaudet *Préréforme* 219ff, 254ff, 302f, *et passim*; P. Debongnie *Jean
Mombaer de Bruxelles* (Louvain 1918) and *Jean Mombaer de Bruxelles, abbé de
Livry, ses écrits, ses réformes* (Louvain 1927).

A LETTER FROM ERASMUS OF ROTTERDAM TO JAN OF BRUSSELS
Affectionate greetings, my beloved brother; for it is thus, respected sir, that
I have chosen to address you, in terms suited not to your rank but to the
affection I bear you. Indeed I do respect your talents and the shining goodness of your life, but I embrace you still more warmly for your civilized dis-   5

    * * * * *

51:16 theology] Erasmus appears anxious at this time to assure his friends in
Holland that he was seriously undertaking the study of theology (cf Ep 48: 24ff).
His apology for not having anything of his own to send the bishop raises the
question of why he had dedicated the *De casa natalitia Iesu* to Hector Boece
rather than to his patron (cf Ep 47 introduction).
17 Jerome] Cf *Epistles* 133:12.

position and for the studies that unite us. The former qualities earn my
admiration; the latter, my love.

I am, then, not writing this time to abbot or prior, but conversing with
a friend in a familiar way. I was extremely pleased to be asked to write to
you and am only sorry, indeed angry, that I am not in a position to do as   10
I should wish. I have just recovered from an illness and am not yet quite
myself, and I have never been busier in my life; in other circumstances I
should be overwhelming you with so many letters, and such long ones, that
you would become quite tired of them, even though you are as much a glutton for letters as I, who find all my friends' letters too short. If at this time   15
you will not pardon me because I am busy, perhaps you will do so because
I am ill. When I have time and am a little stronger I shall be a frequent, and
very garrulous, correspondent; usually there is nothing I enjoy more than
writing to my scholarly friends or reading their letters.

I have sent you my trifling verses printed a year ago, together with   20
Willem's poems; in both you will come across a number of faults, for it happened that in each case I was ill at the time of printing, and as a consequence
could not make corrections in the proof. But you will easily identify those
places.

The Carmelite, Bostius, mentions you in his letter to me; he asked   25
where you were and what you were doing, and I gave him all the news.
If only you were closer to me, Father, and I were freer! Then I should either
visit you or write to you daily and you would be another Willem to me –
the other 'half of my soul.' For though you and I have never been closely
associated, I still somehow feel strongly drawn to you. I am by nature   30
extremely prone to form friendships of all kinds, but so strong is the attraction I feel towards enthusiasts for good literature that I can even love my
rivals. Yet I am bound to regard you as especially precious in view of our
bond in the higher studies which, as Cicero perceived, is by far the most
reliable means of cementing good will and besides which, even without   35
this link, your modesty and kindness, friendliness and honour are enough
to make me love you. Then there is our common Order and its habit and

* * * * *

52:20 verses] The *De casa natalitia Iesu* (cf Ep 47 introduction).

21 Willem's poems] *Silva odarum* (cf Ep 49 introduction).

25 Bostius] See Ep 53 introduction.

29 'half of my soul'] Horace's phrase (*Odes* 1.3.8) is slightly adapted here: Erasmus frequently uses it in referring to friends, as do many of his contemporaries (cf Ep 4:18n).

34 Cicero] Cf *De amicitia* 14.49

what I take to be a considerable similarity in our dispositions, except that
you are more inclined to virtue.

I am not surprised that you find your exile somewhat uncongenial, but   40
in a matter of such a sacred character and of such importance I desire and
urge you to be stout-hearted; and I recommend it too. From the beginning
I have guessed, as I do now, that this charge of yours will lead to countless
blessings in future. Of course it would have been pleasanter to live in lettered ease, but you have chosen the path of Hercules, the path of virtue,   45
and must put on a Herculean spirit. The poets remark, both frequently and
learnedly, that, as Seneca says, the way of virtue is steep and hard, and
winds not through the places where we bathe and sleep and feast but
through sweat and battle and toil. This was Homer's meaning in inventing
a Ulysses buffeted by such dire hardships, and Virgil's, as he describes the   50
grim experiences and perils of Aeneas:

> Though dooms and perils all our way beset,
> We hold a course for Latium, where th'abode
> Of quietness the Fates to us declare.

And this is the meaning of the celebrated Labours of Hercules and Labours   55
of Theseus.

But I have to leave off writing. Farewell, and pray for me: this is my
one ardent request to you.

Paris, 4 February
Your friend Erasmus   60

53 / To Arnoldus Bostius   [Paris, spring 1497?]

Arnoldus Bostius, Boschius, or Bost was a Carmelite of Ghent who was a friend
of Gaguin, Ermolao Barbaro, Cornelis Gerard, and other literary men whom
he encouraged to write and publish (cf Renaudet *Préréforme* 120, 133, 225, *et
passim*).

ERASMUS TO ARNOLDUS BOSTIUS

I have received a considerable number of letters from you, all to much the
same effect: that you suspect I am angry with you. If this were not a baseless
suspicion on your part, I should certainly be angry with you for entertaining
such unloving thoughts about a friend who loves you dearly. Farewell.   5

* * * * *

47 Seneca] Cf *De ira* 2.31.1.
50 Virgil] *Aeneid* 1.204–6
55 Labours of Hercules] Cf *Adagia* III i 1

54 / To Christian Northoff   Paris [spring 1497?]

Despite Erasmus' refusal to earn money by teaching on his return to Paris in September 1496 (cf Ep 48:24ff) and his reassertion of his intention to devote himself exclusively to theology in January 1497 (cf Ep 51), by the spring of that year he was forced to turn to teaching to support himself. Two of his first pupils were the brothers Christian and Heinrich Northoff of Lübeck, who were studying and living with Augustin Vincent, called Caminade (cf Ep 131 introduction). Christian soon returned to Lübeck to become a merchant (cf Ep 61:86ff), but Heinrich remained in Paris till February 1498 (cf Ep 70). The letters Erasmus wrote to his pupils were probably intended primarily as models of Latin style. He also wrote for them a little book of forms for polite conversation, entitled *Familiarium colloquiorum formulae* (cf Ep 130:108–9n, and Thompson *Colloquies* 555ff).

ERASMUS TO HIS FRIEND CHRISTIAN, WHO HAD WRITTEN A LETTER WITH THE
HELP OF AUGUSTIN IN AN ORNATE STYLE
Greetings, to your heart's content. So may God love me, I did not expect such elegance from you, or rather, such eloquence, for I could easily foresee that you would be elegant. This is why your letter gave me especial   5
pleasure, and for the same reason I recommend you to continue in the way you are going for you will soon emerge as your teacher's image. But I advise you to take some definite school of oratory as a standard to keep your style from becoming nondescript and inconsistent with itself, and furthermore to choose for preference the school to which you are specially adapted by   10
nature. If I may venture a guess about you, you seem to come closer to Timon's type than Cicero's, whereas I would rather it were Cicero's. The finest school would be the Attic. You are quite unsuited to the Asiatic school and have no reason to aim at the Rhodian. You appear reminiscent of the Punic, or rather the Allobrogian, which of course is acknowledged to be by   15
far the best blended of all, being a balanced mixture of the Arabian and Spanish schools with 'the toad's blood' meantime disguised by 'Calenian

* * * * *

54:12 Timon's] The reading is probably corrupt; Allen suggests *Tironis,* since Tiro was Cicero's freedman and secretary.

15 Punic] Referring to Carthage; its schools were famous in antiquity.

15 Allobrogian] A mock-designation employed in pure jest; the Allobroges were a warlike tribe of southern Gaul.

17 'the toad's blood'] Juvenal (1.69–70) mentions a woman who poisoned her husband with a toad (according to the scholiast 'toad's blood') in Calenian wine.

wine.' But it is foolish of me to try to teach you this, like the proverbial sow,
when you have a Minerva of your own; his kindness, however, is of so
unprecedented a sort that he will pardon me if I put my scythe to his harvest,   20
as I shall often do. I have no aversion to the kind of learning where the substance is provided by another, while you furnish the words: this very thing
was often done by Crassus, who was no mean orator, but he used ancient
sources. I myself have encountered Horace's crow, whom I should not wish
you to resemble, as you will if you try to be as like your teacher as possible.   25

You mention your love for me, but that is no news: I knew it before.
You need not be troubled about our rivalry, dear Christian; you stand high
enough, unless Augustin is lying to me, which he is not in the habit of
doing. My greetings to you and your Daedalus.

Paris, in the year [1498]   30

55 / To Christian Northoff   Paris [spring] 1497

ERASMUS TO CHRISTIAN

Greetings to my dear friend. Yesterday I did not write at all: deliberately,
for I was a little angry. Do not ask me with whom; it was with you. 'How,'
you say, 'did I deserve this?' I was afraid that you were laying traps for me,
clever fellow that you are, and I was suspicious of that box of yours, in case   5
it might bring us some consequences like those that Pandora's box brought
to Epimetheus in the legend. Then, when I opened it, I was annoyed with
myself for having been inclined to harbour suspicion. 'Why, then,' you will
ask, 'did you not write even today?' Because I was extremely busy. 'Indeed,
and what was the business?' I was watching a play, a very enjoyable one.   10
'A comedy,' say you, 'or a tragedy?' Call it which you like, but no one played
a part in character, there was only one act, the chorus had no flutes, the type
of play was neither Roman nor Greek but down-to-earth miming, all done
on the ground, without dancing, viewed from the dining-room, most excit-

* * * * *

18 sow] Cf *Adagia* I i 40.

20 harvest] Cf *Adagia* I iv 41.

23 Crassus] Cf Cicero *De oratore* 1.154, 5.

24 Horace's crow] Horace, *Epistles* 1.3.19, uses the metaphor of a crow decking
itself in peacock's feathers.

29 Daedalus] A reference to the myth of Daedalus who fashioned wings from
feathers, bound with linen cords and fastened in wax. His son Icarus, using
the wings his father had made for him, flew too near the sun so that the heat
melted the wax and he fell into the sea (cf *Adagia* III i 65). Erasmus seems to
be suggesting the danger of flying too high with wings made by someone else.

55:2 my dear friend] Literally, 'Attic honey'

ing crisis, bloodcurdling final scene. 'Confound you, what is this play you   15
are inventing?' you'll say. Well, Christian, I will tell you the story.

The spectacle we saw today was that of a battle royal between a house-
wife and her maidservant. The trumpet had sounded repeatedly before the
engagement. Resounding insults were exchanged by both sides. At this
stage the contest was indecisive, and nobody carried the day. It all went   20
on in the garden, while we looked on with some amusement from the
dining-room. Now for the denouement: the girl left the battle and came
upstairs in order to make the beds in my room. In the course of conversation
with her, I complimented her on her courage in giving her mistress as good
as she got in insults and abuse, but said that I had wished her hands might   25
have proved as formidable as her tongue, for the mistress, a stoutly built
female who might well have been an athlete so far as appearance went, kept
on boxing the girl's head with her fists. 'Why,' said I, 'have you no nails
at all, to endure such treatment without any response?' She answered with
a smile that, for herself, it was not spirit she lacked so much as strength.   30
'Do you,' I said to her, 'think that the outcome of a battle depends on
strength alone? In every case, the most important factor is planning.' When
she asked what plan I had in mind, I said: 'When she next attacks you, at
once pull off her headpiece' (for the women of Paris are extraordinarily
vain about a sort of black headdress, of false hair), 'this done, go for her   35
hair.'

I then imagined that she took my suggestion in the same jesting spirit
in which it was offered but, just before supper, up rushed mine host, all
out of breath (he was a herald in King Charles' service, commonly nick-
named Gentil Gerson). 'Come, my masters,' said he, 'you will see a gory   40
spectacle.' We ran forward and found the lady of the household and the girl
at grips upon the ground. We had difficulty in separating them. The evidence showed clearly how bloody the fight had been. On one side the
woman's headpiece, on the other side the girl's veil, lay on the earth in
shreds. So cruel had been the massacre that the ground was covered with   45
piles of hair. When we sat down to supper, Madame told us with much
indignation how violently the girl had behaved. 'When I set about correcting her,' she said, 'giving her a beating, I mean, she at once pulled my headpiece off my head.' I recognized that I had not sung my tale to deaf ears.
'Then,' she went on, 'when she had pulled it off, the witch brandished it   50

* * * * *

17–18 housewife] Antonia, the keeper of the boarding house in which Erasmus was living with his English pupils (cf Ep 60). She was apparently a Norman (cf Ep 62:5).
49 to deaf ears] Cf *Adagia* i iv 87.

before my eyes.' That had not formed part of my advice. 'After that,' she
continued, 'she pulled out all this hair you see here.' She called Heaven and
earth to witness that she had never come across a girl who possessed so
much naughtiness in so small a person. We proceeded to urge the vicissitudes of human life, the uncertain outcome of war, and negotiated to   55
establish peaceful understanding between them for the future. In the meantime I was privately congratulating myself that the mistress had no inkling
that my advice to the girl had prompted the affair, else I too would have
been made aware that she was the owner of a tongue!

So much for my amusing story: now to serious matters. You entered   60
upon a twofold contest with me, firstly in writing letters, secondly in sending presents. In one of them you now admit total defeat, inasmuch as you
have begun to fence with me by the aid of hands other than your own –
or are you going to be shameless enough to deny this? I think you will not,
if you have any decency at all. As to the other contest, I have never even   65
entered upon it myself but merely yielded the prize without competing. In
the realm of letters you are hopelessly beaten, indeed you do not so much
as fight, except like Patroclus, with the weapons of Achilles. I have no wish
to begin a contest of gifts with you. Can a poet undertake such a contest
with a merchant? Are we equal at all? But come now: I am challenging you   70
to a fairer, more level wrestling-ground than that. See whether you can tire
me out by sending gifts before I tire you out by writing letters, for this surely
is the kind of contest that would ultimately suit both poet and tradesman.
Get ready, if you have stomach for an adventure – and farewell.

Paris, 1497   75

56 / To Christian Northoff   Paris [spring 1497]

This letter was first published by Gervasius Amenus of Dreux (cf Allen I 442n)
in his *Lucubratiunculae* (Paris 1513–14). Gervasius says in his dedication to Lord
Mountjoy that he found it 'some time ago among the papers in your study.'
It is also included in the *De conscribendis epistolis* (ASD I 2 492–6).

ERASMUS TO HIS FRIEND CHRISTIAN OF LÜBECK
Since, Christian, my excellent friend, I had no doubt whatsoever that your
passion for letters was extraordinarily keen, I thought you needed no exhortation, but only some guidance and, as it were, signposting of the road you
had entered upon. This, I thought, was my duty: to point out to you, as a
person closely linked to me in many ways and highly congenial, the paths   5

* * * * *

68 weapons of Achilles] While Achilles sulked in his tent, Patroclus borrowed
his armour to frighten the Trojans.

I myself have followed from boyhood onwards. If you attend to them with
the degree of care I shall now devote to explaining them, I am confident that
I shall not regret having given the advice, nor will you be sorry that you
took it.   10

Your first endeavour should be to choose the most learned teacher you
can find, for it is impossible that one who is himself no scholar should make
a scholar of anyone else. As soon as you find him, make every effort to see
that he acquires the feelings of a father towards you, and you in turn those
of a son towards him. Not only ought we to be prompted to this by the very   15
principles of honour, since we are no less indebted to those from whom we
have acquired the rules of right living than to those from whom we acquired
life itself, but your friendship with him is of such importance as an aid to
learning that it will be of no avail to you to have a literary tutor at all unless
you have, by the same token, a friend. Secondly, you should give him atten-   20
tion and be regular in your work for him, for the talents of students are
sometimes ruined by violent effort, whereas regularity in work has lasting
effect just because of its temperance and produces by daily practice a greater
result than you would suppose. As in all things, so in literature, nothing
is worse than excess; accordingly you should from time to time abate the   25
strenuousness of your studies and relieve them with recreation – but recreation of a civilized kind, worthy of the vocation of letters and not too far
separated from it in nature. Indeed, a constant element of enjoyment must
be mingled with our studies so that we think of learning as a game rather
than a form of drudgery, for no activity can be continued for long if it does   30
not to some extent afford pleasure to the participant.

You must acquire the best knowledge first, and without delay; it is the
height of madness to learn what you will later have to unlearn. Make it your
rule to apply to the care of your mind the same rules that physicians generally recommend for the care of the body; do not ruin your brain with food   35
that is harmful, or excessive in quantity, for this damages both body and
brain. As for Eberhard, the *Catholicon*, the *Brachiloquus*, and others of that
sort (I cannot recite them all, and it would not be worth while to do so), you
should leave them to those who take delight in acquiring a barbarous style
at the cost of endless pains. What matters at the outset is not how much   40
knowledge you acquire, but how sound it is. But I shall now explain a
method by which you can learn more easily as well as more accurately; for
a craftsman usually obeys certain rules of his trade that make it possible for

* * * * *

56:37 Eberhard, the *Catholicon*] Cf Ep 26:100nn.
37 *Brachiloquus*] Cf Ep 35:89n.

him to produce a given quantity of work, not only more accurately and
quickly, but also more easily. Divide your day into tasks, as it were; this   45
is reported to have been the practice of those universally celebrated writers, Pliny and Pope Pius. First of all, and this is the essential thing, listen
to your teacher's explanations not only attentively but eagerly. Do not be
satisfied simply to follow his discourse with an alert mind; try now and then
to anticipate the direction of his thought. Remember everything he says   50
and even write down his most important utterances, for writing is the most
faithful custodian of words. On the other hand, avoid trusting it too much,
like that absurd man of wealth in Seneca who had come to believe that he
had preserved in his own memory everything that any of his servants
remembered. Do not be guilty of possessing a library of learned books while   55
lacking learning yourself. In order that what you have heard may not vanish
from your mind, go over it again, privately at home or in discussion with
others. And do not be satisfied with these measures alone: remember to
devote a part of your time to silent thought, which St Augustine records
as the most important of all aids to intellect and memory. In addition, the   60
contests of minds in what we may call their wrestling ring are especially
effective for exhibiting, stimulating, and enlarging the sinews of the human
understanding. And do not be ashamed to ask questions if you are in doubt,
or to be put right whenever you are wrong. Avoid working at night and
studying at unsuitable times and seasons; these things quench the light of   65
the mind and are very bad for the health. Aurora is the Muses' friend: daybreak is an excellent time for study. After lunch, take some recreation, or
go for a walk, or enjoy gay conversation; reflect that even such activities as
these can afford opportunity for studying. As to food, eat only what suffices
for health, and not as much as you long to eat. Take a short walk before   70
supper, and again after it. Just before you go to sleep you should read something of exquisite quality, worth remembering; let sleep overtake you while
you are musing upon it and when you awaken try to recall it to mind.
Always keep fixed in your heart Pliny's dictum that all the time which one
fails to devote to study is wasted, and reflect that youth is the most fleeting   75
thing on earth, and that when once it has fled away it never returns.
    But now I'm beginning to offer advice, though I promised only to point
the way. It is for you, my sweetest Christian, to follow this method – or a
better one, if you can discover it. Farewell.
    Paris [1499]   80
        * * * * *

47 Pope Pius] Pius II (Enea Silvio Piccolomini), the humanist pope
53 Seneca] Cf *Epistles* 27.5–7.
74 Pliny] Pliny the Elder; cf Pliny *Epistles* 3.5.16.

57 / To Evangelista   [Paris?] 1497

Allen has been unable to identify this person. He may have been a pupil with
whom Erasmus was reading some classical author.

ERASMUS TO HIS FRIEND EVANGELISTA
About that word *accensi*, which gave us trouble: I have found it in Vegetius,
whose text reads as follows: 'But to serve the judges and tribunes, and in
addition also the magnates (*principales*), those soldiers were appointed who
were known as *accensi*; that is, added to the roll when it was complete (they   5
are now known as *supernumerarii*)'. Thus far Vegetius. It is clear, therefore,
that the *accensi* were named from the act of adding them to the list (*ab
accensendo*). This, then, was the discovery I wanted to share with you.
Farewell.
            1497   10

58 / To Thomas Grey   Paris [July] 1497

In the spring of 1497 Erasmus was tutoring, in addition to the Northoff
brothers, two young Englishmen, Thomas Grey and Robert Fisher (cf Ep 62
introduction) who were living in the same house with him under the charge
of a guardian. After a time the guardian became suspicious of Erasmus' emotional attachment to Grey and requested him to leave. He then moved into the
house of Augustin Vincent, but continued to be interested in Grey's studies
and offered to continue his instruction by an exchange of letters. The scurri-
lous description of the old guardian may have been intended not only to
relieve Erasmus' feelings but also to serve as a model of invective, a common
form of humanist rhetoric. Erasmus' friendship with Grey lasted throughout
his life (cf Epp 829, 1624, 1641). The young man was obviously of good family,
but cannot be traced in the genealogy of the house of Grey.

ERASMUS TO THOMAS GREY; WRITTEN AS A YOUNG MAN
I should have written to you long ago, most generous youth, and most dear
on earth, for even though the fates looked with displeasure on the possibility that you should be called my bosom friend, yet fortune has never deprived me, nor ever shall, of my love for you. Long ago, I repeat, I should   5
have written to you as I greatly desired to do, because of my good will

        * * * * *

57:2 Vegetius] *De re militari* 2.19. Vegetius was a Roman military writer, 4th
century AD.

towards you, and as I knew you eagerly expected, because of your corresponding love for me, but I was afraid that I should inflame the still raw wound newly inflicted on me. So far was this wound from being susceptible of any treatment that I can feel it bleeding again even now at this slight   10
reminder. See how my very real grief makes me burst into floods of tears, though I hoped the injury had healed! No ill-treatment is more unendurable than that which rewards kindness. If only I might drink so deeply of the stream of Lethe that the old scoundrel with the wrong he did me and my services to him might vanish completely from my mind! Whenever I   15
remember him, not only do I grow angry but, still more, I am amazed that there can be so much malice, envy, treachery, and wickedness in a human heart. So may God love me, when I reflect on the fellow's dastardly character it seems to me that the poets, in spite of their usual perspicacity and eloquence in describing human nature, either never knew this kind of poison   20
or failed to find adequate words for it. Did they ever venture to portray a pimp who equalled him in perfidy, a braggart soldier in vainglory, an old man in peevishness, or ever, indeed, create such a monster of sour and envious ingratitude as this elderly humbug who actually seems to himself conscientious and invents the most complimentary terms to describe his   25
own vices?

You will tell me not to feel aggrieved. My dear Thomas, I am in fact exercising the greatest restraint in this revolting business, but one cannot help feeling aggrieved at unpleasantness which crops up in unexpected places, and how could I ever have looked for such extraordinary maltreat-   30
ment from a person who is white-haired (as is evident), of noble birth (as he boasts), and devout (as he pretends), after all my friendliness and helpfulness and loyalty and well-nigh brotherly affection towards him? I have always thought it was the height of ingratitude not to repay kindness with kindness; I had also read of the existence of a sort of person whom it was   35
safer to offend than to befriend. But I would not believe, until forced to by experience, that it was much more dangerous to do good to evil men than to do evil to good men. Since that ungrateful scoundrel was aware that he was under too heavy an obligation to me to be able to show gratitude, he took time off from literature, which for some time he had plagued intoler-   40
ably, and devoted his entire efforts to ruining me by his wicked scheming. Once he had lost hope of making an end of me by such efforts (for he had tried this without success), his next attempt was to quench me by means of a tongue steeped in the poison of hell; and, so far as in him lay, this he

* * * * *

58:14 Lethe] A stream in the underworld the waters of which cause forgetfulness

did. It is to literature that I attribute the fact that I am now alive and well: 45
literature, which has taught me never to give way in the face of fortune's
buffeting. That born criminal is incensed that he could do so little damage.
To him, it is nothing that he ranted at me so wildly to my face, causing me
great distress of mind, and while I avoid him is plotting at a distance to
poison me and wreaking his fury, for hatred of me, upon you who are the   50
dearest part of my soul. Exercising his fury, I repeat, by means of the
weapon that is more effective among human beings than any other: namely
slander, which is a snake's venom, more poisonous than any aconite or
foam from the jaws of Cerberus. To think that a monster of this sort looks
at the sun's light, and breathes the life-giving air, or rather taints it; and   55
that the earth we all inhabit bears the weight of this disgraceful creature.
Never have the talents of poets been capable of imagining a scourge so dire,
so deadly, or so loathsome as not to be easily outdone by this monster. Can
any Cerberus, Sphinx, Chimaera, Fury, or hobgoblin be properly compared
with this pest whom the land of the Goth has recently spewed upon us? Has   60
any scorpion, viper, or basilisk a more noxious poison? Venomous serpents, as a rule, bite only when they are disturbed; lions show gratitude
to those who have succoured them and dragons grow tame by kindness;
but this old man is made furious by the magnitude of my services to him.

So much for his poisonous disposition. Now, in order to give you a   65
picture of him in the round, I will add this: if you should examine a little
more closely his threatening expression and the posture of his whole body,
I am sure you would believe yourself to be looking at a portrait, so to say,
of iniquity of every kind. One must at least praise Nature's wisdom in
clothing an ugly soul in a body suitable to it. Beneath a forest of shaggy eye-   70
brows lurk shifty eyes that always glower at you. His forehead is granite.
There is no vestige of a modest blush, even in the cheeks. His nostrils
are choked with thickets of bristly hair; his breath snuffles through a polyp.
His jowls sag; his lips are pale; so little self-control has he that his voice does
not come out naturally, but erupts and you would swear that when he   75
speaks he barks. His neck is askew, his legs bandy, and in fact there is
nothing about him that nature has not marked with some notable flaw. Just
so do we brand criminals and evil-doers; just so do we hang a warning bell
on dogs that bite, and mark the dangerous bull with straw tied to its horns.
To think that I shared my interest in letters with this abominable monster   80
and wasted on him so much of my life, my talents, and my labour! It would
cause me less grief to have lost them entirely, for now I am conscious of hav-

* * * * *

78 bell] Cf Avianus *Fabulae* 7.8.

ing sown dragons' teeth to grow up and destroy me. It is worse than a waste
of kindness to make a bitter enemy by behaving like a friend; for the tyrant
made use of my help, but since he neither could respond to it in full, nor   85
desired to respond to it at all, this creature, whose talents lay only in the
direction of evil-doing, invented a novel way to ruin not only me, to whom
he dislikes being under obligation, but you too, a young man, of whom this
boy of fifty is disgracefully envious. Is this the famous nobility, of which
he commonly boasts until everyone is sick of it? Is this the reflection of the   90
family he so frequently vaunts? Is this, I ask, a spirit worthy of his heroic
origins? Would anyone really think he even came of human flesh and blood,
rather than deserving Virgil's description:
    Was rock-strewn Caucasus your birthplace then,
    And were you suckled by Hyrcanian tigers?   95
    And this most shameless of men dares to claim openly that he has done
you many services, and me still more, and to indict us both for ingratitude!
He is unaffected by the many witnesses to my kindness and his guilty
knowledge of the wrongs he has done me, and he has the effrontery to live
among mankind after behaving like this. He would have acted more   100
decently had he withdrawn, like Timon, from human society altogether and
betaken himself to the uttermost bounds of the sea, there to live like a beast
among beasts.
    But I must bridle my grief, however legitimate. Yet for all this most
hurtful ill-usage I am not a little consoled by the reflection that he will not   105
escape punishment for these actions. On the contrary, he will presently
begin to expiate his offences to me in person, with heavier penalties to follow. 'What penalties,' you ask: 'for surely he is happy in his own
applause?' Very well; but does it not seem to you to be quite punishment
enough for him to be both a great fool and full of malice, and to be most   110
wretched on both scores? Could any more severe punishment be invented
than envy? For envy is its own executioner and also, as the poet said, its
own punishment. Accordingly, the well-known writer of epigrams
addressed a most envious rascal (like, I think, this old man of ours) in the
following clever and witty words, invoking upon him the worst possible   115
curse – his own sin of envious malice: 'May you envy everyone, and no one
envy you.'
    For myself, I do not yet entertain such a mortal dislike for the fellow

* * * * *

93 Virgil] *Aeneid* 4.366,367
101 Timon] The half-legendary misanthrope of Shakespeare's *Timon of Athens*
116–17 'May you envy ... you.'] Martial 1.40.2

as to wish him so much harm, though he fully deserves this fate or a worse,
if such there be. And I have no doubt that this has long since occurred, if   120
Plautus was right in saying that men receive the treatment they deserve,
for he is wretchedly envious of everybody. You were applying yourself
industriously to letters and so, instead of complimenting you as you
deserved, he became so envious that he suddenly fell dangerously ill. And
does any of his qualities not deserve to be pitied rather than envied: if, that   125
is, obstinate ill-will even deserves pity? Now I shall tell you about the other
penalty, one that no guilty person ever yet escaped. What Furies, think you,
rage in that heart with its guilty burden of crimes? Can you not imagine
the sound of whips, the threatening firebrands, the goads that wound?

Such men receive a punishment severer far   130
Than any Rhadamanth, or stern Caedicius, knew.

That no guilty person is acquitted at his own tribunal was a just observation by a very wise author. This is the everlasting torture that the poets
have devoted enormous talent to portraying in action in the nether realms.
If, therefore, revenge can cure one's sickness of heart, I ought already to be   135
entirely freed from my grief. But I myself think it a more honourable and
generous sort of revenge to take no notice of a wrong, since the guilty are
visited in any case with the appropriate penalty.

However, I should be telling a palpable untruth if I pretended to feel
no annoyance. Nevertheless I do claim that I am no more troubled by the   140
insult to me, though this could not be exceeded, than sorry for your own
situation. I have come off very well, inasmuch as I have finally escaped the
poisoner's grasp. But, alas, I did not escape entirely, having left you, the
dearest part of me, behind. To think that you, dear Thomas, with your honourable nature and your modest and gentle disposition and promising   145
character, are now the servant of savage beasts, and that your intellect,
made by Nature for literature, for virtue, and for great affairs, is crushed
by the malice of a dotard! In your case, supreme goodness has encountered
supreme badness; youth and talent have met old age and stupidity;
friendliness has met ill-will; perfectly civilized humanity has met the most   150
crabbed of natures and, in the words of the ancient proverb, you 'have a
wolf by the ears.' What an unjust fate! Unkind stars, and unpropitious gods!
O youth of fairest hope, what witch or enchantress has harmed your noble
character? Must we believe that Nature herself grudged you her own gifts?

* * * * *

121 Plautus] Cf *Poenulus* 1270.
130-1 Such men ... knew.] Juvenal 13.196–7
151-2 'have a wolf by the ears'] *Adagia* I v 25

For in other respects she seems to have poured forth all her resources in   155
creating you so that in the finished work no perfection should be wanting,
implanting a gifted mind in a handsome body and adding an endearing
grace of manners, contributing high birth, wealth, and ability. In short, she
made of you the kind of person whom in antiquity men used to call sons
of gods. And now, unhappy youth, what evil genius or evil fate has cast   160
you forth into a pit of suffering? Is the blossoming of your distinguished
talent to be choked by a disgusting old man? Is the promise of that highly
fertile soil to be lost? Is the future of so rich a vein to be annihilated? Alas
for the envious malice of old men, the most monstrous vice one could mention or imagine. Having themselves passed their lives, as you would expect,   165
in debauchery, they are wretchedly envious of you, who are young and better endowed and at a better time of life, because you betook yourself earlier
to the humanities. They are envious because the warm blood leaps in your
breast, whereas they themselves have only hearts of lead. And so they
endeavour to delay you as you run ahead, instead of urging you on as they   170
should, while they themselves, unfit to follow, try to take the lead.

But alas, where has the onrush of my grief taken me? Indeed I am doing
you in many ways a great wrong, dearest Thomas, sharpening your sufferings unnecessarily by my complaints, whereas I should have lessened them
by offering consolation. I shall now turn from grief, which I have   175
sufficiently indulged, and devote the rest of my attention to rational considerations.

Sweetest Thomas, I had chosen you – you, I repeat, out of many – to
be the one in whom I should leave behind a finished monument of my skill,
for which purpose I believed that I had now found the most perfect material.   180
But did Fortune begrudge you to me or me to you? She may perhaps have
aimed her blow at me, but you were without doubt more harmed.
Nevertheless I am resolved to carry through as best I may, even in her
despite, the work thus wrested from my hands. For if our separation
involves any loss, we can easily repair this by corresponding often. Only,   185
you must proceed with high courage, keep yourself up to the mark, and act
as your own adviser.

I come now to your letter, which was as delightful to receive as you
are and always have been and shall be dear to me. I was pleased with its
straightforward and unaffected language and with the masculine vigour of   190
its observations – so pleased that I began to wonder whether you had composed it yourself or received the help of an auxiliary force. As for your
remark that you find it hard to bear my absence, you have no reason for

* * * * *

168–9 the warm blood leaps in your breast] Cf Virgil *Georgics* 2.484.

grief, dear boy. If you are grieving on my behalf because of your affection
for me, there is no reason to, since I feel exactly as though I had emerged   195
at last from the lower world, unhappy only because I was not able to bring
my dearest Pirithous out with me. If, therefore, your affection matches
mine, you ought to congratulate your Erasmus on finally, and with difficulty, breaking an adamantine chain. Nor can I see any reason for you to
be unduly vexed on your own account for, if what you object to is the loss   200
of my teaching, there are certain advantages in changing your instructor,
inasmuch as you have obtained a fresh one instead of a tired one, a most
conscientious one for one less exacting, and perhaps a more learned one too:
not, I think, a more loving one. However indifferent the new tutor may be,
still the loss you suffered by my departure was very trifling for, even while 205
I was still with you, you were grudged access to me and were almost deprived of my services. What could I say that was worthy of you, when the
ass at the lyre was endlessly at my elbow? Finally, any loss that did occur
can be easily made up by an exchange of letters between us; indeed, we
can replace it by more than was lost.   210

Only be sure that you do not fail yourself. If you miss me, miss me
only so much that none of your application to study is lost. You used to say,
I remember, that you would wipe all lettered pursuits from your mind the
moment I left your household. Just for once, my dear Thomas, I should like
you to be detected in a falsehood, and not to be so over-scrupulous that   215
you'd be ashamed to tell a lie for my sake. There: I acquit you of any pious
obligation and any sin you commit, upon my own head be it. Forget the
wrong, treat the old man's peevishness with contempt, and erase me too,
if you wish, from your mind, so long as you think of nothing but literature.
Never let hatred or love of anyone assume such importance in your eyes   220
that you are moved to abandon what you have well begun. Dislike the old
man's tongue and his attitude, but be prepared to put up with them; do
not imitate them. Make yourself your own standard, and apply yourself to
whatever is worthy of your family, your character, and your intelligence.
You have a tutor who is as worthy of you as he is unworthy of comparison   225
with the old man, so follow his advice. Do not quarrel with Robert, for I
do not wish to lose his friendship. If you manage not to hate the old man,

* * * * *

197 Pirithous] A type of close friendship. He was associated with Theseus:
cf Horace *Odes* 3.4.79 and 4.7.28.
204 the new tutor] Possibly Pierre Vitré (Viterius) (cf Ep 66 introduction). He
was still in friendly contact with Grey in 1516–18 (cf Epp 503, 528, and 817).
208 ass at the lyre] *Adagia* i iv 35
226 Robert] Robert Fisher (cf Ep 62 introduction).

it will show that you have regard to modesty and patience; though if you could ever love a monster of that kind you would be the most frivolous person alive; for if you did it from the heart, you would be a complete fool, 230 if from servility, a contemptible sycophant. It is as insane to hug an enemy to your bosom as it is ungrateful to neglect a friend. Farewell.

59 / To a friend   [Paris? July 1497?]

The tone of this letter suggests the mood of depression following the events referred to in Ep 58. Allen suggests the friend may have been Robert Fisher, in which case Erasmus' intention to dedicate something to him might refer to the *De conscribendis epistolis*, which he did dedicate to Fisher the following spring (cf Ep 71).

ERASMUS TO A CERTAIN FRIEND
My dear X: I ask you of your kindness to forgive me for not having written anything much, or anything worthy of yourself. Believe me, I was eager to do so, but it is extremely difficult to write in a light vein when one is in the mood of mourning. I have not yet pulled myself together or recovered 5 my spirits, but I am trying with the aid of the Muses to dedicate to you something worthy of you. And so that you will not think that I have been avoiding a small task, undertaken for your sake, I have forced my mind to do my bidding as far as I could and have acted like our little Denise; as you know, she sometimes dances and sings even while she is crying. When I 10 get back my old spirits again, there is no service you will ask me for in vain, provided I can do it. I ask you, on your side, for the sake of our friendship, to devote yourself wholeheartedly to literature, with no doubt in your mind that you are going to achieve much. If you are fond of literature, you will never dislike me, so I am asking you to do this not only for your own sake 15 but for mine. I wish you health. My greetings to all in your household.
    [1498]

60 / To Jan of Brussels   Paris [July] 1497

The reference to the vicar (line 11) identifies this Jan of Brussels with the recipient of Ep 155. He was probably an old friend of Erasmus from his days in the service of the bishop of Cambrai, but also a recent visitor to Paris since he was familiar with Erasmus' domestic arrangements.

* * * * *

59:9 Denise] This person has not been identified.

ERASMUS TO MASTER JAN OF BRUSSELS

I am indeed quite at a loss how to begin my letter to you, and cannot say
which I should blame: the treachery of certain people well enough known
to you, or the foolish eloquence of Antonia, or rather my own credulity. But
it is better to keep quiet about all this. I would say only this, that I have   5
earned dislike on every side because of my friendly services. So Erasmus
is banished from that house; others are reigning there, without Antonia's
agreement as I suspect. But it will be better to talk of these things in person.
In the meantime, stay as well disposed to me as you have been. Please give
my greetings individually to all those former companions of mine who are   10
with you; and particularly remember me kindly to the reverend vicar.
Farewell, and return my love.

Paris, 1497

61 / For Heinrich Northoff, to Christian Northoff   Paris [August 1497]

Christian Northoff had by this time returned to Lübeck, and Erasmus, after
the quarrel with Grey's guardian, had taken up residence with Augustin Vincent. There he continued to tutor Heinrich (cf Ep 54 introduction). This letter
seems to have been intended as a model of epistolary style for his pupils.

HEINRICH TO HIS BROTHER CHRISTIAN; ERASMUS COMPOSED THE LETTER

Dearest Christian, are you anxious to hear what the news is here? I am
dreaming. 'Dreaming of what?' you ask. Dreaming of what I love – literature, my chief joy in life, and next to literature, of Christian, the beloved
part of my soul. Do you suppose that you are absent from me? Nothing is   5
less true:
     No day, no night for me doth pass away,
     But you are there.
When I am alone, I think of Christian; with my friends I delight to chatter
about you. In sleep I dream of you, and no meal is taken here without talk   10
of you; you are with me at the dinner table, in the study, in my sleep. Ah,
Christian, brother far sweeter to me than life itself, what vast plains and
hills and cities and rivers lie betwixt us. Still, though our bodies may be
sundered afar, in no way can our hearts be reft apart. For sleep, which from
time to time is wont to separate those that are joined together, links you   15

* * * * *

60:4 Antonia] Cf Ep 55:17–18n.
11 vicar] Jacob Anthoniszoon of Middelburg (cf Ep 153 introduction).
61:7–8 No day ... there.] Ovid *Tristia* 3.3.18

with me though we be apart. May we suppose that in reality souls love surreptitiously to slip, as it were, the chains of bodies buried in slumber and,
flying away, swiftly cross vast distances to visit the beloved? Or does the
human mind, being made of fire and wondrously nimble in movement,
struggle in its restless impatience to penetrate the sluggish clouds of drowsy   20
vapour that block the pores of all the sleeping body's limbs, and either make
afresh for itself the images that settle there, or out of the variety of eddying
vapours fashion the outward appearances of many objects? Or does, as
poets tell, a certain gracious king and god most loving kind to men, whom
they call Sleep, sprinkle the limbs and senses of mortals, tired by long   25
labour, with the tincture of Lethe, and restore them with sweet rest and self-
forgetfulness, and thereafter send to earth him they call Morpheus, a
wondrous inventor of shapes, who softly glides into the chamber where one
or another lies, and limns for each the forms he knows? Or is it from the
huge elm that visions such as these come forth to us by the twin gates of   30
Sleep? But, if the poet's tales are not all false, I can be sure that a most
delightful dream I had of late must have come through the gate of horn; and
this I should be pleased to relate in due order, so long as you do not find
it tedious in the hearing.

On the first day of August, the brightest day by far that ever dawned   35
on me, after we had dined cheerfully, pleasantly, and extremely well ...
'Who had dined, and how many of you were there?' you will ask. There
were three of us, three souls, the purest and brightest ever born on earth:
Erasmus, already manifestly a friend to both of us, Augustin, who is
everyone's friend but is particularly devoted to you, and I the third, though   40
you yourself were not entirely absent. 'The company was choice indeed;
also, the occasion was a timely one, the place well chosen, and the arrangements well planned.' How often we drank your health, spoke your name,
and said how much we missed you, Christian! Did you feel no tingling in
your right ear? After the second course we went out for a short stroll, to the   45
very place where, as Erasmus proceeded to tell us, he had sometimes
walked with you when you wandered together, drunk on honey-sweet talk
and dodging between the vineyards, while he employed those eloquently

* * * * *

27 Morpheus] The god of dreams

30 elm] The huge tree in the underworld in which dreams nested. Cf Virgil
Aeneid 6.283.

32 gate of horn] True dreams pass through the gate of horn, false ones through
the gate of ivory. Virgil *Aeneid* 6.893–6.

41–3 'The company ... planned.'] Varro *Menippean Satires* 335; quoted in Aulus
Gellius *Noctes Atticae* 13.11

persuasive arguments of his to summon you away from vulgar cares to a
wholehearted love of letters. Do you recognize the spot, Christian? It was   50
there that Erasmus entertained us with a literary recital that was far more
elegant even than the supper: he rehearsed so much ancient lore, in so
charming a manner, that, to speak for myself, he transported me to the
seventh heaven. When we got home, we prolonged our talk about you deep
into the night. It was very late when we finally went to bed and I fell into   55
an especially deep slumber, partly because I had eaten and drunk more
generously than usual, partly because of the exercise afforded by the walk,
for you know how lazy I am. Then, in the poet Claudian's words,

> Every view that meets the sense by day
> Kindly sleep gave back, when all was still.   60

There I was, still walking among those same vineyards, and retracing every
step, but alone; it was all quite true to life. My mind was visited by many
thoughts of you, and I felt a longing to revive our old companionship as
I remembered your more than brotherly affection.

I had already begun to be anxious to hear of your doings and your   65
health, and whether all was well with you, for I had had no word from you
for a great many months, when suddenly you appeared unexpectedly
before me, apparently taking a leisurely stroll, with a bright countenance
and 'skin well cared for.' I now take this, dear Christian, as the first sign
revealing your good state of health. Morpheus had reproduced your whole   70
appearance so well that you are not more like yourself than that image. It
seemed to me that when you saw me you smiled in that affectionate way
you have, which I take as a second sign that you are well. Thereupon we
eagerly rushed together and embraced and, shedding tears of joy, I cried,
'Is it you I have in my arms, my beloved brother, my heart's supreme   75
delight? How is this? What god, or stroke of fortune, has brought you to
me? Do my waking eyes behold you, or am I mocked by a phantom?' And
you replied: 'O thou half of my soul, I have fared well indeed, save that,
since I lacked your beloved companionship, it seemed to me that I was
scarce half alive, with the better portion of my spirit reft from me.' To which   80
I answered, 'Never shall I allow that our separation brought more anguish
to you than to me; but come tell me, what sudden event has made you
anxious to come all this long way back to Paris? For, great as my longing for
you was, there was nothing I less expected than to see you.' Whereupon

* * * * *

58 Claudian] *De sexto consulatu Honorii, Praefatio* 1–2
69 'skin well cared for'] Horace *Epistles* 1.4.15

you said, 'This I will tell you; for I shall not be ashamed to confess the truth.'   85
    'When I returned to those mercantile affairs of mine, I began to be strangely dissatisfied with myself, envious of you, and angry at myself for leaving the Muses' sacred company to return to such profane concerns. I reflected how foolish I had been to set such store on any kind of gain as to prefer it to the holiest of pursuits. At that moment I thought of Erasmus'   90
honeyed words, words by which, among those very vineyards, he made as it were a new man of me, when he spoke of the degrading and unsatisfactory sides of the life of business and at the same time compared good letters with every sort of activity in such a way as to prove that no others whatsoever could be compared with them. He remarked that they alone formed   95
man's proper wealth, wealth that Fortune could neither bestow nor take away; that, in use, they increased instead of dwindling, and grew better instead of wearing out; nor did they decline with age, as bodily strength and beauty do. They were not conferred, like worldly honours, upon the idle and undeserving. They did not distract one from practising virtue, but   100
themselves conferred it. They alone, said he, could give peace to the spirit and abide as a refuge. Finally, without them we could not even be human. But why do I touch on matters he could scarcely dispose of in a two-hours' discourse? Roused by all this, I asked: "Is it to be my fate to leave my own promising beginnings unfulfilled as I sink myself in worldly affairs, while   105
Heinrich grows rich upon merchandise that is fairer by far?" So I gave in to my envy, tore myself away, left all, and flew to you, that I might be no longer a stranger to your company. It remains for you, of your grace, to accept within your camp a fugitive who is ready henceforth to be your loyal soldier.'   110
    Thereupon I marvelled exceedingly. 'Immortal God,' I said, 'what is this story? Can it be true that envy restored you to me, or rather, to yourself? Blest envy indeed! But if I show you now how fortunate you are you will, I think, begin to envy your own lot.' And you said, 'Come, tell me quickly; why are you silent now?' I said – 'Give me a moment, dear Christian; for   115
"Man's trivial thoughts are eloquent; deep thoughts do him benumb." All the stars and divinities of Heaven look kindly upon me, your brother Heinrich. Could one but enjoy this blessed state for ever, the life we have secured for ourselves is verily that of gods.' Then you were still more fired with eagerness to hear, and said, 'So may the Muses love me, I congratulate you,   120
brother; but that I may do so in proper fashion, I beg you to explain quickly.'

* * * * *

115–16 "Man's ... benumb"] Seneca *Phaedra* 607

So I answered, 'Heaven has vouchsafed to me the supreme good, if any such there be in this life: a good that I have never dared even to aspire to. You have, I think, already guessed what the blessing is that I have gained, for what could I have got that was more desirable, or serviceable, than a tutor 125
at once learned and amiable? And my tutor is the most learned, and the most amiable, on earth; I found him after a long and painful search: the celebrated Erasmus! And what is more, I have him entirely to myself; I own him with sole title, enjoying his undivided attention continually by day and night. As a result I have at command, within the four walls of my room, the mount 130
of Helicon itself. If this be not to live as one of the Muses' band, what is? Our whole existence is seasoned with literature, be it play or earnest business or leisure. Our talk is of letters at the noonday meal; our suppers are made exquisite by literary seasoning. In our walks we prattle of letters and even our frivolous diversions are no strangers to them; we talk of letters till 135
we fall asleep, our dreams are dreams of letters, and literature awakens us to begin the new day. It seems to me that I am not studying but playing; nevertheless I now perceive I am studying indeed.

'But in case you scorn us for living like hermits, many others are in the habit of joining us each day at noonday or evening meal; though 140
we ourselves suffice to equal the Graces in number, still we like to invite a variety of guests to share our daily potations. You ask who these are? You must not imagine them to be such as drain their cups dry; they are, rather, some excellent old friends of ours, whom you know, who contribute pleasure without expense: I refer to tried and tested authors. When we are 145
about to begin a feast, we ask whom we should most like to invite. Suppose Macrobius to be our guest; well and good, but let him bring his elegant trifles, not his *Dream*. Or perhaps rather we should invite Aulus Gellius, a more sophisticated guest than Macrobius, who can keep us entertained, with those most charming *Nights* of his, far into the night itself. Or suppose 150
we were to summon Apuleius – a philosopher, but without any trace of a frown. If we prefer poets, Catullus or Martial may come, or if we choose to

* * * * *

147 Macrobius] The early fifth-century author, whose *Saturnalia*, being full of curious information, could perhaps be regarded as 'elegant trifles,' while his Commentary on Cicero's *Somnium Scipionis*, or *Dream of Scipio* is undoubtedly a serious philosophical work (cf Ep 121:5).
150 *Nights*] The *Noctes Atticae*, or *Attic Nights*
151 Apuleius] Rhetorician, scholar and philosopher of Madaura in Africa; (2nd century AD)

listen to the moderns we might invite Campano, a man born for jesting and wit, or let the exquisite Poliziano attend. As for the sternly serious, we invite them to debate with us but not to drink with us. Surely you don't   155
think our banquets could possibly be more elegant, or the guests more congenial, than these? Other guests require not only outlay of money but also the trouble of looking after them, whereas these make a dull dinner gay, a meagre one luxurious, and a tasteless one delicious; and so far are they from being expensive visitors that they even reduce the cost of the enter-   160
tainment while they enlarge its amenities. Think, too, how agreeable and polite they are! They never grumble at being invited; when you ask them, they come; they do not crash in uninvited; they never indulge in backbiting or slander; they do not speak unless they are asked but, if asked, talk just as we wish, on whatever we wish, so far, and for as long as we wish. They   165
never give away any of the scandals that are commonly blurted out by men in their cups, but simply express their own views with courtesy, while they keep our personal secrets with absolute discretion. They converse without uttering a single barbarism or a stupid or ignorant remark; when they tell any tale it is because its great age charms or its novelty pleases them, or   170
because it is brilliant in style or has usefulness to recommend it. Do you not consider me lucky indeed to have acquired, quite unexpectedly, such great benefits as these?'

Then you answered: 'Heinrich, my brother, I think you are in every way more fortunate than Fortune herself. But tell me, who was the deity   175
that favoured you so notably with a visitor so illustrious?' 'It is a "long tale of wrong," Christian,' I replied, 'a tale that "long would take to tell," for which the entire day would not, I fear, suffice. Still, I shall endeavour to abridge it. Do you know an old man of sorts, whose name is such-

* * * * *

153 Campano] Gianantonio Campano, one of the literary friends of Pius II who enjoyed his wit and genial satire and awarded him a bishopric (cf Rossi 233f, and Ep 101:37f).

154 Poliziano] Angelo Ambrogini of Montepulciano, called Poliziano (1454–94), the most distinguished humanist of the second half of the fifteenth century, taught Latin and Greek at the Florentine Studio. His *Miscellanea* (Florence 1489), composed of excerpts from his lectures, held a position in his generation similar to that of Valla's *Elegantiae* half a century earlier. He was a friend of Lorenzo de' Medici and tutor to his children. He also wrote polished verse in Latin, Greek, and Italian (cf Rossi 359–87).

176–7 "long tale of wrong" ... that "long would take to tell"] Virgil *Aeneid* 1.341–2; cf Ep 58.

and-such?' You then stumbled over the unfamiliar and barbarous word, 180
and asked in surprise what demon's name that was; whereupon I said, 'Forbear: this name would seem to you scarcely barbarous enough did you but
know, even slightly, the barbarity of its owner, who is more barbarous than
all the barbarism on earth. He has spent his whole life in the assiduous practice of every known crime, so that he has no further fear of robbery or fraud, 185
the arts by which he has climbed so high in office that in Paris he now plays
the role of a traitor on his own sovereign's behalf, a function for which none
is so suited as he who is himself a prince of traitors. And though there is
no wickedness of which he is innocent, still he claims the honour of being
called by the very opposite terms, as it were.' 'I am not sure,' you began, 190
after hesitating slightly, 'whether I have set eyes on this monster.' And I
said, 'Christian, you will be lucky if you never do; for I myself would rather
look at any Fury there is than at such a portent as he. To describe him to
you in a very few words: imagine a composite portrait of all you ever
remember seeing in human shape that was foul, repulsive, monstrous, 195
crooked, and ugly, and you will then know the old man's precise linea-
ments, for it is not that some monstrosity disfigures him, but that he is all
compact of sheer monstrosity itself. Thus it is evident that, as all the gifts
of all the gods were bestowed, as poets tell, upon Pandora, so all mon-
strosities of all monsters united in his making. If you saw him, you would 200
pronounce him neither man nor beast but Fury herself. In short, he is the
half-Scot who slaughtered our friend Erasmus. Once he had taken a
notion to harass literature it would take long to tell of the many ways in
which this crafty creature has ensnared our straightforward and good-
natured friend.' 205
    Then, begging my pardon, you interrupted to ask 'But how did it occur
to such a dolt as this to give any thought to letters at all? What had a fellow
who had not merely grown old, but had done so in a welter of vices of all
kinds, and who furthermore had a heart of lead and a brain already disordered, to do with literature?' 'As much,' said I, 'as an ass has to do with 210
a lyre, or a jackdaw with a lute, an ox with the wrestling ring, a camel with
the stage, or perhaps less than any of those, for I do believe it would be
easier even to make a philosopher out of a pig than an educated man out
of one who does not so much as look human and has the temper of the

* * * * *

210 ass] Cf *Adagia* i iv 35.
211 jackdaw] Cf *Adagia* i iv 37.
211 ox] Cf *Adagia* i iv 62.
211 camel] Cf *Adagia* ii vii 66.

Furies. But it is unwise to speculate on what came into the lunatic's head.   215
If he was aware at all of what he did, I suppose he merely took a notion to
persecute literature and to make trouble for literary men of whose carefree
condition this monster of envy was, in fact, envious.' Then you remarked,
'Alas for our dear literature, when such creatures can so much as mention
it!' 'You would certainly have thought so, Christian,' said I, 'had you but   220
seen that ass at the lyre. There the fellow sat: grey-headed and wrinkled,
the spittle dribbling down upon his unkempt beard, staring, through a forest of eyebrows, with those wild-beast's eyes of his at the learned tutor
before him while, with head a-shake, lips pale, and teeth decayed, he
breathed the venom of Hell out of that noisome throat. And, to make the   225
marvel greater in your eyes, he used to say he thought of taking holy orders!
Don't you feel that you are watching the popular play in which one of the
characters is the Devil who, in sickness, pretends that he would turn monk?
And of course with his grey hairs, and the tears that he sheds with the readiness of a harlot, he won the confidence of our friend Erasmus; no hard task   230
this, for Erasmus, whose heart is quite guileless, could not have supposed
that such monsters of depravity as this man even existed upon the earth.
He taught him for several months, unaware that he was cherishing a snake
in his bosom. However, poisons cannot lie concealed for ever. In the end
the Furies that lurked in this man's breast broke into the open. Only then   235
did Erasmus become aware that all his many kindnesses had been thrown
away on a scoundrel without a shred of gratitude, and forthwith he abandoned the man, with his evil nature; it was I, inasmuch as I had known Erasmus long and well, who seemed best suited to receive him thereafter. The
wretch, for his part, relies so much on his money that the last thing he fears   240
is that he may be unable to recall Erasmus. All the rest of his household are
calling down curses on the morose old man, and begging with tears for Erasmus' return. Robert, who is wealthy, assails him with promises. Thomas,
a high-minded youth, coaxes him to alter his decision. The master and mistress recall him, while every serving maid and lackey begs that he may come   245
back, so deeply had he attached persons of all conditions to himself by his
immense personal charm. The blockhead already repents of his action, but
it would be dishonourable for such a resolute hero to come to his senses
quickly after a fit of insanity; so he raves on, to the disgust not only of his
own household and the entire human race but even of himself. Erasmus is   250

* * * * *

233–4 a snake in his bosom] Cf *Adagia* IV ii 40.
243 Robert] Fisher (cf Ep 62 introduction).
243 Thomas] Grey (cf Ep 58 introduction).

no more perturbed by these events "than hardest flint, or adamantine rocks": he has enrolled in our household.'

Hereupon you marvelled at the fellow's extraordinary ingratitude, and began: 'Unhappy Erasmus, to encounter such madness; and how loath- some a plague is that old man, who should be banished to the remotest   255 deserts of India!' 'On the contrary, Christian,' I objected, 'I am infinitely grateful to his demented outburst, for had he not thrust Erasmus out I should myself have missed a blessing. Erasmus too takes comfort, he often says, from the reflection that it was God's will he should encounter the evil spirit so that he might thereby learn patience, just as long ago Xanthippe   260 is said to have afforded such practice to Socrates. And so this comedy had a happy ending for both of us, which is why it would be proper for you, Christian, to applaud your brother's exit from the play.' Then you answered: 'My brother, the warmth of the congratulations I feel disposed to offer lies beyond my power of utterance; if my capacity to express my   265 sentiments were equal to it, I should congratulate you in a speech so splen- did, so elaborate, that Cicero himself never rivalled it for elaboration or splendour; but you know how tongue-tied I am. Why should we not go home at once and greet Erasmus?' 'A good suggestion,' said I; 'I, too, think it the best thing to do.'   270

Then, as I was trying to walk on your left, while you likewise tried to place me on your right, and we were thus struggling to outdo each other in politeness, I woke up – and lost my Christian. Erasmus, who shared my couch, noticed that I was somewhat perturbed, and asked what ailed me. I told him the whole story; then he called for his young scribe and wrote   275 this letter, to let you know that I should not even keep my dreams from you. Farewell.

Paris, in the year [1498]

62 / To Robert Fisher   Paris [August 1497?]

Robert Fisher was a kinsman of John Fisher, bishop of Rochester. After study- ing in Paris, for a time as a pupil of Erasmus (cf Ep 58 introduction), he went to Italy in the spring of 1498 where he obtained the degree of doctor of laws. Later he returned to England and received ecclesiastical preferment from the king. Erasmus wrote for him the first draft of the *De conscribendis epistolis* (cf Epp 71 introduction, 72:4n, and 1284) and possibly also his paraphrase of

* * * * *

251–2 "than ... rocks"] Virgil *Aeneid* 6.471
260 Xanthippe] The shrewish wife of Socrates

Valla's *Elegantiae* (cf Ep 23:108n and Allen Ep 2260:85ff where he refers in disparaging terms to a certain Englishman for whom he had prepared it).

ERASMUS TO HIS FRIEND ROBERT FISHER

Just observe how greedy and peevish the female of the species is! The other day my servant came back to me with a long list of complaints from our old landlady. The husband was voicing some grumble or other about both of us; the mother, in order to show herself a true Norman, kept complaining   5
that she had received no acknowledgment for the work she had done for me; the daughter was saying that you had paid very meanly and had forgotten your old acquaintance with her. I myself purchase extra service at a tenfold rate, for I pay for regular work at highly inflated prices, and even so, am in debt for favours. It is when I think about these characteristics of   10
womankind that I feel happy to have hit upon my own kind of life. If this was by chance, I am lucky; if I chose it deliberately, I am wise.

There it is: a dry sort of letter, but the subject was furnished to me by that dried-up stick of a woman. If your are well, I am glad of it: as for me, I wish and now even hope; for the sickness is gradually beginning to subside.   15
Paris [1498]

63 / To Thomas Grey   Paris [August] 1497

ERASMUS TO HIS FRIEND THOMAS

Though I am rather busy, nevertheless, my sweetest Thomas, in order that you might know that I should not allow myself any excuses when it was time for me to write to you, I have decided to converse with you in a letter, even if business interrupts me. From now on, you are not to look in each   5
separate letter for a declaration of my good will, or for compliments on your intellect: I should like you to be assured once for all that I consider nothing dearer or more congenial to me than your affection, in its warmth, candour, modesty, eagerness, and friendly spirit, and that I consider so desirable a blessing as something I certainly would not change for all the wealth of   10
Arabia. Further, as regards my corresponding affection for you, I want you to take the following as if it were an oracle of Apollo: so long as you continue to embrace virtue and good literature as you are doing, this attitude of mine will not be altered by any interruption of intercourse between us or by any stroke of fortune. A lasting affection, based on virtue, can indeed no   15
more come to an end than virtue itself, whereas, if greed be friendship's

* * * * *

62:4 landlady] Antonia. Cf Ep 55:17–18n.

foundation, then when the money runs out so will the friendship, and when pleasure lures men to love, they cease to love when satiety supervenes. Finally, those who seek each other's friendship from some childish freak of mind desert their friends as wilfully as they joined them. But our com-   20
radeship, which arose from far finer causes than these, rests upon bases also far stronger: for we were brought together not by considerations of advantage or pleasure, or any youthful whim, but by an honourable love for letters and for the studies in which we shared. Between good and studious men there is a kind of impersonal but very firm link forged by their enthusiasm   25
for similar things. And since the pursuit of virtue knows not satiety nor is exposed to the hazards of chance, good will between good men is bound to endure.

Since, then, it is this kind of love that unites us, you need not fear that our friendship can be threatened by such untoward events as we continu-   30
ally see imperilling friendships of the common sort. The greater your affection for innocence and literature, the dearer you will be to me. For my part, I shall think I reap an ample harvest from my love for you if I observe that the notable disposition to virtue, which I was the first to remark in you, has with my aid fully ripened. I urge you earnestly to strive toward this with   35
might and main, my dear Thomas. You will achieve it if you choose for your reading the best authors, avoiding like a plague those who are lax and indecent, especially at your present time of life, which is instinctively lewd and prone less to follow the good than the evil way. And what good does it do to read them and harm one's morals, when there is no lack of authors who   40
are considerably more valuable in terms of scholarship and do not give offence by impropriety? Among those whom you should read under this head are Virgil above all, then Lucan, Cicero, Lactantius, Jerome, Sallust, and Livy.

I must stop: unwillingly, so pleasant is the conversation I seem to be   45
having with you as I write this. See, I beg you, how little diminution our friendship has suffered through our physical separation! I see you in my heart; I talk with you in letters, even more pleasantly perhaps than with my voice. So be happy, and farewell.

PS: Do not be surprised at the new colour of my writing; you should   50
be apprised that lovers' letters are written with their blood! For want of ink, I wrote this in mulberry-juice.

Paris, 1497

* * * * *

63:36 might and main] Cf *Adagia* i iv 15.

64 / To Thomas Grey   Paris [August 1497]

Despite his enforced resort to teaching, Erasmus had not given up his intention to study theology and eventually acquire a doctor's degree (cf Epp 48:24ff;
75:16ff). Hence his attendance at lectures in theology, which resulted in an
interruption in his promised exchange of letters with Grey (cf Ep 58:184f). The
scornful comment on the Scotists here strikes a note frequently repeated by
Erasmus throughout his life.

ERASMUS OF ROTTERDAM TO THE NOBLE YOUTH, HIS FRIEND THOMAS GREY;
WRITTEN AS A YOUNG MAN
Greetings, Thomas my excellent friend. The fact that for a few days I have
laid aside my previous habit of writing to you should occasion no alarm.
How true it is that 'love is full of anxious fears!' My love has in no way   5
grown cold. 'What, then, was the reason?' you will ask. I have unlearnt how
to write. 'What was done, or happened, to make Erasmus lose his pen?' 'Why,
something I will tell you about, extraordinary, but true. I, yes I, that former theologian, have lately turned Scotist! May Heaven grant success to the
enterprise; but you too should put up a prayer, if you are on my side. I   10
have been so deeply immersed in the imaginings of one of your countrymen (for though Scotus, like Homer of old, has been claimed as a son by
rival parts of the world, the English lay special claim to him) that even Sten-
tor's voice seems unlikely to arouse me.' 'Oh,' you will say, 'are you writing
this in your sleep?' 'Hush, profane fool: thou understandest not that sleep   15
which is the sleep of divines. *We* not only write in our sleep; we wench,
and tipple, and spread gossip in our sleep. In my experience I find there
are many things that simply would not be believed by those who have never
come across them. There was a time when I thought the sleep of Epimenides
a tall tale indeed; but it excites in me no wonder now that I have found its   20
equal.' At this point you will, I know, remark, 'Confound it, what tales are
you telling me now?' So, though you are not initiated, and ought not to be
admitted to the holy shrine of theology, still I will show the depth of my
love by unveiling our profound mysteries for your sake.

* * * * *

64:2 written as a young man] These words ('scripsit iuvenis'), which appear
also in Ep 58, like the 'scripsit puer' of Epp 26 and 29, were added in the *Epistolae ad diversos* of 1521.

5 'love ... fears'] Ovid *Heroides* 1.12

13–14 Stentor] A Greek soldier before Troy who had an immensely powerful
voice; *Adagia* II iii 37

There was once a certain Epimenides, he who wrote that all Cretans   25
are liars, being a Cretan himself and at the same time speaking quite truthfully. And not only did he live to a ripe old age: long after he died, his skin
was found, marked with the shapes of letters, and some say that at this very
day it is preserved in Paris at the Sorbonne, the holy of holies of Scotist
theology, and is as highly valued as the *diphthera* once was among the Cre-   30
tans, or the Sibylline books in Rome; for the theologians are said to consult
it as an oracle whenever syllogisms fail them. Only those may view it who
have borne the title of *Magister noster* for a full fifteen years. If anyone else
dares to set profane eyes upon it, he immediately becomes as blind as a
mole. The proof that my story is no fairy-tale lies in that very ancient Greek   35
proverb, 'the skin of Epimenides,' which they applied to something secret,
and forbidden to the vulgar eye. And he also published books on theology,
for he was particularly distinguished as a professor of theology, though he
was also reputed as a prophet and poet. In these books he wove such cats'
cradles of syllogisms that even he himself could never untie them, and mul-   40
tiplied mysteries that he himself could never have understood had he not
been a prophet.

It is said that on one occasion he went for a walk outside his city
because nothing at home pleased him. Eventually he entered a deep cave,
either in search of coolness because he already found the heat trying, or   45
looking for a place to rest because he was tired, or because, having lost his
way, as even theologians do, he was afraid night might overtake him in the
countryside and expose him to wild beasts, or else, as seems most probable,
in search of a suitable spot for meditation. It was there, while he was biting
his nails and pondering, at great length, 'instances' and 'quiddities' and   50
'formal qualities,' that sleep came upon him. I know you will not believe me

* * * * *

25 Epimenides] A semi-mythical Cretan philosopher-prophet of the 6th century BC, supposed author of the statement that the Cretans are always liars,
quoted by St Paul (Titus 1:12). The legend of his long sleep, which Erasmus
here embroiders, is in *Adagia* I ix 64.

30 *diphthera*] The skin of the she-goat by which the infant Jupiter was suckled,
said to be preserved as a relic in Crete (*Adagia* I v 24).

31 Sibylline books] Oracular utterances of the priestesses known as 'Sibyls';
a collection of these kept in Rome could be consulted only on the order of the
Senate.

33 *Magister noster*] The common title for a member of the Faculty of Theology.
It occurs constantly in the *Epistolae obscurorum virorum*. Erasmus also uses it
frequently with satirical effect.

34–5 as blind as a mole] *Adagia* I iii 55

36 'the skin of Epimenides'] *Adagia* IV ii 76

when I tell you that he did not wake until evening of the next day, though
even drunkards sleep longer than that. In fact, however, that theological
sleep was prolonged, as all authorities are agreed, for forty-seven years: and
they say there is some mystic meaning in the fact that he woke up just then,   55
no sooner and no later. 'Quite dead!' you will say. On the contrary, it seems
to me that Epimenides was fortunate in that he came to his senses, however
belatedly. Most of our present-day theologians never wake up at all, and
believe themselves quite wide-awake when in fact they are drugged with
mandrake. But let us return to Epimenides' awakening.   60

He awoke, then rubbing his eyes, which were still drowsy with
sleep, and came out of the cave, uncertain whether he was awake or dreaming. Observing that the entire appearance of the surrounding district had
changed, inasmuch as after all those years the river beds had altered, the
trees had been cut down in one place and replaced by new growth in   65
another, plains had risen into hills and hills sunk into plains, and even the
entrance to the cave itself was transformed by overgrowing moss and brambles, Epimenides began to doubt even his own existence. He went to his
city and there found everything new: he could not recognize the walls, the
streets, the coinage, the very people; dress, behaviour, speech, all were   70
altered. Such is the mutability of human affairs. He called out to everyone
he met: 'Ho there! don't you recognize Epimenides?'; but the person
addressed always thought he was being laughed at, and said 'Be off with
you: look for someone you know.' In this way, he walked about, a figure
of fun, for several months, until he fell in with some boon companions who   75
were now well advanced in age, but at any rate recognized him.

But tell me, dear Thomas; what do you think Epimenides' dreams
were of, all those years? Why, of course those very super-subtle subtleties
that today are the boast of the sons of Scotus; for I should be prepared to
swear that Epimenides was reincarnated in Scotus. If only you could see   80
your Erasmus sitting agape among those glorified Scotists, while 'Gryllard'
lectures from a lofty throne. If you could but observe his furrowed brow,

* * * * *

74 someone you know] Literally, a 'guest-friend' (Greek, 'xenos') with whom
any stranger in a Greek city would have ties of hospitality and to whom he
would naturally address himself.
81 'Gryllard'] Unknown. Possibly a playful corruption of a French name; but
see Allen Ep 222:36, on Plutarch's dialogue (*Moralia* 985D-992A) between
Ulysses and 'Gryllus,' who had been changed into a pig by Circe and now
rhetorically expounds the advantages of his swinish condition. Such puns on
names are familiar in Erasmus: see D.F.S. Thomson 'The Latinity of Erasmus'
Erasmus ed T.A. Dorey (London 1970), especially pp 127-8.

his uncomprehending look and worried expression, you would say it was another man. They say the secrets of this branch of learning cannot be grasped by a person who has anything at all to do with the Muses or the 85 Graces; for this, you must unlearn any literary lore you have put your hands on, and vomit up any draught you have drunk from Helicon. So I am trying with might and main to say nothing in good Latin, or elegantly, or wittily; and I seem to be making progress; so there is some hope that, eventually, they will acknowledge me. 90

'What is the point of all this?' you will ask. It is to warn you not to expect from me anything with the flavour of my former studies or character, bearing in mind the company I keep, and sit among, every day; so you must look for another crony. But, my sweetest Grey, I would not have you mistakenly infer that what I have just written was directed against theology 95 itself, to which, as you are aware, I have always been deeply devoted. I merely wished to make a joke at the expense of a few quasi-theologians of our own day, whose brains are the most addled, tongues the most uncultured, wits the dullest, teachings the thorniest, characters the least attractive, lives the most hypocritical, talk the most slanderous, and hearts the 100 blackest on earth. Farewell.

Paris, in the year [1499]

65 / To a friend   [Paris? August 1497?]

Possibly sent to Robert Fisher at the same time as Ep 64 to Grey.

ERASMUS TO A CERTAIN PERSON
You are surprised that I have temporarily ceased to write; but please do not regard this interruption of my former practice as sinister, for I have not ceased to regard you with deep affection, as I always did before. Farewell. 5

65A / From Rutgerus Sycamber   [autumn 1497]

This letter was discovered by P.O. Kristeller and published by him in 'Two Unpublished Letters to Erasmus' *Renaissance News* 14 (1961) 6-9. It had been preserved in a manuscript collection of Sycamber's works, probably autograph, now in the Historisches Archiv der Stadt Köln. The date at which the

* * * * *

87 Helicon] A mountain in Boeotia, famous for its spring, Hippocrene, from which poets drank inspiration.

letter was written can be determined with reasonable assurance from internal evidence. The mention in line 91 of Hermans' odes, which were published in Paris on 20 January 1497 (cf Ep 49 introduction), fixes the earliest possible date. If, as seems almost certain, the 'spiteful Englishman' of line 5 can be identified with the guardian of Thomas Grey and Robert Fisher, Erasmus' letter to Bostius complaining of the Englishman's treachery must have been written not long after the quarrel which took place in the summer of 1497. It was probably more or less contemporary with Epp 58 and 61, when Erasmus' indignation was still at white heat and he was apparently broadcasting his grievance to his friends. Allowing time for the letter to reach Bostius and for him to send it to Sycamber, the earliest date at which Sycamber could have written would probably be some time in the autumn. This hypothesis is confirmed by the fact that the 'one letter' written by Gaguin to Sycamber (cf line 88) was published in Gaguin's correspondence with the date 11 August 1497. Cf L. Thuasne, ed, *Roberti Gaguini epistole et orationes* (Paris 1903) II 49-52.

Rutgerus Sycamber, or Roger of Venray (1451-after 1509), was born in Venray in upper Gelderland, not far from the border of the duchy of Cleve, the ancient home of the early German tribe of Sigambri or Sicambri, from whom Rutgerus apparently took his cognomen. He became a canon regular, attached for most of his life to the monastery of Hagen near Worms. He was a prolific writer and maintained correspondence with other humanists in Germany and the Netherlands (cf Kristeller 'Two Unpublished Letters').

TO THE REVEREND CANON DESIDERIUS ERASMUS FROM SYCAMBER

I have lately read the letter you wrote to Bostius, and could not refrain from laughing to see you complain that they had not kept faith with you and that some spiteful Englishman had let you down. What, I wonder, would   5
become of us if God thought fit to present His account to each of us and upbraid us for our breaches of faith? How few of us there are who keep faith with God who created us, who do not stain the white of our baptismal robe and do not offend against God in thought and word and deed! See how God, though we hurt Him and despise and spurn Him a thousand times, supports us and sustains us, promising us pardon and reward whenever we   10
return to Him; and we complain of some trifling injury done us by some poor mortal, and are very slow to forgive him. And if we do forgive him, we do so with our lips only and not from the heart, as though God were not familiar with our inward parts but could be taken in by our deceptions. Has anything new or unusual happened to you, reverend Father, if some   15

* * * * *

65A:2 Bostius] Cf Ep 53 introduction.

false and cunning man has deluded you? Are we not deceived, and do we not deceive others, every day? It would indeed have been grievous matter for sorrow, very bitter sorrow, if you yourself had deceived someone else; as it is, we may rejoice that you were not the doer but the victim of the injury. Or do you count happy one who wrongs another, and the wronged   20
person pitiable and unhappy? Plato himself did not think so, gentile and pagan though he was, but on the contrary declared the man who suffers wrong less to be pitied than him who inflicts it. And you, a Christian and vowed to the religious life, do you not feel something that was evident to a pagan and a gentile? Return then to right feeling. Think again; be sorry   25
for the man who wronged you, for he did harm to himself but conferred innumerable benefits on you. No wonder that I laughed when I read your letter, which Bostius sent me on purpose that I might learn your style. Indeed I was so much inspired by what you have written that I enclose an essay *De mentis variatione* which, rough as it is, I have dedicated to   30
your distinguished self, not doubting that you will carefully polish and correct it all.

I too was often disturbed to see how untrustworthy and inconstant a thing is man, until I came to understand that in God above is all our trust. From the brethren with whom I live I frequently suffer opposition,   35
although, thank Heaven, there are not many who are hostile to my work. Sometimes I have to endure one of them ill-treating me to such a tune that he rouses others against me as well, and stirs up innocent people by spreading some invention calculated to make brotherly union difficult, and break up peace and concord. If I take it into my head to warn someone in a chari-   40
table spirit, as our custom is, at once there is an uproar: those whose policy is to cause me distress join forces at once with the man of whom I have complained, and strive to turn his heart first to dislike and then to hate me. If this does not succeed they are bitterly hurt, while it really would hurt them if such a scheme succeeded. At length I made up my mind to remain per-   45
petually at arm's length with those whose friendship I could not enjoy with a clear conscience. Truth, virtue and religion must be valued above every friendship, as pagan philosophers and all the poets have maintained. At

* * * * *

21 Plato] Cf *Gorgias* 469B and 509C.

25 Return then to right feeling.] Isaiah 46:8

30 *De mentis variatione*] 'On Changes of Mind.' Kristeller suggests that this may be identified with the *Dyalogus de mutabilitate cordis humani* listed among Sycamber's works at the beginning of his *Dialogus de quantitate syllabarum* (Cologne: Henr. Quentell, 1502). Cf V. Scholderer 'Rutgerus Sicamber and his writings' *Gutenberg-Jahrbuch* (1957) 129–30.

the same time I am much moved by our Saviour's teaching on concord and
the words of the Apostle John about hatred between brothers and so forth,   50
so that from time to time almost against my will I seek for peace; yet I do
not find it. I think that you, reverend Father, must have the same experience, and so must everyone who tries to live a religious life in Christ and
follow in God's ways. Discord and disagreement among brethren is a horrid
thing, I confess, but men differ so much in character and natural gifts and   55
affections that true concord is a rare thing even between those who live
together and are closely united. These unpleasantnesses, these dislikes,
this feeling between monastic brethren (hatred I will not call it) I disregard
or overcome by continually studying, reading, writing something, though
what I produce is of no value. Yet I am satisfied: I pass my time in healthy   60
employment, I keep my fancies and my sorrows at bay. And this I advise
you to do likewise from the bottom of my heart, nor do I doubt that you
do of your own accord what a poor ignorant creature like myself is in such
a hurry to suggest to you. So while the others (if any there still are, for I
begin to think better of my fellows) make ready to put me to the test exter-   65
nally with word and deed and behaviour, I exercise myself within to be
ready to meet them, and prepare in my own mind something that may comfort me, though it may have no comfort for our descendants and successors.
I cannot charm my readers with beauty of style, much as I should like to
one day; but my stubborn nature says no, often though I try to bend it. But   70
you, most eloquent Father, have both the power and the will, I do not
doubt, to write the most splendid things, which both in words and matter
will enchant all your readers. When shall I behold your poems, like some
joyous green grove lovely with the foliage of all kinds of trees? When set
eyes on the meadow of your odes or lyrical pieces, full of fragrant flowers?   75
When shall I turn the pages of your works in prose so full of charm, so rich
in sense, weighty and eloquent in the same breath, gladdening my spirit
as I read? Woe is me that I am compelled to dwell in a place all thorny (rightly
so called) and full of briars, with nothing gay or elegant to read, nothing
to imitate and to equal if I can. Is this really so? 'We speak that we do know.'   80
Great is the power to win a reader's good will exerted by ease and elegance
of style; this I do not, cannot possess, and am rightly dismissed as a provincial. Pray of your kindness display my shortcomings to wise persons
interested in such things, that thus, if nohow else, they may cease to complain.   85
     I hear Robert Gaguin writes wonderful things, including history that

* * * * *

50 Apostle John] 1 John 3:14–17
86 Gaguin] Cf Epp 43 and 45 introductions.

one can trust in the style of Sallust or Livy. I have already found him a
pointed and delightful writer of verse, and I have one letter from him,
purchased at the price of my own entreaty. I have also heard that one Willem
Hermans, your fellow-canon, writes marvellous poems and incomparable   90
odes, which have been printed in Paris. I hope I may see some of them
thanks to Bostius the Carmelite. I am also given to understand that Father
Willem is still quite young, and has produced these mature works in the
first flower of his age. What will he not produce when he is older? I hope
he will fill the whole world with the fragrance of a sweet savour, and will   95
end up as the supreme glory of regular canons, if God grants him long life.
Farewell, dearest Father, and rest your hopes on God.

66 / To Thomas Grey / Pierre Vitré   [Paris? 1497?]

First printed as the preface to the *De ratione studii,* in a volume which also contained the *Epistolae* of Agostino Dati, published by G. Biermans of Bruges
(Paris, October 1511) without Erasmus' knowledge. It was originally composed
for Thomas Grey, as is indicated by the name Leucophaeus (line 17), a Greek
translation of 'grey' (cf Allen Ep 221:34). It was apparently among the papers
entrusted to William Thale in Ferrara in 1509 (cf Ep 30:17n). Thale, on returning
to Paris, had it printed, substituting his own name for Grey's in the preface.
He did not, however, have sufficient knowledge of Greek to detect the significance of Leucophaeus and so left it unchanged. Erasmus was annoyed and at
once republished the *De ratione studii* in an authorized edition, together with
the *De copia* (Paris: J. Bade, 15 July 1512), replacing Thale's name with that of
Pierre Vitré and changing Leucophaeus to 'mi Petre.' The text is in LB I 521ff.
See also the critical edition with introduction by Jean-Claude Margolin in ASD
I 2 79–151.
    Pierre Vitré (Latin, Viterius) was a close friend of Grey and may have suc-
ceeded Erasmus as his tutor (cf Ep 58:204n). He taught for a time at Calais, but
was back in Paris in 1516, where he taught at the Lombard College and later
at the collège de Navarre. Erasmus offered to write a letter of recommendation
for him to Etienne Poncher, bishop of Paris, in 1518 (cf Allen Ep 779: 8ff). Correspondence between them ceased for many years, but just before his death
Erasmus left him a legacy in his will (cf Ep 3101). There seems no very good
reason why Erasmus should have changed the dedication of this letter to Vitré
instead of restoring it to Grey. He remained on friendly terms with both
throughout his life and in 1517 addressed a letter to them jointly (Ep 528).

ERASMUS OF ROTTERDAM TO HIS FRIEND [WILLIAM THALE]
My sweetest [Thale] you have indeed foreseen with skill, and now state
with truth and dignity, that it matters enormously what plan and order one

applies to each action; and that the importance of this consideration, great
as it is in all activities, is particularly so in literary studies. Do we not ob-   5
serve that skill makes possible the lifting of huge weights, which otherwise no degree of force could move? Similarly, in warfare it does not matter
so much how large your forces are, or how massive your attack, as how good
your dispositions are and what order you maintain in the battle. And those
who are familiar with short cuts reach their destination much sooner than   10
those who take the river-bank or the shoreline as their guide, as Plautus
remarks. You ask me accordingly to lay down for you an ordered course of
study so that, following it like Theseus' thread, you may be able to find your
way in the labyrinths of letters. I shall certainly be happy to obey, as far
as in me lies, the wish of a friend so dear to me that I could not possibly   15
deny him any request, much less one so useful and honourable as this.
    ... This, my dear Leucophaeus, is what I had to write to you for the
moment on the method of study. Use it, if you like it; but if you do not,
at least take my diligent efforts in good part. Only go on as you have begun,
and confer lustre on your distinguished birth by equal prowess in letters.   20
Farewell.
    [London, 15 March]

67 / To Robert Gaguin   [Paris, c January] 1498

This and the following letter were probably written during Gaguin's illness
in the early months of 1498.

ERASMUS TO GAGUIN

I am not very clear who are the 'Cereales' and 'Anabasii' in Jerome's *In
Rufinum*. About the Cereales I have some vague ideas. Both words seem to
mean 'investigators sent off in any direction'; but I should like you to inform
me. For some time I have been in need of Lorenzo Valla's *Dialectica*; if you   5
have it, I beg you to lend it to me; or if not, to suggest whom I should ask.
I wish you good health.
    1498

* * * * *

66:11 Plautus] Cf *Poenulus* 627–8; *Adagia* II vii 81.
14 labyrinths] Cf *Adagia* II x 51.
67:2 Jerome] *In Rufinum* 3, 3. Erasmus was already studying St Jerome,
although he had probably not yet begun work on his great edition of Jerome's
correspondence (cf Ep 138).
5 *Dialectica*] Valla's treatise on logic, 1429 (cf Rossi 84f).

68 / From Robert Gaguin   [Paris, c January] 1498

GAGUIN TO ERASMUS

A most painful disease prohibits me from thinking about either the
Cereales or the Anabasii, so bad am I at putting up with pain. I am sending
you the *Dialectica*; please arrange for its return in due course, together with
those little speeches you borrowed from me. I wish you better health than   5
your Robert enjoys.
  1498

69 / To Thomas Grey   [Paris, February] 1498

Erasmus was probably collecting letters for the *De conscribendis epistolis* which
contained a number of letters from himself and his friends (cf Ep 71 introduction).

ERASMUS TO THOMAS GREY

If I have ever earned your gratitude in deed or thought, I beg you to oblige
me by repaying the debt to this extent: please deliver to the servant who
bears this the letters I have written to you; I shall send them back when I
have made a copy for those who insistently demand it. Farewell. 1498   5

70 / To Christian Northoff   Paris, 13 February 1498

ERASMUS TO CHRISTIAN, A MERCHANT OF LÜBECK

You were, perhaps, expecting a long letter, to be sent by your brother's
hand; but you are quite wrong, for it is customary to charge the best envoys
with no written instructions, or only the briefest. Idler, trifler! Ah, how
roughly I should have treated you, had not grief robbed me of energy! I had   5
already planned to write you a letter full of a thousand well-deserved
reproaches. You add crime to crime: not only failing to write, but also tearing Heinrich, the only joy of my life, away from me with your gilded
phrases. Did I say from me? Rather, from the Muses. I believe you envy him
because you yourself have now begun to cultivate Mercury and Janus,   10
instead of Apollo and the Nine Sisters. But woe to you, you ruffian, if you

* * * * *

68:5 speeches] Some of Gaguin's *Orationes* were published with his *Epistolae*
by D. Gerlier and And. Bocard (Paris, 22 November 1498).
70:10 Mercury] The god of profit (and hence of trade)
10 Janus] The god of (lucky) beginnings and ventures. At his 'arches' in Rome
the merchants and money-changers met, as at a sort of Exchange.

do not at once send back my solace. The arrows in my armoury are sharpened, the javelins ranked in readiness; you shall receive invective more bitter than any poison, and after that you may as well devote yourself to looking out for a beam from which to hang yourself. Do you hear me? I command   15
you to liberate Heinrich – who is as much mine as yours – and to send him here instantly, without delaying him any further by your business nonsense. If you do not do so, I declare war on you upon the spot, and no necessity for you to wait for my heralds and the 'pater patratus.' I have spoken! Yet though you entirely deserve to be sent to that place where   20
stone grinds upon stone, and worthless scoundrels knead their daily bread, and dead oxen attack living men, still I am anxious for your preservation, provided you come to your senses. But if you persist in your silence, do you know what words I shall have you dressed in? I shall call you rascal, butcher, gallows-bird, glutton, wretch, scandal, abomination, monster,   25
nightmare, dung, dungheap, plague, ruin, disgrace, slanderer, wastrel, jailer (or rather jail itself), whipping block, kiss-the-rod, and any still more insulting terms I can invent; these, I repeat, are the names I shall use to humiliate you. So you will be forced to write a reply, even while you fume.

I have had my fill of joking on this page; the second page will be   30
devoted to serious matters. But what serious business can one do with you, that is, with a fellow as ridiculous as you? None, I believe. The printers are eagerly waiting for your works, for you are indeed a man of enormous learning. Nor am I laughing at you. For your *Epistolae* are now in the press and Augustin is composing a commentary on them, while Fausto, who is after   35
the same commission, openly envies Augustin his task. There is a report that you have already got something out where you are, but I fancy this has to do with scions, not science: you ought to get the best children you can, to make them as much in your own image as possible – for there is nothing more wicked than you. Do you like this observation; is it witty enough, is   40
it sharp enough for you? But I will give you cause to describe it as honey-

* * * * *

19 heralds] The Roman 'fetiales' (as in Ep 29:24), of whom the 'pater patratus' was the principal one, who actually declared war with the appropriate religious ceremonial.

20–2 stone grinds upon stone ... living men] Plautus *Asinaria* 31–5

24ff This catalogue of insulting names is inspired by Plautus, especially *Asinaria* 297–8.

35 commentary] A public lecture, arranged by a bookseller to launch a new book, was customary. Augustin also performed this service for Hermans' *Silva odarum* (cf Ep 81.29–30) and for Erasmus' *Adagia* (cf Epp 128:39ff and 129:50).

35 Fausto] Andrelini (cf Ep 84 introduction).

sweet if I bring out the others I have in store. These, however, I am keeping
for a regular war; hold me in fear, and be discreet.

Enough of serious matters; now let me return to joking again. What
impels me to love you so very much, dear Christian, is the character of you   45
two brothers – not yours alone – than which I have never in my life seen
anything more open or more upright. I have longed to have you with me,
but in vain. Often I am hard at work on something to present to you; but
you will learn from Heinrich what my fortune has been; he is dependable in
other respects, but do not believe him when he praises me, for he will tell   50
many lies about me, as his way is, through excess of affection rather than
good judgment. I have written to Rodolf von Langen. Please help me, and
my letter, by your recommendation. But this letter is becoming longer than
I intended. Since I have a messenger who is good at talking, I leave the telling of the rest to him. Love me, and farewell.   55

Paris, 13 February 1498

71 / To Robert Fisher   [Paris, March 1498?]

The preface to an original draft of the *De conscribendis epistolis* first published
without Erasmus' knowledge by Siberch at Cambridge in 1521 (STC 10496). As
frequently happened (cf Ep 130:108–9n), Erasmus was incited by the unauthorized publication to issue a greatly enlarged and revised edition (Basel: Froben, August 1522). In it the seventy-six leaves of Siberch's edition were
expanded to more than four hundred pages and the character of the book
changed by numbers of personal remarks, not to mention the insertion of the
Encomium matrimonii, so that it was practically a new book (ASD I 2 170). A preface to Nicolaus Beraldus (Ep 1284) was substituted in this edition for that to
Fisher and in it Fisher was referred to in very derogatory terms, as also in Allen
Ep 3100: 220. Meanwhile, Erasmus had several times undertaken revision with
a view to publication. In May 1499 he told Batt that he was about to dedicate
it to Batt's pupil Adolph of Veere (cf Ep 95:37f). In November of the same year
he sent a copy to Mountjoy from Oxford with a letter that has the appearance
of a dedicatory preface (cf Ep 117 introduction). Back in France, he announced
his intention, in September 1500, of revising it further (cf Ep 130:111f). In

* * * * *

52 Langen] Rodolf von Langen was a Westphalian humanist who would be
about sixty years old at this time. He had just established a school on humanist
lines at Münster. As Münster was on the road from Paris to Lübeck, Christian
may have visited him there and been asked to put him in touch with Erasmus
(cf Ep 72:10–11). Erasmus later referred to him as one of the small group who
revived good literature in Friesland (cf Allen Ep 1237:11).

December he again told Batt of his intention, if it seemed a good idea, to dedicate it to Adolph (cf Ep 138:188). In January of the following year he promised Anna van Borssele, vrouwe van Veere, to send it to aid her son Adolph in his studies, but with no mention of a dedication (cf Allen Ep 145:155f). He was working on it again in Cambridge in 1511 (cf Allen Ep 241:28–9), at which time the copy which fell into the hands of Siberch may have been made. It was laid aside, however, and apparently not touched again till 1522. See the critical edition with introduction by Jean-Claude Margolin in ASD I 2 157–579.

DESIDERIUS ERASMUS TO ROBERT FISHER

Yes, Robert, you have won: here is the method of writing letters, which you have so often begged me to produce. All the same, notice how many disparaging remarks I have exposed myself to in the course of humouring your whim. For what will the critics say – or rather, what will they *not* say – when they see I have ventured to discuss a subject that has already been handled with skill and thoroughness by so many learned authors? They will say 'Do you then essay to weave again Penelope's web? For what can you see that those before you have not seen? After those great men you must of a surety either repeat what they have written, or write worse; now the former is superfluous for the studious reader, the latter even harmful.' To such persons, among many answers I could make, I will make but this one: as I was at liberty to do a favour to a great friend, so are they at liberty, to the same degree, to leave alone what they do not like. All the same, I make you one promise: I will refuse to follow closely in the steps of another, and I will include more appropriate, if not more scholarly, material: not that I do not approve of the purpose of those other authors, who have, as they say, broken the ice and aroused the interest of other men, but that there is not a single one of them in whom I do not find a great deal to be missing. Why this should be so is a topic we may perhaps discuss at another time. For the present, I shall lay down as briefly as possible what I myself have been able to achieve by training, practice, and the imitation of others. Farewell.

72 / To Christian Northoff   Paris [March 1498?]

ERASMUS TO CHRISTIAN

Are you not afraid of your friend's pen, when you have such a presumptuous action on your conscience as the abduction from me of my dear Hein-

* * * * *

71:8 Penelope's web] Cf *Adagia* I iv 42.
18 broken the ice] Cf *Adagia* III v 95.

rich? English Robert also deserted me, but on very different principles; that
is, he acted in perfect disloyalty, which well accorded with his character!   5
But, joking apart, I not only do not find anything to disturb me in your plan,
but am very much in favour of it; for it is more sensible to discard a load
that is too heavy, than to collapse under its excessive weight. I take pleasure
in his courage as if it were mine. See that you follow your brother's example
and show your affection for Erasmus, even at a distance. I should like you   10
to remind Rodolf von Langen to answer my letter and to keep his promises.
Farewell.

Paris [1496]

73 / To Jan Mombaer   Paris [April 1498?]

Mombaer had by this time probably completed the reform of the monastery
at Château-Landon and had begun the reform of the abbey of Livry (cf Ep 52
introduction). This letter survives in a MS in the Bibliothèque de Ste
Geneviève, Paris, the heading being added by the scribe.

A LETTER FROM ERASMUS OF ROTTERDAM TO MOMBAER, AT THE TIME WHEN
ERASMUS WAS A STUDENT IN PARIS

Distinguished and reverend sir, I have received your letter, written a considerable time since. However, your servant Pieter, the bearer of this reply,
had arrived here but a short time before and informed me of all that was   5
happening in your community. I have long since delivered to my lord president de Hacqueville, in Master Emery's presence, the report enjoined upon
me; which, truth to tell, they received with great enthusiasm, together with

* * * * *

72:4 Robert] Robert Fisher left for Italy immediately after the completion of
the *De conscribendis epistolis*. Erasmus had compiled it hurriedly so as to have
it ready for presentation before his departure. Nichols suggests that Erasmus'
charge of perfidy here may have been due to his not receiving as much as he
expected in return for the gift from his wealthy pupil (Nichols I 166). The
charge, however, was explicitly made in jest and could scarcely have been a
serious enough matter to embitter Erasmus' feelings for Fisher many years
later. The friendly tone of Ep 118 is evidence that any possible grievance was
soon forgiven. It seems more likely that the disparaging tone of Erasmus' comments on Fisher after the unauthorized publication of the *De conscribendis
epistolis* (cf Ep 71 introduction) was due to suspicion that Fisher was responsible for letting the hastily written first draft fall into the printer's hands (cf Allen
Ep 3100:23ff).
73:7 de Hacqueville] Nicolas de Hacqueville was a canon of Notre Dame,
member of the Parlement de Paris and president of the Chambre des Inquêtes.
He was so much impressed by the success of Mombaer's work at Château-
Landon that he persuaded the Parlement de Paris and the bishop of Paris in

the gifts sent by your chapter; and heard with marked pleasure the account
I gave of past and present proceedings in your community. I have   10
repeatedly urged our worshipful master, Jan Standonck, to inform you of
these and other matters, and in particular to tell you what message he
thought proper to send to the fathers; and this he has done.

  We have awaited, and still await, the arrival of your reverend Father
in God; we shall take pains to ensure that he is admonished and exhorted   15
by men of undoubted authority who are friendly to you and who, moreover,
as it is quite superfluous for me to say, and as you yourselves must surely
be aware, have the keenest interest in your undertaking and entertain the
greatest good will towards you. The fact that everything still goes forward
at a snail's pace has to be borne without impatience, since it is always an 20
uphill task to dis-accustom those who are accustomed to something. But he
who granted the beginning shall by his grace vouchsafe the ending, so that
in no long time it shall all be made perfect. Come then, prior most worthy

* * * * *

1497 to request the chapter of Windesheim to send a group of Dutch Augustinian canons to reform the abbey of St Victor. He was also active in persuading
Mombaer to undertake the reform of Livry. In February 1499 he acquired the
abbey of Livry 'in commendam' and paved the way for its reform by Mombaer
who succeeded him as abbot after his death in December 1500. Cf Renaudet
Préréforme 182ff, 221ff.

7 Emery] Jean Emery, canon of Notre Dame and one of the most enthusiastic
supporters of the reform movement instituted by Standonck and the Win-
desheimers. Cf Renaudet *Préréforme* 230 *et passim*.

11 Standonck] Jan Standonck was born of poor parents in Mechelen and
educated by the Brethren of the Common Life in Gouda. He studied theology
in Paris and was admitted to the Sorbonne in 1480. In 1483 he was appointed
principal of the Collège de Montaigu, where he instituted a strict reform. In
1490 he acquired an adjoining building to house poor students, the *Domus
pauperum*, in which Erasmus lived for a few months in 1495–96 (cf Ep 43
introduction). For more than twenty years Standonck was the leader of a movement to reform the French clergy in the strictest spirit of the *Devotio moderna*.
Cf A. Renaudet 'Jean Standonck, un réformateur catholique avant la Réforme'
in his *Humanisme et Renaissance* (Geneva 1958) 114–61; and *Préréforme* 174 *et passim*; cf also M. Godet 'La Congrégation de Montaigu, 1490–1580' *Bibliothèque
de l'Ecole des Hautes-Etudes* 198 (Paris 1912).

14 reverend Father] Allen's suggestion in the introduction to this letter that
this may refer to Jean de Mixon, archbishop 'in partibus' of Tarsus, may have
some support in the fact that he was at this time intriguing at the court of Rome
to obtain the abbey of Livry 'in commendam' and that in June 1498 Mombaer
wrote to him to discourage his action. However, in 1498 the abbey was actually still held by Charles du Haultbois who had promised to surrender it to
de Hacqueville but apparently did not do so till Febuary 1499. Cf
Renaudet *Préréforme* 228, 296, 302.

of the name: exhort your splendid troops not to lose heart; take pains to encourage them, that they be not dismayed; for so shall God ordain prog- 25 ress through suffering, to the end that Goliath may not prevail against Israel, but the Philistines may perish root and branch.

Most devoutly I entreat your prayers, with such little humility as I can command. My greetings, Father, to you and your fellow-labourers.

Reverend Father, the enterprise you have begun pleases me in- 30 expressibly. At some distance off, I see a religious end; it seems to be expressed precisely in Virgil's words: 'Yield not to ills, but do more boldly tread/The way that Fate permits thee.' When I have time, I propose to commemorate your achievement in some literary memorial. I am sending the histories, printed in a revised edition. Remember me in your prayers; and 35 so farewell, good Father. Affectionate as I feel towards you, I would have your affection or, if this be too much to ask, at least your good will. From your devoted Erasmus. Farewell, from Paris.

74 / To Nicolaas Werner   [Paris, c April 1498]

ERASMUS OF ROTTERDAM TO HIS REVERENCE, FATHER NICOLAAS WERNER
Reverend Father, I have for a month and a half now been most seriously affected in health, and as yet I see no hope of recovery. What a thing man's life is, what sore pains it encompasses! I have all but died of a low, but daily recurrent, fever. At present the world looks unsatisfactory to me; I have no 5 regard for the very hopes I cherished, and am longing for a life wherein I may in sanctified leisure devote all my time to God and myself alone, and meditate on holy writ, and wash away my past mistakes with my tears. This is my inward thought; and I hope that in time to come, with your aid and counsel, I may yet achieve it. 10

Cornelis of Gouda is making a name for himself here. He is very well thought of by the bishop of Paris, and by the abbot likewise. Farewell.

* * * * *

32 Virgil] *Aeneid* 6.95, 96

35 histories] Gaguin's *De origine et gestis Francorum compendium*, of which revised editions were published on 24 June 1497 and 31 March 1498.

74:5 fever] Cf Ep 75: 2ff. Erasmus complained of a similar recurrent nocturnal fever in April 1500 (cf Ep 124: 10ff).

11 Cornelis of Gouda] Cornelis Gerard (cf Ep 78 introduction).

12 bishop of Paris] Jean Simon de Champigny (d 1502), bishop of Paris since 1492. Gaguin attested his high regard for Cornelis' learning and character in a letter quoted in Renaudet *Préréforme* 226, n4.

12 abbot] Nicaise de l'Orme or de Lorme, abbot of St Victor. For evidence of his special friendliness to Cornelis, see Renaudet *Préréforme* 227, n3.

75 / To Arnoldus Bostius

Cf Ep 53 introduction.

ERASMUS TO ARNOLDUS

Dear Arnoldus: I have for a month and a half been seriously afflicted by a fever, rising at night, that remains low but recurs daily; it has completely crushed me. I am not yet free of the disease, but am a little better now. I am not exactly alive yet, but some hope of living begins to dawn. You ask   5
me to share my thoughts with you; I will tell you one thing, I have long since lost all interest in the world, and find no merit in my own hopes. I only ask to be given leisure to live a life entirely devoted to God alone, in lamentation for the sins of my rash youth, absorption in holy writ, and either reading or writing something continually. This I cannot do in a retreat, or under a   10
monastic regime, for I am the most sensitive man alive. My health can never, even at its best, tolerate vigils or fasting, or hardships of any kind. Even in my present circumstances, living in the midst of such luxury, I sometimes fall ill; what should I do among the toils of a monkish life?

I had previously made up my mind to withdraw to Italy this year, and   15
to study theology for a few months at Bologna, taking my doctorate there, and to visit Rome in the jubilee year; after which I would return to my people and make my life among you. But I am afraid I cannot complete this course in the way I desire. I fear especially that this health of mine may be unable to stand a journey of such length in a hot climate, and lastly I reflect   20
that neither the journey into Italy, nor supporting oneself while there, is anything but very expensive. Even to acquire the degree itself one requires a substantial amount of money; and of this the bishop of Cambrai is a very poor provider. In every way he is more warm-hearted than lavish, more generous with all kinds of promises than with actual help. I myself am partly   25
responsible, refusing as I do to insist on payment; there are so many who go so far as to squeeze him for it. But I shall do whatever seems best according to the situation. Farewell.

In the year [1489]

* * * * *

75:15 Italy] Despite his decision here to give up his cherished plan to visit Italy and take his doctor's degree in theology at Bologna, Erasmus continued to nurse hopes that he might yet be able to carry it out. Cf Epp 78: 6f, 82: 19f, 92: 7ff, 95: 29ff, 118: 10ff, 124: 69ff, 139: 59ff, Allen Epp 145: 106, 157: 58.
17 jubilee year] 1500

76 / To Martin   Brussels [July? 1498]

After his illness in the spring of 1498, Erasmus returned to Holland to visit friends and recover his health. On the way back to Paris he stopped in Brussels to pay a visit to his patron, the bishop of Cambrai, in the hope of raising funds.

Martin seems to have been a physician resident in Gouda, since this letter was included in the collection made for Erasmus by Franciscus Theodoricus, his friend at Steyn, in 1505 (cf Allen Ep 186: 2n).

ERASMUS OF ROTTERDAM TO MASTER MARTIN, THE PHYSICIAN

Most kind Martin, please go on as you have begun, making your friend Erasmus famous by singing his praises. I have detected this, and am now beginning to pay for it: my uncle Theobald has relieved me of one of my two tunics on the strength of your compliments, being eager, I suppose,   5
to oblige his nephew by lightening his baggage when he was about to start out on a long journey. Yes, your zeal on my behalf, dear Martin, is extremely welcome, and gives me much pleasure; but, if reports are true, your praise of your humble friend is not only exaggerated but absurd. You boast how rich he is, but who could believe this of a poet, and one of Fate's unlucky   10
ones too? If you are determined to advertise your new friend by fabricating facts, then pretend he is exceptionally modest, or say falsely that he is an expert on literature; make me out to be something suitable, something I wish to be. For what has Erasmus to do with money?

You have a right to know about the state of my health. All over Holland   15
I tried it severely by the heavy drinking I began when I stayed with you. However, I have weathered all such perils and come through unscathed; my paleness has left me, I have recovered my spirits, and I pray that Heaven may guard its gifts. Dordrecht saw the final gamble with my strength, but it went well: I felt that all my resources were under my command. I was   20
extremely unwilling to be dragged away from there, and am now as reluc-tant to linger here as I was to leave Dordrecht. 'Well, what detains you?,' you may ask. It is, I think, my own evil genius that empties my purse here to no profit. I stayed with the bishop for about ten days: on the third of July

* * * * *

76:4 Theobald] There seems to be no other mention of an uncle by this name. The word 'patruus' means specifically a paternal uncle.

19 Dordrecht] In the *Compendium vitae* Erasmus recalled seeing two of his mother's brothers at Dordrecht when they were almost ninety. This may have been the occasion, accompanied by considerable celebration. Cf Allen I 47 lines 3–4.

he left for England on an embassy, which has done me further harm, since   25
the bishop, overwhelmed by pressure of business and concerned about
financial provision for the journey, and a little annoyed also because Prince
Philip, on whose behalf he is being sent, has given a subsidy of only six
hundred gold florins, has poured upon me a flood of complaints but precious little money. Now – and this is the most irritating thing – I am stuck   30
here, at great expense to myself, with no means of transport or fellow
traveller in prospect, while I ought to get to Paris as quickly as possible.
But enough of all this.

I was most distressed at having missed you on my return. I paid a visit
to Louvain, where I stayed for a night and a day and was entertained most   35
hospitably by certain people, among them Francesco da Crema, an exceptionally well-read person. If you are looking for news from me, I can add that
the supreme pontiff has sent to our archduke the splendid gift of a golden
rose, the workmanship of which is far more remarkable even than the
material. The prince left in company with the bishop on the thirtieth of   40
June, to meet the papal delegate two leagues outside the city. The gift was
brought to Brussels in solemn procession, accompanied by bishops on
either side, the papal delegate in the middle with the rose held aloft in his
hands. The duke accompanied him to his lodging and the company then
dispersed. Next day, being the first of July, the pope's gift was handed over   45
to the prince before a numerous gathering in the church on the Koudenberg. A speech was delivered on the generosity of the gift and in praise of
the prince; it was followed by an address of thanks by the chancellor.

* * * * *

25 embassy] The purpose of the visit to England was kept secret (cf Ep 77: 6–7),
but it afforded Henry VII an opportunity to force Perkin Warbeck to repeat the
confession of his imposture in the presence of Prince Philip's ambassador (cf
Nichols I 161).

28–9 six hundred gold florins] Literally 'sexcentis aureis,' probably
Burgundian-Habsburg gold *florins of St Philip*; at 4s *gros* each, a sum worth
£120 *gros* Flemish. See the Glossary, and Appendix A on gold coinage.

36 Francesco da Crema] A learned Italian lawyer and writer (d 1525) who was
later one of the tutors of Prince Charles

38 pontiff] Alexander VI

38 archduke] Philip the Handsome (Philippe le Bel), archduke of Austria
and duke of Burgundy, son of Emperor Maximilian I and Mary of Burgundy:
mentioned above, lines 27–8

46–7 Koudenberg] The church of the Augustinian abbey on the Koudenberg
near the modern Place Royale

48 chancellor] Thomas de Plaine, Sieur de Maigny (d 1507), chancellor of Burgundy since 1496

I have scribbled down a great deal of trifling stuff, but I enjoyed writing to you in this way, as though I were talking with you. Farewell, and love me as you are wont to do.   50

The bishop's library, Brussels

77 / To Nicolaas Werner   Brussels [9 July? 1498]

ERASMUS OF ROTTERDAM TO THE REVEREND FATHER, NICOLAAS WERNER
I have recovered sound health and all my resources of bodily strength. For many days now I have tarried in Brussels, much against my will, since thus far no means of transport or travelling-companions have been forthcoming. I have spent about ten days with the bishop and the rest of the time with   5
his vicar. The bishop has gone to England with an embassy on behalf of the prince, but what it is about is a close secret. My guess is that the bishop is acting in his own interest as well as the prince's, and is looking for a cardinalate with English help. The English king is most anxious to have him, and he is an especial favourite of the cardinal of England, from whom he   10
lately received the gift of a splendid cope and at the same time a warm recommendation in a letter to the pope and the College of Cardinals. Be that as it may, this embassy has cost me a pretty penny, both because the bishop is wholly distracted by business and because he himself is as anxious as I am about raising journey-money; for he, a man who lives in state, is being   15
sent to a wealthy people, who love pomp, with a subsidy of only six hundred florins from the prince; and the presents customarily given to the heads of embassies are prospective, not ready money.

On the first of July a very beautiful and holy gift was offered to our prince by the supreme pontiff: a golden rose, as remarkable for its work-   20
manship as for its material. I commend earnestly to your prayers my fortunes and myself. I would request your reverence to be confident, for Providence will aid me and guide my bark, I hope, to the desired haven. For the present, though I run before the wind, I shall not quit the rudder. May Immortal God protect you.   25

Brussels [13 September]

* * * * *

77:6 vicar] Jacob Anthoniszoon of Middelburg (cf Ep 153 introduction).

10 cardinal] John Morton, archbishop of Canterbury

17 presents] The bishop received a present from Henry VII of one hundred pounds (cf Nichols I 161).

24 run before the wind] Cf *Adagia* I iv 33

78 / To Cornelis Gerard

Paris [c October 1498]

This letter must have been written shortly after the departure of Cornelis from
Paris. He had been a member of the group of Dutch Augustinian canons,
invited to help reform the abbey of St Victor, who reached Paris in October
1497 and left in August 1498, having accomplished nothing (cf Ep 73: 7n; and
Renaudet *Préréforme* 221ff, 294ff). Cornelis made a very favourable impression
on both the bishop of Paris and the abbot (cf Ep 74: 12nn) but neither supported the reformers strongly. Cf P. Debongnie 'Corneille Gérard à Saint-
Victor' NAKG 17 (1923) 161ff.

ERASMUS TO THE LEARNED CANON, CORNELIS

Has France sent you home so puffed up that you have begun to regard your
humbler friends with distaste? You send letters to satraps, but not to Erasmus. Have I deserved this? But you have an excuse, perhaps a genuine
reason: you say 'I was totally unaware that you had gone back to live in   5
France for at that time you had resolved on, and were getting ready for, a
visit to Italy.' There, I won't argue. I accept your excuse, provided you compensate my loss with an immensely long letter. I have no news to give you:
to say I am very fond of you is ancient history. I wonder what has happened
to Bostius; there has been no reply from him for ages. There are murmurings   10
here about my withdrawal. Tell me all about your journey and how things
are with you; and, if you think that devoted care and attention from me can
help at all at this point, you have the right to demand them boldly. In view
of our close and ancient friendship, it seems wrong to bespeak your interest
in my position. Keep urging my friend, or rather your friend, Willem to do   15
something worthy of his talents. I have no definite news about myself, since
all is in the balance. Thus far I am well – my best regards to you. Please show
warm friendship to my dear Pieter, as you are doing. If I tell you to keep
to yourself what I have confided to you for old acquaintance' sake, I will
seem to have too low opinion of your trustworthiness, and your affection   20
for me. Yet there are some who blame you, I don't know how, on the
grounds that you did not defend my position, when I was away, with com-

* * * * *

78:7 Italy] Cf Ep 75:15 and n.

15 Willem] Erasmus seems to have been worried lest his old friend Willem
Hermans should neglect his literary activities (cf Ep 83: 21ff).

18 my dear Pieter] This probably refers to Erasmus' brother, Pieter (cf Epp 3
introduction and 81:87).

18–19 keep to yourself] Literally, 'give satisfaction to Harpocrates,' the god
of silence; cf *Adagia* IV i 52.

plete loyalty. But I am so rooted in my opinion of your integrity that I would
sooner doubt myself than you, and I should like you to be sure that I have,
and always shall have, a sincere affection for you. Farewell.   25
    Paris [1497]

79 / To William Blount, Lord Mountjoy   [Paris, November 1498?]

This letter introduces one of the important personages in the life of Erasmus.
William Blount, fourth Baron Mountjoy, was at this time about nineteen and
was spending a year studying in Paris with Erasmus as one of his tutors. He
had already attended Cambridge and was accompanied by a Fellow of
Queens', Richard Whitford (cf Ep 89 introduction). On returning to England
in 1499 he took Erasmus with him. For more than thirty years he remained one
of Erasmus' most constant friends and patrons. He had close relations with the
royal court and held a number of official posts (cf *E & C* 216ff).

ERASMUS TO WILLIAM MOUNTJOY

Greetings, my well-named Mountjoy. I ought to have asked pardon, but
have decided to defend myself instead. I admit the charge, I did deprive
you of your lesson today; not, however, because I wished to, but because
I was obliged to. I had to give letters to two messengers at once. Be sure
you do not try to alter the ground of my defence and object that my plea
of necessity is false; for in that event the defendant will become the plaintiff,
and the case at issue, which was juridical, will become conjectural or at any
rate a problem of definition, the question being: what is 'necessity'? But
see what a clever defence attorney I make! I am pleading my own case even   10
before I have been summoned into court, in order that I may be acquitted
since there is then no prosecutor, while I myself am both counsel for the
defence and judge. I bid you farewell, and commend you to the Muses'
friendship.
[1496]   15

80 / To Jacob Batt   Paris, 29 November 1498

Jacob Batt, whom Erasmus had met at Bergen some five years earlier (cf Ep 35
introduction) was now established at the castle of Tournehem as the tutor of
the young Adolph of Burgundy, heer van Veere (cf Ep 93 introduction), grand-
son and heir of Anthony of Burgundy, 'le Grand Bâtard,' illegitimate son of

* * * * *

79:6 ground of my defence] The word *status* has a technical meaning in Roman
rhetorical language; but Erasmus plays on its general meaning also.

Duke Philip the Good. Adolph was now in the care of his widowed mother, Anna (1469?-December 1518), daughter and heiress of Wolfart of Borssele, heer van Veere. The castle of Tournehem was the principal residence of Anthony of Burgundy, and its position on the border of France, between Calais and Saint-Omer, led to his being suspected of disloyalty to the duke of Burgundy. As a result, he and his relatives were kept under surveillance for some time before his death in 1504 (cf Allen Ep 157: 20f).

Batt obtained for Erasmus the patronage of the Lady Anna which, though never very certain or satisfactory, continued until Batt's death and her second marriage (cf Allen Epp 146, 170: 11, 172: 4ff). For the relations of Erasmus to Anna, see Nichols I 176f. This letter replies to an invitation to visit Tournehem to pay court to the Lady of Veere.

ERASMUS TO HIS FRIEND BATT

I am not unaware, dear Batt, how surprised you may be that I did not at once rush to join you, especially since the result was even better than either of us could have dared to hope. But once you know what was in my mind you will be surprised no longer, and will realize that I had your interests 5 as wholly at heart as my own. The pleasure your letter brought me is well-nigh inexpressible: it allows me now to conjure up the wonderful time we shall have. How freely we shall chatter together, and in what ways we shall commune with our Muses! Already I am full of eagerness to fly from this horrible thraldom. You ask what, then, delays me. I shall show you that 10 there are reasons. I did not expect the messenger to arrive so soon; there is a little money owing to me here. But everything like this must surely seem immense to me! I have a number of engagements to certain persons, and these I could not abandon without suffering loss; I have begun my month in the count's service; I have paid the rent for my room; I have some busi- 15 ness with Augustin; my servant-pupil's books have strayed, I do not know where, and I have received neither a letter nor money on his account; the arrangements are a matter of some dispute.

You can see, my dear Batt, that I am unable to relinquish all these com-mitments without expense; and I saw that these interests of mine would 20

* * * * *

10 horrible thraldom] Erasmus' teaching and other hack-work

15 count] Mountjoy

16 Augustin] Augustin Vincent (cf Ep 131 introduction). Erasmus had frequent difficulties with him over financial matters, the details of which are obscure but apparently related to Augustin's activity as a copyist or his services to prin-ters and booksellers (cf Epp 81:30ff, 82:16ff, 95:14ff, 133:11ff).

16 servant-pupil] Cf Ep 82.

Anna van Borssele
Michiel Yssewyn of Mechelen, c 1517
Stichting De Schotse Huizen, Veere

be sacrificed if I moved away before concluding the business. You know
the saying in Terence: 'Where were you, and why did you put up with it?'
Now, while you can see that I was unable to neglect these points, still I was
much more influenced by the consideration that, had I torn myself suddenly away, my treatise *De conscribendis epistolis* would have been lost,   25
inasmuch as Augustin has the only copy. Nor could I have hoped for Valla,
or any of my own compositions: for there is nothing less likely than that
he should send you anything he has while I, for whose sake alone he will
do anything he does, am away. It was only by dint of supreme exertions
that I pushed him into sending you a part of the Valla, and even then only   30
on condition that you should reciprocate by sending some of my letters back
here. He insists on a fair bargain, for hand rubs hand: give a little and take
a little. These were the factors that made me decide to stay here for another
month, until debts due to me are repaid and I discharge my own obligations
and recover my writings. If you approve of this plan, I shall not be sorry;   35
but if you don't, please tell me so as soon as possible. I shall act entirely
in accordance with your wishes.

The bearer of this will tell you a tale of new disasters. He came to see
me on his way and said that he had left his horse at an inn with a sum of
money hidden in the saddle. I told him to run back to the hostelry and take   40
the money out. He went but, as he made his way back in the twilight,
officers of the watch set upon him, punched, kicked, and wounded him,
locked him up, and robbed him of the money. At first I supposed he had
found some boon companions to drink with; but when he had failed to
return by a late hour next day, I was beginning to guess that something of   45
the kind had occurred; he turned up in the nick of time besmeared with
mud and blood and in sorry case. We went straight to a lawyer, and next
to the prefect of the city, a very new bird in those parts; I'd rather enter a
sewer of any kind than that cave of his. I made a complaint in person before
a justice, who then produced a sword broken in the middle. According to   50
the officers, it had been broken when the messenger was cutting off somebody's arm in the street and was caught in the act. We had witnesses to tes-
tify that his sword was broken when he entered the city. It had happened

* * * * *

22 Terence] *Adelphoe* 234
25 *De conscribendis epistolis*] 'On Letter Writing' (cf Ep 71 introduction).
30 Valla] Erasmus' paraphrase of the *Elegantiae* (cf Ep 23:108n).
31 letters] Cf Ep 101:36n.
32 hand rubs hand] (Or 'hand washes hand,' ie 'one good turn deserves
another') *Adagia* I i 33, II viii 8

when the ass fell, not from an ass, but from his horse. The judge replied
that he would pronounce on the case as soon as we produced the authors   55
of the crime; but though these officers were in attendance upon the judge,
they had quietly withdrawn as soon as they saw us enter. Adrian warned
us of this but they had gone already. Consequently we dropped the proceedings.

I might well have been deterred by this ominous event. I desired to   60
keep him here because of his wounds, but decided to inform you as soon
as possible about my plans, and find out what you thought; also, I was so
busy that I hardly had time to sleep. As additional journey-money I gave
him eighteen *douzains*, since he said that he had not received above thirty
from you, and all that remained of that had been stolen by the officers. Also,   65
I changed a pure gold piece for a certain young man, because the messenger
had (he said) changed his gold for gold on the way. Make sure that when
money is sent to him in replacement, as I hear it shortly will be, the exact
sum is repaid to me; I shall repay the senders in the currency of our country,
so that they may transfer it to you.   70

You do not need to be reminded, my dear Batt, for I know how loyal
and conscientious you are, to look after my financial rewards and at the
same time think of my honour. The atmosphere at court rather terrifies me,
and I recognize how badly I am treated by fortune. I rejoice to hear that the
Lady's attitude towards me is as you say; but think what friendliness the   75
bishop used to show to me, and what hopes he used to hold out, and now
he is coldness itself. I really should prefer to find in your letter a definite
sum of money rather than the most ample promises. I shall not confront you
with Virgil's saying:

An ever-changing and inconstant thing   80
Is womankind

* * * * *

57 Adrian] The messenger who frequently carried letters to and from Batt (cf
Epp 95:45, 101:20, 124:75, 130:116, 133:104). Erasmus later called him a 'rascal
for whom no treatment is bad enough' (Allen Ep 146:83).

64 eighteen *douzains*] See the Glossary.

66 a pure gold piece] 'putum ... aureum': possibly a French *franc* or *salut*, 24
carats fine; but such coins had not been struck for 75 and 65 years respectively.
Other virtually pure gold coins then current in this region were the Florentine
florin; the Venetian *ducat*; the Burgundian-Habsburg *toison d'or*; and the English Henricus, Angel, and Ryal nobles, and the Sovereign. See the Glossary and
Appendix A on gold coinage.

69 in the currency of our country] Probably Flemish *gros* (*groots*): in any event,
a sum in silver coin.

76 bishop] of Cambrai

79 Virgil] *Aeneid* 4.569,70

for I class her among Amazons rather than women. But is there a single person, where you are, who admires the literature you and I love? Or is there
anyone who does not actually hate learning of every kind? It is on you that
my whole future depends. But if (and may great Jove avert the omen) things   85
should turn out as neither of us desires, because you are in the grip of debts,
and moreover because of your usual luck may be in this respect all the more
unfortunate, what help could you offer to your humble friend? I will not
allow that you are more ardently affectionate to me than I to you, but I am
firmly of the opinion that the warmth of our affection should not become   90
too heated.

I am writing this, not because I have changed my views or am in two
minds at once, but in order to put you on the alert, since the interests of
both of us are involved. Were it not that I am so confident of your loyalty,
wisdom, and conscientiousness that I feel sure I might hand the whole   95
responsibility over to you and go to sleep easily, I could have been
frightened off by this seemingly inauspicious beginning: I am sent a
liveryman's hack, bought for a halfpenny, and a journey-allowance that is
not merely meagre but almost non-existent. If the first stages exhibit such
coldness, are we to look for much warmth in the conclusion? Surely you will   100
never have a more honourable and justifiable excuse for begging in my
name than now, when my presence is required, and I must leave this city
and abandon my commitments. With so tiny a sum I could not have come
even on foot, much less on horseback with two companions. Now, if support comes, as I believe it does, from the Lady's money, I do not like the   105
opening scene; but if from yours, I like it still less, because it is based not
only on deficient, but on borrowed funds. What could be less suitable for
a person such as you have described me to those about you, than flying to
accept the first hint, especially on terms such as these? Should I not be
universally regarded as feather-brained or foolish or at least an unfortunate   110
wretch, and in any case to be despised?

Did I not love you most dearly, Batt, so far indeed that I consider any
hardships of my own to be outweighed by the pleasure of your companionship, these facts could have made me give up my plan; but as it is they fail
to influence me. I only urge you to be careful to think of my dignity. If you   115
are asking what my decision is, I will tell you. I am going to make everything
ready here, gathering my written work together and finishing my business.

* * * * *

87 usual luck] 'tuo fato'. Allen notes that this phrase was frequently applied
to Batt, who was evidently considered by his friends to be a lucky person. Cf
Epp 87:9, 91:9, 95:56–7, 101:49, 139:25–6.
96 easily] Literally, 'on which ever ear you choose'; *Adagia* I viii 19

As for you, will you please copy out the materials I shall send, and give me
a careful account of all your proposals by the youth who, I hear, will shortly
leave to come here and study. Next, when you have copied out the Valla,   120
please send this boy – I am speaking of Adrian – back again in three weeks'
time to return the Valla and bring me my journey-allowance, together with
a letter in the most explicit terms. I mean a journey-allowance worthy of me.
For I cannot come at all at my own expense, penniless as I am, nor would
it be reasonable to leave here, thus abandoning quite profitable commit-   125
ments. In addition, I should like you to send me, if possible, a better horse;
I am not asking for a splendid Bucephalus, but one that a man might sit on
without being ashamed. You know, too, that I need two horses; for I have
quite made up my mind to bring my pupil, and so have this other one in
mind for him. You can easily persuade the Lady to undertake all this. Your   130
cause is an excellent one, and I am acquainted with the eloquence that
enables you to turn the worst cases into the best. If she makes difficulties
about doing this, how can she be expected to provide a salary after refusing
journey-money? These, then, are the reasons why I have had to put off the
meeting between us which I held in prospect at the beginning of this cor-   135
respondence; I know you will approve.

Such are the matters in which you can protect my position. It remains
for you to expedite the business as far as possible. I shall not sleep here,
while you at your end must be wide awake. Johannes Falco returns your
greetings a thousandfold, and Augustin sends his good wishes. All of us   140
send our love. I need not remind you what to say to the Lady on my behalf.
Farewell, my dear Batt.

ps: Be sure to act firmly, for I have now severed my connection with
the count, despite repeated requests and promises, in order to make it
easier to gather all my possessions together. I should give you lengthier   145
instructions did I not rely on your absolute loyalty. Please give my greetings
individually to Pierre and Master François the physician, and your fine
boys. Farewell, and be vigilant.

From the friend of your heart, Erasmus.

Paris, 29 November 1498   150

* * * * *

118 copy out] Books still circulated in ms, and Erasmus' early works frequently
did so for years before they were printed. He apparently pressed his friends
into service as copyists.

129 pupil] Cf Ep 82.

139 Falco] Cf Ep 87.

147 Pierre, etc.] Cf Ep 123:30f.

81 / To Willem Hermans   Paris [December 1498]

ERASMUS TO HIS BOSOM FRIEND WILLEM

Greetings, my only joy. Provided only that you are happy, I congratulate
you on being where you are; and happy you ought to be, for I am sure you
have mounted Fame's ladder. I am deeply sorry that the letter was not delivered, in spite of my efforts; not so much because I failed to get what I   5
wanted, as because I was deprived of a very pleasant letter from you. I shall
die if you do not cheer me by writing frequently. I have had a letter from
X, in which he opened his heart to me, as I bade him do. He does not venture
to praise my literary pursuits, saying that many disapprove of them and that
he is afraid I might fall into debt and be a burden to my friends. In his usual   10
fashion, he complains a great deal. I have delivered the fellow from his fear,
though he tells me that of course he was not personally afraid of it, but wrote
to placate others. It does seem that he is fond of me, and not averse to you,
for he mentions you affectionately enough. The reply I gave was in
accordance with my own disposition and with whatever authority I pos-   15
sess. I wrote at considerable length about my own situation. I am surprised
at your distress over the bishop, considering that I have already told you
over and over again that his principles are admirable but he gives nothing
while promising much. You say there is much talk of me in your circle. What
kind of talk? If it is good, I am pleased; otherwise, that's their own affair.   20
Here, at least, I am invariably praised, perhaps deservedly. The exhortations to virtue you address to me are worthy of my Willem; and I in my turn,
dear Willem, now exhort you to be stout-hearted in pursuit of both virtue
and learning. If you do this, I am quite sure you are destined to be the chief
ornament of Holland, and it will be easier for you to qualify as a theologian   25
there than for me here. Believe me, this is so.

But now to gossip. What am I doing? you will ask. Playing Ulysses,
as usual: recently, after my journey, I fell ill and I am not yet quite well. A
member of my household has taken a fever but is recovering. From your
expositor, Augustin, I have for some time been estranged. He treats me   30
warily, as I treat him, and there is no vestige of genuine affection between
us, nor ever was, so different are we in temperament. He intends to visit

* * * * *

8 X] Allen suggests a reference to Nicolaas Werner, but the tone seems to
accord ill with the letters written to Werner or the reference to him in Allen
Ep 296:165ff.

29 member] Probably the servant-pupil from Lübeck (cf Ep 82).

30 expositor] Augustin Vincent had given a public lecture to introduce Hermans' *Silva odarum* (cf Ep 70:35n).

you presently, and I should advise you also to be careful in dealing with
him, deferring to him in public, and treating him with all possible generosity. If he should praise you as perhaps he may, please give him a hearing.   35
It will be his last appearance among you, so treat him with respect, for your
own sake. After all, he has a claim: he has expounded your poems publicly
here – and gratis, too. Thank him, but give him nothing; above all, nothing
that could be of use to me. I expressed my desires to you in a previous letter:
if you have carried them out, I beg you to send me the results for it is a matter   40
of no small moment; but if you have not yet done so, I shall relieve you of
some of the drudgery. At all events send me my *Elegantiae*, and be sure to
send also the third book of Valla if the copying is finished; if not, I should
prefer you to take up a different task. Keep me informed, too, about all your
own work. I will now tell you why I am so anxious for this information.   45
    In company with two young gentlemen, I am staying at the house of
a very civilized English nobleman, on terms that could not be more splendid
or honourable at the bishop's palace, even if I were a bishop myself. This
nobleman has the utmost confidence in anything you write; so, if you make
sure that the courier continually brings something new, you will not only   50
please and help me a great deal but do yourself a service also. Above all,
write to him as a friend: praise him for concentrating his admiration on letters, despising all else; say that while few do so, they are a happy few
indeed. Give him an account of the pleasure that literature affords. Extol
the combination of scholarship and morality, putting in a word for me,   55
while kindly offering your own services. Believe me, Willem, it will do your
reputation good as well; for he is a most powerful figure in his own country,
and in him you will find a disseminator of your books throughout England.
I beg you most earnestly to consider this course seriously, if you love me
at all.   60
    I am vexed with you for writing such a short and careless letter. Alas
for me, have things come to such a pass that it seems to you too much to
lose a single night's sleep for my sake? Have pleasures driven all thought
of me from your mind? If so, I should like to share them. But see how ambition has set me back. I am still rolling the stone of Sisyphus; I have plans   65
afoot, but if they come to nothing I shall fly to you. Not that I am apprehensive about finding means to support myself decently, since I am competed

* * * * *

42 my *Elegantiae*] The paraphrase on Valla. Erasmus had evidently been
employing Hermans as well as Batt as a copyist (cf Ep 80:118ff).
47 nobleman] Possibly Mountjoy
65 Sisyphus] Cf *Adagia* II iv 40.

for and courted from all sides; but how I wish you could live with me, or
I with you. You have no notion how tortured I am by longing for you: for
you alone, that is; I have forgotten K and I and C, together with others whom   70
I shall not name, in case they complain to me. My Willem, alone, has stayed
deep-rooted in my inmost heart. I believe you are a sorcerer: for I'd rather
live with you than with the pope himself. Out of concern for my reputation
I am living rather strictly here. Goodbye to the title of theologian, to fame,
and to profitless dignity. I have had a foretaste of what real success consists   75
of – surely, a chat with a dear friend!

For three months now I have paid my respects neither to Fausto nor
to Gaguin. Still, you should write a brief but scholarly letter to Fausto, and
a rather longer one to Gaguin, in which you argue a few points in a friendly
manner, or, rather, give him something to argue about. And use flattering   80
terms in addressing your cousin the courier to make him especially careful
about delivering whatever comes from us, since he is a glutton for praise.
As for providing, I shall look after that: tell me if you want or need anything.
We always have an *écu* or so for you (notice how French we are!). Joking
apart, the business about the bishop of Utrecht has cooled off so far as I am   85
concerned. I understand he is miserly. Tell me all the news: how life goes
with you there, what my brother is doing, and Cornelis and Servatius and
the others. Write carefully and at great length, or rather have a letter ready
always just before the courier calls.

Bostius writes to say that he has had a letter from Cornelis, who asks   90
for your poems; I understand he said nothing of me. I suspect that Cornelis
is out of humour with me; he has never written to me personally, and I wonder what can be wrong. I am fond of him, at least so long as he is fond of
you; about myself I do not care. I have despatched fifteen copies of your
poems; write and tell me what you receive. Also I have sent a rather lengthy   95
letter, written partly before I fell ill and partly after I recovered. I have no
news of the bishop of Cambrai. Farewell.

Paris [1499]

* * * * *

77 Fausto] Andrelini (cf Ep 84 introduction).
78 Gaguin] Robert Gaguin (cf Ep 43 introduction).
84 an *écu* or so] *Ecu à la couronne* or *écu au soleil*. See the Glossary and
Appendix A on gold coinage.
85 bishop of Utrecht] Friedrich of Baden. Erasmus had apparently hoped for
some patronage from him.
87 brother] Pieter Gerard (cf Ep 3 introduction and probably Ep 78:18).
92 never] ie since Cornelis left Paris (cf Ep 78).

82 / To a man of Lübeck   Paris [December 1498]

ERASMUS TO A CERTAIN MAN OF LÜBECK

Greetings, honoured sir. Your son resides with me and is taught by me, the precise terms of the contract being those communicated to me by Heinrich Northoff, who has promised me on your behalf thirty-two *couronnes* and a scholar's gown. The boy had a serious illness lately, but got well again 5 through God's goodness and the help of physicians. He has been in my care for a good many months, during which I have furnished him with such things as he needed. In October, I took him into my household; he is looked after by me as my own son, rather than another's. He is exceptionally intelligent, and his character is docile and tolerable, considering his age. I shall 10 endeavour, so far as in me lies, to send him back to you worthy of me, his tutor, as well as of you, his father. I am surprised that his books have not yet been delivered to my care. That merchant in Antwerp has informed me in writing that he forwarded them by the agency of a certain Parisian merchant, whom he names, but the latter denies this categorically. I have 15 so far received no payment on his account. Augustin, who looked after him when I was away in my homeland because of ill-health, admits to receiving five or six florins from Heinrich. He gave your son board and tuition for three months, since at that period I thought I should presently leave for Italy, and I left that money for him in consideration of his assistance, mak- 20 ing up in addition the costs incurred when the boy lay sick at his house; further, I bore the cost of his clothing. Some kind of intermittent fever began to spread in this vicinity, so I moved to the most open and healthy part of the city. If this disease breaks out again, I may retire still further off, since nothing ought to take priority in our eyes over health and the preservation 25 of life. It is impossible to live well if we are not alive. In this connexion, I am anxious to learn your decision; are you willing for the boy to accompany me? According to Heinrich's account, I should have acted with your approval even had I taken him to Italy with me.

* * * * *

82:2 Your son] The servant-pupil mentioned in Ep 80:16. For the relation of his servant-pupils to Erasmus, which seems to have been rather like that of an apprentice to a master, see Bierlaire 18ff.

4 thirty-two *couronnes*] *Coronati*: see *écu à la couronne* in the Glossary and Appendix A on gold coins. That sum was worth £56 (*livres*) *tournois*, or £9 2s 8d. *gros* Flemish.

18 five or six florins] Possibly once more Burgundian-Habsburg florins of St Philip (cf Ep 76:28–9n): a sum worth £1 0 0d to £1 4s 0d *gros* Flemish; or Florentine or Rhenish florins. See the Glossary and Appendix A on gold coins.

20 Italy] Cf Ep 75:15n.

This ends my complete account of our situation. It now remains for you to inform me fully about your wishes. But I ask you not to send either money or a letter except by a thoroughly reliable messenger, and not to send them to Paris but to that same merchant of Antwerp, in order that they may not fall into the wrong hands if I leave here. I further request you to give me full information concerning the profession you have chosen for your son and the particular course of study you wish him to follow, for in every undertaking an aim ought to be set in advance and that aim should be the point to which all efforts tend, just as troops rally to the colours. Though boys ought indeed to be trained in every kind of literature, it still matters what object they have in mind in their studies, in order that, since it is impossible to learn everything thoroughly, we may at least learn what best suits our needs.

I have written to you to the above effect at greater length than I should; and have also done so in Latin, not because I despise your native tongue and mine but because it would not have been easy for me to write this letter in it, nor would it have been easy for you to understand what I wrote. I pray that you and your excellent lady, and your entire household, are well. Permit me to assure you, and through you the other members of your family, that I shall not lack devotion, concern, or diligence in the education of your son.

Paris [1497]

83 / To Willem Hermans   Paris, 14 December [1498]

ERASMUS TO HIS FRIEND WILLEM OF GOUDA

Of course, the one thing that was lacking to make my unhappiness complete was an abusive letter like that from you, as if I had not sufficient grounds for anguish already. It would have been more worthy of our long-standing mutual affection, and better adapted to my unfortunate situation, had you, my dear Willem, offered me condolences instead of scolding me. Why do you persecute, and even insult, a good friend who has never wavered in loyalty to you and is now in deep distress? In my present situation I could not have borne even encouraging words with equanimity; yet you gratuitously increase the bitterness of my wretched state by actual abuse. When I receive such treatment at the hands of a friend who is closely linked to me not only by very old acquaintance but also by an association in studies, which I regard as the strongest tie of all, what sort of treatment are you telling me to expect from my enemies? I am more inclined to bewail my own misfortunes than to answer your arguments.

At the same time will you please consider how far I deserve your reproaches? Somebody or other has reported to you that I was annoyed with

you when I left. In the first place, why are you so ready to believe informers
of this sort? Next, even should I indeed be annoyed (to use the invidious
expression you yourself employ), why do you not rather inquire into the   20
reason for my annoyance? Quite often in my letters, and lately when we
met, I have complained that you were lying idle in literature, producing
nothing worthy of your talents, and I urged you to take as much thought
as possible for your undying reputation and to produce the kind of work
that the world expected of you, putting your own fame before everything   25
and leaving trivial pleasures to the dull mass of mankind. If my actions in
this case are the product of self-interest, of personal hostility, and of arrogance, I offer no arguments against the justice of your accusation, but if they
proceed rather from love and a burning desire for your reputation entertained by one who thinks even better of you than you do yourself, why are   30
you attacking such a friend as this in the midst of his miseries, and with
harsh language too? If I was angry with you at all, it was simply because
you placed a lower value upon your own ability than I did. 'But,' say you,
'I find your hectoring methods distasteful.' Does a friend then not deserve
pardon for excess of love? Do you not see that this obstinate insistence on   35
my part emanates from a kind of boundless ambition to see you famous?
And now you, who have often put up with my disdain, find it impossible
to endure with equanimity my devotion to your interests!

What, my dear Willem, did you mean when you wrote 'You yourself
are aware, nor am I unaware, what manner of life you live there'? Alas for   40
myself: I greatly fear you may suppose that I am wasting my time here in
frivolity, feasting, and love-affairs. But please picture to yourself an Erasmus who is not frivolous but sunk in unhappiness, and that he whom you
once used to call 'precipitate' is now indeed broken and lifeless. Be careful
not to use either my past character or your own happiness as a standard   45
to judge me now. As for what I said to you in my chatter at Gouda, conversing with an unusual freedom befitting our intimacy: you ought to have
ascribed such unguarded talk either to the wine which, as you know, we
were often obliged at that time to drink heavily, or to that concern for the
full strengthening of my health which had caused me deliberately to relax   50
somewhat the rigour of my former mode of life. But my spirit lacks the wish
to be foolish, even had I the chance; and again my situation quite excludes
the opportunity for it, no matter how inclined to it I might be. Perhaps this
too will make you angry. 'What is wrong with you?' you will ask. 'Are you
destitute? Do you not possess complete freedom to do as you wish?' But I   55
could hardly enumerate all my troubles face to face, much less give an
adequate account of them in a letter so brief as this; I should judge that the
hardships of Ulysses himself could not stand comparison with mine. On

me, certainly, experience has imposed too much familiarity with this kind
of freedom – and on you, just as certainly, too little.   60

But why provoke a very good friend with complaints like these? You
say you have to endure the envy aroused by my reputation; but what does
this amount to? I myself am in a position to do some good to your reputation
here; why should you not also take up the cudgels for me, even at the cost
of unpopularity? Everyone knows that Willem would be favourable to Eras-   65
mus, even in the most unfavourable cause; and though you may fail to do
this, still everyone will expect it of you. Of course, your devotion to me is
bound to be very welcome; but if Fate should prevent me, you at least must
shed all the lustre you can, first upon our country and next upon yourself,
by literary work. Let me assure you of this, dear Willem: there is nothing   70
you cannot achieve, provided that you have the heart for it. But please forgive the affection that makes me once again set about encouraging you.

You ought not to entertain any opinion about Cornelis, save one that
is worthy of a true friend, for his remarks about you were always in the most
loving vein or, if he took advantage of our close intimacy to make any com-   75
plaint about you to me, he did so with very great restraint and in the manner
of one who sincerely loved you. A report was indeed brought to me that
while I was absent, in your part of the world, he was less than honest in
his dealings with the Englishmen; while this might easily be believed of
anyone else (for integrity is rare among human beings, and their hearts are   80
unreliable), in his case I am not disposed either to believe or suspect it.
Besides, I think it better to entertain delusions in such matters as these than
to investigate, with distasteful thoroughness, what had better remain hidden. I implore you upon your honour not to reveal, even by a gesture, what,
relying on your past ability to keep a secret, I told you about X, for it would   85
do you no good, while you would furnish him with a perfectly adequate
reason for being angry with me. I have written to Servatius about Hendrik;
I cannot get over my astonishment at his character, but what is one to do?
These are the customs of the age, and for this reason we simply have to agree

* * * * *

83:79 Englishmen] Perhaps Mountjoy and his two young friends (cf Ep
81:46ff).
85 X] Cf Ep 81:8n.
87 Hendrik] Perhaps the person alluded to in Epp 95:9–10, Allen Epp 190:11
and 296:229.

with the celebrated utterance of Chilon: 'Love as though some day you were   90
sure to hate; hate as though some day you were sure to love.'

You tell me there is much talk of me there, and that it is anything but
pleasant to hear. Well, what I can do, dear Willem, is to keep myself blameless, as I am doing; what I cannot control are the things men say about
me. I am much more concerned about what you think of me, for, upon my   95
soul, I value your opinion above all others. Now, what was the meaning
of the letter in which you appear to censure my way of living? Do you really
wish to learn (for it is proper that you should know every detail of my
affairs) how your Erasmus conducts his life in this place? He is alive, or
rather I think he may be; but alive on the most wretched terms, exhausted   100
by grief of every kind: endlessly intrigued against, cheated of friends' support, and tempest-tost upon waves of disaster. Nevertheless he lives in perfect blamelessness. I know that I shall hardly be able to convince you of the
truth of all this. You still think of me as the Erasmus of old: of my personal
freedom, and of such lustre as my reputation retains; but if I had a chance   105
to speak with you in person it would be the simplest thing on earth to persuade you of its truth. Therefore, if you wish to form a true picture of your
friend, you must imagine him, not indulging in frivolity or feasting or love-
affairs, but distraught with grief: tearful and loathing himself; with neither
a mind to live nor a chance to die; in short, utterly wretched, not through   110
his own fault it is true but through Fate's cruelty: still (for what difference
does that make?) utterly wretched, and yet full of love, devotion, and warm
enthusiasm for you. So may Heaven vouchsafe that these sorrows of mine
be exchanged for a happier fate or end in early death; never has my own
honour been more important, my own reputation more cherished, or my   115
own life dearer to me than yours.

It causes me no surprise if others dislike me; for who does not recoil,
for the best of reasons, from so miserable a wretch? But why should I fear
that my misfortune had caused your love for me to alter? For I have always
depended on your loyalty alone, and cherished you, and thought I was   120
loved by you, not in any commonplace fashion but as men loved in ancient
days. If I am to understand that I am disliked even by such a one, and that
for my misery's sake, what reason have I to wish to live? Oh, my dear Willem, who were long ago my comfort, would that you might so remain: my
anguish well-nigh makes me cry aloud, besides the tears I shed. Had I dam-   125
aged our friendship by some heinous and wicked crime, still out of conside-

* * * * *

90 Chilon] Usually ascribed to Bias, another of the Seven Sages (as in *Adagia*
II i 72), but Chilon is given by Aulus Gellius 1.3.30.

ration for your friend's great misfortune you ought to have greeted him with compassionate tears instead of anger, no matter how righteous; instead of which you are capable of attacking with abuse, of hounding with your reproaches, one whom no disaster or change of circumstance has ever been 130 able to separate from love of you: as if there were not enough enemies to fall upon me with tooth and claw to ruin me, and to wish for my destruction by fire and sword! What was there at Steyn so dear to me that I have not forgotten it among my troubles? You yourself have sometimes seen me act- ing as a young man does and have often laughed at me. You know the heart 135 I mean. For what have I ever loved so tenderly? Now it is remarkable how cold I am. All those common loves proved transient; you and you alone have remained fixed in my heart, so firmly fixed that my affection increased, instead of dying, when the regular converse between us was interrupted. Will you, then, have it in you to spurn in his most wretched state a friend 140 so doggedly attached to you, whom you could not possibly dislike were he prosperous? Yes, I know this is the usual way of mankind; but I am dis- tressed indeed if education proves powerless to rescue you from the habits of the vulgar. What, if so, was your purpose in calling me your Pylades, your Theseus? You ought, however, to have reversed the appellation, and rather 145 called me Orestes or Pirithous.

But enough, finally, of lamentations. I have one entreaty and request to make of you, dearest Willem (since 'most agreeable Willem' I cannot say), for the sake of our old mutual good will and also of my unhappy situation: if you are unable to refrain from disliking me and incapable of pitying me, 150 at least you should refrain from aggravating my wound's cruel pain with insulting words, and accord to a friend, who has in no wise deserved it, at least the consideration you might have owed to a beaten foe. Look after your own health all the more carefully in proportion as mine is beyond hope. Please be sure to give my regards to your father, a man of great kind- 155 ness to whom I owe much, and also to your comrade, Master Jacob. Your friend Jasper has placed me deeply in his debt, and I am ashamed to have been so remiss in greeting such a good friend. Farewell, sweetest Willem.

Paris, 14 December [1497]

* * * * *

132 tooth and claw] Literally 'hand and foot'; cf *Adagia* I iv 15.

144–5 Pylades ... Theseus] Classic examples of friendship who gave aid to their unfortunate friends Orestes and Pirithous respectively

156 Jacob] Allen suggests that this may refer to Jacob Mauritszoon, a dis- tinguished citizen of Gouda (cf Ep 176 introduction).

157 Jasper] This person has not been identified.

84 / From Fausto Andrelini to Willem Hermans   [Paris, December 1498]

Allen notes that this letter may have been written at Erasmus' request to show his friends at Steyn that he was well thought of in Paris.

Publio Fausto Andrelini of Forlì (1462-1518) came to Paris in 1488 and the following year began to lecture at the university. In 1496 he was made royal poet by Charles VIII. He was one of the more worldly members of Gaguin's little circle of humanists with whom Erasmus established friendly relations on his first arrival in Paris.

FAUSTO, POET ROYAL, TO HIS FRIEND WILLEM

As I inwardly reflect, dear Willem, on the eminence of our friend Erasmus not only in learning but in life, a life transparently free from every vice, I cannot surely, cannot, I say, refrain from rejoicing that your community possesses one to whom not only you yourselves but this university of Paris   5
also owe love, honour, respect, and admiration. For what is better or finer or indeed more divine than to discover a man resplendent in dazzling gifts of literary skill and moral character alike; and this in our own time, which is so slothful, corrupt, and detestable that it rather reflects the pleasures of Sardanapalus than the virtues, or character, of Socrates? And I would not   10
have you ascribe this opinion to fawning adulation on my part, since I have ever been averse to fulsome and hypocritical flattery. Nor would I write so, either to yourself or to another, if it were not that Erasmus is a man so great that, to speak with warmth, and of that not a little, not only your Order but your very country is unworthy of him. Farewell.   15

85 / To Nicasius, chaplain of Cambrai   Paris, 14 December [1498?]

Erasmus had evidently met Nicasius, who cannot be otherwise identified, during his trip to the Netherlands in the summer of 1498, possibly in Brussels where he stopped to visit the bishop of Cambrai (cf Ep 76 introduction).

ERASMUS TO NICASIUS, CHAPLAIN OF CAMBRAI

Though you were very dear to me before for literature's sake, my scholarly friend, still it would not be easy to express how enormously the affection I have for you was heightened by our sojourn together. In me you had a

* * * * *

84:10 Sardanapalus] King of Assyria, a by-word for effeminacy; cf *Adagia* III vii 27.

devoted admirer before; now a closer friend by far. However, it is an act   5
of doubtful merit to repay a kindness with mere words. If you should desire
to test my attitude towards you, pray set me some task in my turn. You could
not cast on me any burden so heavy or vexatious that it will not seem very
light, and even pleasant to bear, for your sake.

I conscientiously delivered your letter, and conveyed your greetings   10
to Thomas of Cambrai. See that you keep your promise to write to me as
often as possible. Please be sure to greet my old teacher Michael Pavius,
and especially that host of mine, a man who deserves, I swear, to be a
bishop. His name I have forgotten, but the kind and courteous way in
which he treated me when I was with you is something I have never forgot-   15
ten, and never shall; give him my thanks in your usual attentive way. My
greetings to you and to all your circle.

Paris, 14 December [1499]

86 / To a friend   [Paris? 1498?]

Allen ventures the conjecture that this letter may have been addressed to
Robert Fisher, who was then in Italy (cf Ep 62 introduction).

ERASMUS TO A CERTAIN PERSON

Hearing that our mutual friend X was about to travel in your direction, I
was loath to let him come empty-handed, especially after his persistent
requests to me for a recommendation to you. Accordingly, I beg you to treat
him as befits our old acquaintance. I am not unaware, and he himself   5
knows, how influential you are and how much you wish me well. Grant,
then, that he may not be disappointed in his hopes, nor I in my opinion
of you. Thus you will make in X a new friend and at the same time bind
me more closely to you. Farewell.

* * * * *

85:11 Thomas of Cambrai] Probably Thomas Warnet, a pupil of Jan Standonck,
who was in Paris at this time. Having spoken against the divorce which Louis
XII was seeking in order to marry his predecessor's widow, Anne of Brittany,
he was forced to leave before the arrival of the king on 1 May 1499.

12 Michael Pavius] Michael Pavius had been rector of the university of Paris.
He had connections with Cambrai, of which he became dean in 1506. As there
is no other mention of him in the correspondence, it is uncertain when or
where he may have taught Erasmus.

87 / To Johannes Falco   Tournehem, 3 February [1499]

Erasmus was visiting Tournehem to pay court to his prospective patroness
Anna van Borssele, vrouwe van Veere (cf Ep 80). Little is known about
Johannes Falco, except that he was a friend of Batt's and at that time resident
in Paris (cf Epp 80: 139 and 119: 273). His family apparently lived in Antwerp.
Cf *infra* line 28.

ERASMUS OF ROTTERDAM TO HIS FRIEND JOHANNES FALCO:
WRITTEN IN JEST

Expect no greeting from me. I curse you as often as I think of your insulting
remarks, and recall to mind those grim eyes and that mouth made for
unmitigated abuse. Therefore I clearly cannot love you; but I shall dislike 5
you less if you can manage to prefer good literature to your miserable
profits. Thus far my misfortunes have continued to dog me, for our journey
was quite extraordinarily rough and uncomfortable. The rest I owe to the
good fortune of my friend Batt, for if I should give you an account of my
Lady's kindness, goodness, courtesy, amiability, and modesty, before I had 10
got through more than a fraction of my discourse I would seem the greatest
liar alive to anyone who had not himself known her. How unlucky you are
to have made difficulties about following me! You would have been the
happiest of men. But I am glad you have suffered for your arrogance. In
future, be wise enough to avoid poets' company and seek that of butchers. 15
I shall be with you presently, if Heaven helps me. Keep the things of mine
that you have, and gather together all you can, to avoid delay when I come.

I shall end this letter after giving you a little advice. Wisdom is useless
if one fails to apply it to oneself. Admire and praise literature, but pursue
lucre. Avoid feeling dissatisfaction with yourself; this throws a cloud over 20
your handsome image. Above all, look after your physical well-being.
Always put your personal advantage first; cultivate friendships for your
own interest. Spare little time for learning. Put your heart into love-affairs
and apply yourself only moderately to study. Be generous with words but
tight with money. I should have given you further advice, but I must say 25
farewell to my Lady in courtly fashion and tomorrow I shall take wing for
Holland. I am leaving the better of my two coats behind; do you know why?

* * * * *

87:18 Wisdom is useless] Cf *Adagia* I vi 20.
21 physical well-being] Literally 'have a care for your complexion'; cf *Adagia*
II iv 75

For fear your sisters may tear it up, since I have to go by way of Antwerp.
Now do you think I have no wit, and you yourself a monopoly of cleverness?
I won't look for a letter from you, since I may well arrive there first myself.   30
Live for yourself; and be well for yourself; and love, as you do, yourself
alone.

Tournehem castle, 3 February [1497]

88 / To William Blount, Lord Mountjoy   Tournehem, 4 February [1499]

Erasmus had been tutor to Lord Mountjoy before leaving Paris (cf Ep 79
introduction), but apparently not for long (cf line 62f).

ERASMUS OF ROTTERDAM TO THE ENGLISH COUNT, WILLIAM MOUNTJOY
We have arrived at last, and safely, too, though the gods above and below,
it seems, conspired against us. What a dreadful journey! From now on, I
shall feel superior to heroes such as Hercules or Ulysses. Juno was against
us: she always dislikes poets. She stirred Aeolus up once again and, not   5
content with unleashing the winds' rage at us, used every weapon in her
armoury: biting cold, snow, hail, rain, showers, mist, in fact every mean
trick, sometimes one at a time and sometimes all together. The first evening,
after a prolonged period of rain, a sudden keen frost made the road
extremely hard going; on top of this came a heavy snowfall, followed by   10
hail, and then again rain, which as soon as it touched the ground, or a tree,
turned immediately into ice. Everywhere you would have seen the ground
covered with a layer of ice; and its surface was not even flat, but had horribly
sharp little ridges protruding all over it. You would also have seen the trees
so heavily laden with ice that some of them were bent over, with their tops   15
touching the very ground, while others had branches ripped off or their
trunks split in two, and others again lay completely uprooted. The old countrymen swore to us that they had never seen such a sight in their lives
before. The horses meanwhile had sometimes to walk through deep drifts
of snow or through thickets coated with ice; sometimes in ruts which   20
were doubly difficult going, because first they set hard with frost and then
ice made their edges sharp; and sometimes upon a surface crust which had
covered the top layer of snow and was too soft to bear the horses' weight,
yet hard enough to injure their hooves.

* * * * *

28 Antwerp] Cf Ep 91:21.
4 Juno] A reference to Juno's visit to Aeolus, god of the winds, in Virgil *Aeneid*
1.50ff

How do you think your Erasmus responded to all this? He sat, a ter- 25
rified rider, on a terrified horse. When my mount's ears pricked up, my
spirit fell; and as often as he fell down on his knees, my heart jumped up
into my mouth. I was becoming alarmed at the precedent set by the poets'
Bellerophon, and cursing my foolhardiness in entrusting my life and my
letters at one and the same time to a dumb creature. But I will tell you some- 30
thing you would suppose I had borrowed from Lucian's *Vera historia*, if I
did not have Batt to witness that it really happened to me. When we were
almost within sight of the castle, we found the entire countryside covered
with a layer of ice which, as I have explained, had fallen on top of the snow.
The wind blew so hard that more than one person was blown down and 35
died that day. Since it blew from behind us, I slid down the slopes of the
hills, sailing on the surface of the ice, and from time to time steering with
my staff, using it as a rudder, a new kind of navigation. In our entire journey
we scarcely met a soul or were overtaken by anyone, so wild, indeed monstrous, was the weather. It was only on the fourth day that at last we had 40
a glimpse of the sun. All these difficulties brought us only one advantage:
we stood in less fear of attack by robbers; yet fear it we did, as rich men
should!

So much, my noble young friend, for the story of my journey. Great
as were its hardships, the sequel proved extremely propitious. We made 45
our way, alive, to Anna, princess of Veere. I need not describe to you how
gentle, kind, and generous she is; for I know that men suspect the elaborate
speeches made by rhetoricians, especially men who themselves know
something of the technique. All the same, you must not suppose me to be
employing rhetorical exaggeration, but on the contrary to be saying that 50
this time the truth outdoes our art. The world has never produced a human
being better endowed with modesty, good sense, good manners, and kindness. To put it in one word, her generosity has exceeded my deserts as far
as that old man's spite stood in inverse proportion to them. Without any
prompting from devotion on my part, she has loaded me with favours as 55
great as the insults he heaped upon me when I had done signal services to
him. And what boast shall I make about my friend Batt, the most straightforward and affectionate soul that ever lived? Only now am I beginning to

* * * * *

29 Bellerophon] The legendary rider of the winged horse Pegasus

31 *Vera historia*] 'True History': a series of 'tall tales.' Lucian wrote in the second century AD.

54 old man] The guardian of Thomas Grey and Robert Fisher (cf Ep 58
introduction).

loathe the ingratitude of those others: to think that I enslaved myself to such monsters for so long! Alas that I came to know you so late, only to be torn 60
from you by fate before we knew each other well!

As I write this, I am on the point of leaving for my native country; immediately thereafter I shall pay you a visit, returning to my beloved Paris, perhaps even arriving before the present letter. Beyond this, I am not in a position to set down anything definite about living with you; however, this 65
can be discussed on the spot. At any rate be assured that nobody on earth has a more sincere love for you than your Erasmus. My friend Batt, who shares all my loves and aversions, feels a like affection for you. Every good wish for your health, dear William.

Tournehem castle, 4 February [1497]   70

89 / To Richard Whitford   [Tournehem, 4 February 1499]

Richard Whitford (c 1470-1542) was a Fellow of Queens' College, Cambridge, who accompanied Mountjoy to Paris and probably returned with him. Erasmus remained on friendly terms with him and in 1506 dedicated a declamation to him (cf Ep 191). Whitford was at that time chaplain to Richard Foxe, bishop of Winchester. Shortly after he entered the monastery of Syon, near Isleworth.

ERASMUS OF ROTTERDAM TO MASTER RICHARD WHITFORD, CHAPLAIN TO HIS LORDSHIP, WILLIAM MOUNTJOY

I was all agog to write you a very long letter, my dear Richard, had I not been too busy, and determined to see you as soon as possible. I shall make 5
no excuses for not having written before; this is a case I'd prefer to plead in person, hoping that you will acquit me. Batt and I have had many long talks about the frank and friendly character of both you and the count. I am happy about what you propose, but sorry that I did not know about it sooner. After I have paid a visit to my native land, I shall rush over to see 10
you at once; and then we shall have a mouthful of follies, as the saying goes. Meanwhile look after your health, and enjoy the philosophy you are so fond of. Please give my salutation to the prior of Ste Geneviève, your fellow countryman with whom I dined so often, and Canon William, and moreover convey my greetings individually to the rest of my acquaintance.

* * * * *

65 living] If Mountjoy was the English nobleman mentioned in Ep 81:46ff, Erasmus had been living with him for a time before his departure from Paris.
89:8 the count] Mountjoy
14 Canon William] This person has not been identified.

90 / To Jacob Batt   [Steyn? February] 1499?

After leaving Tournehem, Erasmus paid a brief visit to his old friends at Steyn
(cf Ep 92). This letter was probably written from there to introduce one of the
monks to Batt. This erudite person was already known to the Lady of Veere.

ERASMUS TO BATT

My dear Batt, if you and yours are well there is good reason for rejoicing,
and I hope it is so. Though I think you are sure of our friendship, still I
would urge you to feel absolutely certain that none has a greater affection
or devotion for you than I. Now, if you are fond of me or admire good litera-   5
ture, please receive the bearer of this note in your usual kindly and gracious
manner; there is nobody I like more, or think more well read. And, a very
rare thing nowadays, he combines scholarly excellence with modesty, both
in the highest degree. He is a great favourite of the Lady of Veere, who takes
pleasure alike in his talents and his diffidence. If, therefore, you show your   10
esteem for me in this case, you will do credit to your own kindness and give
pleasure to all of us.

There is nothing to report about my circumstances. As usual, there
were hostile noises from certain carping critics who are not unknown to
you, but I hope that we shall presently get clear of these rocky shores. I wish   15
you and all your family the best of health.

1499

91 / To Jacob Batt   Antwerp, 12 February 1499

Erasmus was evidently making a brief stop in Antwerp on his way back to
Paris following his visit to Steyn.

ERASMUS TO JACOB BATT

Greetings to Batt, my delight and my refuge. If the Lady of Veere, formerly
your patroness, and, now shared with me, is well, and all goes well with
her, it is as I both wish and trust. I could not set down in writing, even if
I dared, and would not dare to if I could, how anxious I am to learn whether   5
she has already left there, and whether she has taken her dear children with
her. Fortunate will you be – Heaven's darling, indeed – if you can get clear
away from that rocky shore and can, without incurring envy, enjoy that

* * * * *

90:14 carping critics] Literally, 'Zoiluses.' The Alexandrian grammarian,
Zoilus, the 'flogger of Homer' (Homeromastix), was proverbial for disparaging criticism; cf *Adagia* II v 8.
91:8 rocky shore] Cf *Adagia* III i 47.

good luck which to me at any rate seems so remarkable. What makes me
think that this will happen is the goodness of the Lady, which I have no   10
doubt will earn Heaven's favour and goodwill. In her case I have the same
experience as I often have with you; my love and admiration increase mar-
kedly with absence. She is amazingly open-hearted and agreeable, for all
her rank, and so gentle, despite the dreadful treatment she has received;
so cheerful amidst deep troubles, so calm in spirit, so blameless in her life,   15
so interested in men of letters, and so kind to everyone. This is why I have
the strongest belief that you are the luckiest of men if you have her support
for as long as you can, and it will surely be forthcoming if you show your
appreciation of her favourable attitude to you by giving her your grateful
service, as you are doing.   20

We reached Antwerp safely. Augustin has already gone on towards
Paris with his party. He promised to wait for me there for a few days; consequently I think I ought to hurry, in order not to miss the advantage of having so reliable an escort. I have no requests to give you; for one thing, I know
how attentive you are to my interests, and for another, my most generous   25
Lady is so very indulgent to me that I am really quite embarrassed when
I reflect how she has loaded me with benefits and yet I have never done her
any good service. But I shall make it my task to consider how I can make
it clear that her kindness has not been completely wasted. Heaven permit-
ting, I shall fly back to you as quickly as possible. I pray that I may find you   30
all safe and well, especially the Lady, upon whom your hopes and well-
being, as well as mine, completely depend.

Do not be surprised at the hurried look of my writing, for I wrote this
on board ship, about to sail, in the midst of a great hubbub.

Greetings to the young master, a likeable youth, and to his sister, who   35

* * * * *

91:21 Augustin] Vincent (cf Ep 131 introduction). In December Erasmus had
written of Augustin's intention to visit Steyn in the near future (cf Ep 81:32ff).
He had evidently concluded his visit and was now on his way back to Paris,
having left Erasmus in Antwerp, but with a promise to wait for him at some
intermediate point so as to escort him the rest of the way. This, at least, seems
to be the only reasonable explanation of the arrangement between them,
although it does not accord with the text, 'Augustinus cum suo comitatu iam
Parisios praecessit; pollicitus est sese aliquot dies illic me opperiri,' which,
lacking any certain alternative, we have translated literally. Clearly either
'Parisios' or 'illic' must be wrong. Nichols (1 189) substitutes Brussels for Paris
as being a convenient meeting place not too far on the way, but this seems
a too arbitrary alteration of the text. Allen suggests as a more probable alternative that Erasmus may have intended to add the name of some town on the
way, but, writing hastily, forgot that he had not done so when he wrote that
Augustin would wait for him there ('illic').

Adolph of Burgundy
Michiel Yssewyn of Mechelen, c 1517
Stichting De Schotse Huizen, Veere

is so like her brother and her mother; my special greetings also to the rest
of your household.

Antwerp, 12 February 1498

92 / From Willem Hermans to Servatius Rogerus [Steyn? February 1499]

This is a reply to a letter from Servatius (cf Ep 4 introduction), who was apparently absent from Steyn at some place where he heard news of Erasmus' success.

WILLEM TO SERVATIUS ROGERUS

The letter I received from you yesterday brought me enormous pleasure.
I am overjoyed, and exultant, that at last my friend Erasmus is enjoying the
success his character and his scholarship deserve; he sought it through
nearly all the world and now, belatedly, has found it. He has been here to   5
visit us perhaps (though Heaven forbid) for the last time; since he means
to go to Bologna after Easter (what a long and difficult journey!) and is now
making financial arrangements for it. If all goes well, he will return in
triumph with his degree; but if anything untoward should happen to him,
it will cause us everlasting grief; to me especially since, as you know, he   10
has always had the highest regard for me.

Our friend Jacob Batt intends to come to Holland, but I have no idea
what will really happen. But of course you are familiar with his exaggerations; he will as usual play the Braggart Soldier's part to perfection. Yet
it is amazing how much Erasmus praises his faithful friendship and frank,   15
dependable character. Come to see me yourself as soon as ever you can, not
only for the reasons you are aware of, but, if other excuses fail, just for my
own sake. Farewell, most constant of friends. In the meantime, work hard
at the most honourable task of all, the study of literature. It suits you and
your life of leisure, and what else can you do that is praiseworthy?   20

93 / To Adolph of Burgundy, heer van Veere   Paris [March?] 1499

This letter, entitled 'Epistola exhortatoria ad capessendam virtutem ad
generosissimum puerum Adolphum, principem Veriensem,' was first pub-

* * * * *

92:7 Bologna] Cf Ep 75:15n.

12 Batt] Hermans' comment on Batt here does not accord with anything suggested in Erasmus' letters to or about him. Perhaps Hermans felt some
jealousy.

14 the Braggart Soldier's part] Thraso, whose name is used here ('aget
Thrasonem'), is a character in the *Eunuchus* of Terence.

lished at the beginning of Erasmus' *Lucubratiunculae* (Antwerp: Th. Martens, 15 February 1503; NK 835). In later editions (cf Ep 164 introduction) it was headed: 'Exhortatio ad virtutem' or 'Oratio de virtute amplectenda.' Although it is in the form of a letter, Erasmus never included it in any collection of his correspondence. Only excerpts referring directly to Adolph are included here.

Adolph of Burgundy, heer van Veere (1490?-7 December 1540), was at this time about ten years old and was living in the castle of Tournehem with his widowed mother, Anna van Borssele, and his grandfather, Anthony of Burgundy, under the tutelage of Jacob Batt (cf Epp 35 and 80 introductions). His father, Philip of Burgundy, had held high office at the Burgundian court. This fact later assured Adolph a favourable reception there and opened the way to a distinguished career as admiral of Flanders and a member of the council of Charles v. In 1513 he married Anna, daughter of Jan van Bergen, the bishop of Cambrai's brother (cf Ep 42:21n).

ERASMUS, A CANON OF THE AUGUSTINIAN ORDER, TO ADOLPH, PRINCE OF VEERE

When I look at the matter closely, dearest Adolph, I do not invariably find that the ancients' habit of praising captains and kings in set speeches, and in their very presence, arose from a morbid and grovelling desire to flatter. Rather I believe that intelligent men, who well understood the nature of the   5
universe and human nature too, could scarely hope that the lion's proud spirit which lurks in every royal breast, or a king's impatient ear, would ever tolerate either the authority of a mentor or the censure of a critic. So, out of regard for the nation's well-being, they altered course, and reached the same goal by a less obvious route. In the guise of a panegyric they presented   10
the prince with a kind of model of the perfect ruler, depicted in a painting as it were, in order that he might measure himself upon the pattern thus offered and privately acknowledge how far he fell below the standard of the prince they lauded. Thus he might discover, without embarrassment or offence, any fault he must reform, and what virtues he ought to display.   15
So one passage would serve two diverse ends, reminding good rulers of what they were doing, bad rulers of what they ought to do ...

But you, my dear Adolph, have been so lavishly endowed with every kind of aid to excellence that Heaven can give that, unless you exhibit all the virtues in the highest degree, it does not look as though you are likely   20
to fulfil either the destiny God sent you or the hopes of those who love you. For, first of all, need I say that you are Fortune's darling in a supreme and exceptional sense? Hardly were you born than she set you, with her own

* * * * *

93:3 praising ... in set speeches] For a defence of the formal panegyric, see Ep 180.

hands, as it were, in the most exalted place. She rather bore you for, than promoted you to, the purple; indeed even before your birth she made you a prosperous prince, bestowing upon you the gift of a lineage distinguished on both sides by famous ancestors; derived on your father's side from Philip, duke of Burgundy, a hero worthy even to be compared with any of the ancients, and on your mother's from the family of Bourbon, that is to say of the kings of France; to make no mention of your ample fortune and glittering power; or the alliances with powerful noblemen contracted by the marriages of your two sisters; or the blessing I could mention, of a mother as devoted as yours, who has by her unbelievable concern for you virtually borne you a second time, and thinks herself no mother if she has not made you perfect in goodness. And I might add that now in your boyish years there are many men high at court, including the illustrious Prince Philip himself, who, in unbounded hopes of your natural promise, vie with each other in devoting themselves to you with auspicious goodwill ...

Even today, in your extreme youth, you exhibit, as it were, the pattern of a doubly distinguished line: that is to say, on one side your father's spirit, prominent in the arts of peace and war alike, and on the other your mother's virtuous character, proof, as Dame Fortune marvels to perceive, even against Fortune herself. And, while your father was borne by feats of arms and 'his fiery manhood, to the skies above,' your mother on her part has joined to her womanly sex a man's strong mind: indeed a rare phenomenon; and has united to the most refined adornments of life, which her destiny, rather than her tastes, required, a wondrous measure of self-restraint; to proud lineage and highest rank, a modesty and kindness that are almost more than a commoner's; in short, she has united the Christian and the courtly life. Thus you already recall both your parents, that most invincible prince, your father, and that supremely modest and dedicated lady, your mother, in a kind of double promise, inasmuch as you are fired with zeal for soldierly exercises and still do not shun the leisured life of learning and the Muses ...

And the hopes we repose in you are mightily strengthened by the fact that, besides your natural goodness of disposition, you have at your command a distinguished tutor in each of these two fields of accomplishment: in military science, your grandfather, who possesses every quality needed by a great general, while in philosophy and, so to speak, the celebrated

* * * * *

28 Philip] Philip the Good

29 Bourbon] Anna van Borssele was a daughter of Charlotte of Bourbon, daughter of Duke Louis I.

36 Prince Philip] Cf Ep 76:38n.

44 'his fiery ... above'] Virgil Aeneid 6.130

Muses' love of Plato, you have Jacob Batt, a man who is Heaven only knows   60
how distinguished for learning, as well as for perfect integrity of life and
outstanding power of expression ...

Just as the famous Phoenix, whom Homer mentions, was given to
Achilles in early boyhood, almost in infancy,

all this to teach: 65

Words to indite, and manly deeds to do;

so also did Batt assume the charge of your infant years, when you were
scarcely yet weaned. He fairly shared with your nurses the task of nourish-
ing you; for while they attended to your bodily needs he moulded your
mind, wherein your mother's purpose was evident: that at the tenderest   70
age, almost with your very milk you might imbibe the great teachings of
the sages; next, that she might pour the balm of philosophy into the new
vessel of your mind, so that it should give forth the fragrance thereof for
the rest of your life; and that she might protect your childish tongue from
the corruption of vulgar discords, by steeping it in the unalloyed nectar of   75
the Muses; and lastly that she might guide, with friendly counsels, that
heart of yours, unformed as it yet was and apt to follow habits good or
evil ...

Now if such an education as this, no matter how brilliant it may be,
is conferred upon a person of humble situation it is to some extent dar-   80
kened, or beclouded, as it were, by the obscurity of his origins. In your station, however, an education of less merit will still achieve brilliance; learning adorns rank, while rank in turn adorns learning. Thus literature itself
appears to me to exult with joy; and I think I can see those sisters upon Helicon congratulate themselves and vie with one another in embracing you,   85
their sweetest nursling, clasping you to their bosoms with kisses, when
you steer your pen with fingers blest by fortune across the sea of paper;
when with lisping and as yet scarce controlled tongue you practise words
in the Greek as well as the Latin language; when with those pretty well-bred
lips and charming voice you even now both declaim in prose or display   90
the rhythms of verse ...

Accordingly, that you may steadfastly continue as you have well
begun, I shall not cease to intone Homer's words in your ear; but why not
rather in Greek, since you are already learning that?

* * * * *

63 Homer] *Iliad* 9.442,443

76 guide, with friendly counsels,] Cf Horace *Epistles* 2.1.128

93 Homer's words] The quotations from Homer may have been inserted later
before publication. It is doubtful if Adolph knew Greek. Erasmus himself was
working on Homer in the summer of 1500 (cf Epp 131:9 and 132.90f) having
begun the serious study of Greek after his return from England (cf Ep 124:72ff).

Thou too – since I behold thee great and fair –   95
Be valiant, friend, that in some distant time
    It may be said of thee that thou didst well.
And since, as I have remarked again and again, you have everything that
can help you to attain the perfection of glory, 'a following wind and sea,'
so act that the words of the same poet be also true: 'A breeze – a helmsman   100
too – her course made straight.' If you do this, it will come to pass, I am sure,
that you will bring great renown and strength to your house and country
and all your friends through learning; and in turn to learning itself by means
of your high position. Finally, I shall add something I would wish you to
lay very closely to heart: let it be one of your firmest convictions that nothing 105
so well becomes the noble and well born as religious devotion. This is no
idle advice, for I know by experience that royal courts contain those who
neither hesitate to believe, nor blush to say, that Christ's teaching is no matter that need concern noblemen but should be left to priests and monks.
Stop your ears to their deadly siren-song, and follow where your mother   110
and Batt are beckoning. And at this moment when you are beginning to
imbibe Christ along with your early lessons, I am sending you a few
prayers: prayers that I wrote at your mother's request and on Batt's urging,
but wrote for you, and so I have somewhat adapted their language to suit
your age. If you use these carefully, you will at one stroke improve your own   115
style and come to despise, not only as most ignorant but also as very super-
stitious, those 'soldiers' prayers' which men of the sort who frequent courts
generally find attractive. Farewell.
    Paris, in the year of Our Lord 1498

94 / To Adolph of Burgundy, heer van Veere?   Paris, 29 April [1499]

The 'Ludolphus' in the address is most probably a misprint for 'Adolphus.'
The present mentioned in line 3 may have been an acknowledgement of the
'Epistola exhortatoria' (Ep 93) sent to Adolph in March. The work mentioned
in line 4 as having been begun was probably the *De copia* (cf Ep 95:39). Mme
Marie Delcourt disagrees with the identification of Ludolph with Adolph but
suggests no alternative (*Correspondance* I 205).

* * * * *

95–7 Thou too ... well] *Odyssey* 1.301,302
99 'a following ... sea'] *Odyssey* 3.300
100–1 'A breeze ... straight.'] *Odyssey* 11.10; 12.152
113 prayers] 'Precatio quum erudita tum pietatis plena ad Iesum Dei Vir-
ginisque filium' (LB V 1210); 'Paean in genere demonstrativo Virgini matri
dicendus' (LB V 1227); and 'Obsecratio ad eandem semper gloriosam' (LB V
1233). These follow the letter in the *Lucubratiunculae.*

ERASMUS TO HIS DEAR LUDOLPHUS

Believe this of me, at any rate, my excellent Ludolphus, I would not be the cause of your appearing to have wasted your present, for I felt sure it came from you. I have begun a work that may considerably help students in acquiring Latin, and will send it to you from Paris when it is finished. After 5 that, I shall keep composing things that may be able to advance your studies. For your part, you should devote yourself wholeheartedly to literture of the best sort, and at the same time continue to give encouragement to scholars. Farewell, my dear boy.

Paris, 29 April   10

95 / To Jacob Batt   Paris, 2 May 1499

ERASMUS TO HIS FRIEND BATT

I have written you two letters already: one I gave to someone unknown to me, the other, and a very long one, was lost, so I shall give all my news in the briefest possible summary. I had bad luck on my journey; a hood strapped to the saddle fell off and could not be found again after long search. 5 It contained a linen garment, a linen nightcap, and ten gold pieces which I had placed in readiness so that I might change them if I had a chance; also my book of hours. The man to whom I had entrusted the money when I left Paris got rid of it with notable success: he lent some and kept some. Hendrik, to whose wife I had made a loan, has fled to Louvain, accompanied 10 by her. A third person, who printed my books, took in money on my behalf for the books he sold when I was away,and hasn't returned me a farthing. Ghisbert had already left. I cannot get gold exchanged at anything like a

* * * * *

95:6 ten gold pieces] Probably *écus au soleil* or *écus à la couronne* of France: in terms of the latter, a sum worth £17 10s 0d *tournois*. See the Glossary and Appendix A on gold coinage.

9–10 Hendrik] Cf Ep 83:87.

11 a third person] Probably Antoine Denidel who had published Erasmus' *De casa natalitia Iesu* (cf Ep 47 introduction and Reedijk 224 and 237ff). Allen is in error in identifying this person with Marchand, who did not publish the *De casa*, although he did publish Hermans' *Silva odarum*.

12 farthing] *obolum*: literally a halfpenny (*maille tournois*), of extremely small value, worth in fact only 25 per cent of the current English farthing. See the Glossary and Appendix B on silver coinage.

13 Ghisbert] Almost certainly to be identified with the physician of that name whom Erasmus mentioned as physician to the abbot of St Bertin (Allen Ep 252:13) and again as physician to the abbot and the town [of Saint-Omer] and one of his good friends (Allen Ep 273:32).

decent rate. Augustin is not back yet. While he was away he caused general confusion, intercepting money sent to me and sending a threatening letter since he was afraid I had got my talons on it. I can see, dear Batt, that the total has already diminished and become smaller than you think. I have sold for five gold pieces the horse I had fattened for about a fortnight: he suffered from foot-trouble. I have put off my journey, not only because I was short of money for it but much more because my supplications had come to nothing. I am living with the count upon the old terms, and made no difficulty about this in order to be more at liberty. He shows me affection and respect. I am on very close terms indeed with Fausto and a certain other poet, who is new; and I have a very keen contest afoot with 'Delius.' I am devoting myself entirely to my books, and collecting my scattered works while I forge new ones, leaving no spare time, as far as my health allows: I find I have impaired it somewhat by the rigours of travel.

So much for my present situation; now let me briefly tell you my plans for the future. I have decided to put off my Italian journey till August, hoping in the meantime to get together whatever is needed for a journey of such length. The count himself has made up his mind to visit Italy too, if his mother allows, but not until a year from now; and there was no mention of taking me. I remember how egregiously disappointed I was before in hopes of this kind. And if I wait here for a year, when am I going to see my friend Batt again? It is marvellous how eagerly my heart longs to fly back to join you. For this reason I have chosen to hasten my departure as much as I can. The book on letter writing is on the anvil again, and when it is

* * * * *

14 Augustin] Vincent, with whom Erasmus had frequent financial difficulties (cf Ep 80:16n).

18 five gold pieces] Probably *écus au soleil* or *écus à la couronne*: in terms of the latter, a sum worth £8 15s 0d *tournois*. See the Glossary and Appendix A on gold coins.

19 journey] Probably the Italian journey (cf line 29 and n).

21 count] Mountjoy (cf Ep 88:65n).

23 Fausto] Andrelini (cf Ep 84 introduction).

23–4 other poet] Perhaps the Scopus mentioned in Ep 103:2.

24 'Delius'] He is referred to in Ep 103:5 as calling himself Delius Volscus, and again in Ep 129:72. Allen suggests an identification with a certain Aegidius of Delft who is referred to as 'Egidius Delius poeta' in a letter by Arnoldus Bostius (cf Ep 53 introduction) in which he quotes a comment by Erasmus on him (cf Molhuysen *Cornelius Aurelius* 27f).

29 Italian journey] Cf Ep 75:15n.

37 on letter writing] *De conscribendis epistolis* (cf Ep 71 introduction).

finished you shall shortly receive a copy, dedicated in fact to your Adolf.
I shall add the *De copia* and the pieces on amplification, arguments, and
rhetorical figures: since these are for use in school, I have decided to   40
dedicate them jointly to you and the boy, but I should prefer to send the
book in printed form, and will attend to it. I have collected a number of my
writings which have by an odd chance come to light, and intend to correct
them and send them to you as soon as I can find a reliable messenger; so
be sure to send Adrian as soon as you can, with instructions to bring with   45
him everything that is mine; see that nothing is left behind. Natalis, the
Minorite theologian, has been with me, and I will send a letter by him to
the Lady and everyone else. The Picard has resolved to pay my Lady a visit
again at Whitsun. I do not find him agreeable; he is Theology itself, or,
rather, he is the mange itself.   50

Please, dear Batt, try to ensure that we can live together at Louvain as
soon as possible; finish what you have begun. I am ashamed to say how
wildly the prospect excites me. I can see that I must repair my capital, which
has already mostly vanished, and must inevitably diminish day by day.
There is not a soul in whom I can confidently repose any hope, except for   55
you alone. I know by experience how much you can do, as long as that lucky
spirit of yours does not fail. You can see what I wish to achieve; and I am
too bashful to load with requests a man from whom I have received so many
kindnesses. If you extend a helping hand, I shall also try hard myself; if not,
I shall follow the winds of fate. There will be adequate grounds for making   60
a request, either because I had to put off my journey for unavoidable
reasons or because it is better that the book should be printed at my own
expense. Please tell me how hopeful you are and how you feel about this.
Farewell.

Paris, 2 May 1499   65

* * * * *

39 *De copia*] 'On Abundance'; cf Ep 260 introduction.

45 Adrian] Cf Ep 80:57n.

46 Natalis] Cf Ep 101:41.

48 The Picard] There is no other mention of this person in Erasmus' letters.
Allen's suggestion that he may have been a certain Eligius de Vaugermes,
Picardus, who was rector of the university of Paris in March-June 1499 seems
unconvincing. He would be unlikely to be planning a visit to Tournehem during the months when he was rector.

51 Louvain] Cf Ep 101:44n.

62 book] The *De copia*. See above, n 39.

63 expense] Erasmus seems to have found it necessary, or at any rate advis-
able, to publish his early works at his own expense, hoping to reimburse him-

96 / From Fausto Andrelini   [Paris, May 1499?]

This and the following four brief notes may have been exchanged to enliven
the tedium of a dull lecture.

FAUSTO TO ERASMUS
I want my dinner to be quite a simple one. I ask for nothing but flies and
ants. Farewell.

97 / To Fausto Andrelini   [Paris, May 1499?]

ERASMUS TO FAUSTO
Confound it, what are these riddles you set me? Do you think I am an
Oedipus, or the owner of a Sphinx? Still, I imagine your 'flies' are fowls,
your 'ants' rabbits. But shall we put off joking to another time? We have
to buy our supper now; so you should stop being an enigmatist. Farewell.   5

98 / From Fausto Andrelini   [Paris, May 1499?]

FAUSTO TO ERASMUS
I can see clearly now that you are an Oedipus. I want nothing but fowls –
small ones will do. Not a word about rabbits, please! Farewell, you first-rate
solver of puzzles.

99 / To Fausto Andrelini   [Paris, May 1499?]

ERASMUS TO FAUSTO
My most witty Fausto, how at one and the same time you made me blush
and that theologian rage! For he was in the same lecture hall as ourselves.
But I do not believe it serves any purpose to stir up a nest of hornets.
Farewell.
                                                                                  5

        * * * * *

self by the sale of copies. The first edition of the *Adagia* was apparently published under some such arrangement, since he sent copies for sale to friends
in the Netherlands and England (cf Epp 133:5n, 138:177ff, and Allen Ep
181:61ff).
97:5 enigmatist] Erasmus seems to have coined the term 'aenigmatista' by
analogy with the currently used terms 'legista,' 'jurista,' 'canonista,' 'artista,'
and 'humanista' in university slang to designate students of the various
academic disciplines.
99:4 nest of hornets] Cf *Adagia* 1 i 60.

100 / From Fausto Andrelini   [Paris, May 1499?]

FAUSTO TO ERASMUS

Everyone knows that Fausto is capable of dying boldly for his friend Erasmus. As for those prattlers, let us take no more notice of them than an Indian
elephant does of a gnat. Farewell.

    Yours, whatever envious tongues may say,   5
    Fausto

101 / To Jacob Batt   Paris [May 1499]

ERASMUS TO HIS FRIEND JACOB BATT

Have you revived only to slay me with an abusive letter? The news came
that you had already taken to your bed, and that the doctor was already preparing to operate and you were waiting for the knife. Meantime I was
mourning for you, and sadly rehearsing your epitaph. Then, of all things,   5
up you sprang and challenged me to a duel of invective! And yet, dear
Batt, I should far rather be fighting a war of invectives, even the fiercest,
with you, than playing the part even of a devoted friend if it involved the
duty of writing your epitaph. Come on, then: let us gird on our swords,
since you are first to issue the call to arms. What desperate rashness! Do   10
you venture, puny creature that you are, to insult and provoke a hero with
such a fortune at his command? And if you have conceived a contempt for
my wealth, surely you are at least afraid of the pen of an Erasmus? You know
the weapons that poets are wont to use: if I should loose one of these against
you in a rage, all would be over for you, and those encircling moats and   15
ramparts and those walls of yours, however well built, would not avail to
protect you. But this, so far, is only the skirmishing; and unless you volun-
tarily sue for peace I shall decide the issue with you in a pitched battle.

    Joking apart, however, I am intensely delighted, dear Batt, that you
have time to laugh; for that lying letter of Adrian's had frightened me dread-   20
fully, so that I was debating with myself whether I should have to hasten
back to you. As for what I wrote about the loss of the baggage that fell, I
wish it might have been set down in jest. You say in your letter that you
can sense where I am going, so I shall make it clear in one word: I shall not
travel the course I had charted but go where cross-winds drive me, unless   25

* * * * *

100:4 elephant ... gnat] *Adagia* I x 66
101:20 Adrian's] Cf Ep 80:57n.
22 baggage] Cf Ep 95:4ff.

you come to my rescue once more. And this, my dear Batt, as you will presently discover in the event, is by no means said in jest. Still, I, at any rate, shall act like a good skipper and pit my seamanship against the weather. However foul the winds are I can still use my sails if I am driven from my course and, though I may not be able to make the particular harbour I 30 intend, no doubt I shall fetch up on some coast or other. Up to the present I have tossed about in journeys hither and yon, and am hardly settled even yet. I am taking great pains to get together all my own works; be sure to send our donkey, fitted out with a pack-saddle, to me as soon as you can, and I will return him to you freighted with papers. And will you please send 35 me, besides the clothes I mentioned, both my own letters and Willem's? Campano is no longer on sale here, and was too expensive while he was; all the same, I shall send a copy of his works, and Sulpizio's too, but not until our own donkey comes, for I would not entrust such treasures as these to an animal I do not know. 40

Natalis, the theologian, conscientiously delivered your greetings to me. He told me that the Lady of Veere has determined on journeying to Rome in company with a sister and talks of wanting to take me with her. I should congratulate you on your imminent departure for Louvain from the castle, if it were not that the unaccustomed freedom is making you so insol- 45 ent. You have become offensive to a degree, no doubt because, having been long pent in durance vile, you have only now seen a faint glimmering hope of liberty. Whatever will happen when you hold court with royal state at Louvain? Tell me of all your plans, and what hope of good fortune you can

* * * * *

36 letters] Erasmus seems to have been collecting copies of his letters and those of Willem Hermans, possibly for inclusion in the *De conscribendis epistolis* which he was revising at this time (cf Ep 95:37ff).

37 Campano] Cf Ep 61:153n. His complete works were published in Rome and Venice in 1495.

38 Sulpizio] Giovanni Sulpizio of Veroli wrote an *Opus grammaticum* (Rome: Steph. Plannck, 5 August 1481) and a treatise *De componendis et ornandis epistolis* (Venice: Christoph. de Pensis, 4 April 1499); cf Ep 117:49. Both were widely used; the former was reprinted by Bade in 1502 (cf Renaudet *Préréforme* 409).

41 Natalis] Cf Ep 95:46.

44 Louvain] No reason is given for Batt's projected visit to Louvain, where Erasmus had hoped to join him (cf Ep 95:51), except that his employer, the Lady of Veere, would be absent. The last line suggests that he was taking his pupil, young Adolph, with him, which might account for his being well received at court.

47–8 glimmering hope of liberty] The language suggests Virgil's *Eclogue* 1, lines 27–32.

offer in my situation, for at the time when I left you seemed not to have dealt   50
at all skilfully with it. I will send letters, by Natalis, to any persons you
name. The count, courteous as ever, sends warm greetings in reply to yours.
I shall never agree to allow the doctor's boy to dog my footsteps as I
dogged his. And now, to avoid filling up much of my letter with the names
of people at court, please greet for me the decorated gentlemen there, those   55
to whom I owe greetings, and in a manner suitable to each. I pray that your
pupil Adolph may be happy. Farewell.

Paris [1497]

102 / To Jacob Batt   Paris [May 1499]

ERASMUS TO HIS FRIEND BATT

See how effective your abusive language is! Defeated by a single letter from
you, I throw in the towel, climb out of the ring, and run off – all the way
to England, where at least I trust I shall be safe from your insults. For if you
decide to follow me there, you will have to transport yourself to another   5
world; and I am familiar with that lazy disposition of yours which makes
you dislike sea-water above all else, though you were born in the midst of
it. Still, if your insulting letters make their way even there, I hear that at
the farther end of Britain there are islands called the Orkneys. I shall flee
to these for refuge, and then to any place that is still more remote, even to   10
the very Antipodes. Now go and arrange a magnificent triumph for your
glorious victory. Farewell.

Paris [1497]

103 / To Fausto Andrelini   England [summer] 1499

In the early summer of 1499 Erasmus was invited by Lord Mountjoy (cf Ep 79
introduction) to accompany him to England for a visit. At some time during
the summer Mountjoy took him to Bedwell in Hertfordshire where his father-
in-law, Sir William Say (cf Ep 105: 4n) had an estate. This letter may have been
written from there, whence the vagueness of the address. The tone of the letter
was suited to the character of the recipient, who seems to have brought out
the frivolous streak in Erasmus' character (cf Ep 84 introduction and Epp
96–100).

* * * * *

102:3 climb out of the ring] Cf *Adagia* I ix 82.

ERASMUS TO FAUSTO ANDRELINI, POET LAUREATE

Great Heavens, what is this I hear? Is our Scopus, suddenly converted from a poet to a soldier, handling dread arms instead of books? How much better he fought with Delius Volscus, as he called himself! If only he had finished the man off: ye gods, what a celebration would have graced that victory!

I too have made some progress in England. The Erasmus you knew has already become quite a respectable sportsman; he is not a bad horseman either, and quite a skilful courtier, for he is distinctly mannerly in his salutations and conciliatory in address; and in all this, quite at variance with his own temperament. But what do I care? for it suits me very well. Do please come over here quickly yourself. Why are you so complacently burying your wit among French dunghills while you turn into an old man? But you say your gout keeps you back; let it go hang, as long as you are well. Still, if you were fully aware of what England has to offer, you would rush hither, I tell you, on winged feet, and if your gout refused to let you go, you'd long to fly like Daedalus. For, to touch on only one point among many, there are in England nymphs of divine appearance, both engaging and agreeable, whom you would certainly prefer to your Muses; and there is, besides, one custom which can never be commended too highly. When you arrive anywhere, you are received with kisses on all sides, and when you take your leave they speed you on your way with kisses. The kisses are renewed when you come back. When guests come to your house, their arrival is pledged with kisses; and when they leave, kisses are shared once again. If you should happen to meet, then kisses are given profusely. In a word, wherever you turn, the world is full of kisses. If you too, Fausto, once tasted the softness and fragrance of these same kisses, I swear you would yearn to live abroad in England; and not for ten years only, in the manner of Solon, but all your life long. The rest of my jesting may wait until we meet, for I hope to see you soon. Farewell.

From England, 1499

* * * * *

103:2 Scopus] Probably a nickname for one of the Parisian humanists. 'Scopa' is Latin for a broom.

5 Delius Volscus] Cf Ep 95:24n.

10–11 quite ... temperament] Literally, 'despite Minerva' ('invita Minerva'); cf *Adagia* I i 42.

17 Daedalus] Cf *Adagia* III i 65; see also Ep 54:29n.

28 Solon] The Athenian reformer and law-giver (c 639–c 559 BC). The code that bears his name contains provision for the exile of a citizen for ten years by popular vote (ostracism).

Henry VIII
artist unknown
National Portrait Gallery, London

104 / To Prince Henry   [Greenwich? autumn] 1499

This is the preface to the *Prosopopoeia Britannie maioris, que quondam Albion
dicta nunc Anglia dicitur, sibi de inuictissimi regis Henrici virtute deque regiae
sobolis eximia indole gratulantis,* a poem written for presentation to the young
Prince Henry, later Henry VIII. Erasmus was staying at Mountjoy's estate in
Greenwich when he was taken to visit the children of the royal family at
Eltham Palace by Thomas More and Arnold (cf Ep 124: 23n) as Erasmus related
in the letter to Botzheim in 1523 (cf Allen I 6). More presented some verses to
the young prince but, apparently with mischievous intent, had not warned
Erasmus, who was embarrassed at having nothing to offer. He did, however,
promise something, and on his return composed a poem of 150 lines in three
days. The poem was printed in the *Adagia* (Paris: Jo. Philippi 1500) and subsequently elsewhere. Critical edition in Reedijk 248–53.

TO THE MOST NOBLE BOY, PRINCE HENRY, FROM ERASMUS THE THEOLOGIAN,
GREETINGS

Illustrious Prince: you ought to remember that those persons who honour
you with presents of jewels or of gold are giving you, firstly, what is not
their own, for such gifts belong to Fortune, and are, moreover, perishable;   5
further, these gifts are such as the greater part of mankind can amply bestow, and lastly they are but what you yourself possess in abundance, and
better beseem a great prince to give away than to receive. Whereas he who
dedicates to you a poem which is the fruit of his own talent and toil seems
to me to offer a present that is more distinguished by far; inasmuch as he   10
lavishes upon you what belongs to himself, not to another, and will not fade
away in a few years but may even bring you everlasting renown, and can
be given to you by few indeed (for the supply of good poets by no means
matches that of wealthy men), and finally is no less honourable for kings
in the receiving than in the rewarding. And while there never was a king   15
who was not overflowing with riches, not so many have achieved immortal
fame. Kings may indeed earn such fame by their glorious deeds, but poets
alone can confer it, in their learned lays; for whereas waxen effigies, and
portraits and genealogies, and golden statues, and inscriptions on bronze,
and pyramids laboriously reared, decay one and all with the passing of long   20
years, only the poets' memorials grow stronger in the lapse of time, which
weakens all things else. Alexander, of vast renown, surnamed the Great,
showed a wise awareness of this fact when he purchased indifferent verses

* * * * *

104:22–4 Alexander ... Choerilus] Cf Horace *Epistles* 2.1.232–4.

at a *Philippus* apiece, as he had agreed, from Choerilus – a poet of no great
competence, to be sure. Clearly, however, he foresaw that both the portraits   25
by Apelles and the statues made by Lysippus would be destroyed within
a few years and that nothing on earth was capable of making a hero's
renown live for ever save those learned authors' works that deserved
immortality for themselves. Further, that there was no purer or more brilliant fame than that which posterity attributes to men's virtue rather than   30
their fortune; fame that proceeds from untrammelled judgment, not from
affection or flattery or fear. Tell me now: would not a man who so recklessly
purchases bad verses at so high a price gladly contract for the lines, not at
a gold coin apiece but at a city apiece, if they were Homer's? And indeed
Alexander is said to have considered Homer his favourite poet, and to have   35
envied Achilles, saying that he was lucky not only in his heroism but especially in having one such as Homer to sing its praises.

    At the same time I am not unaware that most princes in modern times
enjoy literature the less, the more they fail to comprehend it. They think
it equally foolish, equally shameful, indeed, for a nobleman either to be   40
schooled or to receive scholars' praise; as though they themselves were fit
to be compared to either Alexander or Caesar or indeed to any of the
ancients, either in dignity or in wisdom or in services to mankind. The
reason why they think it unseemly to accept a poet's praise is simply that
they have ceased to do praiseworthy deeds, not that this prevents them   45
from accepting the flattery of their parasites, though either they realize, if
they have any sense at all, that these creatures mock them or, if they do not
realize it, they are perfect fools. In my opinion at least, they are stupider
than Midas himself. He was disfigured with ass's ears, not because he
despised poetry, but because he preferred rustic to polished verse. Thus   50
Midas did not lack intelligence so much as judgment. The rulers of our time
lack both. It is because I am aware, most noble Prince, that your generous
nature recoiled from such folly, and that from boyhood onwards you had

* * * * *

24 at a *Philippus* apiece] Quite likely a pun, playing on the names of two gold
coins: the classic gold *stater* or *Philippicus* and the current Burgundian florin
of St Philip, which was then popularly known as the *Philippus*. See the Glossary and Appendix A on gold coins.

36 envied Achilles] Cf Ep 45:122 and n.

46 parasites] 'Gnatones,' persons like Gnatho (cf Ep 44:22n).

49 Midas] The king of Phrygia, best known for the gift of the golden touch.
On the occasion of a musical contest between Apollo and Pan, Midas decided
against Apollo, who thereupon changed his ears into those of an ass; cf *Adagia*
I iii 67.

made it the goal of your endeavours to model your life upon the ancient
rather than the modern ideal, that I have ventured to dedicate this laudatory   55
poem, such as it is, to you. And if it should seem by far inferior to your
royal dignity, as indeed it is, pray remember the smiling good humour with
which Artaxerxes himself, mightiest of kings, accepted the draught of water
which a country workman offered to him in his cupped hands as he rode
up; or again how another king, I believe of the same name, expressed his   60
thanks for an apple, brought to him by some poor man, in exactly the terms
he might use for a sumptuous present, evidently thinking that it is a no less
royal trait to accept small gifts graciously than to bestow great gifts with
generosity. Indeed, do not the gods themselves, who stand in no need of
mortal men's aid, take such pleasure in these small gifts that upon occasion   65
they will spurn rich men's sacrifices of a hundred oxen and yet be satisfied
with the peasant's pinch of salt, the poor man's morsel of incense; for of
a surety they assess our offerings not by the value of what we offer but by
the thought in the worshipper's mind.

So for the present I have dedicated these small gifts to you as toys for   70
your boyish age, intending to bring richer offerings when virtuous manhood, increasing with your years, shall furnish me with richer themes for
my verse. To this I would urge you, were it not that you are thither bound
already of your own free choice, by sail and oar as the saying goes; and
that you have a bard of your own in Skelton, the great light and ornament   75
of English letters, who can not only inspire but perfect your studies.
Farewell. May you illuminate good literature by your high distinction, protect it with your royal authority, and encourage it by your generosity.

105 / To William Blount, Lord Mountjoy   Oxford [October] 1499

This is the first of a series of letters (Epp 105–18) written or received at Oxford
during the last three months of 1499. Erasmus' departure from England had
been delayed by a royal proclamation forbidding anyone to leave the kingdom
(cf Ep 108: 119) and he had decided to spend the time visiting the famous university. Mountjoy had apparently intended to follow him.

* * * * *

58 Artaxerxes] Artaxerxes II (c 436–458 BC), king of Persia; cf Plutarch *Moralia*
172B.

66–7 rich men's ... incense] Cf Horace *Odes* 3.23.13–20.

75 Skelton] John Skelton, scholar, poet and satirist, was tutor to Prince Henry;
cf W. Nelson *John Skelton, Laureate* (New York 1939). Erasmus wrote a poem
in his praise at about this time (cf Reedijk 153f).

ERASMUS OF ROTTERDAM TO THE NOBLE COUNT, WILLIAM MOUNTJOY

What, pray, is the meaning of the rhetorical repetition in the opening of
your letter, 'O, greetings, my teacher; greetings, my teacher?' Was it due
to grief at separation from your dear wife, or out of joy that you are destined
to return to literature, of which you are equally fond? With me at least,   5
though I find everything very uncomfortable here, one purpose remains
unshaken: to put up with all the boredom, and swallow every annoyance,
for love of you. For since you have shown yourself utterly sincere in your
affections, I in turn must not appear to waver in my devotion to your service. I ask you for your part to feel towards me in such a way that you may   10
not be deemed to have unnecessarily deprived your wife of your company,
nor I on my side to have wasted my efforts in enduring all those distasteful
experiences. Farewell.

Oxford, 1499

106 / From John Colet   Oxford [October 1499]

This letter marks the beginning of a friendship which played a very important
part in Erasmus' life for the next twenty years. John Colet (1466?-1519) had
returned from a period of study in Italy about 1496 and since then had been
lecturing at Oxford on the Epistles of St Paul. He was appointed dean of St
Paul's in London in 1504 and founded St Paul's School in 1510. See Erasmus'
biographical sketch (Ep 1211) and J.H. Lupton *Life of John Colet* (London: 1887,
2nd ed 1909), still the standard life.

JOHN COLET TO HIS FRIEND ERASMUS

My friend Brumus warmly commends you in his letter. You have already
been recommended to me by your reputation and by the evidence afforded
by certain of your writings. At the time when I was in Paris the name of
Erasmus on the lips of scholars was one to conjure with. A letter you had   5

* * * * *

105:4 wife] Mountjoy had married Elizabeth, daughter of Sir William Say, in
1497 before he went to Paris to study. Elizabeth had remained with her family
till his return, probably because she was still too young to begin living with
him.

106:2 Brumus] The name Brumus cannot be identified in Colet's circle. It is
probable that his letter, referred to here, was an introduction brought by Erasmus from London.

5 letter] The complimentary letter (Ep 45) inserted in Gaguin's history of
France in 1495. Colet probably saw it when he was passing through Paris on
his way home from Italy.

written to Gaguin in admiration of his accomplishments in French history
furnished me, as I read it, a very pattern and sample of human perfection,
of distinguished literary abilities, and extensive information on many subjects. But what above all recommends you to me is the fact that the reverend
father with whom you are staying, the prior of the house and congregation   10
of Our Lord Jesus Christ, only yesterday described you to me as one who
was, in his judgment, a truly virtuous man, uniquely endowed with natural
goodness. So far, therefore, as letters and knowledge and integrity of
character may go to recommend anyone to a person who rather desires and
longs for these things than can boast of them himself, so far are you, Eras-   15
mus, most highly recommended to me on the strength of these virtues
which exist in you, and so you shall be always. When I meet you, I shall
do for myself in my own person that which others have done for you in your
absence: I shall commend myself to you and to your wisdom, which others
have recommended to me – improperly, since it is the junior who ought to   20
be recommended to the senior, the lesser scholar to the greater. But if there
is any matter wherein I in my small capacity can be agreeable or of service
to you, it shall be bestowed on you as willingly and as generously as your
great reputation both requires and demands, a reputation I am delighted
to welcome to England. I hope you may like our country as much as I think   25
you are capable of benefiting her by your scholarship; while for my part I
regard you, and shall continue to regard you, as a person whom I consider
to be eminently virtuous as well as eminently learned. Farewell.
    From my rooms in Oxford [1497]

107 / To John Colet [Oxford, October 1499]

ERASMUS TO JOHN COLET

Most kind Colet: If I saw anything in myself that deserved even a modicum
of praise I should now be exulting, like Hector in Naevius' poem, at the
receipt of 'praise from the praised', for you are easily the most praised of
men. I have such regard for your opinion that approval from you alone,   5
given in silence, means far more in my eyes than acclamation and applause

* * * * *

10 prior] This must refer to Richard Charnock, prior of St Mary's College, a
house of Augustinian canons regular, founded in 1435. As a member of the
Order, Erasmus naturally stayed there during his visit. He dated Ep 108 from
St Mary's College and in a postscript referred to Charnock as his host. It is not
clear why Colet should have referred to Charnock as 'Prior domus et ecclesiae
Jesu Christi.'
107:3 Naevius] Cf Cicero *Ad Familiares* 5.12.7.

from the populace assembled in the forum in Rome, if I could win that, or
the admiration of a crowd of the ignorant as numerous as Xerxes' army is
said to have been. For just as I have always refrained, following Horace's
example, from hunting the 'votes of the fickle mob,' the mob which dis-   10
tributes praise and blame with equal irresponsibility, so too I have ever
considered it a supreme distinction to earn the plaudits of those who are
highly respected, since their candour makes them unwilling to praise anyone falsely, while their wisdom guards them against the possibility of
deception; men whose scholarship leaves no room for the suspicion of   15
error, and whose lives leave none for that of flattery. But your compliments,
my dear Colet, were so far from rushing to my head that they have caused
me, who am by nature over-modest, to be even more dissatisfied with
myself than before; for when things are said about me that I respect in
others but find absent in myself, then I seem to be reminded of what I   20
should be like.

I know very well indeed just where the shoe pinches in my own case;
all the same, I have no fault to find with the obligingness, or the kindliness,
of those who have recommended me so affectionately to you, nor do I disparage your amiable readiness to accept that recommendation, since, just   25
as it is the mark of a civilized temper to think well of persons one does not
know, the readiness to believe one's friends reveals a charming and amiable
character. As for your praise of me in citing my own writings: this, I suppose, implies either that you wished to spur me to achievement by a courteous eulogy, or else that through unbelievable modesty on your part it came   30
about that while you took undue pleasure in other men's work you were
excessively displeased with your own. Accordingly, though I gladly
embrace, as I should, and respect and welcome, your enthusiastically
favourable and kindly attitude towards me, still I greet your verdict with
affection for its friendliness, without approving it for its truthfulness; not   35
because I consider you, a man of extraordinarily good sense, unqualified
to judge me or prone to insincerity, for I know well how honest you are;
but partly because, beguiled by affection, you were too ready to believe
those eulogies of me, partly because you were induced by your extraordinary candour and modesty to lend a too ready ear to other men's praises.   40
Still, dear Colet, this mistake of yours ought to be all the more agreeable
to me in that it arises from the kind of disposition I have always found most
delightful: civilized, agreeable, open-hearted, and at the opposite pole

* * * * *

9 Horace] *Epistles* 1.19.37
17 rushing to my head] Literally 'raising my crest'; *Adagia* I viii 69

from any taint of envy. So I would rather you were lovingly mistaken about
me than conscientiously right.   45

However, in order to stop you from complaining afterwards that unknown goods were thrust upon you by a fictitious testimonial, and to give
you a chance to put selection before affection, here is a description for you
of myself – all the better for the unrivalled familiarity I have with my subject.
The person you are to confront is of slender means, or rather, none; knows   50
nothing of ambition, but has a great disposition towards affection; enjoys
but little experience of letters, but admits to a consuming passion for them;
is scrupulous in respecting others' moral excellence, having none himself;
yields pride of place to all in scholarship, to none in loyalty; is straightforward, frank, outspoken, incapable alike of pretence and concealment; in   55
character humble but sincere; no great talker; in fact, one from whom you
should not look for anything, except a friendly attitude. If you, Colet, can
love a man of this sort, if you consider him worthy of your friendship, then
pray stamp Erasmus as the most securely yours of all your possessions.

Now, one of the many reasons why I find your England most agreeable   60
is this in particular, that it is well supplied with that without which life itself
is disagreeable to me: I mean men who are well versed in good literature,
amongst whom I account you easily the leader, as nobody would deny; for
your scholarship would earn you the right to everyone's admiration, even
were it not commended by your morals, while your saintly character could   65
not fail to win you everyone's love, respect, and reverence even if you had
not learning to back it. And moreover, excellent sir, I need hardly add that
your style: calm, tranquil, unaffected, flowing like a pellucid stream from
the great riches of your mind; even and consistent, clear and simple and
full of modesty; without a trace of anything tasteless, involved, or confused, 70
moved me and delighted me enormously, so that it seemed to me that I
could clearly perceive a kind of image of your personality, reflected in your
letter. You say what you mean, and mean what you say; your words are
engendered not in your vocal chords but in your heart, and they choose to
be the servants, not the masters, of your thought. In fine, you have a happy   75
knack of pouring forth with ease what another man could hardly express
with much labour.

But I shall desist from praising you, at least to your face, in order not
to spoil your friendly feelings toward me while they are fresh and new. I
know how reluctant to be praised are those who alone deserve everyone's   80
praise. Farewell.

Oxford [1498]

* * * * *

59 stamp] *Adagia* I viii 51

108 / To John Colet   St Mary's College, Oxford [October 1499]

This letter and the three following arose out of an argument between Colet and
Erasmus concerning the nature of Christ's agony in the garden of Gethsemane
and hingeing on Christ's words: 'Father, let this cup pass from me; yet not as
I will, but as thou wilt' (Mark 14:36). Colet was unwilling to admit that Christ
was referring to his death on the cross. Instead he maintained, following St
Jerome (See Jerome on Matthew 26:39), that Christ meant the agony of witnes-
sing the guilt of the Jews in causing his death (cf Epp 109: 149 and 111: 60ff).
Erasmus regarded this explanation as far-fetched and preferred the simpler
and commonly accepted meaning that Christ in his human nature feared a
cruel death. After the discussion, which took place in the presence of Prior
Charnock (cf Ep 109: 16), probably in St Mary's College, Colet wrote a letter,
which has been lost, reproaching him for following the interpretation of the
current theologians. Erasmus replied at once with this letter and a restatement
of his own argument in Ep 109, which he further developed in Ep 111. Later
Erasmus revised, rearranged and enlarged these two letters and published the
resulting treatise, with this letter as preface, under the title *Disputatiuncula de
tedio, pavore, tristicia Iesu, instante crucis hora, deque verbis quibus visus est mortem deprecari: 'Pater, si fieri potest, transeat a me calix iste,'* in the *Lucubratiunculae* (Antwerp: Th. Martens 15 February 1503; NK835), which also included
Ep 93 and the *Enchiridion*. There were numerous later editions.

DESIDERIUS ERASMUS TO THE LEARNED AND ELOQUENT DIVINE, JOHN COLET
Most learned Colet: I no more deserve the reproof in your last, than the
praise you bestowed on me in your earlier letter. All the same, I can tolerate
your undeserved reproaches with a good deal more equanimity than your
previous compliments, the justice of which I was unable to recognize. For   5
if one is accused, then not only may one clear oneself with no disgrace
attached, but one is blamed for failing to do so; whereas the studious rebuttal of compliments, on the other hand, appears to betoken a nature starved
of praise, hungry for it, and not sincerely endeavouring to avoid it but really
seeking more frequent or more lavish praises. What I suppose you were   10
seeking to do was to try me out in both kinds: to see whether I was complacent when a testimonial from such a great man reflected glory on me, and
again whether the provocation of a petty jibe showed that I had a sting to
use. Surely you must be the most dependable of friends, when you are so
very cautious, thorough, hesitant, and experimental in forming new friend-   15

* * * * *

108:3 earlier letter] Ep 106

ships. But I have indulged a fancy to jest with you over this. In fact, I am as glad to accept reproof from a true friend now as I was earlier to be praised, even falsely, by the most highly praised of men. So in future you may praise or scold your friend Erasmus as you wish, so long as a letter from you flies to me here every day, which is the pleasantest thing that could happen   20 to me.

Now let me briefly turn to your letter, in order to make sure that the boy who brought it shall not return to you empty-handed. When you tell me that you dislike the modern class of theologians, who spend their lives in sheer hair-splitting and sophistical quibbling, you have my emphatic   25 agreement, dear Colet. It is not that I condemn their learned studies, I who have nothing but praise for learning of any sort, but these studies are isolated, and not seasoned with references to any well-written works of an older age, and so they seem to me likely to give a man a smattering of knowledge or a taste for arguing. But whether they can make him wise, others   30 may judge; for they exhaust the intelligence by a kind of sterile and thorny subtlety, in no way quickening it with vital sap or breathing into it the breath of life; and, worst of all, by their stammering, foul, and squalid style of writing, they render unattractive that great queen of all sciences, theology, enriched and adorned as she has been by the eloquence of   35 antiquity. In this way they choke up, as it were with brambles, the way of a science that early thinkers had cleared and, attempting to settle all questions, so they claim, merely envelop all in darkness. Thus you can see her, once supremely revered and full of majesty, today all but silent, impoverished, and in rags; while we are seduced by the attractions of a per-   40 verted and insatiable passion for quibbling. One quarrel leads to another, and with extraordinary arrogance we quarrel over insignificant trifles.

Moreover, lest we seem to have made no progress beyond the discoveries of the early Fathers, we have had the effrontery to lay down a number of fixed procedures that God used, we claim, in working out his   45 hidden purposes, though it would sometimes be more pious to believe in the fact while conceding to the omnipotence of God alone the knowledge of how it comes to be. Further, in our eagerness to show off our knowledge, we sometimes debate questions of a sort intolerable to truly religious men, as when we ask whether God could have taken the form of the Devil or an   50 ass. Perhaps one ought to put up with such things when a youth dabbles in them slightly for the sake, as it were, of whetting his mind's edge; but

* * * * *

42 insignificant trifles] Erasmus uses the proverbial 'goat's wool' (non-existent, and would be worthless if it did exist); *Adagia* I iii 53.

these are the things over which we grow old – even die – as upon the rocks
of the Sirens, relegating all literature to an inferior place in comparison with
them. And moreover, nowadays practically no one devotes himself to the   55
study of theology, the highest branch of learning, except such as, having
sluggish or disordered wits, are scarcely fit for letters at all.

Now, I would wish to say these things not of good and scholarly professors of divinity, for whom I have an especially warm regard and respect,
but only of the squalid mob of carping theologues, who hold all men's cul-   60
ture worthless save their own. Inasmuch as you, Colet, have undertaken
to do battle with this invincible tribe, for the sake of restoring to as much
of its early splendour and dignity as you can that ancient true theology,
overgrown as it is with the entanglements introduced by the modern
school, as God loves me, you have assumed a responsibility of the most cre- 65
ditable sort, one that is a true labour of love towards theology herself, and
will enormously benefit every studious person, and this most flourishing
university of Oxford in particular, yet nevertheless is, to be quite honest,
an extremely difficult and unpopular undertaking. Your difficulties,
indeed, will be surmounted by a combination of scholarship and hard   70
work; as for unpopularity, your generous nature will manage without trouble to overlook that. Even among divines themselves there are, too, not a
few who could and would offer assistance to endeavours as honourable as
yours; or rather, everyone will lend a hand, since there is not a soul, even
among the doctors, in this famous university who has not listened with the 75
greatest attention to the lectures you have given on the Pauline epistles for
the past three years. In regard to this, which should one praise more: the
modesty of the professors, who are not abashed to appear merely as audience at the lectures of a man who is young in years and unprovided with
the authority of the doctorate, as it is called, or your own unequalled combi- 80
nation of learning, eloquence, and moral integrity, which they judge to be
worthy of this honour?

What surprises me, however, is not that you have taken so heavy a

* * * * *

53–4 rocks of the Sirens] Virgil *Aeneid* 5.864
76 Pauline epistles] Colet's lectures on the Pauline epistles, which interpreted
them in their historical setting, rather than as a treasury of proof texts to be
taken out of context and used in dialectical construction of dogma, were
revolutionary and attracted large audiences despite his youth and lack of a doctorate. E.H. Harbison has called them a milestone in the history of Christian
scholarship (*The Christian Scholar in the Age of the Reformation* (New York 1956)
58). Cf P.A. Duhamel 'The Oxford Lectures of John Colet' JHI 14 (1953) 493–510,
and *E & C* 16ff.

burden upon your shoulders – your strength is fit to match it – but that you
are inviting my insignificant self to share in this grand undertaking. For you   85
urge, or rather almost demand with threats, that, just as you are doing by
your lectures on Paul, so I should try this winter to set alight the enthusiasms of this university, which you say are cooling down, by lecturing
either on old Moses or on that eloquent stylist, Isaiah. However, I have
learned to live with myself, and am well aware how scanty my equipment   90
is; and I can neither lay claim to scholarship enough for the prosecution of
such high aims, nor suppose myself to possess strength of character enough
to be able to endure the ill-will of all those determined defenders of their
own. This no assignment for a recruit, but for a highly experienced general. Please, however, do not call me shameless for declining the tasks   95
you suggest; I should be utterly shameless did I not do so. It is you, dear
Colet, who are less than wise in demanding water from a stone, as Plautus
puts it. How could I ever be so brazen as to teach what I myself have not
learned? How can I fire the cool hearts of others, when I myself am trembling
and shivering all over? I should think myself more irresponsible than irre-   100
sponsibility itself if in a matter of such importance I plunged in wholeheartedly at a venture and, as the Greek proverb has it, began to learn pottery
on the largest size of jar. But, you will say, I had relied on you; and you
will complain that I have disappointed your hopes. If so, you should
reproach yourself and not me; for I have not deceived you, inasmuch as I   105
never promised, or even held out a prospect of, anything of the kind; it is
you who have deceived yourself, in refusing to believe me when I told you
the truth about myself. And I have not come to these shores to teach literature, in verse or in prose. Literature ceased to have charms for me as soon
as it ceased to be necessary to me. As I reject this task because it falls below   110
my purpose, so I reject your proposal because it is too great for my powers.
In the one case, dear Colet, I do not deserve your reproaches, because I
never intended to become a professor of what is called secular learning; in
the other case your exhortations are wasted on me, since I am only too well
aware of my inadequacy.   115
    But even were I fully adequate to the task, I should still be in no posi-
tion to undertake it, for I am shortly returning to Paris, whence I came. As
I am kept here for the present, partly by the winter season and partly because

* * * * *

90 live with myself] Persius 4.52; *Adagia* i iv 87
97 Plautus] *Persa* 41; *Adagia* i iv 75
102–3 began ... jar] *Adagia* i iv 15

the recent flight of a certain duke prevents my leaving safely, I have betaken
myself to this celebrated university in order to spend a month or two in the   120
company of men like yourself rather than of those decorated gentlemen
at court. And so far am I from wishing to oppose your honourable and pious
endeavours, that I promise I shall diligently encourage and support them,
since I am not yet qualified to work with you. For the rest, as soon as I feel
myself to possess the necessary stamina and strength, I shall come person-   125
ally to join your party, and will give devoted, if not distinguished, service
in the defence of theology. Meanwhile, nothing could afford me greater
pleasure than daily debates between us on the subject of holy writ, continued as we have begun either face to face or by means of letters. Farewell,
dear Colet.   130

    PS My host and our common friend Richard Charnock, that kind and
reverend gentleman, has asked me to add warm greetings on his own
behalf.

    Oxford, at the college of the Augustinian canons, commonly called St
Mary's   135

109 / To John Colet   Oxford [October 1499]

Lines 1–41 form the opening passage of the *Disputatiuncula* as printed (cf Ep
108 introduction), but from line 42 on Allen has followed the version of the
original letter contained in the Gouda MS 1324 (cf Allen I App 9), which he published for the first time, rather than the conflation and amplification of Epp
109 and 111 printed in the *Lucubratiunculae* of 1503 and later editions, including LB V 1265-94.

ERASMUS TO HIS FRIEND JOHN COLET
In the course of our sparring match yesterday afternoon, Colet, while you
made a great many observations characterized by weight as well as wit, I
was not fully convinced of the soundness of your position, yet found it
easier to record my dissent from it than to refute it, my own impression   5
being that my weakness lay not in the view I espoused but in my presentation of it. As for you, in your modest way you put aside argument for the
time being, but as I took my leave you begged me to think the matter over

* * * * *

119 duke] Edmund de la Pole, Earl of Suffolk, was the eldest son of Elizabeth,
sister of Edward IV. Guilty of treason, he fled to Calais in the summer of 1499
and on 20 August a royal proclamation forbade anyone to leave the kingdom.
He was, however, soon allowed to return (cf Gairdner II 377; and Mackie 167ff).

privately with closer attention and greater precision, and said you had no
doubt that if I did so I should forthwith proceed to vote for your point of   10
view. Here you did rightly, in my opinion; for you were aware that (as the
famous writer of mimes, Publilius Syrus, so wisely remarked) the truth is
sometimes lost sight of when arguments go on too long, especially when
the whole discussion is conducted in the presence of men whose opinion
of our own scholarship we consider crucially important. Now, on this occa-   15
sion Prior Richard Charnock was present; to you he is a very old friend,
while he has only recently been host to me, but he has virtually the same
love and admiration for each of us. Again, there are times when the passion
for debate which nature implants in us, and the eagerness to maintain one's
own position, seize hold even of gentler temperaments; you may find some-   20
one who will give up his ancestral domains, but 'No man alive his brain-
child e'er would quit.' So I was happy, dear Colet, to follow your instructions: I went over the whole discussion again privately and looked at it in
a harder and more concentrated way, freeing myself from every shred of
prejudice while I put together and weighed the arguments on both sides;   25
indeed I altered things round so as to adopt your arguments exactly as if
they were my own and criticize my own no less severely than if they had
been yours. Nevertheless, in spite of these measures I was visited by no
new considerations, and repented of nothing I had said. Accordingly, I
shall attempt if possible to record the entire controversy in writing and, so   30
to speak, repeat the perfomance – not because I am better equipped than
I then was, but with a view to expressing in a slightly more orderly and sys-
tematic form the thoughts I then voiced haphazard, not being prepared. For
even if your resources are adequate, it still makes a great deal of difference
how skilfully you fight, once battle is joined. Let us, however, proceed   35
chiefly by the method of proof, since under present conditions I lack the
help of texts to fall back on. You are, of course, luckier than I am in this
respect; but why should I mind? In a literary battle the wise soldier would
rather be defeated than win; that is, he prefers learning to teaching. If I am
overthrown I come away better instructed, while if I prevail over you I shall   40
not lose any of your affection.

... Very well then, you will say, I grant you that, as man, Christ was
deeply saddened at the prospect of death, found it repugnant, and viewed
it with terror. This he did by reason of his nature, not of his will, not as

* * * * *

109:12 Publilius Syrus] Called Mimus (as often) by Erasmus; this is line
416, quoted by Aulus Gellius *Noctes Atticae* 17.14.4.
21–2 'No ... quit'] Martial 8.18.10.

rejecting death, but as enduring it. Yet why does he pray for deliverance   45
from death? And what is the nature of the 'will' that he subordinates to the
will of his father? If he ever declined death, his love was imperfect; but if
he never declined it, why does he ask to be delivered from that which he
willed? Surely at that moment he spoke as a man, for men, to men, and in
the words of men, expressing man's fears; so that the 'will' in question is   50
but the natural dread of death, which nature has so deeply implanted
within us that it is as natural to be alarmed at the prospect of death as it
is to be hungry when deprived of food. Just as every propensity to anything
is a kind of will or choice, so, in my view, to be repelled or to shrink from
anything is in some sense an act of rejection. Anyone who is hungry wishes   55
for food by the very fact of his hunger; yet it is possible for a hungry man
not to desire food even with a lesser part of his 'will.' However, the very
fact that his physical constitution longs for food is a kind of 'will.' Similarly,
our innate fear of dying is itself a kind of avoidance of death, implying will
or choice no further than does the fact of hunger. For a man who is by no   60
process of reasoning unwilling to die may still be terrified by death; none
the less this is, in a sense, unwillingness. It was this natural aversion to
death that Christ, speaking after the fashion of men, expressed when he
said: 'Father, let this cup pass from me; yet not as I will, but as thou wilt
...': as though he were to pray, 'My Father, I am conscious within myself   65
of the nature I have taken upon me, a nature that violently dreads a cup so
bitter; but let thy will, not mine, be done, since whatever is thy will is mine
also. I am in no way moved by this anguish of spirit to be unwilling to drink
the cup. Rather, I thirst deeply for it; for, exceedingly bitter as it must be
for me, it is to bring salvation to those whom I love, and it cannot do so   70
unless it be bitter for me. Therefore I wish to drink it, but the will whereby
I wish this is thine, not mine, for my steadfast desire to do so comes not
from myself but from thee, by whose gift I am what I am.'

I think, Colet, that my explanation meets all the needs of the case. But
I shall add just one observation, in order to answer your challenge more fully   75
still, since you are highly delighted by the liveliness of affection in which
our entire discussion originated, and immediately thereafter I shall desist
from the debate. I contend that among the whole army of martyrs there
never was such holy joy as Christ had in that hour when he sweated drops
of blood. At that very moment he rejoiced with inexpressible gladness that   80
the time, ordained by his father before time was, had now come to pass,
when he should reconcile fallen mankind to his father by his death. Never
was there any man whose longing for life made him wish as ardently to live
as he wished to die. Never did anyone seek the kingdom of Heaven as passionately as he thirsted for death. And you can still further enlarge upon   85

this, if you will. As for me, I am unable to find words adequate to the thoughts that occur to me. But, you ask, how does an eager thirst for death agree with the dread of death? There is no reason why one soul should not experience different sense-impressions by way of different organs, above all in Christ, and (as I have already remarked) the senses never obstruct 90 the operation of other senses, nor the feelings other feelings. To this extent, Our Lord's soul, where it approached most closely to his bodily feelings, was sensitive to the agonies that torture the body, while on the other side, where it lay nearest to Godhead, it exulted with ineffable joy. Yet that feeling of grief did not impede his joy, nor did that joy diminish or alleviate 95 the experience of terror.

I cannot see what else you could ask, Colet, unless you are still troubled by that particle of doubt why Christ gave no sign of a joy so great as this, whereas he exhibited such clear proof of his terror. I shall try to rid you of that mote, not mountain, of difficulty. Christ's purpose was not to set us 100 an example of courage, though joy such as he experienced is not required even of a hero, any more than we look for the heroic words ascribed by a philosopher to the truly wise man, who ought to cry out even in the horse of Phalaris, 'It is pleasant; it does not hurt.' Our Lord's purpose was to be a pattern of gentleness, mildness, patience, obedience, not fearlessness. If 105 you trace his entire life from the cradle upwards, you will find many gentle and obedient actions, a great many instances of mildness, none of quick temper. Does it not seem to you that he furnished ample evidence of his long-suffering nature when he severely rebuked Peter, who urged him to run away from death? Or when at the Last Supper he received his disciples 110 so lovingly, not bemoaning his own situation but comforting their weak spirits? Or when he neither banished from the feast the friend who betrayed him, nor refused to accept his kiss? Or when he gave himself up freely to the messengers of death, and remained silent when he was accused, and was led as a sheep to the slaughter? Moreover, that joy was not likely to be 115 of great service to us, but his sorrow brought us gain; it was essential that he, who paid the penalty of death for our sakes, might be held to be very man. This last has at many times and by many persons been denied; how much more doubtful it might have seemed had Our Lord suffered with great

* * * * *

104 Phalaris] Phalaris, tyrant of Agrigentum in the sixth century BC, roasted his enemies inside a brazen bull, as Erasmus well knew (*Adagia* I x 86); he is perhaps using horse, 'equus' in the sense of 'instrument of torture,' for which classical Latin uses the diminutive 'eculeus.'

joy upon his countenance and in his words, as if he lacked human feelings?   120
Who, then, would not have said that he inhabited an unreal body? Who
would have believed that he was God? It is certain that he who took death
upon him for our sakes loved us deeply; and there is none to doubt that
he who stood in dread of death was very man. This patient, rather than
resolute and fearless, endurance of his ordeal was more conducive to prov-   125
ing the truth of his human nature. In the same way it was better suited to
our feelings, for he had determined to win our love, rather than admiration;
and, whereas we admire fortitude, we love and affectionately embrace that
which is gentle and weak. And it was more accordant to the utterances of
the prophets, who so represent Christ's character as to compare him to a   130
gentle lamb, or to depict him bruised by blows, disfigured, abandoned, and
an outcast, but never show him as joyous, proud, or highspirited. They represent him as quiet, not boastful. Now, it is for the proud and haughty to
face torture undismayed, and perhaps even to make a fine speech upon the
rack itself. But Christ desired that his own death should be of the most   135
humiliating kind; while reserving the glorious crown of joy for his martyrs,
for whose sake the head became weak so that the limbs might thereby be
strengthened. Lastly, he did not exhibit, in himself, that joy amidst great
agonies which, since it is opposed to nature, he does not expect of us, but
he set us an example of the patience and gentleness which he bade us learn   140
from him, and did so by the tokens that are most familiar to men's senses.
The more obvious were the signs he gave of dread, the clearer was the proof
of his truly human nature and the more cogent was the example of obedience he set. If then the consequence of his dread be no loss to us but rather
great gain; if our Redeemer's love be not diminished but rather much   145
increased thereby; if we acquire from it a pattern of obedience more suited
to us; if, in short, all the facts accord with this interpretation, why should
we abandon the universally accepted view to follow Jerome's commentary,
not his doctrine, and Jerome's alone, especially since neither the substance
nor the expression affords us the means of adducing even the slightest   150
proof?

I am quite convinced by my own arguments, but possibly, Colet, I may
not yet have won over your judgment. What I have urged might be rather
more carefully defended, and also expounded at somewhat greater length,
but I know to whom I am writing. At least I have taken pains with my   155
argument; it rests with you to accept it in good part, such as it is. It is my
desire to produce in your sight these first exercises by my tyro's hand, for

* * * * *

120 and in his words] Reading 'vocis alacritate' for 'voce et alacritate'

the sake of earning praise not for my skill but only for my industry; for my
present struggle is not with you, or with Jerome, but with Paul. And I have
so little confidence in these prattlings of mine that I should not judge them   160
to deserve any attention at all unless they should earn your approval. If you
grant this (and you cannot do so, nor would I wish you to, save upon sober
consideration and their just merits), then I shall put them back upon the
anvil and reforge them with somewhat greater care. If, however, they
should be as displeasing to you as they are to me, they must be destroyed   165
by any doom you like – offered as a sacrifice either to Venus' husband or
to Achilles' mother. Notice, Colet, how well I observe decorum in ending
such a theological argument with poetic myths. But, as Horace says,
'Though ye pitchfork Nature out, sure she will run back again.'
    Farewell; and, I beg you, refute me both carefully and sharply, and   170
show me my own faults.
    Oxford

110 / From John Colet   [Oxford, October 1499]

At the time of publication of the *Lucubratiunculae* of 1503, Colet's replies to
Erasmus' arguments were not available, but his first reply, that to Ep 109,
turned up later and was published in the Froben edition of 1518, as 'Responsio
ad argumenta Erasmiana,' with this letter as a preface (cf LB B 1291–4).

FROM JOHN COLET TO THE ELOQUENT THEOLOGIAN, ERASMUS
Most learned Erasmus: Your letter is not only decidedly long but, even more
decidedly, very well expressed and highly agreeable. I can see in it a retentive memory and a faithful account of our argument; in it, too, that brilliant
intellect of yours, which penetrates everywhere with as much ease as suc-   5
cess; and there, too, I see a style worthy of a philosopher, competent, accurate, full of meaning, illuminating the bare facts, and, as far as the dryness
of the subject permits, rendering them pleasant. Consequently, your letter
taught me a great deal, and entertained me too, as I read it. All the same,
despite the vigour of its argumentation and also the fact that it is laden with   10
a cargo of powerful examples, as weighty as they are numerous, it still does
not, thus far, either rob me of, or lessen in my eyes, my own opinion, which
I have thoroughly absorbed from Jerome. Not that I am wilful, or hardened

* * * * *

166–7 Venus' husband or Achilles' mother] ie, to Vulcan (god of fire) or the
sea-nymph Thetis (representing water)
168 Horace] *Epistles* 1.10.24

in perverse obstinacy, but that, rightly, as I believe, I regard the point of
view I am adopting and defending as being either the truth or a fair approxi-   15
mation to it. For this reason I cannot be as willing to concede your counter-
arguments, powerfully persuasive as they are, as I am to refute them. Truth
herself makes me refuse to let her be unworthily crushed and overborne by
the reasoning of a clever and eloquent man, reasoning which is brilliantly
expressed and resourceful, rather than true. In her defence, as I myself hold,   20
I have to call for help upon the same deity whose help you seem to me to
have invoked in attacking truth.

But I would not for the present wish to take issue with your letter as
a whole, for I have neither the time nor the energy to join so fierce a battle
at once and on a sudden. Yet I should like to try to carry by assault its first   25
part, its front line, as it were, which in war, as it seems to me (reasonably,
I think), is the stronger. Will you therefore please listen patiently for a
while, and let us both catch any sparks that may be struck out when the
flints clash. For it is truth we are seeking, not the defence of a mere point
of view; and perhaps, as argument meets argument, truth will shine forth,   30
just as fire does from steel when it strikes upon steel ...

Farewell meantime.

111 / To John Colet   Oxford [October 1499]

> This letter was printed by Allen for the first time from the Gouda MS 1324. It
> represents Erasmus' actual reply to Ep 110 (cf Epp 108 introduction and 109
> introduction).

ERASMUS' REPLY TO JOHN COLET'S LETTER

Most learned Colet: Since your freedom in refuting me has given me the
greatest pleasure, I in turn request you not to be offended by the directness
with which I defend myself. I shall do so as briefly as I can, since you find
the source of verbosity mere barrenness of thought; and indeed I share this   5
opinion.

First of all, in claiming, as you do in your letter, to have routed the
front rank of my line of battle, you appear to me to be quite in error. I am
confronting you not on equal terms as one commander against another, but
as a young soldier in training under you in the tilting-yard, subject to in-   10
spection and report by you as my master-at-arms. However, suppose that
I were indeed pitted against you in a regular battle; what you have done
is not to dislodge the front line of my army, but to ambush some straggling
soldier, or rather camp-follower, when he wandered too far, and too carelessly, away from the rest of the force; and what you do with him is more   15

your affair than mine. For, as I have occasionally and incidentally remarked, the mysteries of scripture can yield different meanings because of their rich abundance, and we must not reject any interpretation so long as it is probable and not contrary to the faith. Now, I supported my statement with some evidence, which you do not refute; and I made it, not for the sake of affirming a proposition but to moderate one; in a word, not for my sake but for yours. My desire was that my fight should be as bloodless as possible, and that I should conduct my defence in such a way that neither Jerome nor anyone else might become a casualty. But I see you have preferred to contend for higher stakes, so that either you make good the opinion from Jerome, in which case everyone else must perish in a general massacre, or else, if I win, then your favourite Jerome must fall. What if it were impossible for you, on those terms, to defend your Jerome without hurting him? What if you are inflicting numerous wounds on him for the sake of saving him from this one trivial injury? He uttered this only once, and then not on his own authority, whereas he is quite often in agreement with my view. You would rather he had been mistaken on many occasions than on only one! What I maintain is that he was nowhere mistaken but, using the legitimate freedom appropriate to a commentator, made a variety of remarks on the same point. Now, who has Jerome's interests at heart – you or I? Is it you, I ask, who first injure him and then challenge him to risk his neck, or I, who wish to see him safe and sound whatever the issue may be? At this stage, then, when you fight so wordily with me, you fight not with me but with yourself – and I do not fight back, since it has nothing to do with me. This does not mean that I have nothing at all to say in reply: for the case is such that, even were there no rational proof, it could be upheld by the consensus and number of the authorities; while in fact is is supported by rational proofs so powerful that even in default of a single authority your arguments could be, if not overthrown, certainly undermined. Accordingly it does not matter to me how much you are prepared to hazard Jerome in the contest, for I am already in sheltered waters.

Now, when you laboriously resolve the trivial questions I had sent ahead like scouts, you suppose that you have already penetrated both my wings and are routing my centre, whereas you have hardly as yet made contact with my line of skirmishers. In this situation, Colet, it seems to me that you are not acting like a theologian but are making use of a sly rhetorical

* * * * *

111:17 scripture can yield different meanings] Cf LB v 1267A.
46 sheltered waters] Literally 'my voyage is now in harbour'; *Adagia* I i 46

kind of artifice; in accordance with Quintilian's precept, you are leaving out the proofs and aiming again at my unguarded and lightly protected sides – and with some exaggeration, too – while you are inflating and exaggerating your own case. This is the kind of cunning I used in alluding to your 55 arguments, but in such a way that I added to rather than detracted from them.

But I do not think it worth while to reply here to each point in turn, since these things lie outside the debate; I shall merely touch on a few issues. You are very surprised at my question why, if the words of the 60 prayer for deliverance refer to the Jews (for this is your account of my statement), their salvation is not more explicitly discussed; you think that I am blinded when all around is light, for to you it appears clearer than day that the Jews are referred to, since the passage names the cup which the Jews intended to offer to Christ, and that 'Let this cup pass from me' means pre- 65 cisely 'Let not my death be a cause of death to the Jews.' This is the point at which you insistently urge me to lift up my eyes and to behold the light, which you claim to be so bright. Well then, Colet, at your behest I do raise my failing and bleary eyes, and, at least in the words in which you represent Christ as speaking, I do see a great deal of light. But even now I cannot see 70 in Christ's discourse anything that has to do with the Jews. However much you may illuminate that discourse by your comments, you surely cannot deny that it contains a modicum of obscurity, to occasion such doubt among many distinguished scholars. So you ought not to be surprised if I am blind where, as you know, Augustine and Ambrose and Leo and Gregory, and 75 indeed everyone else, one and all appear to have failed to see clearly. It is hardly strange if an owl's vision be poor where eagles are totally blind, or that Tiresias cannot clearly see what it baffles an Argus to discern.

But if this is a conjectural topic, so that we have to put authorities aside for the moment and pursue our inquiry by the method of inference, let us 80 now assemble those circumstantial facts upon which all reasoning by inference rests. The crucifixion lay threateningly close at hand, while the guilty soldiery approached, led by one guiltier still. Christ, to whom there was nothing that was not known, knew what was afoot; he sought privacy, and began to be discomfited and sad, to sweat, to be deeply downcast. His dis- 85 ciples' eyes, too, by reason of their grief were exceedingly heavy with sleep. He bade them watch and pray lest they should fall into temptation, for 'the

* * * * *

52 Quintilian] *Institutiones oratoriae* 5.13.27
78 Tiresias] The blind prophet
78 Argus] The watcher with a hundred eyes (Ovid *Metamorphoses* 1.625ff)

spirit indeed is willing, but the flesh is weak.' He too prayed, thus showing
by example what he had enjoined in words, namely that whenever we are
overtaken by a severe storm of misfortune we too should have recourse to   90
prayer, in order that our heavenly father may, if it please him, drive away
the tempest, or endow us at least with a courageous spirit.

If rational proofs are derived from probable inference, do not all these
facts, taken together, loudly proclaim that here is a man, who stands in fear
of death? The preceding passage contains a quite explicit mention of flesh   95
and spirit, but not a word about his sorrow over the Jews. He had before
this lamented the destruction of Jerusalem, but in terms that admit of no
ambiguity. Upon the cross, he prayed for his murderers, but in such a way
that his meaning is easy to grasp. And anyone who finds this instance of
Our Lord's mercy greatly to his liking will, I think, have no difficulty in   100
accepting the fact that he on one occasion lamented the destruction of the
ungrateful race, and that for them he prayed upon the cross. Since no preceding or simultaneous or subsequent fact gives occasion for even the
shadow of any such inference, but on the contrary all the circumstances
unite to proclaim a very different conclusion, without a single dissentient   105
voice, what then is there to suggest to us that we should wish to distort this
into a reference to the Jews? Especially when we thereby do wrong to the
host of eminent authorities who disagree, if to hold a different opinion be
to disagree, with Jerome, and are as scholarly as he, if scholarship is what
we should trust, and as devout too, if we prefer to place our trust in piety.   110
This, Colet, is what I meant, though I am not sure whether I said so in my
letter: when the inference is so obvious, and the number of famous
authorities so large, it is not proper to join Jerome in disagreement with the
received and long-established interpretation unless one has, I do not say
merely proofs, but the most positive proofs as well. Otherwise your   115
interpretations are but dreams.

At this point I insist once more that you demonstrate to me the existence of even slight grounds for inferring that these phrases should be connected with the Jews. I wish you would make more evident to us that perfectly plain light which only you can see. You answer, 'Do you not hear the   120
mention of the cup? Nothing can be plainer than that!' But is this light
entirely confined within that cup alone? 'The Jews,' you say, 'proposed to
offer the cup of death to Christ; he prays that they should not offer it to their
own destruction, using these words "My Father, let this cup pass from
me." ' But why should the reference to the cup be connected with the Jews,   125
as offering it, rather than with Christ who was to drink it? Suppose I demonstrate that the very phrase to which you attribute perfect light tells strongly
against your view? Recall his words to Peter: 'Shall I not drink the cup which

my Father hath given me?' If the father gives the cup to drink, and Christ receives it to drink, do you not see that the Jews are excluded? Compare 130 the verse 'Shall I not drink the cup which my Father hath given me?' with the verse 'Let this cup of thine pass from me – this cup of thine, I say, that is thine own, O Father' (of course you are familiar with the delicate shade of meaning in the pronoun). What he is plainly conveying is this: 'My Father, thou hast given me this cup to drink, and exceedingly bitter it is. 135 Man, whose nature I have put on, shrinks from it; yet since thou wilt that I drink it, I do not refuse; whatever thou dost will, I will.'

I could develop all this at some length, in the manner of a rhetorician, were I not concerned to be brief and were not my correspondent the most scholarly of men. But, to make you a present of all your assumptions, let 140 us stretch the word 'cup' so as to apply it to the Jews, in that they were to offer it. How will it be possible for us to squeeze out the sense you want: 'Let this cup pass from me' meaning 'I would not that my death should bring death upon the Jews,' or 'Let this cup, this suffering, which the Jews are preparing, pass from me'? He names himself; as for the Jews, he does not 145 so much as allude to them. 'The Jews are to put me to death; I do not, indeed, refuse to die; but I pray, my Father, that my death should cause the death of no one': this, you maintain, is what Christ meant. But who but a diviner could take your meaning from the words 'Let this cup pass from me?' What is their message but 'Let my Passion pass from me?' As a rule you are averse 150 to forced interpretations, but what pronouncement could be more forced or strained than this interpretation of your own? Yet you are driven to it, as if driven on to the rocks, by an incorrect deduction from what I myself wrote. You say, 'if he prayed to be delivered from death, at some point he was unwilling to die; thus the joy of his supreme love is circumscribed and 155 diminished.'

It may be, Colet, that the point you refer to was one that, for lack of the power to express myself, I did not sufficiently explain, though I think I devoted ample space to it and showed by the clearest arguments that this interpretation, adhered to by me or rather by everybody, in no way 160 diminishes either Christ's courage or his love, but even makes them appear decidedly greater. Since you failed to offer any reply to these arguments, it seemed to me, to speak frankly, that you either had not read my discussion or at least had forgotten about it. If the only point in my own view that

* * * * *

134 pronoun] Erasmus' Latin, following that of the Vulgate, has 'iste' 'that cup (of yours)' not 'ille'; the distinction of pronouns does not exist in Greek.
142 squeeze out] Reading 'emungere' (the ms reading) for 'emergere.'

causes you difficulty is your belief that it obscures Christ's love, and if I have   165
so far removed that difficulty as to show that it even augments the love, is
there any reason why we should take refuge in that unnatural explanation,
casting all others aside, in the teeth of the very words of the text? I have
no mind to reply to the minor points of your argument one at a time, nor
need I do so. The argument that seems to you decidedly absurd is one that   170
I interposed casually, as something beyond the scope of the discussion.
What does it matter whether he prays for deliverance from death, or prays
that he be not put to death by men? In this, you go so far as to call me 'rather
imperceptive' if between matters so closely similar, as you put it, I am
unable to distinguish with a particularly discerning eye. If the similarity   175
appears to you so close, why do you call me imperceptive? And yet, dear
Colet, you are quite close to my own opinion if I, who to myself appear to
see nothing, to you appear to see very little. But, all the same, let us now
see how far we can catch any glimmering of light through this obscurity.
I myself observe as most distinct those things which you suppose to be most   180
similar, while those you consider as separable only in logic, I can perceive
as differing in substance and nature as well. For it is possible for one to die
without being put to death by men. Here, I believe, you can see the blind
man making a more evident distinction than you, with your Argus-eyes,
had made. And it would be useless for you to challenge me by objecting: 185
'But Christ could not die save by being slain, otherwise he would have been
no sacrifice.' For, taking into account the laws of nature, nothing could be
less true; he was mortal, and fated to die even though no one slew him. 'But
he willed to be slain, and had to be.' True; but what has this to do with the
distinction we made?
                                                                                        190
    Let us however abandon the foregoing considerations; now I shall take
a closer view. Christ could not be put to death as a victim if he were not
put to death by men. And indeed he himself willed to be put to death; but
he would not that the Jews should kill him. This, forsooth, was the 'close
similarity,' in respect to which I was blind. Is anyone so illiterate as not to   195
know the difference between passive and active, suffering and doing?
These concepts are distinct, not merely logically, as you claim in your letter,
but generically as well. The purpose of my argument was not to prove that
the two concepts appeared the same to me, but that one followed upon the
other in such a way that the latter might be inferred from the former. This   200
is no novel method of proof, invented by me; it is extremely familiar to
rhetorician and logician alike, and very ancient: they call it the argument
from the antecedents. 'She conceived, therefore she lay with a man. She
give birth, therefore she conceived. He died, therefore he must have
lived.' Surely it does not follow that I identify conception with giving birth,   205

life with death? By no means; I only wished to indicate that the one was a consequence of the other. Nor am I blind to the possibility that a woman may wish to conceive but not wish to give birth, or wish to give birth but be unwilling to conceive. However, no sane woman will pray that she may give birth if she is unwilling to conceive. Similarly no one who detests sea-voyages will long to be shipwrecked. And no one will desire to be slain yet wish nobody to slay him.

But since this argument, as I have remarked, is extraneous to my case, I will refrain from setting forth my view. I will merely touch on those points which affect the soundness of my argument. Next, Colet, the matters you discuss so skilfully and eloquently, urging that Christ willed both that the Jews should put him to death and equally that they should not; that he exercised one and the same will, both when he willed the event and when he willed the opposite; and that he willed the opposite precisely because he willed the event (so that you may appear to have set us a riddle!): all these are irrelevant to my exposition. Even so, I cannot agree with you even about this. For it cannot by any means come about that we both wish something and wish its opposite. Christ wished to be put to death; he knew that the Jews were to be the cause of his death, but did not wish it. It was good that Christ should be put to death; but it was evil to kill him. Now, Christ does not by any means desire evil. Have a care lest your analogy of the rich man, which you employ as a weapon of argument in the Platonic manner, might conceivably be turned against yourself. You say that the rich man desires to have no losses, yet tolerates a certain measure of loss in the hope of increasing his profits; therefore, the same person is both willing and unwilling to suffer a loss, and it is the same avarice that prompts him to accept that small loss and to reject loss in general. On the contrary, he does not desire the loss for its own sake; he desires it for the sake of profit. What does it matter under what heading he wishes it, if wish it he does? There are many things which we desire for quite different reasons. I myself wish to be in France; if this be sufficient reason for setting out upon a sea-voyage, I wish also to go on a voyage: not that sailing by itself affords me any pleasure, but that it earns my conditional approval under the circumstances. We give up sleep, we study, we fast, we say our prayers, we observe celibacy; none of these do we desire for its own sake, yet we still desire to do them. If a good man were to be asked whether he wished to have a mistress, what would he answer? That he both wished and did not

* * * * *

212 wish nobody to slay him] Reading 'uolet' for 'nolet.'

wish it at once; or rather 'I should wish it,' says he, 'if it were permitted; but since it is not permitted, I do not wish it.'

Let us then assert that, of those two events which were destined to happen to Christ in succession, not through any inner connexion but just as they occurred – that he should die, and that he should be put to death by the Jews – he desired one (that he should die), but did not desire the other (that the Jews should put him to death, to their own hurt). For it was possible that he might be assassinated by lunatics; it was possible that his murderers might be forgiven their sin, for there is no crime so terrible that it cannot be pardoned.

I pass over many considerations, deliberately. On this last point I have merely touched, in order that you may devote especially careful thought to pondering the rest. So far, you have not even come to grips with my argument. When you have refuted it, I will either frankly admit defeat or offer a stout defence of my position. You gave the splendid counsel that we ought to combine in catching any sparks that were struck out when the flinty rocks of our two arguments clashed together; but it seems to me that thus far you have not touched my flint with your stone. Surely you do not suppose that truth, which is buried deep within the innermost strata, can flash forth at once on the first feeble contact? Nay, she is forced out only after a long and arduous struggle.

Farewell, dearest Colet.

Oxford

112 / From Johannes Sixtinus   [Oxford, c 27 October 1499]

This letter and the following are an introductory exchange of compliments similar to those exchanged between Colet and Erasmus (cf Epp 106 and 107). Johannes Sixtinus (d 1519) was a native of West Friesland, where he owned estates. He had come to Oxford to study and he remained in England till his death, except for some four or five years in Italy after 1504 where he studied law at Bologna (cf Allen Ep 244: 19) and secured an LLD at Siena. He also revisited Friesland occasionally (cf Allen Epp 273: 13 and 291: 2ff). In Italy he acquired a copy of the *De copia* which in 1511 caused some slight strain in his relations with Erasmus (cf Epp 235 and 244). See Emden BRUO III 1675.

JOHANNES SIXTINUS TO THAT MASTER OF LITERARY STYLE, DESIDERIUS ERASMUS
Our most gracious master, Prior Richard Charnock, showed me today some poems written by you which showed uncommon grasp of metre; had they been carefully finished off they would, I think, deserve to earn some little

reputation, but, considering that they are said to have been worked out and   5
composed by you extempore, one can hardly believe that a single critic, of
any talent at least, after he has finished reading your verses, will fail to
award you a place upon the level of the distinguished poets of antiquity.
For they are fragrant with a kind of Attic charm, and with the extraordinary
sweetness of your mind. Therefore I urge you to continue, and to awaken   10
the melodious Muses you possess, in order that the world may learn from
you and others like you what has hitherto seemed incredible, that the
abilities of the Germans are in no respect inferior to those of the Italians.
Farewell, my sweet delightful poet.

EPIGRAM TO ERASMUS, BY SIXTINUS   15
Great poet, here are my verses unkempt;
Sure you will laugh at so crude an attempt,
Quietly murmuring, 'Eminent men
Scorn such deplorable fruits of the pen!'
'Cosmus am I,' you may add, 'and prefer   20
No chilly robe, but rich togas to wear;'
Violets, Sixtin, are not for a boor,
Nor must a tribute to Caesar be poor;
Yet, most renowned of the bards of our age,
Good may transpire from so humble a page: 25
If it earn praise in your critical eye,
Paradise waits for its author. Goodbye.

113 / To Johannes Sixtinus
Oxford, 28 October [1499]

DESIDERIUS ERASMUS OF ROTTERDAM TO MASTER JOHANNES SIXTINUS
OF FRIESLAND
Sixtinus, your honest straightforwardness leaves not the slightest room for
the suspicion of flattery – an accusation from which you would be shielded
by the authoritative testimony of Prior Richard, or equally of John Colet,   5
even if your character were not there to support it, or else (if neither man's
testimony were available) by your character alone, a character entirely free
from every vice, and so much a stranger to falsehood and pretence that
directness itself could not be more direct, or freedom more free. If it were
not so, I should imagine that you were laughing at me, since your praise   10

* * * * *

112:20 Cosmus] The name of a celebrated perfumer mentioned by Juvenal and
Martial, seems to be used more generally by Sixtinus for a person of luxurious
tastes.
113:5 Prior Richard] Charnock (cf Ep 106:10n).

of me is so unlimited though its occasion is so limited, or rather so trivial and insignificant. As God loves me, I am ashamed that those trivial verses, whatever they were, that I threw off not only carelessly but altogether absentmindedly, in the process of trying out a new pen, are given the name not merely of poetry but of accomplished poetry. Had you criticized it   15 adversely, I should still have taken it as a great compliment for the very reason that you did so. Distinguished practitioners do not generally consider trifles of this sort as deserving even their censure, so that blame itself is a kind of praise, when it emanates from men like you. Yet you, Sixtinus, actually admire my more-than-trivial nonsense so much that things which   20 seem to me rank goatherd stuff have for you a flavour of true Attic charm, and things which in my opinion exhibit a kind of Scythian barbarity seem to you to reveal a wondrous sweetness. And, so please the Muses, you think, on the strength of such rubbish, that I even deserve to be compared with the ancients! I tell you once again, I should suppose I was being   25 laughed at, if it were not Sixtinus who wrote all this. For surely this is just like the story in Quintilian about the pigmy who pulled on the boots of a stage Hercules and pretended that a gnat was an eagle?

But in case I should seem altogether to refuse to acknowledge your compliments, Sixtinus, it is true that there is something Attic in my verses: 30 they are sparing of emotions, and seldom meddle with them at all, while they completely abstain from those violent disturbances which are known as passions. You will not find in them any tempest, any river bursting its banks in spate, any wild exaggeration. They practise remarkable economy in the use of words, preferring to stop short of, rather than exceed, the   35 mean, to run aground, rather than make for the high seas. They have not a vestige of any dye: their complexion is natural, certainly, but 'old and weasel-coloured' (what care I?); and they conceal their artistry so successfully that you could not detect a trace of it, even with Lynceus' eyesight! This, in fact, is the one creditable quality in which I am even slightly   40 superior to the Attic writers. They merely conceal their art enough to deceive others – I, enough to deceive myself as well. They simply take pains to see that nothing stands out in high relief, or hits the eye; it can be detected, not perhaps by the mere listener or careless reader, but certainly by him who reads with attention and in a spirit of rivalry, when the author,   45

* * * * *

27 Quintilian] *Institutiones oratoriae* 6.1.36; *Adagia* III vi 67
38 weasel-coloured] Cf Terence *Eunuchus* 688–9.
39 Lynceus] *Adagia* II i 54

in Horace's words, 'sweats long and toils in vain'. But if anyone is so foolish as to attempt to analyse my poems he will find when he has done so how devoid of artifice they are. To this extent I show myself Attic; for just as Ennius' hero wanted to philosophize, but only slightly, so I approve of Atticizing in principle but not to excess. I am frightened off by the manner 50 in which Theophrastus was stigmatized by an old crone's derision for his hyper-Attic way of speaking. To avoid this stigma I try to season the Scythicism of Anacharsis with some Atticism of my own. I am not the man, like Ennius, 'never to rush to tell of arms / In cold sobriety'; nor do I try to challenge the ancient Muse; I write when I am sober, and the verses I write are 55 so level-headed that they fail to possess the least trace of Apollo's inspiration.

So far am I from being ashamed of this, that I am actually quite complacent about it, having just this one trait in common with Cicero – otherwise I should have none at all. Do not suppose that I am anything but sincere 60 in saying this; for 'what forbids, 'mid mirth the truth to tell?' In fact I have slipped into writing a kind of poetry that is dry, feeble, lacking both blood and vital sap, partly through a certain poverty of talent, partly through lack of taste. Cicero is quite right in supposing that men's natures are transformed by their surroundings above all. When I was a lad, I wrote for the 65 ears of men not of Cosenza but of Holland: that is, for very dull ears. I sang my songs to Midas, and, paying too assiduous court to men of his kind, in the end all that I achieved was failure to please them, or scholars either. I was trying to kill two birds with one stone, and please the unlettered with the straightforwardness of my discourse, while at the same time not entirely 70

* * * * *

46 Horace] *Ars poetica* 241

49 Ennius' hero] Neoptolemus: Cicero *Tusculanae disputationes* 2.1.1; *De republica* 1.18.30

51 Theophrastus] Cf Cicero *Brutus* 46.172; Quintilian *Institutiones oratoriae* 8.1.2.

53 Anacharsis] A 'Scythian' philosopher; traditionally one of the Seven Sages (cf Diogenes Laertius 1.101ff)

53–4 like Ennius] Cf Horace *Epistles* 1.19.7–8.

59 Cicero] His verses were commonly regarded as uninspired.

61 'what forbids ... tell'] Horace *Satires* 1.1.24–5

64 Cicero]Cf *De divinatione* 1.36, 79.

66 Cosenza] As Lucilius, the satirist, said he did (Cicero *De finibus* 1.3.7)

67 Midas] *Adagia* I iii 67 (of 'stolid persons with no taste')

69 kill two birds with one stone] Literally, 'whitewash two walls from one pot'; *Adagia* I vii 3

displeasing the world of scholarship by my graceful style and incisive intellect. Clever as this idea seemed to me at the time, it has turned out a failure;
for I write too learnedly to win the approval of unlearned men, and too
unlearnedly to merit the approval of scholars.

So much then, most learned Sixtinus, for my own opinion of my   75
verses. But the extent to which I differ from you in the matter is equalled
by the warmth with which I welcome your enthusiasm, so that whatever
is lost to the truth is added to the sum of your affection for me, since the
less I can recognize the picture you paint of my qualities, the more it follows
that you love me. This is why it was the most delightful thing possible to   80
receive a complimentary address from one who is both very affectionate
and wholly honest; if it was true, I am in your debt for a recommendation;
if false, for a kindness. For it is really only he who is praised without cause
that is done a kindness, since anything done for a person who deserves it
is not a kindness, but a right. Still, I deeply wish the advertisement you give   85
me were quite true, or at least that it seemed true to me. I am preening
myself so much about it that, diffident to a fault as I am, I have almost begun
to be complacent already on the grounds that I have satisfied you; that is,
have satisfied Roscius; anyone who does not arouse your active contempt
is not to be classed among the poorest performers. And I am even trying   90
to win myself over by a seductive chain of reasoning: 'Why,' I tell myself,
'should you disparage yourself when you seem worthwhile to Sixtinus?
Inasmuch as he admires you, he must be either lying or mistaken. But he
is not lying, for he is a most straightforward person; he is not mistaken,
for he is a consummate scholar and a man of the keenest judgment.   95
However, he loves you, and lovers are blind. Yes, he loves you, but because
his sight is good. For what was it that Sixtinus loved in me but literature?
And if he really detected that in me, and loved me for that reason, he is not
blind; if it be otherwise, he does not even love me if the thing for the sake
of which alone he was ready to love me is once removed. But if he does not   100
love me and also praises me falsely, he must certainly be either flattering
or deriding me; and if these faults fit Sixtinus' character less well than sloth
suits that of Hercules, then his praise was as true as it was affectionate.'

How expert I am at the petty wiles of self-flattery! But then, once again,
it seems excessively brazen of me to acknowledge such generous compli-   105
ments as true; yet at the same time I have no taste for replying, and so, in

* * * * *

89 satisfied Roscius] The greatest actor on the Roman stage; hence proverbial
for the best man at anything (*Adagia* iv vii 69).

the old proverb, I have 'a wolf by the ears,' and do not know how to let it
go or hold it. If I acknowledge them, I shall be generous to myself; if I decline
them I shall be ungenerous to you. If I reject them, I diminish either your
loyalty or your good sense; if I allow them, I take too much upon myself.   110
If I accept what is offered, I shall be extremely arrogant not only in my eyes
but in others'. If I refuse it, I should pronounce a clear indictment against
either your wisdom or your moral character, so that you would seem either
to have failed to see things clearly, or to have failed to declare honestly what
it was you observed. Thus I am driven into a dilemma where if I escape   115
Scylla I must inevitably encounter Charybdis; that is to say, I must either
make myself ridiculous by acknowledging your praise, or insult you by
spurning it.

My conclusion from all this, my dear Sixtinus, is that in future you
ought either to praise your Erasmus in metaphorical language (and you are   120
expert in the turns of speech commonly employed for this purpose) or at
least to lay your praise before others; for although in praising me to myself
you do me a most agreeable service (for what could be more desirable than
praise from one whom everyone praises?) still it is a service I can neither
accept without shame, nor decline without insulting you, whereas to others   125
you might even represent me as a god without imperilling either of us! I
do not in fact belong to the class of men who prefer to be judged by others,
who never plumb themselves nor bring into their own view 'the part of the
knapsack that lies behind them,' and depend wholly on the votes of others,
swelling with pride like a peacock when they are flattered; but even if I did   130
belong to it, I should not be injured by praise of which I was unaware.
Moreover, those to whom you trumpet the praises of your good friend will
think the better of me if they believe you, and if they refuse to believe you,
then at least they will have no occasion to think any worse of me. Again,
so far as you yourself are concerned, if men believe you, you will appear   135
in a kindly light as one who in no way envies other men for their good qualities, while, if they do not, you will still earn praise for courtesy in prefer-

* * * * *

107 a wolf by the ears] *Adagia* i v 25, citing Terence *Phormio* 505–6
116 Scylla] *Adagia* i v 4
127 judged by others] *Adagia* i vi 89
128 plumb themselves] Cf Persius 4.23 and 24; *Adagia* vi 90.
128–9 part of the knapsack that lies behind them] Erasmus' words are quoted
from Catullus *Carmina* 22.21. According to Aesop's Fable 266, each man went
through life wearing a 'mantica,' or double knapsack, full of human faults;
the part containing his own faults lay on his back (and so out of view), but
the part that held others' faults hung in full view upon his chest.

ring to commend others for their supposed virtues, rather than to censure their real vices. As you can see, this course benefits both of us to some extent, and harms neither, whereas, if one praises a friend to his face, even   140
though one does it out of an overflow of affection, so to speak, yet observe how much disservice one may do by an ill-judged kindness of this sort. One will be supposed either to be investing that particular morsel of praise in the hope of reaping a dividend, like those who only pay compliments in order to receive them back again, or to be a flatterer of present company,   145
or else, to put the best construction on it, to be yielding to affection. The result is that one's account is reckoned either as untruthful or at least as falling short of the truth. Then again, should the recipient of the compliment say nothing, he will appear to be happy to acknowledge it, for all its falsity; yet if he repudiates it he will seem to desire a more elaborate eulogy; and   150
if he should answer in kind, there will be cries of 'Scratch my back, and I'll scratch yours!'

But, in elaborating on this point at too great a length, I have forgotten my Atticism. And you ask me, 'Why, pray, do you go on so long?' So that you, my dear Sixtinus, may be assured that your eulogy of me was, as I have   155
said, extremely pleasant, since if I deserve it, as I do not think I do, I rejoice in the favourable opinion of a very fine scholar; if not, I still rejoice in the affection of a very good friend. Nevertheless, in order to avoid giving a handle to those profane illiterates, that is, strangers to the play of poetry, for the purpose of slandering the literate, I suggest that though we ought certainly to exchange letters as we do, still we should confine ourselves more   160
or less to subjects of the following kind: if one of us should come upon something new in the course of his reading, he shares it with the other; or else we have a battle royal about something that merits an argument between men of letters; or else we lighten the dull drudgery of our studies   165
by telling witty or charming stories; finally, we should discourse lightly of anything under the sun, so long as we refrain from this pretentious and over-popular kind of writing. But confound it, Sixtinus, in case you should mistake my drift, I would rather that you praised me, rather indeed that you abused me, than that you should keep silent.   170

As for your urging me to rouse my Muses from slumber, you must understand that it would take the wand of Mercury to wake them. I don't know whether it is lethargy or true sleep; but in either case, I think, it would be better if they went on sleeping: they are good-for-nothing, noisy, loquacious, distracting females. There is nothing riskier than challenging Pan to   175

* * * * *

151–2 'Scratch my back ... yours'] Literally 'one mule scratches another'; *Adagia* I vii 96

sing. Once 'the leech, that will not leave you, till he's full of gore,' has taken hold of a man's skin, it will be the death of him.

Indeed I did awaken them recently, much to their indignation, from a sleep of more than ten years' length, and forced them to utter the praises of the king's children. Unwillingly, and still half asleep, they did indite a strain of a kind, a ditty so somnolent that it could lull anyone to sleep. Since the piece vastly displeased me, I had no difficulty in allowing them to slumber again.

To proceed: the task of ensuring that mankind should be made aware that German brains are in every respect just as good as those of Italians is something that you if anyone, Sixtinus, should be able to accomplish. You were born in Friesland; and that most fertile mother of distinguished intellects, that very Africa which ever gives birth to some new phenomenon of this sort, has obviously found in you a son expressly made for the purpose of struggling, like a second Hannibal, with the Romans for the primacy in scholarship. In fact you, Sixtinus, possess gifts which lead us, inevitably, to form unbounded hopes of you. Your intellect is keen and bright, firm and manly, your power of memory capacious, ready and quick; your mental processes are efficient and versatile, while your tongue is articulate and fluent; and you have a character to match all these good qualities, with the result that you appear to have been born for literature alone. Besides which, your introduction to these studies was not delayed, as it is in most instances. You were reared in the very lap of the Muses, as it were, and drank the pure wine of letters, instead of milk. And you are still so young in years that, even if you had yet to take your first steps in literary study, it would still be reasonable to expect nothing less than the highest achievement from that brilliant intelligence, that well-furnished memory, that tireless industry of yours. Now you have come to the point where you have left behind you a mighty horde and there are only a few in front. So up, Sixtinus, and arm courageously; show yourself a Hannibal in rivalling the works of Italian genius, or a Hercules in slaying the monsters that are, alas, laying siege to the citadel of sound learning, and I shall look on and applaud. Your own poem appeared to me to be exactly such as you insisted that mine was; and it pleased Prior Charnock as much as you yourself are dear to him. Farewell.

Oxford, on the feast of Sts Simon and Jude [1497]

* * * * *

176 The leech ...] Horace *Ars poetica* 476
179 praises] Cf Ep 104 introduction.
188 Africa] Alluding to the proverb 'Ex Africa semper aliquid novi'; *Adagia* III vii 10

114 / To Thomas More   Oxford, 28 October 1499

Thomas More (1478?–1535) had met Erasmus in London or Greenwich probably through Mountjoy (cf Ep 104 introduction). This is the first surviving letter in the correspondence between the two men, who were to remain close
friends for the rest of their lives.

ERASMUS TO HIS FRIEND THOMAS MORE

I can hardly find any expressions strong enough to do justice to the exe-
crations I have poured on the head of this messenger, whose carelessness
or dishonesty I blame for the fact that I have been cheated of the letters from
my dear More to which I was so greatly looking forward. For I must not,   5
and would not, suppose that you have been remiss in the duty of writing;
though I have reproached you about this in previous letters with just a
shade of indignation. Nor am I afraid that my plain-speaking may have
upset you, for you are quite well aware of my Spartan habit of sparring until
I draw blood. But, joking apart, dearest Thomas, I ask you to cure, adding   10
a bit of interest, the sick mood that I have caught from yearning too long
for yourself and your letters. Really what I am looking for is not a single letter but a huge bundle of correspondence, such as might break the back of
an Egyptian porter. If there are any enthusiasts for sound learning where
you are now, your function shall be to provoke them to write to me, of   15
course with the object of completing the circle of my friends; but I should
not dare to be the first to rouse them.

I think, you see, that it makes no difference to you in what strain I write
to you, since you are an easy-going fellow; and I have come to believe that
you have, besides, a considerable affection for me. Farewell, my dearest   20
More.

Oxford, on the feast of Sts Simon and Jude, 1499

115 / To William Blount, Lord Mountjoy   Oxford [November 1499]

Mountjoy had intended to follow Erasmus to Oxford and to resume his studies
(cf Ep 105), but had been detained by both public and private responsibilities
(cf Ep 117: 7ff).

* * * * *

114:14 porter] The Egyptians were despised as bearers of heavy burdens
(*Adagia* III v 48); Erasmus uses a Greek word which he found in Aulus
Gellius *Noctes Atticae* 5.3.2.

ERASMUS TO THE NOBLE COUNT, WILLIAM MOUNTJOY

If you, your noble lady, your kind father-in-law, and the rest of your household are well, I have great cause for rejoicing. I am in excellent health here,
and daily better. Your England is beginning to charm me inexpressibly,
partly from acquaintance, which softens all harsh experiences, and partly   5
because of the kindness shown to me by Colet and Prior Charnock. They
are the gentlest, sweetest, most lovable people imaginable, and with their
friendship to support me I should agree to dwell in furthest Scythia itself.
And I have learned by my own experience the truth of Horace's saying that
'oft the mob sees true.' You are aware of the vulgar proverb 'hard beginning   10
makes good ending.' What could have been more ill-omened, so to speak,
than my arrival? But now everything goes better as the days go on. I have
rid myself of all the depression in which you once saw me wallowing. For
the rest, my sweet friend, I pray that, just as once when my own courage
failed me you sustained me with yours, so now, when mine does not fail,   15
your own may not be wanting.

As for your failure to come on the appointed day, I have no mind to
reproach you with it, nor do I hold that I have a right to do so. What detained
you I know not; I only know that whatever it was that prevented you, it was
a good and sufficient reason, since I do not doubt your intention to come,   20
nor can I see any cause why you should have wished to invent an excuse.
The honest straightforwardness of your noble nature is such that, however
urgent the reason, you could not feign even if you wanted to, nor desire
to do so even if you were able. It is not for me either to persuade or dissuade
you, or, rather, I ought to prefer dissuasion. Follow the way your interests   25
urge you to go. I long for you, but in such a way that I would still wish you
to act in the meantime as those interests dictate. If you will be here presently, I am happy; but if anything is keeping you back, provided it be no
misfortune, I shall cheerfully await your coming, just as I have hitherto
done.   30

Please send my money, carefully sealed with your seal-ring. I am
already considerably indebted to the prior, who supplies my needs with
equal kindness and speed; but since he has acted like a man of the friendliest disposition, it is right and proper for me in my turn to play the part
of one who feels gratitude, and give back, as generously, what he so gener-   35

* * * * *

115:2 father-in-law] Sir William Say (cf Epp 103 introduction and 105:4n).
9 Horace] *Epistles* 2.1.63
12 arrival] Possibly in England, but more probably in Oxford (cf Ep 105).

ously gave. I believe a man ought to be sparing in the demands he makes on his friends, as with all precious possessions. Please write and tell me any news there is where you are. Farewell.

Oxford [1498]

116 / To Johannes Sixtinus   Oxford [November 1499]

This letter records a second discussion on a point of biblical interpretation in which Colet and Erasmus were involved, and, as on the previous occasion (cf Epp 109–11), found themselves on opposing sides. Colet had apparently invited Erasmus and Prior Richard Charnock to dinner, probably at Magdalen. The company included a theologian and a lawyer, who cannot be otherwise identified, and a number of Fellows. When the biblical discussion had gone on too long and become too serious, Erasmus introduced a lighter note by offering an alternative version of the story of Cain which he seems to have invented on the spot. It has recently been suggested that what Erasmus had done was to turn the myth of Eden into the myth of Prometheus. R.H. Bainton *Erasmus of Christendom* (New York 1969) 57.

ERASMUS TO MASTER JOHANNES SIXTINUS

How I wish you had been at that recent feast of ours, as I thought you were going to be, for it was a true feast of reason and no drinking-party. I, at least, have never experienced anything more pleasant, civilized, delicious. Nothing was lacking. In the familiar words, 'the company was elegant, the   5 time and place well-chosen, the arrangements well-planned.' It was seasoned by such refinements of comfort as might have delighted Epicurus and by conversation such as might have charmed Pythagoras. The company was not only elegant but brilliantly so: fit to make an Academy, not merely a banquet. You will ask me who these were. Hear, and you will be all the more   10 sorry that you were not there. In the first place, Prior Richard, that high-priest of the Graces; secondly the theologian who had delivered a lecture in Latin on that day, a scholarly and modest person; next, your friend

* * * * *

116:3 feast of reason] Erasmus plays on the word 'convivium' (literally, 'living together'), contrasting it with 'symposium' (literally 'drinking together'), although the two words are, in common usage, practically synonymous.

5 in the familiar words] 'Ut inquit ille,' literally, 'as he [the author whom you know] remarks.' The reference is to Varro *Menippean Satires* 335; quoted in Aulus Gellius *Noctes Atticae* 13.11 (cf Ep 61:41–3n).

11 Prior Richard] Charnock (cf Ep 106:10n).

Philip, a charmingly humorous fellow. Colet, as the defender and champion of the ancient theology, presided. On his right hand sat the prior, whose   15
multifarious grasp of learning in all its kinds is, I swear, as remarkable as
his combination of perfect kindness with perfect honesty; on his left, that
newly arrived theologian; while, in order to make sure that the feast had
its poet, I sat next to the theologian, on the left flank, with Philip opposite,
to ensure the presence of a lawyer. The other places were occupied by an   20
indiscriminate and nameless throng.

When the ranks were thus arrayed, war broke out at once, over our
cups of drink, but not from them, and not a drinker's war. While there were
many subjects on which there was little agreement, we quarrelled particularly fiercely over the following. Colet asserted that the sin by which   25
Cain first angered God was that, as though he lacked faith in the Creator's
good will and placed too much trust in his own efforts, he was the first to
plough the earth, whereas Abel pastured his sheep, in contentment with
things that grew of themselves. Two of us argued separately against this,
the theologian using syllogistic logic while I employed the methods of   30
rhetoric. The Greeks maintain that Hercules himself cannot fight against
two; yet Colet, single-handed, had the better of us all. He seemed to become
intoxicated with a sort of holy frenzy, and to exhibit in his bearing something of superhuman exaltation and majesty. His voice was altered, his eyes
had a different look, and his features and expression were transformed; he   35
'greater seemed, possessed by deity.'

In the end, since the discussion had gone on rather long and had
become too serious and too rigorous to suit a dinner party, I decided to play
my part, that is, the part of a poet, with the object of getting rid of this con-
tentious argument and introducing some gaiety into the meal. And so,   40
'This,' I said, 'is a most ancient subject, for which we have to consult the
very oldest authorities. I will tell you what I have found out about it in the
course of my own reading, if you first promise me that you will not regard
what I am about to tell you as fictitious.' When they had promised, I said:
'Once upon a time I came upon an extremely old book; its title and author's   45
name had been effaced by time and eaten away by worms, those perpetual
enemies of sound learning. In it there was one page that had not either
rotted away or been gnawed to shreds by worms or mice (because, I believe,
the Muses always guard their own property), and I can remember reading
there an account, either true or, if not, at least a very plausible approxima-   50

* * * * *

14 Philip] This person has not been identified.
31 Hercules] *Adagia* I v 39
36 'greater ... deity'] Virgil *Aeneid* 6.49–50

tion to the truth, of the very subject you are fighting about; and I will tell
it to you if you like.'

They asked me to do so, and I began: 'This Cain,' said I, 'was not
merely a hard worker but greedy and avaricious as well. Now, he had often
heard his parents say that in the paradise they had been forced to leave   55
bountiful crops grew of their own accord, with ears of generous size and
enormous seeds and stalks so tall that they matched an alder tree of today,
and not a tare or thorn or thistle growing among them. He laid this well
to heart and, as he observed that the soil he was working at the time
grudged him even a mean and meagre crop, he added a dash of cunning   60
to his hard work. Approaching the angel who stood watch over the gate of
the garden, and laying siege to him with artful tricks, he managed, by making extravagant promises, to persuade the angel secretly to make him a gift
of just a very few seeds from its more abundant harvests. He claimed that
God had ceased to pay heed or attention to the matter for some time past,   65
and that, even if he were to find out, it would be easy for the angel to escape
punishment as it was an affair of no consequence so long as hands were
not laid upon the actual fruit, to which alone God's prohibition under penalty had applied.

"Now, then," he said, "you ought not to show an excess of zeal in your   70
capacity as gatekeeper. What if your over-conscientiousness is positively
unwelcome to the Lord, and he wishes you to be deceived and is likely to
be more gratified when mankind displays brains and hard work then idleness and sloth? Do you get any satisfaction from your present post? God
has turned you from an angel into an executioner so that you might cruelly   75
keep us poor, lost creatures out of our fatherland. He has chained you to
the door, sword and all, a function that we have begun lately to assign to
dogs. It is true that we are most unhappy, but it seems to me that you yourself are in considerably worse case; for, while we are deprived of the garden
for tasting too-sweet fruit, you for your part have to miss both Heaven and   80
garden alike, in order to keep us out, and are more wretched than we, inasmuch as we at least can wander hither and yon wherever we choose. And,
in case you are unaware of this, even the place we dwell in now contains
within it means of solacing our exile: groves of vivid green foliage and trees
of myriad kinds for some of which we have hardly as yet found names; little   85
streams that gush from hills and cliffs everywhere; rivers of clear bright
water lapping on grassy banks; soaring mountains, shady glens, and teem-
ing seas. And I feel sure that deep inside the inward parts of the earth there
lies concealed some precious commodity; to dig this up I will investigate
every vein of Earth's body or, if my own life suffice not, at least my descen- 90
dants will do so. Here, too, there are golden apples, plump figs, and crops
in great variety; and so profusely do many things spring up uncultivated

that, could we but live here forever, we should not miss your garden much. Disease indeed attacks us, but man's industry will find a remedy even for this. I observe that there are herbs exhaling marvellous properties. What if some herb can be found, in this same world of ours, to make life immortal? For I cannot see the importance of your tree of knowledge, and what concern have I with matters that are irrelevant to me? Still, I shall persevere in this endeavour, for there is nothing that will not yield to determined applica- tion. Thus, while we have obtained the wide, wide world in exchange for a single narrow garden, you, banished from both of them, enjoying neither garden nor Heaven nor earth, chained for ever to this door, and endlessly waving your sword, are but fencing with the wind! Very well then, why not be sensible and act in your own interest as well as ours? Give us what you can give without any loss to yourself, and take in exchange the things we are offering to share with you. Let our unhappiness, our banishment, our condemnation arouse sympathy in you who are unhappy, banished, and under a still worse damnation.''

Cain won his wicked case – a thoroughly bad man, but a consummate orator. He took the handful of seeds, surreptitiously given, and buried them with care. They grew up and multiplied; again he sowed the seed and yet again, and so on, until before many seasons had elapsed he had filled a vast and extensive area of farmland with this seed-crop; until it became too obvious to escape the eye of Heaven, and God was greatly angered. And God said, ''So far as I can see, this thief enjoys toil and sweat; and with these things shall he be surfeited.'' No sooner said than done; God sent upon the crop a horde of ants, weevils, toads, caterpillars, mice, locusts, swine, birds, and other plagues of the kind, to eat up the harvest either in the seed or in the blade or in the ear or in the barn. And from Heaven, besides, came a disastrous hailstorm and winds so strong that the grain-stalks, thick as the trunks of oaks, snapped like dry and brittle straw. The angel was replaced by another sentinel, and was clothed in a human body for his sym- pathy with mankind. And when Cain endeavoured to atone for it to God by making a burnt offering of his crops the smoke arose not to Heaven, so Cain fell into despair for he saw that God's anger was not to be appeased.'

This then, Sixtinus, is the story, told over our cups and born among the cups – even born of the cups, if you like – which I decided to set down

* * * * *

109–10 bad man ... consummate orator] Erasmus alludes to, and jokingly rebuts, Cato's definition of an orator as 'a good man, skilled in speaking.' Cicero *De oratore* 2.85: Quintilian *Institutio oratoria* I. Praef.9

for you; firstly in order to avoid an empty letter, for I recognized that it was my turn to write to you since I received your letter after I sent you one, and secondly to make sure that you had at least some share in that delightful dinner-party. Farewell.   130
    Oxford [1498]

117 / To William Blount, Lord Mountjoy   [Oxford, November 1499]

This letter was obviously sent to accompany a copy of the revised version of the *De conscribendis epistolis* (cf Ep 71 introduction). Whether it was simply that or was intended to be a dedicatory preface, as Allen suggests, is debatable.

ERASMUS TO THE NOBLE YOUTH, WILLIAM MOUNTJOY
My noble and distinguished young friend: When you demanded of me a copy of the enlarged and improved *De conscribendis epistolis* and did so with diffidence, as became your modesty, yet in such a way that I could eas-ily perceive the depth of your enthusiasm for the subject, I was highly   5
delighted with your sentiments, and at the same time bound to give my warm approval to your judgment. I am very glad to see that though you have suddenly become involved in all those private and public affairs, and also are naturally preoccupied with your recent marriage, you still have not turned away from your former attachment to sound learning. Whether this   10
is because you thought it was in your own interest that I should write a treatise on the subject, so that you, following the example of the princes of antiquity, might devote any leisure you secured, either on the completion of your business or even during its course, entirely to honourable pursuits, and not to frivolity as most men do; or because you wished as far as possible   15
by means of this work of mine, which labours for your sake throughout, to further the cause of study in your own England, to the end that you might there see Latin learning flourish more and more as the days go by, this attitude of yours, dear William, is one that is both worthy of you and destined to afford support as well as satisfaction to all lovers of sound learn-   20
ing, and so I praise it, as I am bound to do, and, as I have said, welcome it gladly. Equally do I congratulate you on your wise and shrewd judgment in correctly grasping two facts: first, that none of the many authors who have hitherto given instructions for letter-writing has done justice to this great theme, and second, that no single branch of study is of wider applica-   25

* * * * *

117:9 recent marriage] Cf Ep 105:4n.

tion than this, or contains an equal degree of utility or pleasure. All the more to be blamed are those who have compiled such scrappy and inaccurate, not to say uneducated, handbooks on a subject of such richness and importance as this.

I say nothing meanwhile about the pocket manuals which for a long time circulated in the grammar schools but which in recent days have almost vanished, as the mists vanish before the rising sun, when a more polite kind of literature began to flower again. What is the point of boys reading Francesco Negro? Not only are his rules pedantically petty and not even based, as they should have been, upon the fundamental texts in the authorities on rhetoric, but there is not a single letter of his in existence which is even in good Latin, let alone written with taste and charm. Again, the work that circulates under the name of Mario Filelfo seems to me entirely muddled and disorderly, and, to speak fairly candidly, defective both in scholarship and in suitability to the purpose in hand; for, disregarding the fact that it contains synonyms of the most puerile kind, we might have endured his irritating insistence on imposing a different style on each kind of letter had he not done so incompetently, pronouncing the weightiest kind of letter to be that which is wordiest and most heavily dependent on irrelevant assumptions. And what was the use of repeating, at the very beginning of the book, the rules of rhetoric which are so often given extensively elsewhere? Was it to make children abandon the books of Cicero and Quintilian in order to read this man's rubbish? I do not despise the scholarship of Sulpizio or of Perotti; in the works which they themselves call books of grammar, not of rhetoric, their purpose was to give a set of samples, so to speak, of this particular skill. Farewell.

[1498]

* * * * *

34 Negro] Francesco Negro (d 1513) was a Venetian scholar who wrote an *Opusculum scribendi epistolas* (Venice: H. Lichtenstein, 5 February 1488).

38 Filelfo] Giammario Filelfo (1426–80), eldest son of Francesco Filelfo (cf Ep 23:77n) and like his father noted for bare-faced flattery of his patrons, was a prolific poet and taught briefly in nearly every important city in Lombardy (cf Rossi 45). His *Novum epistolarium* was written in 1477, but not published till after his death.

49 Sulpizio] Giovanni Sulpizio of Verole (cf Ep 101:38n).

49 Perotti] Niccolò Perotti of Sassoferrato (1430–80) was an admirer of Valla and had studied under Guarino and Vittorino da Feltre. He was secretary to Cardinal Bessarion and lectured at the university of Bologna. His *Rudimenta grammatices* (Rome: Sweynheym and Pannartz, 19 March 1479) was reprinted more than fifty times before the end of the century. It contained a section 'De componendis epistolis' (cf Rossi 90f).

118 / To Robert Fisher   London, 5 December [1499]

Robert Fisher had been a pupil of Erasmus in Paris, but had gone to Italy in
the spring of 1498 to study law (cf Ep 62 introduction).

ERASMUS TO THE ENGLISHMAN, ROBERT FISHER, RESIDENT IN ITALY
I was a little shy at the prospect of writing to you, dear Robert, not because
I thought that the great distance between us in space and time might have
eroded your friendship for me, but because you are in a country where the
very walls are more scholarly and articulate than human beings are with us,   5
so that things which men in these parts regard as beautifully finished, elegant, and charming, in Italy cannot escape seeming crude, vulgar, and lacking in wit. This is why your own country, England, looks to find you not
only accomplished in the science of law but also equally fluent in Latin and
in Greek. You would have seen me too in Italy long before now, had not   10
Lord Mountjoy swept me away to his native England when I was just on
the point of leaving. Where, indeed, would I not follow a young man so
enlightened, so kindly, and so amiable? I would follow him, as God loves
me, even to the lower world itself. You had sung his praises to me and given
me a most lively description; but, believe me, every day that goes by he   15
surpasses not only your exposition of his qualities but the opinion I had
formed about him.
    But, you ask, 'how does our England please you?' If you trust me at
all, dear Robert, I should wish you to trust me when I say that I have never
found a place I like so much. I find here a climate at once agreeable and   20
extremely healthy, and such a quantity of intellectual refinement and
scholarship, not of the usual pedantic and trivial kind either, but profound
and learned and truly classical, in both Latin and Greek, that I have little
longing left for Italy, except for the sake of visiting it. When I listen to Colet
it seems to me that I am listening to Plato himself. Who could fail to be   25

* * * * *

118:7 in Italy] Erasmus' cherished plan to go to Italy to study (cf Ep 75:15n)
seemed about to be realized in the spring of 1499 (cf Ep 92:7), but just before
Mountjoy invited him to go to England he had decided to put it off till August
(cf Ep 95:29).

14 praises] This suggests that Fisher may have been responsible for introducing Mountjoy to Erasmus, although he had apparently left Paris before
Mountjoy arrived.

25 Plato] Colet was strongly influenced by Platonism and Neoplatonism,
especially in its Florentine form. Cf Sears Jayne *John Colet and Marsilio Ficino*
(Oxford 1963) and L. Miles *John Colet and the Platonic Tradition* (La Salle,
Indiana 1961).

astonished at the universal scope of Grocyn's accomplishments? Could anything be more clever or profound or sophisticated than Linacre's mind? Did
Nature ever create anything kinder, sweeter, or more harmonious than the
character of Thomas More? But why need I rehearse the list further? It is
marvellous to see what an extensive and rich crop of ancient learning is   30
springing up here in England; and therefore ought you all the more to hurry
home. The count is fond of you, and keeps you so much in his thoughts
that he speaks of no one more often, or with greater pleasure, than of you.
Farewell.

From London, in haste, the fifth of December [1497]   35

119 / To Jacob Batt   [Paris, February 1500]

Erasmus arrived back in Paris on 2 February after a series of mishaps. As he
was leaving England on 27 January (cf Allen Ep 145: 52ff), the customs officials
confiscated nearly all his money (see line 9n). From Dover he crossed to
Boulogne and then went to Tournehem where he spent two nights with Batt
(cf Ep 120: 30ff). Here he apparently secured some money, possibly from
Antoon van Bergen, abbot of St Bertin in the nearby town of Saint-Omer (cf
Ep 143 introduction). He then set out for Paris and reached Amiens in the afternoon of 31 January. From here on the narrative is rather confusing. In Amiens
he hired horses and with the hirer's son-in-law accompanying him reached
a village where he spent the night. The following day, 1 February, he went
on to a village which he calls Saint-Julien. Here the hirer himself appeared
unexpectedly (lines 40–54). The narrative then returns to recount suspicious
events of the preceding day (lines 54–114) and then resumes where it had left
off. After a night spent in fear of robbery and a lengthy altercation in the morning over changing their money and settling their account, Erasmus and an

* * * * *

26 Grocyn] William Grocyn (c 1449–1519) was one of the first to teach Greek
in Oxford, both before and after a visit to Italy, c 1488–90. In 1496 he was given
a living in London, where he taught More and was a member of the small
humanist circle. Erasmus probably met him there before he went to Oxford.
He was a close friend of Colet though he disagreed with him over the authorship of the works ascribed to Dionysius the Areopagite. In 1501 he gave a series
of lectures at St Paul's rejecting the traditional ascription which Colet still
accepted.
27 Linacre] Thomas Linacre (c 1460–1524) had spent several years in Italy
studying medicine in Padua, where he took the degree of MD, and in Venice
helping Aldus with his edition of Aristotle. He returned to England about 1499
and settled in London practising medicine and maintaining close relations
with the humanist circle.

Englishman who was travelling with him left the horses and the suspected hirer and finished the journey to Paris on foot. The narrative furnishes no entirely convincing proof that Erasmus was in real danger of robbery or murder, but that he believed he was is evident from later references to his danger on this occasion (cf Allen Ep 145: 59 and a letter inserted in the *De conscribendis epistolis*, ASD I 2).

In all the printed editions Ep 128 is added to this letter as an integral part of it, but since it refers to events some months later Allen has separated the two parts, assuming that they were joined together as the result of an editor's error.

ERASMUS TO BATT

I am bound to thank you, dear Batt, for many reasons, inasmuch as you have sent me my lucubrations, that is to say my wealth, not only in good time – which you are not in the habit of doing – but also, as usual, most conscientiously, and, lastly, have sent them by the hand of a messenger who is not only diligent but also articulate, so that I had to reward him not merely for his trouble, but also for making a good speech. But I have been witty at wit's expense, 'Cretanizing against a Cretan,' as the ancient proverb has it.

My English disaster has pursued me to the very gates of Paris. Here is a second dreadful story for you, more dismal even than my first. On the 31st of January I arrived at Amiens – and what an uncomfortable journey, ye gods, that was! I suppose some deity like Juno had once more stirred Aeolus up against us. When I was already so exhausted from travelling that I was positively alarmed lest I might fall ill, I began to make plans to hire

5

10

* * * * *

119:3 lucubrations] Probably a parcel of Erasmus' papers left at Tournehem because they were too bulky for him to carry on foot.

8 'Cretanizing against a Cretan'] Cf *Adagia* I ii 26.

9 English disaster] Erasmus never forgot the loss of the money on which he had counted to continue his studies. When he was leaving England the officials at Dover confiscated his money to the value of twenty pounds (cf Allen Ep 279). Their action was in accordance with a statute of Edward IV, re-enacted by Henry VII in 1499, forbidding the exportation of gold or silver from England. Recounting the incident in 1523 he asserted that 'More and Colet had mistakenly assured him that there was no danger unless he were carrying English coinage and in fact he had none that was English, or gained or received in England' (cf *Catalogus lucubrationum* Allen I 16). That none of the money was received in England seems improbable. It is more likely that some of it consisted of gifts from Mountjoy and other English friends. But there is a suggestion in Ep 139:117–18 that some at least came from the Lady Anna van Borssele. Erasmus mentioned the incident again in the first edition of the *Adagia*, but dropped it in later editions (cf Phillips 53f).

horses, thinking it considerably better to spare my poor body than my slen-   15
der store of ready money. At this point, all the circumstances were ripe for
disaster. As I was making for an inn where I am in the habit of staying, I
happened to pass by a sign that read 'horses for hire.' In I went, and the
hirer was called, a fellow who suggested the figure of Mercury so exactly
to the life, that at the very first moment of our meeting he caused me to sus-   20
pect him of thievery. We agreed on a price; I hired two horses, and rode
off about evening, accompanied by a youth (the hirer claimed him for a son-
in-law) who was to bring the animals back. On the following day, a long
time before nightfall, we reached a village by the name of Saint-Julien, an
ideal spot for a robbery. I recommended going ahead, but the brigand's   25
apprentice made excuses, saying that the horses ought not to be taxed
beyond their strength, and that it would be better to spend the night there
and to make up for lost time by departing before daybreak next morning.
I was not unduly reluctant to do so, for I had as yet no suspicion that crime
was afoot. We had almost finished our supper when the serving-woman   30
called aside the youth, who was sitting with us at table, alleging that one
of the two horses was in some trouble or other. The youth went off, but you
could see from his expression that what he had really been told was something different. At once I called the girl back and said, 'Tell me, young
woman, which of the two horses is sick, this gentleman's, or mine?', for   35
my travelling-companion, an Englishman, was there. 'And what, pray, is
wrong with it?' The girl, unable to keep up her guilty pretence, smiled and
admitting that it was a lie told us that someone she knew had come and
called the youth away to talk with him.

Shortly afterwards, the horse-hirer himself, he who had planned to   40
sacrifice our necks, came into the dining room. We expressed surprise, and
asked what had happened to bring him thither so unexpectedly and
unforeseen. He said that he brought sad news: his daughter, the youth's
wife, had been so severely kicked by a horse that she was nearly at death's
door, and he himself had made a forced journey to call the young man home.   45
From this point I began to detect an odour of fiction about the story. I
observed the expressions and gestures of both of them with particular
attention, and noticed a kind of shiftiness in the horse-hirer, and dullness

* * * * *

24 Saint-Julien] The most likely identification of this place appears to be that
offered by Allen in an addendum printed in iv xxi, where he recommends
Saint-Just-en-Chaussée, 'a small town on the main road to Paris, 31 miles from
Amiens and 9 from Clermont. With his indifference to accuracy in trivial
details, he [Erasmus] might easily have remembered its name as St Julien.'

in the youth, who sat opposite, and at once called to mind Cicero's remark, 'You would not act thus, were it not that you lied.' My only object, now,   50
was to be rid of the fellow, since every one of the circumstances had, I thought, a flavour of robbery. My suspicion began to be increased by reflecting on previous events – how at Amiens, when we agreed on a price, he carefully asked me what sort of currency he was to be given. Suddenly there appeared (I know not from where) people who supported the tale with   55
their chatter. They praised the hirer to me, and congratulated me on my pleasant companion, while they praised me in turn to the hirer. The hirer more than once asked whether I had a *postulaat*, – a rather rare kind of coin. I said I had none. I took out one or two *écus*, and although they were treated as quite acceptable, still he insisted, in an ingratiating way, that I should   60
give him just one very fine specimen out of the many he supposed I had. For the first rule of this most unscrupulous practice is to investigate how much money each traveller is carrying. I showed him the coins I had with me, and he kept the finest of all for himself.

My apprehension that mischief was brewing had been increased by   65
certain things the youth said and did on the way, which would appear to have been deliberately arranged in advance by his father-in-law. One of the two horses was extremely lazy, so it would have been of no service as a means of escaping. The beast on which I sat had a huge open sore, still covered with ointment, on its neck. We were not very far from the city when   70
the youth asked permission to ride pillion behind me: the beast, he said, was used to carrying two riders, and I need not fear for the horse's sake. 'We left late,' said he; 'this will enable us to arrive sooner.' I allowed it; and we began to talk of various things. He spoke about his father-in-law as though he entertained no very high opinion of him. This, too, is one of the   75
holy secrets of the robber-tribe. In the meantime, my purse slipped on to the animal's back; there were about eight gold *couronnes* in it. He returned it to the pommel; and when it slipped down again he replaced it once more, warning me always to keep my eyes on my money-bag. I laughed, and said 'What is the good of keeping watch over an empty purse?' It was already   80
dark night when we made our way through a wood and at length came out

* * * * *

49 Cicero] *Brutus* 80.278

58 a *postulaat*] One of a series of highly debased imitations of the Rhenish gold florin. See the Glossary and Appendix A on gold coins.

59 one or two *écus*] See the Glossary on coinage and Appendix A on gold coins.

77 about eight gold *couronnes*] *Ecus à la couronne*; a sum worth £14 0s 0d *tournois*. See the Glossary and Appendix A on gold coins.

into a village; the youth gazed about him and, pretending not to know our whereabouts, took us into some house or other. I told the young man to look after himself in his usual way, while both of us went hungry to bed. The Englishman fasted for religion's sake, I for my health's, since I was much 85 distressed in my stomach at the time. The woman came up while, as she thought, we were sleeping soundly, and had a long, and very intimate, conversation with the youth, whom she had pretended not to know. At length, on a hint from the youth, the rest of the conversation was conducted in whispers, so that I might not overhear it.   90

Before daybreak I drove the party out on the road again. Throughout the journey I treated the young man with great kindness. When we came to the town named Clermont, I set myself to go in thither, not with the intention of spending the night there but to change gold, lest that business should delay us if we stayed overnight in a village. The youth urged me 95 not to do so, claiming that he had sufficient change in silver. Accordingly, we went ahead, leaving the town behind us on the left. When we were very close to a village, it so happened that the Englishman had gone ahead, together with the youth, while I followed, 'as is my way, / Thinking upon some all-absorbing nonsense.' In the meanwhile, unknown to me, the Eng- 100 lishman had dismounted, and the youth had led the horse to a pair of doors where there never had been an inn. When I perceived this, I expressed surprise, wondering what was in his mind. He looked about him, and said he had not been in the place for fourteen years. He asked me what hostelry I fancied. 'Suppose we stay here,' he said, and pointed out the house he 105 had in mind. I made no protest, remembering that I had once had a pleasant enough reception there. I was not aware, however, that the landlord had changed. As the custom is, we were given a private chamber. Wine was served, but it had a disagreeable taste, although the moment after we entered I had seen that unknown youth being served in the kitchen with 110 a glass of wine so attractive in hue that I congratulated myself on our lodging; and accordingly, disappointed in my hopes of this, I went downstairs and complained to the landlord. The wine was changed. Even at this time I was rather surprised than put on my guard by these incidents.

So then, to go back to the course of my story which I have interrupted, 115 since my suspicions about robbery were now confirmed, I began to seek means of escaping the knife. 'What is your purpose, then?,' said I. 'It may be,' he replied, 'that I can escort you as far as Paris; but my son-in-law here

* * * * *

85 religion's sake] 31 January 1500 was a Friday.
99–100 'as is my way ... nonsense'] Horace *Satires* 1.9.1-2

must of course rush back home.' 'No,' I said, 'I can suggest a more con- 120
venient plan. Since you have had a dreadful misfortune that has well-nigh
deprived you of a daughter and the young man of a wife, I will do this for
your sake: I have paid you an *écu* with the sun emblem, and there are fourteen miles to go; simply deduct from the agreed sum an amount proportionate to the remaining distance, and go home. We shall either go on foot the
rest of the way or obtain a change of horses.' The fellow shook his head and 125
went downstairs, leaving the youth behind, with the extraordinary cunning of the robber's trade, so that he might use him to spy out what we meant
to do. At this point I called the youth to me and said 'Now then, tell me
the truth; what is this about your wife, please?' He admitted that the story
was a fiction, but maintained that his father-in-law was obliged to go to 130
Paris in order to obtain repayment of a debt. 'Do not be put out by what
he says,' he went on, 'just mount your horses as soon as it is fully light
tomorrow, and we shall both go with you.' 'Still,' I replied, 'it cannot be
by chance that he is following us for such a long distance at such extremely
short notice, and on so holy a day too'; for the following day was that of 135
the Purification of the Virgin Mother. 'And what,' I went on, 'was the point
of stringing all those lies together?' The youth bid me be of a good courage,
and said that they would do everything as I wished. 'But,' he said, 'even
if my father-in-law should prove reluctant, still I will not leave you till my
heart fails me': all this with that asinine expression of his. In this way, he 140
made a pretence of being secretly on my side against his father-in-law; after
which, he too went downstairs, no doubt with the sole intention of report-
ing the conversation to his master in thievery.

In the meantime, when we had a moment alone together I asked the
Englishman what he himself thought about it. He replied that he could not 145
see any explanation except that they were getting ready to rob us. 'But what
can we do?' I asked. It was already late at night; the innkeeper's wife had
meanwhile come to make the beds. I asked where exactly we were to sleep,
and she pointed to a bed. 'And where,' said I, 'will the other two sleep?'
She answered, 'In this other bed here' – which was in the same room. I then 150
said, 'I have to discuss some trifling business privately with my companion; let us sleep alone in this room and you shall be paid for both beds.'
Then the witch, who was well aware what was afoot, at first began to urge
us rather to share the room. The others, she said, were decent men, and
there was no reason why we should be unwilling to let them sleep in our 155

* * * * *

122 *écu* with the sun emblem] *Ecu au soleil.* See the Glossary and Appendix
A on gold coins.

room. If, she said, we had any business to discuss privately, this could be done in our native language, while if we were anxious about our money, we could entrust it to the management for safe-keeping, the sheep to the wolf, as the saying goes. And suiting her words to her evil character, she falsely pretended, with obvious disingenuousness, that the other bed-rooms were already occupied, though apart from ourselves there was not a single guest in the building. In short, though we won the argument, she stubbornly refused to do as we requested. I therefore bade her open the doors and turn us out to go somewhere else. But even this she swore she would not do; and went downstairs, cross and grumbling, and told that assassin all about it while I listened from the stairs.

The Englishman had neither heart nor wit nor tongue, for he possessed absolutely no knowledge of French. To me, at first, it appeared the wisest course to bar the door of the room with an iron bolt, adding an enormous oaken bench as an additional barrier; however, I soon abandoned this plan as I began to reflect that there were but the two of us facing a larger number in this huge building, and it was already very late at night and no cry could have been heard anywhere, except where the room gave upon the street, and the building opposite was the church belonging to a certain monastery. In the meantime, as I was looking for a better idea, without much success, the maidservant knocked at the door. Stealthily I pulled aside the bench, and asked what she wanted. She replied in a cheerful voice that she was bringing something. I opened the door, and flattered and teased the girl in order to conceal my fears. So, for the time being, my companion and I sat like two sacrificial victims awaiting the knife! But we agreed to converse in a leisurely and serious fashion at the fireside, without drinking, until we should take turns to sleep and to watch, in our shirts and hose. Shortly afterwards, in came the honest fellow looking as though he knew nothing about the whole business. I watched him carefully; and the harder I looked, the more I was convinced he was a robber. After he finally got ready for bed, together with his apprentice, we followed their example; and we did not notice anything during the night, except that when the Englishman woke up he found his sword, which he had placed beside his pillow, moved a considerable distance away, in fact, to the very furthest corner of the room. Between the two of us we possessed only a single sword and a single gauntlet of mail; these constituted our entire armament.

Long before dawn I rose, opened the windows and doors of the bed-room, called out that it was getting light, shouted, and aroused the household. When I didn't stop, the robber asked, in a voice you would hardly call sleepy, 'What are you about? It's hardly five o'clock yet.' By way of reply

I called out that the sky was veiled in extremely heavy clouds, and that bright daylight would presently emerge. Most of this went on at the windows. To be brief, a lantern was brought, and in the meantime I rushed downstairs to see what was happening in the lower storey of the building; and, walking to and fro and looking about me, I came across the robbers' horses standing ready saddled, as they must have stood all night, since everyone was in bed, except the girl who had just been roused. Finally, our murderers also got up; whereupon a circumstance, at the time seemingly inconvenient, came to our rescue; for the robber's greed had been aroused simply and solely by his idea that we were enormously rich, and the fact I speak of was enough in itself to persuade him of our slender means. We had rather too little silver money to pay the innkeeper for our supper and forage for all the horses; and so I gave instructions that either the innkeeper should change a gold piece, or the horse-hirer should pay him on my behalf the small sum I was short, five *douzains*, on the understanding that he was to be repaid when we reached Saint-Denis. The innkeeper's wife swore that she had no scales in the house, and that there was nobody there who could change a gold piece. The robber asserted that he would do all this according to law if I deposited a gold piece with him as a security; the innkeeper's wife, whose impudence and folly matched her wickedness, earnestly begged me to do so, and as a result of this we had a bitter and protracted wrangle. I insisted that she should open the door for me, saying that I would go myself to the prior of the monastery opposite in order to change the gold; but this she refused to do.

So we haggled, until it grew quite light. At length we were told to produce the gold we wished to have changed; this I did. One of the coins was short in weight; another was alleged to be of inferior metal; another, less than pure, no doubt with the intention of forcing us to disgorge any gold we had hidden away. I took a solemn oath that I had no gold coins except those in sight. 'But why,' he said, 'do you not tell your companion to bring out his, since I can see that he is very comfortably off?' He then repeated his request, this time in a more engaging manner; but I swore, with the

* * * * *

209 a gold piece] Probably an *écu au soleil* or *écu à la couronne*. See the Glossary and Appendix A on gold coins.

210 five *douzains*] *Quinque duodenarios*: a *douzain* was worth 12d *tournois*; and so this sum amounted to 5 *sols* or 60d *tournois*. See the Glossary and Appendix B on silver coins.

honest look and tone of a man speaking truthfully and sincerely, that my
companion had nothing but a letter of credit. Finally, a man with some
scales was produced, and the innkeeper also came upon the scene; we spent   230
an hour and a half there, weighing the money, and there was not a single
gold piece that was not a few scruples short; some lacked the proper weight,
others gave rise to objections on grounds of impurity. Eventually I realized
that both the scales and the weights were false; and, as luck would have
it, I took up in my hand the heavier of the two weights, a fact of which the   235
innkeeper was still unaware. The only thing left was to weigh the money
against the other weight, and immediately my gold piece recorded a heavier
weight on either side. No matter to which pan you moved it, down went
the scale, for it was a very old piece, with an excess of weight above the
legal minimum, so universal is the phenomenon of decline.   240
     By this time our throats had been saved by one means or another and
the rascals had only one remaining object, to scrape a miserable profit for
themselves by prevaricating. Whereupon the robber, all but baffled in his
hopes as he was, either because he began to realize that we were not so
splendidly off, or because he saw that he was now distinctly suspect in our   245
eyes, and I was actually using threats, and finally because the day was now
well advanced, took the innkeeper, his only too familiar friend, aside from
our company. 'Where,' do you ask? Why, into the chamber, believe it or
not, into which the robber had withdrawn alone; you see how loyalty and
kindness are almost more prevalent among thieves than among the rest of   250
humanity. They made change for my gold piece between the two of them,
taking as much as they wanted for the supper and the horses; I received

* * * * *

239–40 the legal minimum] Because of the imprecisions, imperfections of
mediaeval minting techniques, a coin's official weight was prescribed not in
terms of specific metrological units (as *grains, deniers, onces*), but in terms of
the *taille* or number of coins to be cut from the *marc* weight (= 8 *onces*) or other
standard of mint weight; and for this *taille* a certain degree of error or
'tolerance' (*remède*) was permitted. It was thus quite common to find that a certain percentage of the coins from any given minting – the standard deviation
from the mean, in the language of statisticians – weighed less than the official
mean weight, and a certain percentage more. These heavier coins, with a
higher intrinsic value, were frequently culled from circulation and hoarded or
exported as bullion, thus leaving predominantly short-weight coins in circulation. Erasmus' comment about the 'phenomenon of decline' refers partly to
such circumstances and partly to the considerable debasements of the French
(and Burgundian) coinages, by reductions of both weight and fineness, during
the fifteenth century.

twenty-three *deniers*, glad enough of this for my part, and, concealing my intentions as far as my straightforward nature allows, said, 'Why should we not mount now?' But the horse-hirer still stood idle. 'What are you thinking of?' said I, 'Why do we not get on our way? Are you not ready yet?' 'No,' he replied, 'not until you pay me the whole amount.' 'How much, do you want?' I asked, for three *douzains* were due to him over and above the *écu*. He quite shamelessly demanded the sum he fancied; a sum that it fitted the character of an impudent highwayman to demand. 'Well then,' said I, 'take me to Paris, as you have contracted to do, and there we shall settle up and you will get your due.' But he replied, 'What are you likely to give me in Paris, when you argue with me even here?' He was wise not to let himself be distracted from his trade of robbery, for on my part this was only a pretence: I had not the slightest intention of letting myself travel further in company with those butchers. After a short argument, since he refused to budge, I pretended to be going off to church, but in fact I crossed the river and made directly for Paris; and we stood in fear of the robber's poniard all the way, until St Denis gave us refuge within his walls.

It was on February the second that I arrived in Paris, very tired from travelling, and with an empty purse. And though I had no business there except to demand the return of my cloak, even this gave me considerable trouble. What precious humbugs the French are! Falco on his departure had gone so far as to set down in writing that the garment was to be restored to me immediately I got back. So I went and claimed it. Those hypocrites asserted that the garment had been left there as security, and I should get it back if I paid a franc. But when I went on to investigate in some detail, they returned it to me along with the written instructions, and thereby convicted themselves of obvious fraudulence. All I have left are three *écus*, all

255

260

265

270

275

* * * * *

253 twenty-three *deniers*] Worth 1s 11d *tournois*. See the Glossary and Appendix B on silver coins.

258 three *douzains*] Worth 36d or 3 *sols tournois*. See the Glossary and Appendix B on silver coins.

259 *écu*] See the Glossary and Appendix A on gold coins.

273 Falco] Cf Ep 87 introduction.

277 if I paid a franc] If Erasmus indeed meant a gold coin, then the franc à cheval, currently worth about £1 13s 2d *tournois*. But more likely he simply meant a *livre tournois*, for which the word franc had come to be synonymous. See the Glossary, and also Appendix A on gold coins.

279 three *écus*] If *écus à la couronne*, a sum worth £5 5s 0d *tournois*; if *écus au soleil*, £5 8s 9d *t*. See the Glossary and Appendix A on gold coins.

very short in weight. I have set up house with my old friend Augustin; we   280
are living the literary life, on slender means, it is true, and yet we do not
envy you your castle ...

120 / From Jacob Batt to William Blount, Lord Mountjoy
Tournehem [February] 1500

This letter was probably written at Erasmus' request to reinforce his own letter
(cf Ep 128: 36) telling of his loss at Dover and expressing his gratitude for past
favours. It was probably written before Batt received Ep 119, since it does not
mention Erasmus' misadventures on the road to Paris.

JACOB BATT TO THE NOBLE YOUTH, WILLIAM MOUNTJOY
The return of my friend Erasmus is something I looked for and longed for
ardently, not because I envied you his company, but because my affection
for him was boundless. At the same time, I could not fail to be most distressed by the news he gave me of that dreadful misfortune he had suffered,   5
a misfortune I foresaw long ago. Of course I always was apprehensive on
his behalf, and dreamt of worse mishaps still. As a matter of fact, at the very
time when his letter was delivered to me I was worrying about his fate.
Whatever the result, I am happy; happy, my kind and noble lord, because
I have recovered, albeit battered and tempest-tost, one who is so desirable   10
a part of myself; though of course I am not so selfishly affectionate that I
would not rather have seen him remain safely in your care than return to
me so robbed and dreadfully insulted as he has been. Heavens, cannot even
the arts and literature be protected from those vampires? When Plato was
accused of a capital crime, it did him some good in the eyes of the people   15
of Aegina that he was a philosopher; while even that monster Phalaris
behaved both with intelligent kindness and with generosity towards his
physician (the philosopher Pythagoras) and the poet Stesichorus. But what
is the good of complaining too late, when the hope of success has been
abandoned? What cannot be changed must be endured, not railed at, espe-   20

* * * * *

280 Augustin] Augustin Vincent (cf Epp 54 and 131 introductions).
120:14 Plato] Cf Diogenes Laertius 3.19.
16 Phalaris] Tyrant of Agrigentum in Sicily, 6th century BC. For his alleged
relations with Pythagoras, see Iamblichus *Life of Pythagoras* ch. 30; with
Stesichorus, see Aristotle *Rhetorics* 1393 b 9 (cf Ep 109:104n).
20 What cannot be changed] Publilius Syrus 201

cially because I consider it discreditable in me to be too dispirited when he himself took his mishap in such a good spirit and with such composure.

What a wonderful thing is philosophy, which he has always preached as well as practised! It was my duty to alleviate his distress with comforting words; but instead he smiled and checked my tears and told me to be cheer- 25 ful. He said that he had no regrets at having gone to England. He had not lost that sum of money without receiving great rewards in its place, because in England he had made such friends as he preferred to the wealth of Croesus.

We spent two nights together. He spoke with passionate enthusiasm, 30 and great eloquence, of the graciousness of Prior Richard, of the erudition of Colet, and of the sweetness of More, with the result that if I were free I should myself like to visit men as scholarly and affable as these. As for you, my right good lord, he gave a picture of your entire character from head to foot, as they say, so that while I had conceived a warm admiration 35 for you before, now I would not take second place even to Erasmus in affec- tion for you, and that too although he loves you more than his own eyes. He is so far from blaming you, that he also lamented your condition to me, inasmuch as you were impelled to take such trouble, and to incur such expense, for his sake. When finally he took his leave he charged me with 40 great emphasis to write to you as often as possible. And although I had some reluctance to do this, since you are so accomplished a scholar and I so com- pletely a tyro, still I have written you this letter, such as it is, in order to avoid failing in my duty; and, if I should find that it has given you no offence, I shall write to you fairly often. God grant that we may possibly 45 have the pleasure of your presence closer at hand; Erasmus held out some hope of this. I am immensely grateful, and shall remain so as long as I live, for your extreme graciousness and goodwill towards my friend Erasmus; if anyone does him a service, I think myself more obliged than if he did it to me.
50

My respectful greetings to the noble lady your wife, and to your excel- lent father-in-law, and to the rest of your family.

Tournehem castle, 1499

* * * * *

31 Prior Richard] Charnock (cf Ep 106:10n).

35 head to foot] *Adagia* 1 ii 37

46 your presence] Batt had reason to expect that Mountjoy would be appointed commander of the castle of Hammes near Tournehem. His father had held that post until his death in 1485, and it was again vacant. It was not, however, given to Mountjoy until June 1503.

121 / To Robert Gaguin   Paris, March [1500]

This letter and the following one indicate that Erasmus was busily borrowing
books from his friends to aid in preparing his forthcoming edition of the
Adagia (cf Ep 126). On Gaguin, see Ep 43 introduction.

ERASMUS TO ROBERT GAGUIN
Your unmatched kindness – a quality in which you earn as many laurels
for distinction as you do in scholarship itself – gives me confidence to dare
to solicit your help in this bold fashion, quite undeserving of it as I am. I
have to commune for a few days with Macrobius, a man of passing excellent   5
wit, as you well know. My request is that you should instruct this Macrobius to forsake your learned library and come to me; for you will not miss
him, where he is but one among such a wealth of excellent authors, while
he will bring the utmost delight to me in my poverty. Farewell: I am already
tied to you by many bonds of obligation; please increase my debt by   10
another.
        Paris, 1499

122 / To Robert Gaguin   [Paris, March] 1500

ERASMUS TO GAGUIN
Greetings, distinguished sir. What remarkable effrontery your Erasmus
possesses: he never thinks of his Gaguin, except when he wants something.
For just a few days, I need the work of George of Trebizond entitled *De
rhetoricis praeceptionibus*. I am not asking whether you have it; I know there   5
is not a single good author whom you do not own. Please be kind enough
to place it at my disposal. I wish to compare the Quintilian with him, and
I shall send both of them back to you safely and speedily. Farewell; continue
to love me.
        1499   10

123 / To Jacob Batt   Paris [March 1500]

ERASMUS TO HIS FRIEND BATT
I have sent you back a part of my Valla, along with my letter, by the messen-

* * * * *

121:5 Macrobius] Cf Ep 61:147n.
122:4 George of Trebizond] Cf Ep 36:3n.
123:2 Valla] Cf Ep 20:100n.
2–3 messenger] Cf Ep 119:5.

ger whom you employed to send me my compositions; and I gave the messenger eight *deniers*, as you had directed me to do. I have no other news to report. The usual thing is happening in my case: the wound I suffered 5 in England is only now beginning to give pain, when it is no longer fresh; and it is all the more painful because, though it was accompanied by treatment of the most insulting kind, I have no chance of paying off the score, for how could I fight against all England, or its king? Yet England has in no way deserved my rage, while I believe it would be the height of madness 10 to write against the king, who has it in his power not only to banish, but to kill. In this affair accordingly I long, with Themistocles, to acquire the art of forgetting. In fact I am engrossed in literature; I plan to compile a thesaurus of ancient adages, working in great haste, it is true. I foresee that there may be some thousands of them, but intend to publish only two, or 15 at most three, hundred. I shall dedicate them to your pupil Adolph; but I am still wondering whether I can find a printer, and you know that my own resources are less than nothing.

I am surprised that you have sent no message by François's brother, who has just arrived. Be sure to keep a sharp look out for my parcel, for that 20 'Galba' is an Englishman, as you are aware. When you do receive it, please forward it carefully to me. It contains a black garment, lined partly with black and partly with dark grey; also a cloak, which was bought by you, and a violet-coloured pair of hose; also Augustine's *Enchiridion*, written on parchment, and Paul's Epistles, and other things I cannot remember. My 25 readings in Greek all but crush my spirit; but I have no spare time and no

* * * * *

4 eight *deniers*] See the Glossary and Appendix B on silver coins for *deniers tournois*.

5 wound] Cf Ep 119:9.

12–13 Themistocles ... art of forgetting] Cicero *Academica* 2.1.2; *De oratore* 2.74.299, 2.86.351; *De finibus* 2.32.104; cf *Apophthegmata* 5 (LB IV 244B).

14 adages] Cf Ep 126 introduction.

16 Adolph] Adolph of Burgundy. As in the case of the *De conscribendis epistolis* (cf Epp 71 introduction and 95:38ff), this promise of a dedication to Adolph was not fulfilled.

19 François's brother] See line 29.

20 parcel] Clothing and books which Erasmus had left in England with instructions to have them sent on to him in care of Batt (cf Ep 124:21ff)

21 'Galba'] It probably refers here to an agent in London. Erasmus held him responsible for the loss of his money at Dover and also for discouraging Mountjoy's generosity (cf Ep 135:72f). The Dover incident apparently still coloured Erasmus' conception of the English character.

25 Paul's Epistles] Erasmus may already have begun work on his commentaries on St Paul (cf Ep 164).

means to purchase books or employ the services of a tutor. And with all this commotion to endure I have hardly enough to live on: and this is what I owe to my studies! Please be sure to give my greetings to Master François and Pierre de Vaulg, the philosopher, and your own Pierre, and to Jean, the   30
chamberlain. Farewell, my dear Batt.

PS I beg you not to let my complaints disturb you; it was just my usual fancy to pour out my mind's distress in your ears; but I am not going to lose heart easily, and, in the ancient proverb, 'while I breathe, I shall hope.'
Paris [1498]   35

124 / To Jacob Batt   Paris, 12 April [1500]

ERASMUS TO HIS FRIEND BATT
Dear Batt, I wish you the health I lack myself. From the day I returned to Paris I have been in quite a frail and delicate state, because the severe hardships which in my winter journey I met with on land and sea were not followed by any rest-cure, but by endless work at night; thus I have not rid   5
myself of hardship, merely altered its nature. Then there is the season, inclement in itself, but particularly unkind to my state of health, for I do not remember that since I have lived in France a single Lent has ever gone by without bringing me a bout of sickness, and when I recently changed my abode I was so badly put out by my new surroundings that I clearly felt   10
the symptoms of the nocturnal fever which two years since all but laid me in the grave. I am combating it with all the proper precautions and with the aid of physicians, but am hardly out of danger, for my health is still in a very unreliable condition. If this fever attacks me once again, then, my dear Batt, it will all be over with your friend. Nevertheless I do not   15
altogether despair, for I trust in Ste Geneviève, whose ready help I have more than once enjoyed; particularly since I have obtained the services of Wilhelm Cop, a physician who is not merely highly skilled in his profession

* * * * *

29–30 François ... Jean] Friends at Tournehem

124:11 fever] Cf Epp 74:4f, 75:2ff, 126:12ff, 139:116. In January 1501 he wrote that fever left him four months at the most to work (cf Ep 146).

16 Ste Geneviève] Cf Ep 50:6n.

18 Cop] Wilhelm Cop (c 1466–1532), a native of Basel, was a distinguished medical man who was listed in the records of the university of Paris as physician to the German nation, 1497–1512. Later he was court physician to Louis XII and Francis I. He had also a considerable reputation as a humanist, having studied Greek with Lascaris, Erasmus, and Aleandro in Paris. He published Latin translations of Hippocrates (Paris: H. Stephanus, 1511) and Galen (ibid 1513). He had treated Erasmus before (cf Ep 50:6n). They remained friends and continued to exchange letters till at least 1526 (Ep 1735).

but friendly and loyal and, a most uncommon thing, devoted to the Muses. I enclose an extempore letter of his composition. 20

About the parcel, while you think I have given the matter insufficient attention, I in turn find that your memory is at fault. I personally explained to you that I delivered it, not to a sailor, but to Arnold Edward, a lawyer, who was to give it, for conveyance, to the first sailor he met who appeared suitable. His is a name that is known to everyone in London. He lives on 25 London Bridge, in the house of his father Edward, a merchant. It makes no difference whether you send to him or to Thomas More, who resides in Lincoln's Inn. I am surprised that this Arnold can be unknown to you, since I have given you – by that talkative courier by whom I sent the Valla – a letter from me, addressed to him. I assigned him the task of making 30 enquiries about that robber of ours, but he has not made any report to me, nor have you written to me on the subject. My intention in so doing is not, of course, to bring the rascal to the gallows, but all the same to give him a fright and remove him from the city. Augustin says that you have in your possession the other books of Valla which you ask for. It is not that he is 35 reluctant to send them; but look and see what you do in fact lack, and it will be sent immediately.

I crave your pardon, dear Jacob, for failing to send the other things you ask me for. And I wish the situation were such that you could justifiably call for my services in regard to them, and that I had not quite such a good 40 case to plead. First of all, what special appropriateness would there be in my writing long letters when you are personally at hand, ready to negotiate *viva voce*, as the saying goes; and what could I achieve, even by the most carefully composed letter, that you could not greatly improve on in conversation? In the second place, however appropriate it was to write, I have been 45 forbidden the expenditure of effort it calls for, and simply dare not risk this damage to my health. I know from experience how much easier it is to avoid sickness than to get rid of it once it has taken hold; and by signs I know only too well I can feel it creeping upon me already. Also, I am getting ready my work on adages, which is to be published, I hope, directly after Easter; 50

* * * * *

21 parcel] Cf Ep 123:20ff.

23 Arnold Edward] Allen suggests that Erasmus may have reversed the names and that he is referring to the son of a Richard Arnold, author of a *Chronicle* and merchant who lived in the parish that included London Bridge. If so, he may be identified with the Arnold who accompanied More and Erasmus to Eltham Palace in 1499 (cf Ep 104 introduction).

29 Valla] Cf Ep 123:2n.

34 Augustin] Augustin Vincent (cf Ep 131 introduction).

46 forbidden] Cf Ep 126:10ff.

and, I may tell you, it is a work of no small extent, costing endless pains, for my collection consists of about eight hundred proverbs, partly Greek and partly Latin. This I shall dedicate to your pupil Adolph, if it seems appropriate.

I am delighted that you are hastening away to see the Lady, especially   55
upon her invitation. I have no doubt that it was partly for my sake that she invited you, since I sent her an account in bad French of the whole affair. So I shall bide my time for another month, supporting myself on credit, until some good news arrives from you; otherwise, I should have come back myself to join you. Please, dear Batt, put on once more the spirit you used   60
to possess; if only you try hard enough I know there is nothing you cannot achieve. Still, I am annoyed with you for just one reason: ever since I once wrote you a 'lying' letter from England, you imagine all my statements are lies. Yet in that letter, which you suppose to be a tissue of lies, may I die if I told a single untruth. So you must rid yourself of this prejudice you have   65
about me, and refuse to believe that anything I write, especially to you, is untrue or insincere. When I have finished my present work I intend to devote all my efforts to finishing off my Dialogue, and to bestow the whole of the coming summer on literary composition. If there is a chance, I shall set out for Italy in the autumn with the intention of obtaining a doctor's   70
degree; and it is for you, in whom my hope resides, to see that liberty and leisure come my way. I have turned my entire attention to Greek. The first thing I shall do, as soon as the money arrives, is to buy some Greek authors; after that, I shall buy clothes. Let me know your views about sending

* * * * *

53 Adolph] Cf Ep 123:16n.

55 Lady] Anna van Borssele. She was evidently away from Tournehem, possibly at Veere.

57 bad French] There is ample evidence that Erasmus could speak French of a sort. He could scarcely have talked to serving-maids and inn-keepers otherwise (cf eg Ep 119). He was, however, hesitant about writing French.

63 'lying' letter] When Erasmus was trying to break away from the hospitality of his English friends he seems to have written to Batt to rescue him with a fictitious letter recalling him to Paris (cf Ep 139:8ff).

68 Dialogue] This may refer to the *Antibarbari*, which was cast in the form of a dialogue. He was still working on it years later in Italy (cf Ep 30:17n). Allen's suggestion that it might refer to the *Familiarium colloquiorum formulae* (cf Ep 130:108–9n) seems unlikely, as in that case he would have used the plural, as in Ep 163.

70 Italy] Cf Ep 75:15n.

Adrian, or someone else, to England. There are many reasons, in my opin-   75
ion, why the opportunity should not be lost. The moment I hear from you
about this I shall send you a handwritten copy, together with a letter. As
for that lampooner from Gelderland, my own opinion is that he ought to
be arrested and thrown into chains, for he is, beyond doubt, an impudent
buffoon who would stop at no kind of crime. Farewell, dear Batt, and do   80
come to my rescue. Then, when my health is patched up, I will attend to
it all.

    Paris, 12 April [1498]

125 / To an unnamed person   [Paris, spring 1500]

    The tone of this letter and the context suggest that it was originally addressed
to Batt's young pupil Adolph of Veere. Allen's suggestion, however, that it
was a preliminary dedication to the *Adagia* addressed to Adolph is not
altogether borne out by the last paragraph. An equally plausible explanation
is that it was simply a friendly letter to the lad from whose mother Erasmus
had hopes of financial support. It begins with an apology for not having written more often and ends with a report on work in progress at a time when the
collection of adages was still unfinished and when he thought that it might
eventually amount to several thousand, although he had no intention of publishing more than a few hundred immediately (cf Ep 123: 15f). The concealment of the name of the addressee in the printed editions may have been
caused by some feeling of embarrassment at having dedicated the work to
Mountjoy after having indirectly promised it to Adolph (cf Epp 123: 16f and
124: 53f). In any case, the letter was first published in the *Farrago nova epis-*
tolarum (Basel: J. Froben 1519), by which time Erasmus' connection with
Adolph was less close.

TO A CERTAIN PERSON
I should have written you more often, my most agreeable X, since I am
keenly devoted to the habit of serving my friends in this way; but I was
afraid I might possibly appear to be pestering you, instead of wishing you
well, if I caused an interruption in your studies by breaking in upon them   5
with my letters, or if you should perhaps not take quite the same pleasure
in that sort of friendly exchange. But at this point, truth to tell, I could positively restrain myself no longer; not because I had plenty of spare time –

    * * * * *

    75 Adrian] Cf Ep 80:57n.
    78 lampooner from Gelderland] It is uncertain to whom this refers.

a commodity I have come to deny myself altogether – but in order to make sure that the break in our personal contact should not appear in any way 10 to have diminished my former affection for you. In fact, dear X, the manner in which I regard you implies that I am miles out in my reckoning if you do not entertain the warmest feelings towards me.

Perhaps you wonder what I am up to. My friends are my occupation; and in their company, which I enjoy enormously, I refresh my spirits. 'What 15 friends are you boasting of to me, you frivolous fellow?' you ask. 'Would anybody wish to see, or listen to, anyone so insignificant as yourself?' For my part, I am ready to acknowledge that successful men have troops of friends; yet even poor men do not lack them; indeed the latter possess friends that are considerably more pleasant in character, as well as firmer. 20 With such friends, then, I closet myself in some secluded nook and in their company, avoiding the fickle mob, I either indulge in some delightful musings, or else listen to their whispers, speaking to them as freely as to myself. Can anything be more agreeable than this? They, on their side, never hide their secrets, and observe perfect loyalty in the keeping of secrets entrusted 25 to them. They never blab abroad such remarks as we commonly voice freely among close friends. When you call for them they are at once at your disposal, yet never thrust themselves upon you uninvited. They speak when they are bidden to, and otherwise keep silence. Their conversation is what you will, as much as you will, and for as long as you will. They never flatter 30 or feign or dissemble. They are frank in telling you your faults, but never complain of them to anyone. What they say is either for pleasure or for profit; in prosperity they curb one's vanity, while in adversity they offer consolation. They do not alter as one's fortune changes. They go with you into every perilous situation, and stay by you until the very end of life, 35 while their relations are perfectly amicable. From time to time I exchange them, taking up first one and then the other, in fairness to all.

These then, my dear X, are the friends with whom I am burying myself at present. Tell me, what wealth, what royal sceptre, would I take, in exchange for leisure such as this? But in case my metaphor escapes you, you 40 must understand that, in all I have hitherto said about my good friends, I was speaking of my books; it is their friendship that has made me perfectly happy, my only misfortune being that I have not had you to share this happiness with me. My advice to you, superfluous though it is, will always be to devote yourself wholeheartedly to studying the best works and withhold 45 your admiration completely from anything that is common or of poor quality. Strive ever towards the heights. I hope some day you will allow that on more than one occasion I gave you honest and affectionate counsel.

I have plans for a work on witty sayings, proverbs, and maxims. You

have received from me a few samples. I am confident that in a short time   50
I shall run up a total of more than three thousand. I foresee that it may be
a work that will give pleasure and also be extremely useful, and one that
nobody has previously attempted. If I hear from you that you like the idea,
this will give me reason to undertake more eagerly and more willingly the
drudgery it involves. In the meantime, farewell; and continue to regard me   55
with affection, as you do.

126 / To William Blount, Lord Mountjoy   Paris [June 1500]

The first edition of the *Adagia* was a slim volume of 152 pages, containing 818
adages, published under the title *Adagiorum collectanea* (Paris: Jo. Philippi
1500) with this letter as preface. The decision to dedicate it to Mountjoy was
probably made after the book was set up in type, as the preface appears on
unnumbered pages at the front of the volume. This preface was replaced by
a new one (Ep 211), also addressed to Mountjoy, in the vastly enlarged Aldine
Adagiorum chiliades of 1508. The *Collectanea*, with twenty adages added in the
Bade edition of 1506, was frequently reprinted, even after the appearance of
the *Chiliades*, at least twenty-six times in Erasmus' lifetime. Cf Phillips 41–61.

DESIDERIUS ERASMUS OF ROTTERDAM TO THE NOBLE COUNT,
WILLIAM MOUNTJOY, GREETINGS

Here you are, dear William: instead of the letter which, modestly, by the
way, you asked for, your friend Erasmus sends you a book, and a real book
at that. I wish it were good enough to suit either the obligations you have   5
placed me under, or my good will towards you; and good enough, moreover, to feel no qualms at facing your sharp and trenchant judgment. I am
well aware how little your refined palate savours even the dishes which
appeal most of all to the general taste; much less do those over-confident
productions stand a chance of pleasing you, which are so far below attain-   10
ing a craftsmanlike polish that they have not as yet received the final touch
of the first drafting hand. For, since I was suffering from a persistent, rather
than acute, fever that I had caught the moment I left, I have dictated this
work instead of writing it, and, in doing so, I have given my doctor the slip,
for he solemnly warned me against having anything at all to do with books.   15
But I agree with Pliny that every moment not bestowed upon study is

* * * * *

126:13 fever] Cf Ep 124:11.
14 doctor] Wilhelm Cop (cf Ep 124:18n).
16 Pliny] Pliny the Elder; cf Pliny *Epistles* 3.5.16.

Desyderii Herasmi Roterdami veterū maximeq̃ insignium paroemiarū id est adagiorum collectanea: opus qum nouū tum ad omne uel scripture uel sermonis genus uenustādū insigniendūq̃ mirū in modū cōducibile. Id quod ita demū intelligetis adolescētes optimi: si huiusmodi deliciis et litteras vestras et oratione quotidianam assuesceris aspergere. Sapite ergo et hūc tam rarū thesaurū tantillo nūmulo venalē vobis redimite: multo prestantiora propediē accepturi: si hec boni cōsulueritis. Ualete.

· In noie sctē trinitatis

Duobus in locis libellus hic prostat: In magistri Iohānis philippi officina: cuius quidē tum industria: tum sumptu nitidissimis formulis est emaculatissime impressus: In uia diui Marcelli ad diuine trinitatis signum: Rursū in uia diui Iacobi ad Pellicani quem uocant notam:

Erasmus *Adagiorum collectanea* title page
Paris: Jehan Phillipe 1500
Houghton Library, Harvard University

wasted, and so thought it improper that my sickness should make away with such an important enterprise, especially in view of my belief that this our life holds no charms without the traffic of letters. So I put aside my nightly labours over a more serious work and strolled through divers gardens of the classics, occupied in this lighter kind of study, and so plucked, and as it were arranged in garlands, like flowerets of every hue, all the most ancient and famous of the adages. It was, in part, your wishes that spurred me to undertake this task. At the same time I was encouraged by an appeal from Richard Charnock. What a civilized and honourable man he is! He appears to me, indeed, to be the supreme pride and glory of the clergy of England, just as you yourself are of its nobility. Also, I foresaw that while this labour of mine might bring no credit to its author, nevertheless it was likely to bring some profit and pleasure to its prospective readers: those, I mean, who dislike the current jargon and are searching for greater elegance and a more refined style.

Meantime the reluctant asses, that is, those dull donkeys who believe themselves born for the purpose of carping at other men's toil, influenced me not a jot, so long as young people of sense took my effort, such as it was, in good part. I felt sure that though they might not admire it as a work of great artistry, at least they would be glad to welcome it on the ground of extreme usefulness. What, indeed, is so serviceable for adorning a prose discourse with a kind of debonair gaiety, or lightening it with scholarly jests, or seasoning it with sophisticated wit, for setting it off with a few jewels of metaphor, or illuminating it by flashes of epigram, or giving variety to it by employing tiny gems of allegory and allusion, or, finally, garnishing it with all the allurements of Antiquity, as to possess an ample supply, a well-stocked storehouse, as it were, of proverbs of this sort? You may draw upon it for all purposes; to find something that will charm by means of a clever and apposite metaphor, or bite with incisive wit; give pleasure by pointed brevity, or delight by brief pointedness; have either age or novelty to recommend it; attract by means of its variety, or else arouse pleasure in one who recognizes the subtle allusion; or, in fine, awaken the nodding reader by its very obscurity. Now it is surely common knowledge that, as far as prose style is concerned, its resources and its pleasures alike consist of epigrams, metaphors, figures, paradigms, examples, similes, images, and such turns of speech; and while these devices always add considerably to the distinction of one's style, they confer an exceptional

* * * * *

25 Charnock] Cf Ep 106:10n.
32 reluctant asses] *Adagia* I iv 83

amount of elegance and grace when they have come to form part of the
accepted idiom and the daily coin of language, inasmuch as everyone gives   55
a ready ear to what he recognizes; but especially is this true when there is
the additional recommendation, so to speak, of antiquity. Proverbs
improve with age exactly as wines do.

And they do not merely decorate your style; they are equally helpful
in giving it strength as well. For this reason, Quintilian not only includes   60
them among the means of relieving judicial tedium, and also among the
figures of oratory, but considers that the proverbial example is one of the
most effective methods of proof whether your aim be to convince, or to
refute your opponent by means of a witty adage, or to defend your own position. For what statement gains readier approval than one that is on   65
everyone's lips? And could anyone remain unmoved by the consensus
among so many generations and races of mankind? It might seem that I
maintained this point of view out of affection for my own work, were it not
that in all branches of literature the facts themselves proclaim the most eminent authors to have been those who took the keenest delight in proverbs   70
of this sort. To take a prime example: is there anything in the world more
splendid than Plato's philosophy, or more eloquent than his style? Yet he
interrupted his dialogues, even though their theme was serious enough,
Heaven knows, with adages inserted like highlights at frequent intervals.
To me at least the result is that this philosopher's argumentation affords   75
more pleasure than any comic play. Again, take Plautus, that leading light
of the theatre: how he overflows with adages at every point, uttering
scarcely a single remark he has not either borrowed from the speech of ordinary people, or else turned into a byword the moment it was pronounced
on the stage. It is this faculty above all that has given him title to be com-   80
pared with the Muses themselves for eloquence. Terence, who is a better
literary craftsman than Plautus, does not use proverbs quite as indiscriminately; but those he does use are choicer. Did not that consummate
scholar, Marcus Varro, derive such pleasure from proverbial witticisms that
he made them the sole source of subjects as well as titles for his Satires?   85
Some of them are still quoted nowadays: 'The ass at the lyre,' 'Know thyself,' 'Old men are twice-childish'; or again, 'Thou knowest not what the
eleventh hour may bring forth' and 'Scratch my back and I'll scratch yours.'

* * * * *

60 Quintilian] 5.11.37 and 41 (quoted in the Introduction to the *Adagiorum
chiliades* LB II 7 D-E)
84 Varro] Author of the *Menippean Satires*, first century BC
86ff It has not seemed necessary to identify by reference to the *Adagia* the
numerous adages cited as examples in this letter.

Deprive Catullus of his adages and you will take away a great deal of his
charm. Indeed, for all the variety and incisiveness of Horace, are not most 90
of his verses either proverbial in type or cast in a proverbial mould? And
his imitator, Persius, copied this leading feature of his model, as he copied
Horace's other devices, to the best of his ability. Passing over Martial and
Ausonius, and coming to a different kind of literature: that man of multifarious learning, the elder Pliny, reveals how enthusiastic he was about 95
this kind of stylistic ornament; for example, in the celebrated preface to his
history of the world, in the composition of which this most industrious of
writers frequently seems to me to have, in Horace's words, 'scratched his
head and bitten his nails to the quick' and moreover to have tried with
might and main, as the saying goes, to ensure that the preface should as 100
much as possible avoid the appearance of being written in a humdrum
style; and for this reason to have besprinkled it from head to heels with the
highest possible concentration of adages. Or another example: in that vol-
uminous work of his, he has taken considerable pains to note down such
proverbs as come his way. Among the Greeks, too, there has arisen a large 105
body of authors of considerable note who have even made it their stated
object to compile anthologies of proverbs: Apostolius of Byzantium or
Stephanus, for example, or Diogenianus. I myself have been unable as yet
to find out anything about them except their names, apart from a few frag-
ments of the compilations of Diogenianus, and these were so mutilated and 110
so jejune, having no authors' names or references attached to them, that I
gained little help from them. Furthermore, as far as I am aware, no writer
in Latin before me has attempted a task of this kind, not because writers
have not thought it worth while, for why should such an enterprise have

* * * * *

98 Horace] *Satires* 1.10.71

100 with might and main] Literally, 'with hands and feet.' *Adagia* I iv 15

112–13 no writer in Latin before me] The *Collectanea* was not the first collection
of proverbs. Polydore Vergil's *Proverbiorum libellus* (Venice: Chr. de Pensis 10
April 1498) was earlier, but Erasmus was apparently unaware of it at this time.
Later when Vergil's work was called to his attention he again asserted that his
own edition was the first, having been published some months before Vergil's
(cf Allen Ep 531:408ff). He may have seen only the third edition of the *Proverbiorum libellus* (Venice: Chr. de Pensis 6 November 1500). Whatever the
reason, he continued consistently to the end of his life to deny Vergil's claim
to priority and to refute his charge that Erasmus was merely following in his
footsteps (cf Allen Epp 1175, 2305:36ff; 2773). The charge of plagiarism at least
was false, as a comparison of the sources of the two collections demonstrates.
Cf T.C. Appelt *Studies in the Content and Sources of Erasmus's 'Adagia'* (Chicago
1942) 68.

earned the contempt of those who thought they did something worth while   115
when they wrote almost fussily about isolated letters, and the derivation
of words, and even more trifling things than these? In fact, you may conclude how little they despised it from the behaviour of Aulus Gellius, a person of refined literary tastes, and also of his follower Macrobius, and
Donatus too, and Acron, with his imitator Porphyrion, to omit mention of   120
Greek commentators for the moment. Whenever they detected the underlying presence of a proverb in the text, they did not suppose that they had
'hit upon something in the bean,' as boys cry out sometimes, but on something which, they thought, deserved to be marked with an asterisk and
explained with some care, inasmuch as they were aware that it often hap-   125
pens that an adage, couched in two words, would produce a great deal of
obscurity if it were left in darkness, but a great deal of illumination if it
should be aptly explained.

If at this point you look for a single instance, among the multitudes
that you will meet with everywhere, here in front of your very eyes is one   130
that I have for better or worse commented upon: 'Let us laugh sardonically,'
to be found in Cicero's letters. Into what devious explanations, what mazes
of error does it not send the commentators? If, again, as Christians we feel
more drawn to an instance taken from a Christian writer, then I should not
hesitate to put forward Jerome to represent this numerous class, for his   135
scholarship is so profound and so various that, compared with him, the
others appear able neither to swim, as the saying goes, nor to read and
write. And, furthermore, his power of expression is so great, he writes with
such authority and incisiveness, and possesses such a rich and varied
equipment of metaphor and allusion, that in comparison with him one   140
would pronounce other theologians to be mere Seriphian frogs. Now, you
will find in Jerome's books a greater number of adages than in the comedies
of Menander, and extremely witty ones too, such as these: 'The ox taken
to the wrestling-ring,' 'A camel has danced,' 'A hard wedge for a hard knot,'
'To drive out a nail with a nail,' 'The weary ox more heavily doth tread,'   145
and 'The cover suits the dish.' Again, his allegorical sobriquets ('The Christian Epicurus,' 'The Aristarchus of our generation') have a very strong
natural resemblance to adages. I note also that Basil shared his interest in
them. To bring my rapid survey down to modern times, there are certain

* * * * *

123 as boys cry out] *Adagia* II ix 86
132 Cicero] *Epistolae ad familiares* 7.25; *Adagia* III v 1
141 frogs] The frogs of Seriphos, an island in the Cyclades, were supposed
to be dumb; *Adagia* I v 31.

authors, Ermolao Barbaro, Pico della Mirandola, and Angelo Poliziano,   150
whom I should not hesitate to include among the greatest. All of these were
so dissatisfied with the scholarship and literary standards of their own age
that, as it seems to me, they decided to challenge Antiquity on its own
ground, and I believe they actually did better than a great many of the
ancients themselves; Pico by virtue of his amazing intellectual powers,   155
Ermolao by means of devoted and painstaking work, and Poliziano in the
marvellous brilliance and almost more than Attic loveliness of his style.
These writers, sharing an ambition to avoid as far as they possibly could
the common, that is, mean, jargon of the day, thought that this aim would
be fully attained only if they adorned their prose at all points with ancient   160
adages and with those figurative expressions which exhibit a family resemblance to the adage. Ermolao had such a wholehearted devotion to them that
he did not even fight shy of blame for undue affectation, as though he would
not consider as an educated piece of writing anything that was not seasoned
with some adage or other. Poliziano would never have introduced a   165
number of proverbs into his *Miscellanea*, where he had no intention of
allowing anything to appear below the highest standards of perfection, had
he considered this was a matter for schoolmasters alone.

But – not to extend the list too far – the whole point of this verbose
review was to show that the amount of attention paid by authors to prov-   170
erbs is in proportion to the distinction of their literary style, so that we puny
critics should not feel that we had a right to despise the genre. Yet in spite
of this, no doubt some 'dismal Elder Statesman' (as they call them) will come
forward, anxious to seem full of proper scruples (and to seem a theologian

* * * * *

150 Barbaro] Ermolao Barbaro (1453–1493?) was a Venetian aristocrat who combined diplomacy with scholarship. As professor of philosophy at Padua he did
much to revive the knowledge of Aristotle in Greek and to free his philosophy
from mediaeval tradition. His meticulous scholarship was also demonstrated
in his most famous work, the *Castigationes plinianae*, in which he corrected
thousands of errors in Pliny's *Naturalis historia* (cf Rossi 319–21).

150 Pico della Mirandola] Giovanni Pico, Count of Mirandola (1463–94), the
young philosopher whose erudition and intellectual brilliance dazzled his
generation, was a member of Ficino's circle in Florence. He combined Florentine Neoplatonism with a thorough grounding in scholastic Aristotelian
philosophy and was learned in Hebrew and Arabic as well as Latin and Greek.
His search for the truth common to all philosophies and religions was cut short
by his early death. Cf E. Garin *Giovanni Pico della Mirandola* (Florence 1937).

150 Poliziano] Cf Ep 61:154n.

173 'Elder Statesman'] Literally, member of the Areopagus (the highest court
at Athens); *Adagia* I ix 41

Pico della Mirandola
artist unknown
Galleria Uffizi, Florence

too, for a good part of theology is commonly deemed to consist in censori-   175
ous looks) and he will raise his voice loudly in opposition to me and say,
in the tones of a reproving uncle, 'Away, if you please, with those childish
frivolities; I have no more use for rhetoric – the entire science, I mean – if
it includes such meretricious trimmings, than a donkey has for gold, or a
cock for a precious stone.' Well then, let us even humour a person of this   180
sort, and reply to his strictures after the following fashion: 'If you are
ashamed to be described as a rhetorician, still you desire to be, and to
appear to be, a man of wisdom, and a theologian, too. Even if you provi-
sionally assume what no sensible person believes, that it is irrelevant to take
trouble over how one expresses oneself, yet it is just this metaphorical style   185
of expression that has always been the special distinguishing mark, not of
professional stylists, but of philosophers and prophets and divines. And
this was easily the favourite among many objects that the sages of ancient
days strove to attain. We today, alas, are as far behind them in wisdom as
we have outrun them in garrulity. Yes, these fathers of wisdom took so little   190
pleasure in the talkative ways of the sophist that they reduced the ancient
and celebrated secrets of philosophy to a few very brief adages, deliberately
adding a dash of obscurity by employing either a metaphor or a conundrum
or something of the kind. These apophthegms were invariably grasped at
as eagerly as oracular pronouncements, and circulated rapidly in every   195
quarter; they gained currency in popular jingles and could be seen displayed in front of temple doors; all over Greece they were preserved in mar-
ble inscriptions and in public monuments engraved on bronze. Examples
of them are: 'Stir not the fire with a sword,' 'Know thyself,' 'Hunger is the
best sauce,' and 'What is above us need not concern us.' Have you not at   200
any rate observed how in the esoteric writings of the Hebrew prophets
many adages are even quoted explicitly, while their entire discourse is
crammed with figures of speech akin to proverbs? As for example: 'Thou
dost lean upon a staff of reed,' 'The smoking flax shall he not quench,' 'He
falleth into the pit that he hath digged,' 'He falleth into the net he did   205
spread,' and thousands of sayings like these. You must surely have read
how King Solomon put several riddles of this sort to the wise men of Tyre,
and how he solved certain others that they propounded. And do not his

* * * * *

179–180 donkey ... stone] For both adages see *Adagia* IV viii 38. The imaginary
Areopagite's double use of the device he condemns will not escape the reader.
195 oracular] *Adagia* I vii 90
206–8 You must ... propounded] Cf Jerome Epistle 70; also used in *Antibarbari*
(ASD I 1 112).

books, called the Proverbs of Solomon, full as they are of profoundly mys-   210
terious utterance, affect any and every reader by their very title? Does not
that of the book called Ecclesiastes, and also that known as Ecclesiasticus,
point to the same kind of subject-matter? And since adages are met with
in large quantities, both in the Pauline Epistles (I do not suppose you are
so enamoured of Scotism that you never open these!) and also in the Gospels
themselves: for example, 'A dog returneth to his vomit,' 'The sow wallow-   215
ing in the mire,' 'Beating the air,' 'A tinkling cymbal,' 'We have piped to
you and ye have not danced,' 'Thou dost remove the mote from thy
brother's eye, yet hast a beam in thine own,' 'With what measure ye mete,
it shall be measured unto you again,' 'Shall he give them a stone for bread,
a scorpion for an egg?' and 'Sellers of oil.' When these are found, I repeat   220
(and I need not list them all), does it never occur to you that this manner
of expression contains not merely vain display but rather a genuine element
of sanctity, appropriate to religious topics? So for many reasons it seemed
to me I had undertaken no vain or unprofitable task in attempting to
instruct, or at least interest, studious youth, as well as I could, in a method   225
of composition which a great many learned and pious authors have found
good reason to pursue. These, I think, are the arguments which might
appease the critic's sternness and make him either take my part or at least
cease to harass me.

It remains, I think, for me to give you an account of the method I have   230
followed in this new work. It may be that as soon as they read its title some
readers will jump to the conclusion that I have laboriously but unskilfully
accumulated a vast number of aphorisms from this or that source, and so
compiled a sort of lexicon: sayings such as 'Love conquers all,' 'We cannot
all do everything,' 'Every man has his own opinion,' 'Loyalty is never sure,'   235
or 'Truth is lost when strife is bitter.' This was not my object, and I do not
hold that every aphorism is necessarily a proverb, or vice versa: to take an
example, 'Envy, like fire, attacks the high places,' is a maxim but not a
proverb, while on the other hand 'My bark is in harbour' is a proverb, not
a maxim; but 'Truth in the wine-cup' is both of them at once. Now, to make   240
it a proverb two things appear necessary: first, that its conclusion should
be distinguished in some way, either by a metaphor (for example, 'Kick
against the pricks') which form the great majority, or by an allegory (for
example, 'Dionysius at Corinth' or 'We Trojans are finished'), or by a conundrum (for example, 'The half is more than the whole'), or by any other   245

* * * * *

243 great majority] Virgil *Aeneid* 6:611
244 'We Trojans are finished'] Virgil *Aeneid* 2.325

figure of speech; or else by a witty and seemly brevity, if the image be a straightforward one, as for example 'Each to his taste.' The second requirement is that it must already have gained currency in the common speech, or be borrowed from the theatre, or be derived from some philosopher's saying, of which this is an example: 'Anacharsis commits a blunder in 250 Athens, but so do Athenians in Scythia.' Or else it may be recited as a quotation from some poet (Macrobius informs us that in antiquity isolated tags from Homer were popularly bandied about as proverbs), or extracted from some moral fable, for example, 'The mountains laboured and brought forth the mouse,' or from a remark heard by chance, as for example 'My steed 255 doth bear me, while the king doth feed me'; or it can be derived from some new and important event, like the famous saying 'There's many a slip 'twixt the cup and the lip,' or metaphorically applied in relation to the character of a man or a nation, for example, 'Phalaris' tyranny' or 'Sybarites in the streets.' But I do not indiscriminately lump together, with the white 260 dividing-line on a white ground, as they say, everything that falls under this heading; no, rather do I follow the Greek adage: 'not all, nor everywhere, nor from all men.' First of all, I leave popular maxims to the populace, with very rare exceptions; secondly, I have refrained from tacking on anything that is not ancient, or not distinguished by a certain grace. 265 Besides this, I have pointed out, as briefly as I could and merely as it were with the finger, what the adage meant and how it was used.

But now, before we come to the main task, let us block all the routes of attack open to those hostile quibblers by, as it were, strengthening our defences on every side. If these persons complain of a lack of eloquence in 270 my compilations, why, 'My very theme repudiates adornment; / Instruction will suffice her.' If there should be any who are offended at this discussion for the reason that it is too rhetorical, they will be confronted by me with the adage 'To a pig, even sweet marjoram stinks.' If anyone detects a lack of arrangement, Gellius paid no attention to it. Or if, to another critic, 275 I seem too brief, brevity suits the annotator's rôle. If I am called too verbose, this is a venal fault in a tyro. If I am blamed for copying other men's flowers, anyone who cites his own remarks is not citing adages. Some of my sayings will be described as old-fashioned, but age is a recommendation in a proverb. Some of them will be regarded with distaste because of excessive 280

* * * * *

250 Anacharsis] A 'Scythian' philosopher; one of the 'Seven Sages'
252 Macrobius] *Saturnalia* 5.16.6
254–5 'The mountains … mouse'] Horace *Ars poetica* 139
260–1 white … ground] Cf *Adagia* I v 88.
271–2 'My very theme … her'] Manilius 3.39

obscurity, but it is the nature of adages to be obscure. Others are a shade too obvious, but if you cannot learn from them, at least they will admonish you. A few are a trifle frivolous, but in a crowd of this size there is a place even for such as these. Some will appear over-elaborate, but the jewel that sparkles on the finger does not show up so well upon a dunghill; while those that, taken by themselves, seem tastelessly elaborate, become attractive when they are placed in their proper setting. The serious-minded will take little pleasure in my frivolous adages, and the frivolous little in my serious adages. I have written for the average man. If anyone deems that my offerings are too scanty, I managed to assemble them by dictation within two months when I was not well, and moreover had other tasks to distract me. If on the other hand I am held to have included too much, well, I have left out quite a few things. And there will be no lack of critics to whom this whole enterprise appears mean and petty, but even small enterprises occasionally yield a great deal of credit and profit. If anyone says that some of it is still too jejune and poverty-stricken, he should patiently await my final revision; for I have published this sample merely in order to see, at comparatively little risk and expense, what this novel work is going to look like. Anyone who points out my mistakes, provided that he does so in a friendly spirit, will earn my warm thanks; and even if he does so out of ill-will, I shall still give him my attention. But anyone who foolishly blames what he fails to understand shall be met with Apelles' adage, 'Let the cobbler stick to his last.' And there will surely be some critic who will like nothing in the book: but I did not write it for him.

There you are, dearest William: a letter full of verbosity and also of proverbosity, since it is about proverbs. I am afraid that while I was writing it I forgot that very ancient adage, 'Nothing too much,' and that by now you must already be sick of adages, and likely to lose your appetite for the rest of the book, as being warmed-over cabbage. Accordingly I take my leave, noble young sir, with greetings to you and to the wife so worthy of you, asking you to regard with fair and friendly feelings this sample of a work still to come. If you find in it some vestige of genuine promise, I shall carefully polish the specimen you now see before you, and will append a good deal more. Later I will add a second book – written 'under my own Mars.' You'll say 'What, more adages?' Not so; they will be, not adages, but something very like them; and I know they will please you much better. Farewell.
    Paris

127 / From Fausto Andrelini   Paris, 15 June 1500

Erasmus had probably sent proofs or an advance copy of the *Adagia* to his friend Fausto (cf Ep 84 introduction) in time for this letter to be printed with

the preface on the unnumbered pages at the front of the book on the verso of
the title page (cf Ep 126 introduction).

FAUSTO ANDRELINI, THE KING'S POET, TO HIS FRIEND ERASMUS
My dear Erasmus: It gave me the greatest of pleasure to read the adages
which you have sent me. In my humble opinion they are such as might win
the approval even of a hostile critic; so perfectly do they combine usefulness
and charm, that they quite certainly deserve to be endorsed by the votes   5
of everyone. I do not merely encourage you, I go so far as to command you,
by the privilege of friendship, so to say, to publish these agreeable and
profitable effusions and not to give the impression of total distaste either
for your own labours or for the publication which we have so long awaited.
Nor need you be in any fear of those critics who make a habit of sneering   10
at other men's works; for yours, destined as they are to provide a considerable amount of delight as well as edification, need not be afraid of any
supercilious carper alive. Farewell; please give my greetings to Augustin
Caminade, who is more than 'the half of my soul.'
    Paris, 15 June 1500   15

128 / To Jacob Batt   Paris [July 1500]

This letter forms the conclusion of Ep 119 in all printed editions, but refers to
a period after the publication of the *Adagia* and so some months later. By the
summer of 1500 Erasmus found himself more than usually desperate for
money. Not only had he lost the money he had in England, but he had returned
to France fired with determination to learn Greek, which would prove expensive, and to devote himself wholly to biblical and patristic scholarship and
literature (cf Ep 138: 46ff). The importunate tone of his begging letters for the
next year or so reflects a growing confidence in the importance of his work,
if only he had the means to carry it on (cf especially Ep 139).

... I have nothing to send to my lady, and accordingly I have pushed this
youth off to England to see if I can possibly scrape something from the

* * * * *

127:4–6 combine ... everyone] Cf Horace *Ars poetica* 343.
13–14 Augustin Caminade] Augustin Vincent (cf Ep 131 introduction).
14 'the half of my soul'] Horace *Odes* 1.3.8
128:2 youth] The young man, whose name was Jean (cf Ep 133:76), also carried
some copies of the *Adagia* for sale. Cf Epp 129:60ff, 130:115f, 133:5ff and 76ff,
139:189ff, 146.

count, though my instinct tells me I shall not be lucky. I am aware that the
scheme is a piece of effrontery and totally unsuited to my character; but
Necessity, that strongest goad of all, obliges a man to try everything. If he   5
should send just a little, will you for your part see that you prise away something from her or from another source, so that I can make up thirty gold
pieces in all. I am not making such strenuous efforts over this without
reason, dear Batt, for it is clear to me that my health will be imperilled if I
prolong my sojourn in these parts, and if anything happens, which God for-   10
bid, both I and all my small contributions to learning will perish; while if
my doctorate is deferred, I fear that my courage may fail before my life ends.

So I entreat and implore you, dear Batt, if you have a single spark left
of your former affection for me, to give your most earnest consideration to
saving me. With your agreeable, easy-going disposition, you possibly   15
believe that you have left me well off; however, I seem to be in a worse state
of ruin than ever before, since X offers no bounty, my lady merely extends
promises from day to day, and the bishop goes so far as to turn his back
upon me, while the abbot bids me be of good hope. In the meantime, not
a soul comes forward to give, save only X, whom I have already squeezed   20
so dry, poor fellow, that he has not a penny more to give me, while the
plague comes between me and the regular source of income upon which
alone, as I have remarked, I was relying. At the same time I have many
thoughts to ponder: Where shall I flee, without a rag to my back? What if
I fall ill? Granted that nothing of this kind happens, what will I be able to   25
achieve in the literary field without access to books? What can I hope to do
if I leave Paris? And finally, what will be the use of literary productions if
I have no recognized position to back them? Will monsters like the person
I encountered at Saint-Omer be able to laugh at me, calling me a prater?

I write this not with the intention of wearying you with my complain-   30
ing, but to arouse you from your somnolent attitude, and in order that we
may achieve at long last the object we have been vainly striving for, and

* * * * *

7–8 thirty gold pieces] Possibly *écus à la couronne*, for a sum of £52 10s 0d
tournois; if *écus au soleil*, worth £54 7s 6d *tournois*. See the Glossary and Appendix A on gold coinage.

12 doctorate] Cf Ep 129:67n.

17 X] Possibly Mountjoy, since he is the only one of Erasmus' regular patrons
not mentioned here. He is, however, mentioned in line 3. The second X (line
20) seems to refer to someone else, possibly Augustin Vincent who, though
not exactly a patron, did help Erasmus out occasionally.

18 bishop] Hendrik van Bergen, bishop of Cambrai (cf Ep 49 introduction).

19 abbot] Antoon van Bergen, abbot of St Bertin (cf Ep 143 introduction).

return in the end to the happy companionship we used to enjoy. Farewell, dear Jacob.

PS: I sent an answer by the messenger who brought the parcel. If you   35
still have the letter I wrote to Mountjoy when I was with you, please give
it to this youth. Greetings to those to whom I owe them. You can depend
on the young man to be reliable if you should have anything to entrust to
him. Augustin is giving public expositions of the *Adagia*, which are very
well attended; so far they have had a splendid start. If you think you can   40
sell off a few copies at Saint-Omer, take them out of the bundle. Farewell
once more.

Paris [1499]

129 / To Jacob Batt   Paris [beginning of September 1500]

The plague was raging in Paris during the summer of 1500, emptying the city.
Batt invited Erasmus to come to Tournehem, but for reasons not altogether
clear he preferred to flee to Orléans. He remained there till mid-December and
from there Epp 130–40 were written. The period of Erasmus' stay in Orléans,
and indeed the whole of 1500, was marked by an unusually intensive exchange
of letters with Batt. As we have only those written by Erasmus, and by no
means all of them, many of the references to persons or events are obscure.

ERASMUS OF ROTTERDAM TO HIS FRIEND BATT
On the day of writing I am about to leave for Orléans. There is always some
imp of mischief at hand to interrupt my studies. My inclination was rather
to come to you, partly because I should be closer there to my homeland,
partly because it would give me, I thought, an opportunity of helping for-   5
ward your studies to some extent, or at least of encouraging them. On the
other hand, I have had many reflections of a contrary sort: as that I could
scarcely find a suitable lodging there, for while I approve of the one you
showed me at Pierre's I still have a reservation, which you know, about such
a situation, not because I fear for either my continence or my reputation but   10
simply to ensure that no dubious reports filter back to Pierre as a result; for,
as you know, the mass of mankind, especially at court, dislikes members

* * * * *

35 parcel] Cf Epp 123:20n and 124:21ff.
36 letter] Cf Ep 120 introduction.
39 public expositions] Cf Ep 70:35n.
129:9 Pierre] the friend at Tournehem to whom he frequently sent greetings
(cf Epp 80:147, 123:30, 138:193).

of the literary profession, and would gladly accuse us of the vices they themselves habitually practise. Secondly, I reflect that there might be some who
would wonder why I kept rushing back to see you; and lastly, I call to mind   15
how lukewarm you are, for I remember that your advice to me to take refuge
with you was coolly and almost timidly given. Indeed, I am not sure
whether you even take pleasure in literature any more; for you have fallen
into a love of a different sort in which, though its allurements whet the
appetite, fulfilment does not, as in other kinds, bring a surfeit. You take   20
my meaning.

Now, I am not quite unaware that you have begun distinctly to favour
Willem, and are devoted to the purpose of advancing him. I am so far from
feeling envious that I am even ready to confess a debt to you on this score;
but when you, who laid the foundations of my rescue, desert me now, is   25
not this like a readiness to beget a son and then, though you have acknowledged him as your own, to expose him to die? Whereas my lady presented
Willem with a travelling-allowance of generous size, she sent me away
empty-handed, even though he was returning homewards, while I was outward bound; and moreover I was hastening to libraries, he to libations. No   30
doubt you will answer that she is well enough off to endow both of us; but
you know what courtiers are, and what fickle breezes guide the female temperament. However, I say no more. Whatever comes of it, even if I am
cheated of promised help, I am glad if it be given to my dear Willem instead
of me. And if my suspicions on this head are unjustified, as indeed I ear-   35
nestly hope they may be, and you are your usual friendly self, then see that
my lady is as good as her word, and makes me the gift of a benefice as well,
considering the latter as a present to you rather than to me; for in this way
we shall have found a means by which you can enjoy a living without being
ordained. I shall explain to you why I am so very anxious to have these   40
benefits. My intense desire is to leave France as soon as possible and live
among my own people. This, I foresee, will further my reputation more,
and also be better for my health, for at present my fellow countrymen at
home believe that I am glad to be away, in order to be free, while those who
reside in Paris suspect that I am not popular with my own nation and am   45
living here in a kind of enforced exile. Lastly, even if I had no other reason,

* * * * *

20–1 You take my meaning] Batt undoubtedly did know what Erasmus
meant, but the modern editor is not so fortunate. Here, as in some other places,
Erasmus is wilfully obscure, possibly from fear that the letter might fall into
the wrong hands.
23 Willem] Hermans (cf Ep 33 introduction).

yet what would still count enormously in my eyes is the desire to see you, and my dear Willem too, quite often.

About the book I have printed I can report this: it cannot be disposed of here at present, because Augustin has given up his expositions, and people are running away everywhere from the plague. Yet if it is not sold off as soon as possible, I shall not find a printer for my work on literary style, on which I am now engaged. So, dear Batt, be sure to bend every effort and strain every muscle and cudgel all your brains to come to my aid in this business. I have written a somewhat elaborate letter to the lord provost, sending him a copy of my *Adagia*, and Willem's odes, and also a trifling poem I printed long ago, entitled *De casa natalitia Iesu*. When I hear Josse has returned I shall send letters to him and to the abbot, for I have found a suitable topic on which to write to both of them.

I sent a youth to England with some books for sale; I am surprised he had not reached you by the time the physician took his leave. When he comes back from England (he is absolutely reliable, and will certainly follow me to Orléans), please send me a full report on the whole situation and what I can expect. As soon as I finish anything in the shape of a book I will send it to you at once, in order that if anything should suddenly happen to me you may keep the products of my brain from perishing. If either Mountjoy or my lady sends me any gift, I shall take a doctorate; if not, I shall give up hoping for that honour, and come back to you all whatever my situation may be. I am long since wearied of France. Farewell, dear

* * * * *

50 expositions] Cf Ep 128:39ff.

52 literary style] '*De literis*.' This could refer to the *De copia*, on which Erasmus was working at this time (cf Epp 95:37 and 145) or to the *Antibarbari* which was a defence of good letters and on which he also seems to have been working (cf Ep 124:68n). See also Ep 31:88 where he refers to the *Antibarbari* as 'de literis.'

55 lord provost] Nicholas of Burgundy (cf Ep 144 introduction).

56 Willem's odes] The *Silva odarum* (cf Ep 49 introduction).

57 *De casa natalitia Iesu*] Cf Ep 47 introduction.

57 Josse] Perhaps Josse Blysell who was at Saint-Omer in 1500

58 abbot] Antoon van Bergen had recently been appointed councillor to Archduke Philip, which probably explains his trip to the court of Brabant (cf Ep 143 introduction). He did not return until December (cf Ep 137:2ff and 55ff).

67 doctorate] Erasmus had now, at least temporarily, given up hope of being able to obtain his doctorate in theology in Bologna (cf Ep 75:15n), and had decided to take it in Paris if he could afford the expense (cf Ep 128:12). He had earlier commented on the high cost of a degree in Bologna (cf Ep 75:21ff). It was probably no less expensive in Paris.

Batt. My health is so-so; not as good as I should wish. My friend Augustin   70
sends you his greetings.

ps: I have sent you a poem on 'Delius'; but it is extempore and not
worth any but perhaps a single hurried look: reckon it as a member of the
species *unedo*; it were more than enough to taste it once. I enclose one copy
of the *Adagia* for your pupil Adolph; if I notice him taking a genuine   75
pleasure in literature, I shall later present him with some creations of my
own. And, my dear Batt, I am very anxious that you should know Greek,
both because I find that a Latin education is imperfect without it, and also
to heighten the pleasure we take in each other's society, as would happen
if we both enjoyed precisely the same range of study. Give your pupil   80
Adolph a taste of the first lessons, too. You will say 'Send me the book'; well,
it is for sale here, and cheaply too; but my short answer is, that I haven't
a penny. You will, of course, guess the rest, what slavery I am enduring,
and you know me well enough to realize how badly I put up with slavery.
But, as I wait to see what the end of all this will be, I remain hopeful.   85
Another thing: I am glad that the man about whom we were concerned for
his daughter's sake has been acquitted. Farewell again and again, dearest
Batt – or rather farewell just once, and let it be *really* well.

Paris [1498]

130 / To Jacob Batt   [Orléans, September 1500]

ERASMUS TO HIS FRIEND BATT: A LETTER WRITTEN IN AFFECTIONATE JEST,
FULL OF IRONY

I can see that you were annoyed by my letter; you say that it was a peevish
one, whereas I think its tone was merry enough; any gall it contained was
poured out not upon your head, but merely in your ear, prompted by the   5
quite proper anguish I felt. Yet I acknowledge my mistake, and it was a
twofold one, since I failed to consider either your good fortune or my own
desperate situation. Of course the proper expression to assume, when one
is in such dire straits, is that of supplication, not of jesting, much less of
witty audacity, especially towards a person who is in the full flood of good   10
fortune and to whom one is oneself indebted on several accounts. Also, I

* * * * *

72 'Delius'] Cf Ep 95:24n.

74 *unedo*] The strawberry-tree (*Arbutus unedo*) bears fruits so unpalatable that
one is enough (Pliny *Naturalis historia* 15.24–99).

86 man] Cf Ep 130:71ff; there is no further information about this intriguing
case.

am conscious how to some extent it is a characteristic of people at court that from men whom Dame Fortune has deserted, and whom they have reduced to dependence by some trivial donation, they are quite incapable of tolerating any insolence, and indeed can scarcely bear to hear even the abashed tones of a suppliant. They actually look for gratitude from the poor wretches whom they themselves have cowed into submission. Still, in my bitter anguish I have been experiencing something that generally accompanies severe disease: the patient loses consciousness. Thus, though my grief was at its most violent, I do not recall being unhappy. And I used to think that as Batt's friend I had liberty to behave towards him with perfect freedom. For hitherto, let me admit it, I have simply loved and not feared you, and you are quite aware that deep affection agreeth not with fear. But my love, which was indeed blind love, has taken me too far. I can see that I have sinned, and will abide punishment most dire if I reform not. In future I shall love my Batt only as a friend, a benefactor, and a scholar. I shall respect him as my teacher and as my sovereign, in whose hand it lies either to destroy me or to render me happy. I accept chastisement even with blows if hereafter you detect in my letters a single word that is, I will not merely say impertinent or free-spoken, but in the slightest degree wanting in unctuousness or deference or unsuitable to the condition of a slave, if he be in fear of mortal punishment. Nay, I am grateful besides, dear master, that you have brought me to self-awareness and put me in mind of my low condition.

I shall now make certain replies to your most gracious epistle; and I beg you not to find it irksome to grant me a calm and sympathetic hearing. First, I intend to rid myself utterly of that habit I had of writing peevishly; and if you deem it too little merely to repent of my error, then I will undergo any punishment, so long as you will take me back into your favour, not of course the favour I once enjoyed, for I am not so brazen as to dare to ask for that, but it will be a very great privilege if I can but secure a place on its uttermost margin. For the provost's sincere good will towards me I claim no credit to myself; I render homage to the indulgence towards me that led you to recommend me to so great a man, and I embrace it gratefully. And when you promise to grant your active and loyal patronage on my behalf in my lady's sight, then, most distinguished Batt, what can I possibly promise to you in return for such devotion? Must I not promise myself? Yet I have long been one of your slaves. Besides, when you sent me Willem's

15

20

25

30

35

40

45

* * * * *

130:41 provost] Cf Ep 129:55n.
47 Willem] Cf Ep 129:23ff.

letter you seemed to me to be commanding me to choose, with the least possible delay, a tree from which to hang myself. I have known for some time that, if he succeeds as he has done, all is over with me. But why do I exhibit such a lack of self-control in my reaction to my sufferings, which I have brought upon myself by my own folly? I am now ready to endure even crucifixion at your hands; though even this I consider a less dreadful fate than to see Willem preferred to myself. I do but entreat you most humbly, both by your good fortune and by the gods' anger towards me, that if you are resolved to destroy me you do not postpone the end by long-drawn-out tortures.

As for my failure to write to the abbot, please do not suppose that this was due to laziness on my part. I simply could not think of any subject to write about, and you know how slow I am to move; a reprehensible fault, certainly, but what is one to do with a donkey? Besides, I was reckoning on the assumption that he would be away in Brabant for some considerable time. I have written to Master Antonius, in case you should suppose me to be neglecting all my obligations. On this occasion, too, I was unable to think of a suitable topic. I know, you see, that it is positively harmful to send letters to people who are eagerly interested but who lack an education to match; however, since I was prompted and prodded by your reproaches, I wrote to him, not as well as I wished, but undoubtedly as well as I could, choosing rather to offend him with a poor letter, than to arouse your anger by failing to send one.

For the saving of the man whom they tried to represent as a heretic, I offer congratulations: first to his daughter, whose deeply filial tears tore at my heartstrings, secondly to you, inasmuch as the prayers you offered up for her sake were effectual, and lastly to the hero of the episode himself, since he has had a change of heart. How much more deserving of the punishment was that scoundrelly Dominican suffragan, the most corrupt, grasping, and insolent fellow alive! In fact, my dislike of him moved me to take up this man's case all the more enthusiastically with the abbot.

You make a request for the purchase of some copies of Terence,

* * * * *

58 abbot] Cf Ep 129:58n. Erasmus did finally write to the abbot (cf below, 124). For the reception of the letter, see Epp 137:82ff and 143.

63 Antonius] Antonius of Luxembourg, steward of the Abbey of St Bertin (cf Ep 137 introduction).

71 heretic] Cf Ep 129:86.

76 Dominican] Jean le Vasseur (d 1508) was a Dominican, suffragan to the bishop of Thérouanne and prior of the Dominican convent at Saint-Omer.

together with Willem's odes. I shall make sure that you regard me as a profit-   80
able slave. But pray excuse me for not rushing back to Paris in person to
buy these; much as I longed to do so, I was hindered by sudden floods of
rain. The road is hardly passable even for horses, once it becomes water-
logged. Besides, the messenger claimed that you had given him a piece of
tin money and that he left it at home; I myself had nothing to give him, and   85
nobody whom I could ask for a loan, and I was unable to pledge my credit
in a strange city. Still, I shall try to see, if any god chooses to rescue me,
whether I can manage to send you what you ask for.

In inviting me to the castle if the plague should drive me from here,
you have, most merciful Batt, restored to me my hope of survival. Why   90
should I not, at this point, rush to embrace your knees and fall on my face
to kiss your feet? I can see that you wish for my preservation; my death from
starvation is not what you wish, for would not this be the most painful and
disgraceful of punishments? Ah, my liege lord, here at this moment we are
sore pressed by the plague, and I long to fly to that fortunate castle of yours,   95
more even than I long to fly to Heaven; but, pray pardon my fears, I am still
somewhat alarmed, lest the fire of your anger against me be not yet out.
When I feel sure that it has ceased to rage, then at last, and not before, shall
I quit this sanctuary. For the nonce, allow me to be absent a while for
shame's sake; afterwards I shall come back, when I have found some friends   100
who will intercede for me.

Your remark that you were so pleased with your friend Willem's poem
gives me once again to understand how I have failed; and I have none,
among gods above or below, to appeal to, except yourself, who for me take
the place of any and every god. Caminade is most grateful to you for deign-   105
ing to mention him in your most elegant letter; as soon as he received your
decree, he swept out all the lumber in a search for something to send you.
Believe me, he has nothing you do not already have, except a few daily conversational sentences, such as we use on meeting each other and at table.

* * * * *

105 Caminade] Augustin Vincent (cf Ep 54 introduction).
108–9 conversational sentences] Augustin Vincent had evidently still in his
possession a collection of forms of polite conversation which Erasmus had
written two or three years earlier for the use of his students, particularly Christian Northoff and his brother who were then living with Augustin (cf Ep 54
introduction). Later the manuscript passed into the hands of Lambertus Hol-
lonius (cf Ep 904 introduction) from whom it was purchased by Beatus
Rhenanus, who published it, together with other of Erasmus' early *opuscula*
(cf Epp 56 and 260 introductions), without Erasmus' knowledge as *Familiarium
colloquiorum formulae* (Basel: Froben, November 1518). Annoyed by the

If you command these to be sent to you, they shall be sent, once they are   110
corrected and also augmented. I am about to revise the work *De conscriben-*
dis epistolis and will send this too if you bid me. And if you have any further
orders, I shall stand ready to carry them out.

Thus far I have answered your letter; now a few remarks not connected
with that letter. I sent a youth, bearing a load of books; but I conjecture that   115
your letter was already written before he arrived. Then I wrote by Adrian,
but much regret having done so, for I wrote somewhat peevishly (and I am
sorry and ashamed I did so), not having received your letter at the time.
But please forgive me – so may you ever have the luck to live in riches and
prosperity in that court of yours. Farewell; I shall be hungry enough here,   120
as I deserve.

I gave the messenger three *douzains*, which I begged with difficulty,
and some shame, from Augustin; and I told him where he could purchase
the books. I have written to the abbot: the letter will do no good, unless
you read it out; so be sure to be present.   125

Farewell, my very dear and delightful Batt. I am not refusing your invitation to come and stay with you; for I have made up my mind to flee to
you, should plague break out here as well.

[Saint-Omer, 1499]

131 / To Augustin Vincent   [Orléans, September 1500]

This is the first extant letter addressed to Augustin Vincent, called Caminade,
whose name, however, appears frequently in the preceding letters. He was
apparently a North German, probably from Kamin in Mecklenburg-Schwerin,
whence his cognomen Caminadus. He had connections with Lübeck and

* * * * *

unauthorized publication of his early work in uncorrected form, something
which had happened on other occasions (cf Epp 66 and 71 introduction), Erasmus published a revised edition (Louvain: Th. Martens, March 1519) which
was reprinted by Froben in May and October of that year (cf Ep 909 introduction). It was reprinted in successively augmented editions until it had grown
beyond recognition and become the *Colloquia familiaria* as we have it (cf LB I
615ff). The original *formulae*, in which Christian, Augustin, and Erasmus are
the principal speakers, are translated in Thompson *Colloquies* 555ff. Cf P.
Smith *A Key to the Colloquies of Erasmus* (Cambridge, Mass. 1927).

111–12 *De conscribendis epistolis*] Cf Ep 71 introduction.

116 Adrian] Cf Ep 80:57n.

122 three *douzains*] Worth 36d or 3 *sols tournois*. See the Glossary and Appendix
B on silver coinage.

tutored young men from there (cf Epp 54 introduction and 82: 16ff). Aside from tutoring, he supported himself by doing odd jobs for printers and book-sellers (cf Ep 70: 35n) Erasmus lodged with him from time to time (cf Epp 58 introduction and 119:280). He also gave Vincent instruction in return for services and occasional support. Some of Erasmus' early MSS which Vincent retained may also have been regarded by him as payment (cf Epp 80: 25, 130: 108–9n). Despite their long intimacy Erasmus' feeling for Augustin was decidedly ambivalent and frequently marked by distrust (cf Epp 80: 16n, 81: 30ff, 95: 14ff, 133: 10ff, 138: 14ff, and F. Bierlaire 'Erasme et Augustin Vincent Caminade' BHR 2 (1968) 357–62. On his arrival in Orléans Erasmus stayed with Augustin for a short time until one of the pupils who lodged with him became ill and Erasmus left to avoid contagion (cf Ep 133: 25ff). For the next three months he lodged with Jacob Voogd (cf Ep 137: 35ff; Allen Ep 147: 47ff).

ERASMUS TO AUGUSTIN

So – is it to humour some leech or other of yours that you are robbing me of the only consolation (for I dare not utter the word 'gift') I possess in my dreary situation? Indeed my affection for this particular author is so warm that, even though I should fail to understand him, I should still derive   5
refreshment and sustenance from the very sight of his work. Nevertheless, I consider it most unfair to oppose you in any matter, even under difficult conditions, especially when you are undergoing misfortune, so I am sending you one part of my Homer, in order that the importunate demands of that doctor of yours may be met and yet I myself be not wholly bereft of   10
solace. For the terms on which I live with Master Jacob amount to living in solitude, hence I ardently look forward to the time when you and I may resume the intercourse we used to have. Indeed, I foresee that this may happen soon, for I hear that the youth is greatly recovered. For the present my request to you is that we should enact a semblance, as it were, of our inter-   15
course, simply by interchanging letters.

I cannot prevail on you to send me the collection of letters, though it

* * * * *

131:2 leech] Probably Pierre d'Angleberme (cf Ep 140 introduction), certainly the physician to whom Ep 132 is addressed. Augustin had evidently asked Erasmus to return a copy of Homer he had lent him in order to give it to the physician, presumably the one who had attended his sick pupil.

11 Master Jacob] Voogd (cf Ep 152 introduction). The name means 'guardian' ('tutor' in Latin). Erasmus sometimes plays on the word, as when he speaks of 'meus Tutor'; and as in Ep 137:38.

17 collection of letters] The De conscribendis epistolis. Erasmus had complained two years earlier that Augustin had the only copy (cf Ep 80:26).

is of such great importance to me, and also, to some extent, to you. As far
as Jacob is concerned, I shall at all hazards commit myself to promising you
that I will not pass a single syllable on to him. I have trained the fellow not   20
to take the slightest notice of what I am doing. Greetings and farewell, dearest Augustin; be manful, as you are wont, in face of the misfortunes we both
endure.

     PS Greetings from Jacob, your friend, and mine too, because he is
yours. I am waiting for that collection of letters; if not in its entirety, at least   25
a couple of volumes, so that at least a beginning may become possible. This
is one work that I think I could polish off in the meantime. The others cannot, so far as I can see, be brought to completion without an enormous
number of books to refer to. Look after yourself, my dear Augustin.

     [1499]   30

132 / To a physician for a friend   [Orléans, September 1500]

This was evidently written to accompany the Homer to be sent to Pierre d'Angleberme, the physician mentioned here and in Ep 131. It may have been written on behalf of Augustin's pupil who had been ill and to whom the Homer
may have belonged.

A LETTER WRITTEN BY ERASMUS TO A PHYSICIAN
ON BEHALF OF A CERTAIN FRIEND
Most learned sir: It has at length been brought home to me by actual experience that the bitterest discomfort a grateful person can suffer is to have no
chance of repaying, in even the slightest degree, men to whom he owes   5
infinite gratitude. This is exactly what has befallen me in respect of you.
When, in my heart, I review your extraordinary services, as I do unceasingly, looking anxiously to see whether in any way I could respond to all
your kindness towards me, if not equally, which I may not hope to do, at
least in part, then I rage and curse at my fate, which has elected that I should   10
be born into a station in life where I must become the recipient of infinite
kindness from men like you, without having the ability to make the very
slightest return for what I have received. Indeed it is in this single respect
that I chafe under the cruelty of fortune, and my innermost spirit is overwhelmed by a flood of emotion when my heart is eager to return the good   15
deed and yet at the same time I reflect how little it is that my slender means

        * * * * *

27 others] Probably the *De copia* (cf Epp 95:39, 136:57f), or possibly an
augmented edition of the *Adagia*, either of which would have required access
to a number of books.

can manage, and how vast the gift your kindness deserves. Who, indeed, no matter how rich, has ever fully paid his debt of gratitude to a physician? You cannot make fair return to God; no more to a physician. God gives us our lives; our physician, as it were, gives us those lives again. If from the Supreme Creator of the universe we have received the gift of life, yet it is by a physician's care that it is preserved so that it be not lost, and again is saved when otherwise it would have perished. Wherefore I would not reckon a man of medicine as 'one worth many,' in Homer's words, but rather would deem him to deserve to be regarded by mankind as a sort of god upon earth. 20 25

Yet I also consider you to be as far above the common run of medical men as the physician excels the rest of mankind; so my debt to you is that which is due, not merely to a physician, but to a physician who is the prince of his profession, whose loyalty is exceptional and well-nigh unbelievable, whose care and concern exceed a father's, and whose kindness is marvellous to behold. To find all these qualities united in a single member of the profession may well be a prodigy no less rare than the phoenix of poetic fame which has become a byword for rarity; but not only are they all present in you, they are present in the highest degree, for there exists no abler diagnostician, none whose judgment is more keen and sure, none whose decisions are announced with less arrogance. In these respects, not only do you far excel all the physicians of our own day but you are fully entitled to be ranked with the very founders, godlike, as the ancients used to call them, of the art of medicine itself. Then again, you possess absolute loyalty to patients; if a physician's professional skill fails to be augmented by this quality he is indeed a dangerous creature, but yours is so tried and tested that as a result all the princes of this world vie with one another to entrust their lives' safety to you, as to a parent rather than a doctor. Again, your thoroughgoing attention to even the tiniest details, and your ability to endure drudgery without the slightest display of irritation, are such as to place you upon the same level as the most loving of mothers. Besides this, you are unsurpassed in kindness, a quality that has rightly meant that everyone admires you, and not only admires but loves you. Your skill arouses amazement in your fellow professionals; your loyal conduct appeals to princes, your conscientious care to those who are suffering, and to each and everyone your kindness and extraordinary good manners. And in my supreme peril, when I, a person whom you hardly knew, was in well-nigh desperate straits, or at least in the deepest distress, you displayed all 30 35 40 45 50

* * * * *

24 Homer's words] *Iliad* 9.116–7

these qualities in a way that could not have been more thoughtful had I been   55
your brother; consequently I was restored to life as if from the nether world,
entirely by your skill.

So I am clearly conscious of the debt I owe, though in fact I cannot fully
grasp its extent in my imagination, much less express it in words. But I am
beginning to think, as I should, of making a return, and there is plainly no   60
way of balancing debits and credits in the account. How could I pay a just
sum out of my small competency? It is extremely slender; a true poet's
purse, which is to say miserly, almost non-existent in fact, while what you
have bestowed on me is a gift of greater value than even Croesus, if he
emptied his entire treasury, could match; or, if I possessed streams of gold,   65
as in the poetic tale, or some sort of Tagus or Pactolus, rolling down its
golden sands. Even when Phalaris, who was a despot and enormously rich,
had sent lavish presents, quite worthy of a king, to his physician Polycletus,
he made excuses for the meanness of the gift, declaring that he was unable
to match what Polycletus had done for him. As things stand, I believe that   70
I am in no position to pay off even the least part of my debt, even if I pledge
myself for every penny I am worth, or go so far as to put my estate up for
auction; but I am sure that your need of this kind of gratitude is as small
as my capacity to repay it. Sometimes, however, as Seneca says, 'true
gratitude is repayment,' for did not Aeschines leave Socrates more in his   75
debt by a grateful and modest speech than Alcibiades, whose riches were
equal to his generosity? But I recognize how far I fall behind you in this
respect also, for your services to me are such as to outrun any possible
degree of eloquence, and nobody could make a speech that was splendid
enough not to seem jejune compared with your kindness; moreover my lack   80
of rhetorical skill is such as to make me incapable of the proper treatment
even of indifferent subjects. Finally, your own intellectual refinement is so
great, and your judgment so acute, that it cannot possibly find satisfaction
in anything that is not superbly finished, exquisite, and perfect.

Since, then, I am bound to be outdone either way, unable either to   85
repay any of my gratitude, or to express it adequately, I shall for ever continue to do the one thing that it lies within my resources to achieve: that
is, I shall remember and love and be grateful as far as I can, and repay

* * * * *

66 Tagus, Pactolus] Gold-bearing rivers in modern Portugal and in Asia
Minor; *Adagia* I vi 75
67 Phalaris] The cruel tyrant of Agrigentum; cf Ep 109:104n.
74 Seneca] *De beneficiis* 2.30.2 and 35.1
75 Aeschines] Cf Seneca *De beneficiis* 1.8.

gratitude to the extent of finding it utterly impossible to seem ungrateful. And it is not by way of payment on account, but as a token of my gratitude, that I send you a Homer in Greek, that I have filched from a very good friend, with an eye to increasing your friendly feelings to me. Farewell.

133 / To Jacob Batt   Orléans [end of September 1500]

ERASMUS OF ROTTERDAM TO HIS FRIEND BATT
Best greetings, my delightful Batt. My present situation is such that I have neither inclination nor opportunity for affectionate banter or playful indig- nation. I shall tell you how my news goes, so I ask for a dash of your usual friendly spirit. The youth I spoke of, whom I sent to you with a load of books, promised he would be back in four weeks, yet he has already been missing for eight. Now, I am not unaware of the unexpected accidents that befall wayfarers: sickness and robbers and fresh business and, in short, myriad causes for delay. Still, it is not without some reason that I have been gripped by a profound anxiety in case a deep-laid plot underlies this cir- cumstance. In the first place, you are familiar with Augustin's nature and those old tricks of his; secondly, I am told that the youth is substantially in debt here, and besides not very sensible or reliable; and that in addition he is a close accomplice in Augustin's most secret plans. All this has only now come to light – as usual, after the party is over, as the saying goes. Per- sonally, I have often wondered at Augustin's sudden flood of generosity; how could the fellow have been transformed so instantaneously from one who always was in the habit of filching other men's property into one who now lavishly gave away his own? For most recently he has begun to expend on me rather more than he got from me. Sometimes I began covertly to sus- pect that I was being lured with bait, so that once I was caught I should dis- gorge everything for my captor's benefit. If I am not utterly mistaken, this slight suspicion is about to prove fully justified: to make this clear to you I will tell you what happened.

In alarm at the plague, I retired to Orléans, whereupon one of Augus- tin's two young charges fell sick a few days later. As to whether this sickness

* * * * *

133:5 youth] Cf Ep 128:2n. The suspicion of him expressed in this letter is understandable in view of his failure to return, although Erasmus had earlier declared him to be entirely reliable (cf Ep 129:62f). He was still missing four months later (cf Ep 146). The loss was a serious one for Erasmus, involving the prices of 100 copies of the *Adagia* for which he still had received nothing as late as December 1504 (cf Ep 181).

15 after the party] *Adagia* I ix 52

was contagious or not: I think it may have been, but am very far from being
certain, for it is the hardest thing on earth to put your finger on this elusive
cuttlefish which withdraws into an inky darkness of his own manufacture.
But when the boy had been vomiting and suffering from continuous   30
diarrhoea for four days and more, I became apprehensive about contracting
an illness from the noxious odours that resulted, and represented to Augustin that there would be some advantage to be gained if I withdrew
elsewhere for five or six days, leaving more room for him as well as affording
some relief to my nostrils, and then returned. At once Augustin grasped   35
at the opportunity I had afforded him to take umbrage at this, for all his
vigorous pretence to the contrary. He said he had no advice to give me and
I must do what I thought best; he had no feelings about it, and nothing to
suggest. The point of this lay in his belief that I did not then possess a penny,
and without money should be unable to do anything, so that I should   40
either have to remain against my will or meet with disaster. I entered into
a connexion with one Master Jacob Voogd of Antwerp, a doctor of canon
law, who is an extremely civilized young man and deeply attached to me,
an enthusiastic admirer and champion of my literary works; but it was on
the understanding that I should go back to Augustin when the youth recov-   45
ered. Thereupon Augustin not only began to show anger, but also envy
towards Voogd, and to convey to me, partly by his silence and partly by
those mysterious riddles in which he expresses himself indirectly, that I
was barred from returning to him. Though I had guessed this for some time,
I had an increasing desire to clarify the matter. He put up several different   50
pretexts, in his usual way, but the authors of numerous lies cannot always
remember what they have said. In short, I discovered in him the spirit of
an enemy, a traitor, a robber and, to sum everything up, an Augustin, I
mean the old Augustin whom I have partly described to you.

I can detect that his purposes are hostile, treacherous, wily, in fact   55
worthy of himself; particularly the one purpose he tries most strenuously
to conceal, namely to intercept, without my knowledge, the youth we sent
to England, so as to make away with any money or letters he may be carrying, and afterwards, of course, to send him off upon another errand; I know
of many reasons he could easily give for doing so. I shall be told a tale to   60
the effect that the young man has run off and nowhere come to light; meanwhile some action will be taken: either Augustin himself will run away
somewhere, or at the least he will ruin us in some way or other. Believe me,
Batt, at his hands I look for no treatment save what one usually expects from
a deep-dyed assassin. Indeed, I am horribly anxious in case the youth has   65
already got back and the brigand already has his booty; that it has been

seized, I am convinced, even by the following proof alone: Augustin himself, telling a parcel of lies as usual, recently let slip the remark that he had
had some news of the youth's arrival, to the effect that he was already on
the way and would be coming back not by way of Paris but by another   70
route. The object of this was to prevent me from meeting him and cutting
him off as he returned. At once I began to press him to tell me from what
sources he had heard this. At first he prevaricated and tried to change the
subject; but when I would not stop asking questions and pressing him, he
said he had it from So-and-So (naming him). At once I sent a message to   75
ask the latter if he had heard any news of Jean. He gave me no information
except that with which Augustin himself seemed to have furnished him;
so I remonstrated with Augustin, asking him why he had directed me to
an 'informant' whom he had himself informed. The fellow blushed and
changed the subject; at length, when I insisted, he confessed he himself was   80
drunk when he said this, for it was he who had told the man the whole story.

There were a great many tricks like this, which I might mention; but
be assured that I have never been so certain of anything as I am that Augustin will try to bring about my ruin if he can do so undetected, and that he
first of all intends to lie in wait for this sum of money. So, if you wish for   85
my deliverance, please be vigilant in the matter and spare no labour or
expense. Once I get clear of this reef I am sure the rest will be plain sailing.
Accordingly this – or anything better you can think of – is what I want you
to do. If the youth is not back from England yet, it may be that he has crossed
to France at another place on the coast, on his master's instructions of   90
course. If, therefore, you have in your possession any books, or money from
the sale of books, do not let them out of your hands, but keep what you
have. But if you have sent him off to Zeeland or elsewhere and he is not
back yet, try as hard as you can to recall the young man and relieve him
of all that he carries; especially in anything that has to do with me, do not   95
trust him with a penny. Say to him that you know for certain that I shall
be with you in a few days. If you can make a decent excuse to do so, keep
Augustin's property also, since I have not yet got back all my possessions
from him. If the youth is back already and has visited you, please send me
a written statement, by fully reliable messengers, of the date when he left   100
you, what money he carried and on whose account, and what letters he had,
so that I may make some trouble for that wolf Augustin. Add in your letter
some persuasion that may frighten even a man who is most sure of himself,
as this man is; or else send Adrian to greet me, if he wishes, and to follow

* * * * *

104 Adrian] Cf Ep 80:57n.

up every track of the runaway youth. I beg you, dear Batt, to lavish on this   105
affair every trick, every device, every kind of attention you can command.
Even if the young man now comes back to you from England after doing
everything quite honestly, keep all my belongings in your care, and do not
trust him with so much as a feather, making the pretext I spoke of. And if
the youth has long since left you and has in fact brought some money, and   110
it appears clear that Augustin has been up to his tricks, then send someone
straight away to England to probe into the matter, if you agree that it is right
to do so. And whatever you get from the youth should please be sent by
the Saint-Omer courier, with explicit instructions and warnings not to go
to Augustin; but send him either to the abbot's brother, Master Dismas,   115
or to Master Jacob Voogd of Antwerp, with whom I share a dwelling, or else,
if there seems sufficient reason, send Adrian. Farewell, my dear and
delightful Batt. I am surprised that you did not send me any note by the
hand of this young man, who escorted the governor's son to Orléans, since
there was so much to write about. Farewell.   120
      PS: Greetings to you from my good friend Master Jacob. Rid me of this
groundless alarm, if I am wrong, or calamity, if my suspicions are justified.
      Orléans, in the year [1499]

134 / To Fausto Andrelini   Orléans, 20 November [1500]

Fausto had already written a complimentary letter which was printed on the
verso of the title page of the *Adagia* (cf Ep 127; and line 48 below). The testimonial Erasmus was now requesting was probably intended for circulation or
display in the bookseller's shop to promote sales, which had been dropping
off since Augustin had stopped his public lectures and the plague had emptied
Paris (cf Ep 129: 50ff).

ERASMUS TO FAUSTO, THE KING'S POET

My servant, acting on your instructions and using words prescribed by
you, has called me craven for moving to a new territory out of fear of some
trifling plague or other. This would be an intolerable insult if it were
addressed to a Swiss guardsman, but it fails to make any impression on one   5
who is a poet, fond of a sheltered and leisured existence. Really, I consider
a total absence of fear, in situations such as mine, to be the mark not of a
valiant fellow but of a dolt. When one is faced with an enemy who can be

* * * * *

115 Dismas] Cf Ep 137:15n.

driven off or thrown back or defeated by active resistance, it is then that
anyone who wishes to show himself a hero may do so, as far as I am con-   10
cerned. But the celebrated hydra of Lerna, the last and most difficult of Hercules' labours, could not be mastered by the sword, yet could be overcome
by Greek fire. What, I ask, are you going to do with an invisible and invincible pestilence, like this one? Sometimes escape is better than victory. Hero
as he was, Aeneas refused to come to grips with the Sirens, but steered his   15
course well away from that dangerous shore. But, you tell me, there is no
actual danger. Yes, but I see plenty of men dying without falling foul of danger. I am like the fox in Horace,

> ... terrified
> Because those footprints mostly point to you   20
> And none point back.

Such being the aspect of things, I should have no hesitation in fleeing,
not merely to Orléans but west to Cadiz, by the Pillars of Hercules, or north
to the remotest of the remote Orkney islands; not because I am timorous
and effeminate, but to avoid a genuine reason for fear; not to shun death,   25
for to die are we all born, but to avoid dying by my own fault. Inasmuch
as Christ bade his apostles escape the swords of persecutors by moving
occasionally from town to town, shall I not evade an encounter with a foe
so deadly when I am able to do so with ease? Even so, it is partly my Muses
who are urging me to go back, for they feel the cold acutely here, in the com-   30
pany of Accorso, Bartolo, and Baldo, and partly this keen and cruel frost,
which is only too well adapted to killing off completely all vestiges of the
disease. But still I have some reservations on account of those traces of the
fierce conflagration, smoke and smell, ash and even perhaps sparks 'neath
treacherous cinders hid.'   35
I know, my kind Fausto, that I am wasting your time in begging you

* * * * *

134:15 Aeneas] Cf Virgil *Aeneid* 5.864f.

18 Horace] *Epistles* 1.1.74–5

30–1 in the company of] The university of Orléans owed its great reputation to
its faculty of law, hence Erasmus' suggestion that his Muses might find a rather
chilling atmosphere dominated by such legal authorities as the three mentioned. Francesco Accorso (1182–1260) was a Florentine jurist, author of *Glossa
ordinaria,* an attempt to arrange methodically the commentaries on the *Corpus
juris civilis.* Bartolo da Sassoferrato (1313–56) was one of the most distinguished
jurists of the fourteenth century. Baldo degli Ubaldi (1327–1400) was a pupil
of Bartolo and author of commentaries.

34–5 'neath ... hid'] Horace *Odes* 2.1.8

to do something which you yourself continually do of your own accord.
Still, I shall make a request: would you write a complimentary piece to
embellish with your own testimonial those adages to which I have recently
given premature birth, in order to get them sold more quickly? If you do   40
this, you will make a gift, not so much to the work itself as to our friendship,
for I am not such a self-flatterer as not to perceive its poor quality. But the
unsatisfactory goods one is inclined to push need puffing all the more for
their lack of merit; and I shall owe you not a little more on that account if
you adapt your verdict of approval not to your judgment but entirely to our   45
mutual good will. Not to say, meanwhile, that you have left yourself no
opportunity of refusing to praise my trifles, to which once before, in the
panegyric letter you prefixed to them, you attributed every virtue under the
sun. Consequently you have to choose between continuing to compliment
me on them, or being censured for inconsistency. Lastly, I will take great   50
pains to see that the same work, which was merely roughed out at the first
attempt, will be not simply filed into smoothness but put back on the anvil
and entirely reforged; and it will finally come out in such a handsome dress
that you will have no regrets in commending it, nor will it in turn be
ashamed of your tribute, as being undeserved. In this last respect, indeed,   55
I intend to employ you not merely as a critic but also as an architect.
Farewell.

Orléans, the morrow of St Elizabeth's day [1499]

135 / To Jacob Batt   Orléans [November 1500]

ERASMUS TO HIS FRIEND JACOB
I ask you for your old kindness' sake not to take it amiss that I am staying
here, contrary to my former decision. I did not change my plan without
good reason, for in the first place I had no journey-money save what I could
have borrowed, and secondly I had only just recovered from an illness. At   5
the same time, I was a little alarmed at the prospect of a winter journey,
especially this year, when I have been a frequent and unlucky traveller. And
the plague has now practically died out, I am told. Another consideration
was the gossip that might spread among ill-natured persons if I went back
so often to see you. Lastly, the other Jacob, who resembles you in disposi-   10
tion as well as name, is treating me so lovingly, that this fact in itself might

* * * * *

135:3 former decision] Cf Ep 130:126ff.
10 Jacob] Voogd (cf Ep 131:11n).

suffice to fetter me to the place, even were there nothing else. Besides, the abbot is so pressing in his invitations that he almost makes me terrified to come and, however fond of me he may be, I still do not know how he will take this terror of mine. Then too, since his spirits are not as heavy as lead (I will not say light), he will like me better in absence if he likes me at all, while if he is going to act like his brother it behooves me to keep the greatest possible distance between us. I am ashamed to complain to you, dear Batt, about this brother's frivolousness, or rather perhaps ill-will. How unlucky my poor literary efforts were, to find an anti-Maecenas like him, one who not only fails to encourage but even passionately resents them. As you know, Jan Standonck returned the other day from Louvain accompanied by a master of humble condition, a native of Mechelen; to whom that serious-minded bishop allotted the task of scenting and ferreting his way through all the secret places of my life in Paris, and of sending him a written report on what he discovered, with the promise, to boot, of a rich reward for the informer. In his brazen folly he added that he was surprised at my impudence in remaining in Paris without his permission. If he was utterly insane to entertain any such idea, was it not greater lunacy still to share it with a needy clerk? I suppose the man's rage is aroused partly because he imagines himself to be slighted, but partly also – mostly, indeed – because he fancies I am complaining about him either to his brother or to others, who perchance think poorly of him on my account. But this kind of behaviour is so far from discouraging me that I am all the more eager, while I am in Paris, to bring off some splendid feat that may burst his spleen with envy.

　　These, then, are the reasons that prevented me from coming to you; otherwise I should have longed to do so. I hope you will endorse my decision. Now, I have sent my former servant-pupil Louis to you, with the intention that he should enter the service of Josse, who has, I suppose,

* * * * *

13 abbot] Antoon van Bergen (cf Ep 143 introduction).

17 brother] Hendrik van Bergen, bishop of Cambrai (cf Ep 49 introduction). Erasmus felt that the bishop had been cooling toward him for some time (cf Ep 128:18). Erasmus' first patron, he may well have resented his growing independence.

22 Standonck] Cf Ep 73:11n.

39 Louis] Cf Ep 167 introduction.

40 Josse] Cf Ep 129:57n.

already got back; if not, please recommend the youth to someone else for the time being, or in the last resort take him into your own charge if you possibly can, which is what he himself would prefer. He is dependable enough to be entrusted with anything, a great virtue this in a boy; and he writes a neat and speedy hand in French, and also in Latin. He is fairly well 45 versed in grammar, willing to work hard, very obedient, and without a vicious temperament. He might be useful as a copyist of books, even to you. And so, if you can take care of him, you will oblige me greatly and also help a boy who now has nobody to help him; if you have no place for him, see if the abbot has any room. If, however, you keep the boy with you, be sure 50 to hand over my little sum of money as soon as possible to the Saint-Omer courier, with instructions to deliver it to me; also the Augustine on parchment, together with anything else you think I may find useful.

For some time past I have been reconciled to Augustin by force of circumstances. He admits his various liabilities, but claims he has no means 55 of paying me; and I believe him, more or less. I am already a few *écus* in debt to my other Jacob; so please send me not only all the money standing to my credit in your possession but anything with which you are able to furnish your friend by way of a loan. 'Who is to repay me?,' you will ask. Why, my lady, who will never be so unfeeling as to let Christmas slip by. 60 It is unavoidable, dear Batt, if you wish me to be rescued; nor are these idle words I write. However, if you see no prospect of making provision for this boy, do not allow him to linger with you but send him back immediately, carrying a letter from you and the money and the book and anything else you have, for you could not send a letter or a package by a more reliable 65 messenger. The extreme care you take when you write is something I approve of, but rest assured that in his case you can gossip as freely as you like. Please pay him at my expense a special allowance of ten or twelve *douzains* as journey-money; and, whether he stays with you or is sent back, give him that black coat of mine which you have in your possession, if it 70 has not already been given away, so that he may have some reward for his services to me. As you say in your letter, Mountjoy is very parsimonious

* * * * *

52 Augustine] The MS had been in the parcel expected from England in the spring (cf Ep 123:24).

56 a few *écus*] See the Glossary and Appendix A on gold coins.

68–9 ten or twelve *douzains*] Worth 10s (120d) to 12s (144d) *tournois*. See the Glossary and Appendix B on silver coins.

70 black coat] This was also in the parcel from England (cf Ep 123:20).

72 Mountjoy] The name is replaced by 'N' (X) in all editions after the first. (Cf the similar omission of Mountjoy's name in Ep 128:17n.)

about giving: this I put down to that dolt Galba. It was through his folly, too, that my money was lost in England. But I shall keep quiet about this for the present; some day I shall have a chance to even the score with him. 75 All the same I shall keep to my chosen programme of writing. I regret sending the *Adagia* to your country for sale, since it fetches a higher price here, and sells in greater quanties too. My friend Jacob here, who is quite a second Batt, asks to be remembered to you, in the most affectionate way possible. Believe me, he deserves your wholehearted friendship; and since 80 he loves you so warmly, you ought to take care not to be outdone in displaying your affection. Farewell, dear Batt.

PS: I have written this rather carelessly, not wishing to upset my health, which is still delicate.

Orléans [1499]   85

136 / To Augustin Vincent   Orléans, 9 December [1500]

Erasmus' quarrel with Augustin, described in Ep 133, had now been made up. One of the 'circumstances' that led to the reconciliation (cf Ep 135: 54) was undoubtedly Erasmus' need for a place to stay when he returned to Paris, and this letter was designed to make sure of the arrangement. The reconciliation, however, was based on expediency rather than trust (cf Ep 138: 15ff).

ERASMUS TO HIS FRIEND AUGUSTIN

All you tell me about Fausto and Gaguin and Emilio is bright and cheerful, though none of it is new – yet, again, it is just as welcome as if it were. Am I not bound to set a high value on the good will of such men as these and their authoritative tributes to my quality? It is the same with your own 5 devotion to my reputation. I gladly acknowledge that it is of long standing, yet welcome it as much as if it were new, though the exaggeration Fausto perpetrates, when he insists that I alone preside over literature's holy place, gives me no especial pleasure, both because unrestrained praise is unsuitable to my modesty and my limited talents and because, generally speak- 10 ing, images of this sort are insincere, and tend to make one very unpopular.

* * * * *

73 Galba] Cf Ep 123:21n.

136:2 Fausto] Andrelini (cf Ep 84 introduction).

2: Gaguin] Robert Gaguin (cf Ep 43 introduction).

2: Emilio] Paolo Emilio of Verona (c 1460–1529) was one of the Italian humanists who promoted the revival of classical studies in France. He came to Paris in 1483 and remained there the rest of his life, during the last twenty years occupied in writing a history of France under Royal patronage.

Finally, too, they verge upon irony, just as those expressions in your letter, however flattering: 'My revered teacher, as your devoted pupil I consecrate myself to you; command me as you please; I have nothing of my own but consider all I have as yours' still fails to attract me greatly. All language of this sort should, in my opinion, be excluded as completely as possible from true feelings of good will; for when love is sincere, as it is, I believe, between us, what purpose is served by using such phrases? And when it is not sincere, those very phrases are apt to be seized upon as grounds for suspecting that ill-will exists. So you will greatly oblige me if you completely eliminate such attractive exaggerations from your correspondence, and leave straightforward affection to talk its own language, remembering that you are addressing a very close and good friend, not a despotic ruler. I am surprised and distressed to hear that, even now, Fate is giving a niggardly response to your desires and even to your deserts; but I am glad that she is beginning to relent. Indeed, unless I am quite wrong, that dreadful storm is going to be followed by another spell of fair weather. You have only to be stout-hearted as ever, dear Augustin,

And upon thy way
More boldly press, by fortune circumscribed.

Your letter leads me to suspect that Paolo Emilio is about to come back to us; yet I should much prefer him to stay there, since I cannot see any reason for sticking in this place myself. Please, however, be sure to send me a full account of your circumstances and tell me whether your small competency can bear the slight burden of our living together, since you desire me not to doubt your readiness, nor can I after it has been tried and tested by so many proofs and perils. Accordingly, please tell me quite frankly, that is, with the freedom our close friendship demands, if there is any reason why a visit from me appears likely to be untimely or inconvenient, and my affection for you will not be diminished by one jot. So may all the gods love me, my object is not so much to improve my own fortune, though this is part of my intention (and why should I deny it?) as to complete your education, which, your letter tells me, I was responsible for spoiling. And if you still keep your attitude, or rather if your are in a situation that may allow each of us to find his own advantage to be associated with the other's, then bid me come; while even if it is not so, it is still very important for me to know this, so that I may quickly think of another plan to serve my interests; even though I prefer the former alternative. There is nobody with whom I should prefer to complete my own studies than with you to

* * * * *

29–30 and ... circumscribed] Virgil *Aeneid* 6.95–6

whom I gave a first introduction to good literature and with whom I   50
returned to those studies I had already virtually set aside, and in close
association with whom I spent so many years. But if one cannot do what
one likes, one must like what one is able to do.

I have some faint prospect of a visit to Italy, and my heart hankers after
it not a little, but I can decide on my own plans as soon as your letter reaches   55
me. To Nikolaus Bensrott, who, you tell me, greets me warmly, I in turn
send my warm greetings. I am thrashing ahead with my *Copia*, but I think
the Muses are unpropitious. What fine work indeed can I do, with not one
good book at hand to consult? Also, once I get deep into the work I find it
more extensive than it appeared to be at the outset. All the same, I labour   60
on; what else can I do? In fact, of course, my object is to avoid idleness, the
most disgraceful condition of all. Look after yourself, dear Augustin, and
preserve your affection for me.

At Orléans, the morrow of the Feast of the Conception [1499]

137 / To Antonius of Luxembourg   Orléans, 11 December [1500]

Antonius of Luxembourg was steward of the abbey of St Bertin at Saint-Omer,
and chaplain to the abbot (cf Allen Ep 143: 236). Later he was made a canon
of Notre Dame at Saint-Omer (cf Allen Ep 273: 31). He remained a friend of
Erasmus for many years, and as he had great influence with the abbot, Antoon
van Bergen, Erasmus frequently addressed requests to his patron through him
(cf Allen Epp 147, 148, 150, 161).

ERASMUS TO HIS FRIEND ANTONIUS OF LUXEMBOURG
I was on the point of writing to that cultivated gentleman, the lord abbot;
but since I had heard very recently, in a letter from my friend Batt, that he
was not yet back from Brabant, I thought I should put off writing until I had
news of his return. I have written to you instead, not because I had anything   5
new to relate, but in order to show by means of friendly correspondence
that my affection for you was unchanging and enduring. For you, my
delightful and amiable friend, are as much, or at least very nearly as much,
beloved by me as is my Batt himself, not only as a result of your myriad
kindnesses to me and of your charming nature, but also because of a kind   10

* * * * *

52–3 if one cannot ... to do] *Adagia* I viii 43
54 Italy] Cf Ep 139:37ff.
56 Bensrott] Cf Ep 158 introduction.
137:4 Brabant] Cf Ep 129:58n.

of innate good will which makes it impossible for me to forget you, even
if I would.

I am going back to Paris, since I hear the plague has quite died out.
While I was staying here, a great deal of attention was paid to me by the
abbot's brother Dismas; and I in turn derived much pleasure from his com- 15
pany. I solemnly declare that I have never in my life met a more gifted,
agreeable or modest youth; and, my dear Antonius, I do not say this to curry
favour. It is exactly what I have found by experience. It befell that, in the
words of the Book of Wisdom, he 'had a good spirit,' and besides he is, as
the Greeks say, εὐφυής – of a high, that is, and fortunate birth. His talents 20
are of the keenest, his disposition the truest, his manners most agreeable,
and his modesty extremely engaging. He has an admiration for literature,
and with it he delights to occupy his time, always to his intellectual gain.
As this boy seems to have been made by nature for the highest pursuits,
he deserves the very best tuition we can find for him, in order to prevent 25
his gifts, which are of no common sort, from being reduced to the common
level of dreariness. Yet he is living, uncared-for, in a kind of 'tutelage,' for
so it is called: far too close a tutelage indeed, for it means most unappetizing
food and dirty surroundings, among a group of lazy ruffians who hate
books and educated speech more than anything else, who prowl the streets 30
at night and drink during the daytime, and from whom he can learn nothing
but disgraceful behaviour. And you are well aware how easily boys of his
age are lured into bad habits, for they catch the infection by contagion from
their associates, and 'he that toucheth pitch shall be defiled therewith.'

There is here one Master Jacob Voogd, a man of completely upright 35
character and distinguished learning, who is full of zeal for study and is a
doctor of canon law besides. He is bringing up several well-born youths
under his supervision in his own house, and is doing so in no tutor-like
fashion, but in great refinement. I stayed with him myself for three months.
Now, he is as fond of Dismas as any father is of his son, and receives filial 40
love from him also. So, if the lord abbot would have this youth's interests
well served, as I am sure he would, he ought to remove him speedily from

* * * * *

15 Dismas] A half-brother of Antoon and Hendrik van Bergen, one of the
thirty-six bastards of Jan van Bergen (cf Ep 42:21n).
19 Wisdom] Wisdom 8:19
33–4 they catch ... associates] Cf Seneca *Epistles* 7.7.
34 'he that ... therewith'] *Eccles* 13:1
35 Voogd] By recommending him as tutor for Dismas, Erasmus hoped to gain
favour with the abbot and the bishop and at the same time secure a noble pupil
for his friend.

his present tutelage, where he exists miserably and at great cost and, worst
of all, in the company of men who may corrupt but cannot teach him, and
to place him in the care of the aforesaid Jacob, who, let me assure you, is   45
one to whose praises no tribute of mine could do proper justice. He for his
part will be delighted to have one to whom he can freely impart his teaching, and whom he can completely fill with zeal for good studies; while Dismas will have a man with whom he can live exactly as with a father, and
in whose house he will hear no dishonourable or ignorant word.   50
     Perhaps you will be surprised at the earnestness with which I urge
this. Certainly it has nothing at all to do with me, for I have no axe to grind.
But since I had become aware of the squalor of the tutelage, and the dangerous companions and general corruption surrounding the boy, and had an
affection for his excellent disposition, and also because I owed everything   55
to the lord abbot's great kindness to me, I decided that I could not, without
doing a very great wrong, omit giving a warning by a letter of something
I realized to be vital to Dismas' well-being and was very well aware of. For
I am quite sure that if the lord abbot had the least inkling of how things
actually stand, he would not tolerate his staying in that household for half   60
an hour longer. And you need not worry that, if he lives with a man of my
own nation, he will learn little French; Dismas' knowledge of French is
good, and he can already speak it fluently. He will never be in want of
people to give him practice in listening to French; but he will also learn letters, and virtue too. If you can persuade the abbot (and you, Antonius, can   65
surely do so), you will bind the youth to you by an eternal debt of gratitude.
And I feel certain that all his well-wishers, among whom the lord abbot
holds first place, will for the future be extremely grateful to me for giving
timely warning. So do not rest until this is accomplished.
     Please commend me very warmly, as best you can, to Father Antoon,   70
your patron – and hence mine, for your sake – and give him my apologies
for not sending him any message by this courier; I shall write to him from
Paris when I hear he has got back. Farewell, my dearest Antonius, and continue in your affection for me.
     Please give my greetings to that very kind gentleman, the head of the   75
hall, and those others who wish me well.
     Orléans, 11 December [1500]
     PS: Do not be surprised, dear Antonius, at my having said at the begin-
ning of this letter that I was not writing to the abbot, though in fact I have

* * * * *

52 axe to grind] literally 'here I neither sow nor reap'; *Adagia* I vi 82
75–6 head of the hall] 'praefectum Aulae'

written. For when the other courier had eluded me and this youth unexpec-   80
tedly turned up from Batt, I changed my mind, particularly since Batt urged
me to. It was from Batt's letter that I learned how kind a reception that
gentleman had accorded my own letter, something I hardly dared hope for,
knowing as I do how little there is in my writings to make them deserve
to be read by prominent men.   85

Please make every effort to help me in what I have suggested to you
concerning Dismas. It is absolutely vital to his well-being, and I am afraid
that if it is not done we shall all, and the boy especially, regret our failure
to act. You see, the story I told was no vague report but something I had
seen with my own eyes. I have no object in view except the boy's welfare,   90
and he is at an age when one can easily be influenced in the direction either
of high distinction or of complete moral ruin, so that in my opinion we must
be watchful and act speedily. Farewell.

138 / To Jacob Batt   Orléans, 11 December [1500]

ERASMUS TO HIS FRIEND BATT

My dearest Batt, it seems an age since I had any word from you. One single
thing gives me an acute dislike of that castle of yours: the extreme rarity
of messengers, whether from there to here or vice versa. If you were staying
at Louvain, or in Zeeland, we could assuage the pain of missing each other   5
by exchanging frequent letters. I sent you my former servant-pupil Louis,
bearing a letter from me; his failure to return appears to indicate that he
has either remained with you or gone off in another direction. However,
as I am unwilling to set out on a winter journey myself, partly with a view
to sparing my health, partly to avoid a further interruption in the task of   10
compilation which wholly engrosses me at present, and also since I am
under greater pressure than I had expected, I have specially engaged, for
a fee, the courier who bears this.

Now I shall briefly outline my intentions. Augustin has gone back to
Paris. Whether he is friendly or hostile I am not quite sure, even yet; one   15
cannot safely trust either his looks or his words. But I do not altogether
despair, in this respect, preferring to appear to think too well of him rather

* * * * *

80 youth] Louis, with an answer to Ep 135, to which Erasmus replied with Ep
139
82 Batt's letter] Probably the one mentioned in Ep 130:114f
138:6 Louis] Erasmus had urged Batt to find a place for Louis at Tournehem
or Saint-Omer (cf Ep 135). He remained with Batt for a year (cf Ep 167 introduction).

than to harbour petty suspicions. For myself too, returning to Paris is not only the wisest but even a necessary course, both in order to continue the studies in Greek which I have begun there and to finish the works I have in hand. There are other reasons too, reasons I have decided not to put down in a letter, and I cannot either remain idle here or go away unless you yourself should happen to advise me to go back of my own accord, after those dreadful scenes of anger, indeed those bitter quarrels, and cast myself on Augustin's mercy, confessing myself beaten, I suppose, and unable to bear his usual playing fast and loose with me. But even if I were so pusillanimous as to be able to endure such humiliation, the worst possible treatment, in other words, still I am not sure whether he himself would accept my humble petition. Consequently, it would be better to die than to undergo such an ordeal as this. Of course I shall take whatever he offers. From whom after all should I rather accept favours than from him for whom I have done so much to earn them, and who owes everything he is to my favour? Yet the last thing I ought to do, in my opinion, is to slip into the galling obligation to choose between submissively begging for his help and doing without it, to my great shame, as well as inconvenience.

So, although I did it with a certain distaste, I summoned up my resolution and settled down here once more, to wait until you should send me a little money that might make it possible for me, once I go back to Paris, either to benefit from any largesse that Augustin should bestow on me honourably and freely, or to disdain it and pay him out for it, if he should somehow show the false and feigned colour of his kindness. Now, even if the business should turn out exactly according to my wishes, and I do not so much hope for this as refuse to despair of it, still I must scrape together from each and every source a small sum of money to clothe myself and to buy the complete works of Jerome, on whom I am preparing a commentary, and a Plato, and to get together some Greek books, and also to pay for the services of a Greek tutor. Although I think you are quite aware how much all these things mean to my reputation, indeed my survival, yet I ask you to trust me when I state them as facts, out of personal experience. My mind

* * * * *

45 Jerome] This is the first mention of the work on Jerome to which Erasmus was devoted at this time (cf Epp 139, 141, 149) and which was to occupy so much of his time during his years in Cambridge (cf Epp 264, 270). It culminated in his great edition of Jerome's correspondence (Basel, Froben, 1516). Cf Ep 396 introduction.

46 Greek] the expense of acquiring Greek books and a Greek tutor aggravated Erasmus' desperate need for money at this time (cf Epp 128 introduction, and 149).

is burning with indescribable eagerness to bring all my small literary works   50
to their conclusion, and at the same moment to acquire a certain limited
competence in the use of Greek, and thereby go on to devote myself entirely
to sacred literature, the discussion of which has long been an ardently
sought goal in my mind. Heaven be thanked, I am well enough, and hope
to continue so, and thus I must this year stretch all my sinews to ensure not   55
only that the present objects of my labours see the light but that by editing
works of divinity I am able to bid my multitudes of hostile critics go hang,
as they deserve. For a long time past, whenever I promised great achievements I have been held back, either by my own listlessness or by some
unlucky mischance or by the state of my health. Now, at last, I have to   60
awaken my heart and stiffen the sinews, so that I can eventually boast, with
my dear Horace, 'Above envy I am,' and 'No more by envious tooth am I
assailed'; or, to put it another way, so that I can suppress the ill-will of malicious individuals by the bright light of goodness; and this, with Heaven's
blessing, I trust will come about, if I can only be spared for three years.   65

But virtually my entire future rests in your hands, so it is for you to
help me, by matching your efforts to mine, as you must for a variety of
reasons: firstly, because it was from you that the origins of my good fortune
arose; secondly, because we have for long been linked by a bond of friendship so close that it is impossible any closer could exist between two human   70
beings; thirdly, because you are aware that the survival of your own reputation is linked to the immortality of my books, so that in so far as my talent
will enable me to spare my works from perishing, the memory of your kindness likewise shall not perish. So rouse yourself, my dearest Batt. Stir up
that heart of yours, devoted as it is to friendship and the Graces, and strain   75
every nerve of good will; so that if ever you have had thoughts of giving
friendly succour to your Erasmus, as you always have, you now bestow all
your efforts on the matter.

But there: I have been seriously slighting our friendship for some time
by making such elaborate requests to you, when simply to remind you   80
would have been more than enough. I shall not, therefore, pray you to hold
me in affection, for this you do with the greatest possible warmth; or to promote my well-being, for this you consider before your own; or to grant me
your loyalty and devotion in attending to my affairs, for in these respects
you outdo even me; but the one thing it is really important for me to per-   85
suade you to do is a very little thing: that you should not suppose that the

* * * * *

58 promised] reading 'minantem'
62 Horace] *Odes* 2.20.4 and 4.3.16, cf *Adagia* III i 1 and III i 22.

written accounts of my affairs which I send to you are but verbal embroidery
or artistic fictions, designed for the furtherance of my own interests. And
if in moments of leisure I have ever indulged in jesting or improvisation,
there is a time and place for such things, dear Batt; but my present situation   90
affords me no opportunity whatsoever for the exercise of wit, and I have
no reason for telling anything contrary to the truth. So may Heaven vouchsafe that we may both grow old in happiness and mutual love, and that
even among posterity the memory of our unalloyed affection may endure
through long ages. I have not set down in this letter a single jot that dis-   95
agrees with the feelings of my heart. What secret indeed is there, that I could
not safely, or should not freely, share with you, who are my very soul? So
I beseech you, dear Batt, not to suppose that any of the things I say in my
letter are meant to deceive, whereas in fact they are said even more seriously
than either of us might desire – that I may not completely recall that tag in   100
Horace, and, when my leg is really broken, be laughed at by everyone and
helped by none. If I can establish this one point, I know you will look after
the rest.

Will you please deliver to a reliable messenger, or to Louis, anything
my lady has sent, together with my small sum from England? Or, in the last   105
resort, if you cannot find a more dependable courier, I think it would be
all right to give it to the bearer of this; he has a wife and children in Orléans,
and carries letters belonging to a great many people. But if nothing has
arrived from her, or you do not fancy the messenger, even so be sure to give
the bearer the bits and pieces of money from England, so that I can use them   110
to hie me back to Paris; I have decided to do this after the Christmas
holidays, and am completely on the rocks at present.

'And what, then,' you will ask me, 'is your friend Jacob going to do?'
Everything you yourself regularly do, dear Batt, and with the very looks and
attitudes you practise too. His love is of the warmest, in admiration he is   115
supreme, while his praise is ceaseless and unrestrained. What little money
he acquires, he shares so promptly and generously that one may say his
readiness to do a kindness exceeds that of all the rest of mankind to receive
one. I will not seek to exaggerate: he is yourself, or, at any rate, a second
Batt, so precisely does he reproduce your benevolence and charitable spirit   120
and, in short, that heart of spotless integrity which is your own. But there
were a great many things to draw me back to Paris, and my sense of decency
recoiled at burdening the slender means of a friend so generous and hon-

* * * * *

101 Horace] *Epistles* 1.17.58f
112 am completely on the rocks] Literally, 'no rock can be barer than I.'

ourable as he is, for his substantial fortune lies rather in the future than in
the present. What he does possess is barely sufficient for maintaining him-   125
self, but might be too limited to maintain me: though one fact I should like
to see marked with a pearl of dazzling whiteness is that I have found here
a friend who is not simply most agreeable, as so many are, but utterly
dependable, as are very few others, perhaps none at all. Believe me, he is
already as warmly attached to you as he is to me. Your name is continually   130
upon his lips, and whenever I sing your praises he is all agog to see you
and embrace you. You ought to return his affection, as one Jacob to another,
one generous friend to another, one scholar to another, and one almost
excessive admirer of myself to another. If you prove to have wasted your
time, upon my head be it.   135

Send me, at the same time, what there is in my bundle on how to write
letters, for this is the work I am endeavouring to finish off; also the parchment manuscript of Augustine, and a copy of my prayer to the Virgin
Mother, for Augustin is away with my own. And tell me what I may expect
from my lady, and how the provost's affections stand towards me, and how   140
the abbot, after his return from his unfriendly brother, regards me and
whether my *Adagia* is securing any favourable reception, and what news
there is from England. As Cicero puts it, I am waiting to hear 'everything
about everything.'

I have sent a letter also to Antonius by the bearer of this, at the   145
instance, as a matter of fact, of the abbot's brother Dismas, for the following
reason. Young Dismas himself has such an excellent disposition that I cannot remember ever before encountering anyone to equal him for talents or
for modesty; his respect for scholarship is unsurpassed, and he appears in
every way to merit consideration as too good for a run-of-the-mill educa-   150

* * * * *

136–7 on how to write letters] Probably some materials to be used in revising
the *De conscribendis epistolis* (cf Epp 71 introduction, 130:111 and line 187 below)
which were in the parcel from England, along with the Augustine and other
books and papers (cf Epp 123:22ff, 135:52).
138 prayer] Cf Ep 93:113n.
140 provost] Nicholas of Burgundy (cf Ep 144 introduction), to whom he had
sent a copy of the *Adagia* in September (cf Ep 129:55ff).
141 abbot] The abbot had just returned from a stay at court where he would
have met his brother, the bishop of Cambrai (cf Ep 129:58n). For the bishop's
hostility, see Ep 135:17n.
143 Cicero] *Epistolae ad familiares* 12.20 and 15.17
145 Antonius] Antonius of Luxembourg. The following paragraph repeats the
recommendations for the education of Dismas in Ep 137:14ff.

tion. But he is living under conditions of neglect, in a kind of so-called tutelage, on a squalid diet of unclean food, among men who are rather buffoons
than scholars; who fancy swordplay in preference to study, and think it a
finer thing to spend their evenings in drunken revels in the streets than at
their books; and you know how easily boys of his age can be corrupted by   155
bad company. The youth himself feels an increasing attraction to learning,
partly because of his good disposition and partly as a result of association
with me; and he is passionately anxious to leave that pigsty of idle young
men and join my friend Jacob, for there is a remarkable bond of affection
between them. Jacob is eager to have someone out of the ordinary, who is   160
wholeheartedly eager to pursue the higher studies, and to whom he can
impart his own learning, while Dismas longs to find one in whose house
he can live in a decent manner while he devotes himself entirely to letters.
So will you please, as occasion may dictate, afford your assistance to the
abbot in detaching Dismas from that household and attaching him to my   165
friend Jacob Voogd; thus, you will bring happiness to the youth and
pleasure to our Jacob, while I have no doubt that the abbot will be profoundly grateful to all of us for this action. Please therefore prompt
Antonius, to whom I have written, to bring it to the abbot's attention. I have
changed my mind, and have not sent any letter to the abbot himself, nor   170
do I plan to do so until I hear from you. Please go yourself to Saint-
Omer for a further account of the whole affair.

I am sending you a letter written to me by our friend Willem, in order,
of course, to amuse you, since it is extremely witty and rhetorical. Notice,
if you please, his roundabout turns of phrase, his changes of direction this   175
way and that, all directed to the final conclusion, reached as if absentmindedly, that I should send him some copies of my *Adagia*, at my own risk,
that is. He will of course, he says, be conscientious in sending me the proceeds later. Not devoid of business sense, is he? He knows how to make a
profitable deal for himself, at another's risk and expense. My friend Jacob   180
has sent him the Greek grammar as a present; for I am desperately anxious
that he should get a taste of this kind of study. Your role will be to spur him
into activity by a brisk correspondence. He is somewhat sluggish by nature;
but the kind of life he has led, with no fellow students, none to emulate or

* * * * *

154 to spend ... in the streets] perhaps 'grassari' for 'grassationibus'
173 Willem] Hermans. Erasmus' suspicion had been aroused by fear that Hermans was replacing him in Batt's affection and Anna van Borssele's favour.
(cf Epp 129:22ff, 130:47ff). Despite his suspicion, however, Erasmus sent some
copies of the *Adagia* to Hermans (cf Ep 139:196).

applaud or encourage him, without glory or rewards, would surely turn the   185
keenest enthusiasm into profound apathy.

At present I am fully occupied with my work on rules for letter writing;
I shall, if you agree, dedicate it to your Prince Adolph. Likewise, I shall try
to finish off my *Copia*. The messenger who delivered this letter seemed to
me fairly reliable; so you would be justified in entrusting to him whatever   190
you like. Even if you have already sent Louis back to me, kindly send a note
to say just what you have given him. Please be sure to convey my greetings
to your most amiable Pierre and his excellent wife. Will you please also give
my remembrances to your pupil Adolph? Jacob Voogd, your second self,
sends warm greetings to his second self, that is, to you, and wishes to be   195
cordially remembered to you. He is one whom you can regard, believe me,
with no courtly love but a love of your own Battic sort.

Farewell, my very dear and delightful Batt.

Orléans, at dawn on 11 December [1499]

139 / To Jacob Batt   Orléans [c 12 December] 1500

This is an answer to a letter brought by Louis and received by Erasmus after
he had finished Epp 137 and 138 (cf Ep 137: 82n). Batt's letter so annoyed Erasmus that Jacob Voogd had to persuade him to send a reply back with Louis
(cf Allen Ep 146: 23ff).

TO BATT

I am very much at a loss to know what could have made you suspect me
of playing the conjuror with words in my letters to you; that is, of being
hypocritical and affected in style, instead of straightforward and honest.
Dear Batt, I wish you would once for all realize that I detest nothing so much   5
as hypocrisy, and that it is not my way either to invent falsehoods when
I write to my friends or to take any pleasure in other men's falsehoods.
When I wrote from England I asked you to rescue me, in fact, with a fictitious letter. This trickery was designed to catch the Englishman, not you,
for you were not taken in. But as for the letter I sent afterwards   10
about my intentions, I swear it was sincerely written. In the same way,

* * * * *

188 Adolph] He had already promised the dedication of the *De conscribendis*
epistolis to Adolph in May 1499 (cf Ep 95:37ff). For the various dedications of
this work, see Ep 71 introduction.
193 Pierre] Cf Ep 129:9n.
139:9 letter] Cf Ep 124:63n.

I myself believed that your letter which, as you afterwards confessed to me on my return, was your 'fictitious reply to a fictitious epistle' had been written sincerely. Now, however, it is quite clear that the letter I wrote from Orléans on the subject of my dire financial straits appears to have been com- 15 posed with the same degree of artificiality; for if it were not so, you would not have sent Louis, who bears this, back to me laden with a mere three nobles. I omit advisedly to mention here both how different was the treat- ment I expected of you and in what measure you have increased my happi- ness. If I seem to you, when I write like this, to be joking, I cannot see why 20 I should ever write to you.

But an end to all this. Since I have no doubt, dear Batt, that everything you do is done from the kindest of motives, I ask you to extend your old familiar self in the effort to secure my happiness; and certainly you will be entirely successful, if only you will bring to bear the spirit that nature gave 25 you. Send Louis straight away to my lady and, if it is convenient, go there yourself with a view to supporting my letter by your eloquence. Encourage Adolph to appeal to his mother's heart by the pious claims of a first request, but take care that his wish be not for a mere trifle, since it is his assistance too that will enable us to be successful in appealing for quite a large benefac- 30 tion. If you really care sincerely for my well-being, then you must act as fol- lows: speak to her in conciliatory terms, apologizing for my diffidence as though it had been impossible for me, because of my disposition, to confess my poverty to her directly. And you must send her a letter to explain that I am now reduced to the direst straits, since my escape to Orléans cost me 35 a great deal, for I had to leave those from whom I had been receiving some- thing by way of subsidy. Further, that there is no better place to take a doc- torate than Italy, while the journey to Italy, for a man in poor health, is impossible without a large amount of money; especially since I am posi- tively unable to live in miserable surroundings now that I have a literary 40 reputation, such as it is. Please explain to her how much greater is the glory she can acquire from me, by my literary works, than from the other theologians in her patronage. They merely deliver humdrum sermons; I am writing books that may last for ever. Their uneducated nonsense finds an audience in perhaps a couple of churches; my books will be read all over 45

* * * * *

17–18 a mere three nobles] English gold coin: either the Henricus, Angel, or Ryal nobles. If the first, as seems most likely, then a sum worth £1 7s od sterling, or about £11 5s od *tournois*. See the Glossary and Appendix A on gold coinage.

26 my lady] Anna van Borssele was apparently absent from Tournehem, pos- sibly at Veere. Adolph, however, was still with Batt.

38 Italy] Cf Ep 75:15n.

the world, in the Latin west and in the Greek east and by every nation. Say that there is everywhere a huge supply of such uneducated divines as these, while such a one as I am is scarcely to be found in many generations – unless you are so excessively nice in your scruples that your conscience forbids you to employ a few small fibs in the interest of a friend! In addition, explain 50 to her that she will not be any the poorer if she spends a few gold pieces on subsidizing the restoration of Jerome's now corrupt text, or the revival of a genuine science of theology, when such a proportion of her wealth is miserably wasted as it is.

When you have elaborated all this, and put in a good deal about my 55 character, and my promise, and my feelings of affection for her, and my modest reserve, then you can add that I have written to say I must have at least two hundred francs as an advance on next year's salary. This is anything but a fiction, dear Batt, for it seems to me hazardous to set out for Italy with only a hundred, and not all of them full weight either, unless I am pre- 60 pared once more to make myself over to someone as his servant, and I should rather die than do that. Again, it can matter but little to her whether she gives it now or in a year's time, while to me it makes an enormous difference. Urge her also to be sure to think of my claims to a benefice, so that when I come back from Italy I may have a literary retreat. And do not be 65 content to urge it; explain to her the most convenient method you can think of, to ensure that she gives me the first choice among a large number of livings; a satisfactory living, even if not the best, which I can exchange for a richer one as opportunity offers. Of course I know there are many who aspire to benefices, but you can say that I am the person who by himself 70 alone, if you compare him with all the rest, etc. You know how enthusiastically you used to fib about me! Please see that a letter to the same effect is sent by your pupil Adolph, with melting words of entreaty – dictated, of course, by you. Please also make sure that the promise of a hundred francs is confirmed without delay, and if possible with your Adolph's knowledge 75 so that if anything should happen to snatch away his mother (*absit omen*), I may get it from the son. Finally, add that I have written you to complain, as Jerome more than once does in his letters, that my studies are impairing

* * * * *

51 a few gold pieces] Probably *écus, à la couronne or au soleil*. See the Glossary and Appendix A on gold coins.

57–8 at least two hundred francs] Erasmus here undoubtedly means two hundred *livres tournois*, in the same sense as in Ep 119:277n. See the Glossary on coinage. (If Erasmus indeed meant the gold coin, the franc à cheval, then a sum in current values worth about £331 4s 0d *tournois*. See Appendix A on gold coinage.)

my eyesight, and it looks as though, like Jerome, I shall have to begin to
study by the aid of ears and tongue alone; and, in the wittiest language you   80
can muster, try to induce her to send me a sapphire, say, or some other gem
that is good for strengthening one's eyesight. I should have told you myself
what jewels possess this power, but I have no Pliny at hand; you can find
this out yourself from your doctor.

These measures, dear Jacob, do not appear to me either selfish or   85
unlikely to succeed, so long as you are able to equip yourself with that old
spirit which brings me luck. Also it seems to me that now more than ever
I have to seize Opportunity by the proverbial forelock, when such an honourable pretext presents itself. Again and again reflect, dear Batt, what close
friends we are, so close that if one of us should be in a position to help the   90
other, even at heavy cost to himself, he could not possibly refuse him anything. In the present circumstances, when you are able to confer so great
a benefit on your Erasmus, whom you have always positively surpassed in
affection, without any inconvenience to yourself at all, it seems to me that
to deny him your help would be the act not so much of one who fell short   95
in friendship as of a person who was actually hostile. And you need not
let your heart be assailed by the scruple that says 'If she gives this now, how
can I have the effrontery to request what I must ask for on my own behalf?'
I know that you yourself stand in urgent need of her help. I should like you
to bear in mind, however, that it is impossible to achieve these two ends   100
satisfactorily at once. For the moment, while the chance presents itself, you
should act in your friend's interest, postponing your own. Later you will
attend to your own interest in due time, without any disadvantage. And
you need not fear that a trifle like this may exhaust her resources.
Remember, at the same time, that you are in a position to make requests   105
every day, whereas in my case it is not so.

Possibly you think I am well enough off if I can avoid beggary. But
my own attitude is this: either I must obtain, from whatever source, the
essential equipment of a scholar's life, or else I must to abandon my studies
completely. And that essential equipment includes a way of living that is   110
not utterly poverty-stricken and miserable. Yet how far was I from beggary;
rather, how far am I now, without a penny in my purse? The rest I am
ashamed to set down. Just look about and see the wealth commanded by
illiterate donkeys. Does it then appear too much, if Erasmus should escape

* * * * *

83 Pliny] Pliny, *Naturalis historia* 37.10.140, attributes this power to the Indian
agate.

starvation? And what if he falls sick, for every year he has a recurrence of   115
fever, practically on the same date, or falls a victim to the numerous other
ills which, as your experience tells you, assail the life of man? Have I ever
yet had anything from my lady but promises? Yes, you will say, but my
money was lost in England. It was not your fault that this happened, but
not mine either, for I did not go there without due consideration, or arrange   120
my departure without care. But one cannot control accidents.

As for your loud complaints that I myself send nothing, I confess they
surprise me. As though either it was likely I should hide anything I had in
my possession that could be sent, or I were slumbering and needed to be
awakened. Believe me, there is no idleness here. On the contrary, I am pay-   125
ing scant regard to my very health as I help my friends; I compose for some,
read to some, correct for others, and meanwhile read, compile, emend, and
compose on my own account, and practise my Greek, which in any case is
very difficult. After which you (supposing me to have as much spare time
as yourself) shout at me 'Dedicate a book to So-and-So,' or 'Write hundreds   130
of letters,' as if my brain were made of steel. I imagine that it is because
you have little experience of the exertions demanded by this kind of exercise
that it all looks so easy to you. Find out for yourself what is involved in writing a book and then, if you like, accuse me of sloth.

Your letter contains certain remarks which you consider funny but I   135
regard as insulting or at any rate ill-timed. My dearest Jacob, do let us, I
beg you, avoid wit of this kind, which has a flavour of carping rather than
humour. On the other hand, if we have a fancy now and then to indulge
in scholarly witticisms, let us so engage in them that, until time permits,
there is no dereliction of work on the part of either of us. And I further beg   140
you, by our friendship, not to think of attempting to see whether I am in
a position to disregard even that hope which alone is left to me; and let us
not cloud our delightful affection by misplaced frivolities. I am quite sincerely dedicated to the single aim of acquiring the most perfect scholarship
I can command, and that is why I vehemently despise the superficial kind   145
that is fashionable for I am aware, and have long been aware, how insane
the popular notions are. My books, however, will not immediately take
to the air. I would rather win fame that is a little delayed, but endures, than
a speedier reputation which I must afterwards regret, as I notice has hap-

* * * * *

116 fever] Erasmus regarded fever as an annual event, occurring every Lent (cf
Ep 124:8 and 11n).
118–19 my money ... England] Cf Ep 119:9n.

pened to many men. For this reason, I beg you to give me liberty to handle   150
this matter as I think best. I for my part shall not want either enthusiasm
or courage; as for you, only see to it that I am not entirely bereft of resources.
This you can ensure without any loss to yourself, and indeed perhaps with
considerable profit. I do not say this as if I thought you needed any prompting; all you required was encouragement to raise your spirits to the utmost   155
extent. We must not ask noble patrons for trifling gifts, and there is nothing
you may not honourably attempt for a friend's sake. Believe me, if you set
about the business intelligently it will prosper. If, however, you hold out
no hopes at all, do not try to comfort me with false prospects. Let me search
for other sources of hope.   160

I hope, dear Batt, you will not think my language too harsh in what
I have written above, but rather take it in good part, as being quite plainly
spoken. I had to use serious words on a serious subject. Now listen while
I tell you what I should like you to arrange in addition, so that you can
relieve the abbot of a small donation. You are familiar with his feelings: 165
invent some modest but persuasive reason for your request. Say that I have
a large project on hand: to restore the entire text of Jerome, which has been
spoiled and garbled and confused by the ignorance of divines, for I have
found many passages in his writings that are corrupt or spurious, and to
restore the Greek. By so doing I shall cast light on the ancient world and   170
illuminate his literary achievement, which I venture to say nobody hitherto
has appreciated. For this task I need a considerable number of books, and
also the help of Greek tutors; ask him for a subsidy. There will be no need
for you to tell lies in this connexion, dear Batt, for I really am working at
this.   175

If, however, you do succeed in getting a large sum of money from my
lady, and I feel sure you will, please send Louis back to me at once. If on
the other hand she gives only ten or a dozen *écus*, or nothing, Louis is not
to come back, but anything you have should be handed over to Jean, unless
it happens that the boy volunteers to go. Louis himself knows the date when   180
Jean will arrive in Zeeland. As to your unduly scathing remarks about the
coat, do as you wish. However, it seems to me absurd to keep a boy in food
but not in clothing. To beg tiny favours like this from my lady is not greatly
to my taste, but, as I have said, it is for you to decide. Even if you do not
receive as much as you want from her, make sure that at least a few *écus*   185
are conveyed to me along with your own money. To be very hard up for

* * * * *

179 Jean] Cf Ep 128:2n.

books, have no spare time, and be in poor health – could you yourself write books amid such conditions?

About Jean as a messenger, I can see that there is no certainty. So please decide for yourself whether you prefer that my Louis should come back here. But don't send him with only a couple of nobles. And, dear Batt, please hurry. You should give Augustin's books to Louis, so that he can take them to my very good friend Thomas at Veere, selling any he can, even on the journey. The remainder should be forwarded by Thomas to X at Gouda, by a reliable boatman; while he in his turn should keep some for local sale and as soon as possible send some to Willem for sale at Haarlem. I shall also send a letter by the courier.

Farewell, my dearest Batt; put your whole self into this business: your friendly self, I mean; you may leave out the sluggish one!

Orléans, 1500

140 / To Pierre d'Angleberme   Orléans [c 13 December] 1500

Pierre d'Angleberme was a physician, probably Augustin's friend to whom he sent a copy of Homer (cf Ep 131: 2n) and to whom Ep 132 was addressed.

ERASMUS OF ROTTERDAM TO THE PHYSICIAN, PIERRE D'ANGLEBERME

Confound me, my dear Pierre, if I think the nectar of the gods would be any sweeter than your sample of cordial; in great measure, of course, through its potent spices and that health-giving power in which you surpass everyone else 'on white horses,' as the saying goes, just as you do in kindness; but vastly more because it owes its exquisite bouquet to your own friendly and engaging qualities. Indeed I am now experiencing, even more in action than in words, your marvellous openness of heart and wellnigh incredible kindness, things I was familiar with and came to love before when your friend Augustin talked of them, now that you have given me such a delightful and expensive and altogether suitable present. For Seneca's advice is right when he says that it makes a very great difference, in sending presents, who gives what to whom. Since, moreover, the works

* * * * *

192 Augustin's books] Apparently copies of the *Adagia* in Augustin's possession, or being handled by him (cf Ep 172).

193 Thomas] Perhaps Thomas Warnet (cf Ep 85:11n).

196 Willem] Hermans. Erasmus had sent him some copies, in the hope that he could sell them (cf Ep 138:179ff). There was evidently some misunderstanding as a result (cf Ep 142).

140:5 'on white horses'] *Adagia* I iv 21

12 Seneca] *De beneficiis* 1.6.1 and 1.11

of poets everywhere unite in praising Bacchus as the giver of eloquence,
and aromatic spices restore and repair the vigour and vitality of the heart,   15
what gift, pray, could you as a medical man more suitably have given to
a man of poesy and a diligent wielder of the pen than the very wine which
by the vulgar indeed is styled 'Hippocratic,' but which scholars know
sometimes as *trimma*, sometimes as *aromatites*, unless you would rather call
it 'myrrh-wine' or 'spiced wine'? I only wish I could, as easily as I should   20
like, find some suitable gift to give in exchange for your memento; if only
the opportunity equalled the ardour of my desire.

However, to avoid the appearance of being quite empty-handed as far
as gifts are concerned, and of owing double thanks and yet paying none,
I now express my gratitude in writing, in the manner of poets, who, as they   25
have no wealth but their own pages, are generous with these; answering
your present with a letter, though it is neither so well seasoned nor so
exquisitely made; I obviously get in exchange, as Diomedes does in Homer,
'Gold for bronze, large offerings for small.' If you cannot see your way to
balance these against each other, as being severely unequal in value, then   30
see whether the addition of this supplement suits you. I place wholly at your
service, such as he is, that puny mortal Erasmus. So long as you do not feel
reluctant to include him in your property, you are very much mistaken if
you think anything you own ever belonged to you more completely, or can
more freely be used and disposed of as you please. Meanwhile I am   35
delighted to have an excuse to write to you as I have been longing to do
for some time. When I return to Paris (and I am getting ready to set off
tomorrow) I shall be happy to lend your son my assistance in his studies
in any way I can. Farewell.

Orléans, 1500

141 / To Greveradus   Paris, 18 December [1500]

Nothing seems to be known of this person, except what is to be deduced from
this letter. Allen suggests that he may have taken his name from the town of
Greverath, about 25 miles NE of Trier. His friendship with Heinrich Northoff

* * * * *

28 Homer] *Iliad* 6.236; *Adagia* I ii 1
38 son] Jean Pýrrhus d'Angleberme (d 1521) studied Greek under Erasmus at
Paris, then returned to Orléans, where he lectured on law till 1515. When he
was dean of the university in December 1510, he brought Girolamo Aleandro
to Orléans to teach Greek, which Aleandro did until June 1511 (cf Ep 256
introduction). D'Angleberme was a prolific writer, the author of a number of
books on law as well as translations of Plutarch and Lucian. Erasmus corre-
sponded with him at intervals for years (cf Epp 256, 725).

of Lübeck (cf Ep 54 introduction) suggests a German origin. He was at this time
living somewhere near Paris (cf line 13 below). This letter is further evidence
of Erasmus' enthusiastic commitment to the project of editing Jerome's correspondence, although it is not clear what kind of aid he hoped for from
Greveradus. Possibly he was seeking a patron or a collaborator, although the
latter seems less in character.

ERASMUS TO GREVERADUS THE ADVOCATE

Dear and honoured sir: I beg you not to ascribe to lack of manners my temer-
ity in venturing to address without previous notice a person with whom
I am unacquainted, but rather to welcome the good will of which it is a sign
and the resulting confidence. At the same time, surely you could not in fact   5
be unknown to me, inasmuch as Heinrich Northoff, the most truthful man
alive, has so often described to me in conversation your mind and character
and interests that I seem to see a picture of you, exactly as if it were framed
and in front of me. Since our admiration of moral excellence and scholarship
is such a potent force that we feel some who are almost at the furthest ends   10
of the earth to be nevertheless linked to us by the closest bonds of affection,
if they are good men and scholars, am I not bound to pursue a person so
honourable and studious, and so near a neighbour, who holds sound learning in such respect and esteem? Now, I do not propose to open a friendship
with you in any common fashion. Associations between scholars are sac-   15
rosanct and have to be inaugurated by a kind of holy pledge, the nature of
which I shall now briefly describe.

I have long had a burning desire to write a commentary on the letters
of Jerome; and some god is now firing my spirit and impelling me to dare
to contemplate this massive enterprise, never before attempted by anyone.   20
What prompts me to this is the goodness of the saintly man who of all Christians was by common consent the best scholar and best writer, whose works
deserve to be read and got by heart by all mankind, whereas only a very
few read them and fewer still respect them, while fewest of all understand
them. Great Heavens: Scotus and Albertus Magnus and still more   25
unscholarly writers than these are noisily preached in every school, while
Jerome, the supreme champion and expositor and ornament of our faith,
who has earned unchallenged celebrity, is the only one among all the
Fathers of whom no mention is made. But I consider it most disgraceful that
Jerome should be forgotten for the very reason that earned him his title to   30
be remembered. That very excellence of style, which benefited our faith,
has done harm to its creator. Many are put off by the profound learning
which ought to have been the especial source of his fame; so there are few
to admire an author who is comprehended by few indeed. But if this great
Father can be provided with adequate commentaries to explain him, I   35

foresee that the reputation of Jerome will shine forth far and wide, as if a new day had dawned, so that everywhere in schools and lecture halls, in churches and homes, in public and in private, he may be read and become familiar.

Yet of course I am quite well aware what a rash enterprise I have taken 40 upon myself. First of all, how difficult it will be to wipe away the errors which in the course of long ages have so profoundly penetrated the text. Secondly, look at the classical learning, the Greek scholarship, the histories to be found in him, and all those stylistic and rhetorical accomplishments in which he not only far outstrips all Christian writers, but even seems to 45 rival Cicero himself. For my part at any rate, unless my affection for that saintly man is leading me astray, when I compare Jerome's prose with Cicero's, I seem to find something lacking in even the prince of prose writers. There is in our author such variety, such solidity of content, such fluency of argument, and while it is very difficult to demonstrate this kind 50 of artistry in the works of good stylists, it is nevertheless extremely helpful. This is what I trust I may be able to do, provided the saint himself comes to my aid; and I hope that, as a result, those who have hitherto admired Jerome for his reputation as a stylist may now admit that they never before understood the nature of his stylistic power. 55

For my part I shall conscientiously do for Jerome all that can be done by devoted attention, a moderate degree of scholarship, and the possession of some little intelligence. But just as one needs auxiliary troops to fight a major war, so I realize that one needs a leader and protector for such a ticklish business as this. And nobody can tell me better than you can whom 60 I am to select as best of all for this commission, partly because you have had a constant and special affection for this author, so Heinrich used to tell me, partly because it was my desire to begin the present friendly association between us on the strength of this very bond. Come then, my dear sir, join with me, and with me address yourself courageously to this splendid enter- 65 prise. The saint will help us, and bless the defenders of his own works, works that were the fruit of many hours of midnight toil; nor shall such pious endeavours as ours be cheated of their own reward. Farewell.

Paris, 18 December

PS See how much your character induces me to trust you, so that I am 70 not afraid to write to you so carelessly, just like an old and familiar friend. The rest of the news you will hear from the bearer of this, Augustin

* * * * *

141:72 Augustin] Although Augustin and Greveradus had a friend in common in Heinrich Northoff, they apparently had not met each other. Augustin made frequent journeys on business, and on such occasions might act as a letter-carrier for Erasmus.

Caminade, who is a very good scholar and a close associate of mine; he has earned a considerable reputation as a professor of the humane letters, as they are called, in the city of Paris. Receive him in your usual kind fashion, for he fully deserves your affection.   75

    Paris [1499]

MONEY AND COINAGE OF

THE AGE OF ERASMUS

An historical and analytical glossary
with particular reference to France, the Low Countries
England, the Rhineland
and Italy

JOHN H. MUNRO

The weights of all the coins listed in the glossary are expressed first in terms of the medieval notation of this era: the taille, literally the number of coins cut, struck from a marc or pound or other mint-weight unit of precious metal of the decreed fineness. The theoretical mean weights are then given in grams, or, for English coins, also in Troy grains. Because of the crudity of minting techniques of this era, the frequent and fraudulent practice of 'clipping' and 'sweating' coins, and simply their normal wear and tear in circulation, one should not expect to find that any high percentage of these coins had or maintained weights actually approaching the theoretical mean. Furthermore, coins heavier than the legal mean were frequently culled from circulation to be hoarded or exported as bullion, thus again reducing the average weight of such coins in circulation. Finally, the intrinsic precious metal contents of the coins in this glossary are described in grams of 100 per cent pure gold or silver.

ANGEL

English gold coin which Edward IV first struck in March 1465: $67^1/2$ to the Tower pound (qv) of the traditional $23^7/8$ carats fineness, so that each was to weigh 80 Troy grains and to contain 5.157 grams fine gold. The device stamped on its obverse was the angel St Michael, trampling on the dragon; that on the reverse, a ship similar to that on the former Henricus nobles (qv), containing the royal Yorkist arms, with the sun on one side of the mast, and a Yorkist rose on the other, but no king as formerly. The angel furthermore received the money-of-account value of 6s 8d sterling (= $^1/3$ pound) that had traditionally been assigned to the noble; and so it was originally called the noble-angel. Half angels or angelets, worth 3s 4d sterling, were also issued from this date, and these gold coins retained their sterling values until Henry VIII's first debasement of September 1526 necessarily raised them.

ARGENT-LE-ROY

The standard of commercially fine silver employed in France and the Burgundian-Hapsburg Low Countries, containing 12 deniers, each having 24 grains, which in total was $^{23}/_{24}$ths or 95.833 per cent pure silver.

BILLON

Heavily alloyed, base, petty silver coinage; monnaie noire; copper coinage. But paradoxically 'billon' in medieval French ('billio' in medieval Latin) meant precisely 'bullion,' or those precious metals that were legally required to be brought to the prince's mint for coinage.

BLANC

French royal silver coin first struck by John II as the blanc à l'épi in January 1352. From August 1360 its successor, the blanc à la couronne (which effectively superseded the old gros tournois from 1364), was issued consistently at a value of 10d tournois (qv) through various debasements and *renforcements* until November 1475, when the coin was transformed into the douzain of 12d tournois. The word 'blanc' itself, however, continued in common parlance to signify the former money-of-account value of 10d tournois.

CARAT

The universal measure of the fineness of gold, by which 24 carats signify pure, unalloyed gold. The term was borrowed, probably by the Venetians, from the Byzantine monetary system, in which 1 gold bezant (hyperper) = 12 silver miliarisia = 24 silver keratia.

CAVALIER. See PHILIPPUS

COURONNE = crown. See ÉCU À LA COURONNE

CRUZADO

Portuguese gold coin struck from 1457 at a fineness of $23^3/4$ carats and a weight of 3.780 grams (= taille of $64^3/4$ to the marc de Troyes), thus containing 3.741 grams fine gold. Its continued success was evidently based upon Portugal's rich gold discoveries in West Africa, from the early fifteenth century.

DEBASEMENT

The act of reducing the precious metal content of a coin by decreasing its fineness (titre) or weight, or both together. The result of such reductions was to raise, inflate the money-of-account value of any given weight of the pure precious metal, silver or gold; or conversely to diminish the amount of precious metal represented by any unit of money-of-account.

DENIER

From the Latin denarius, a Roman silver coin = 1 Attic drachma. A penny, one pence (1d) = $1/12$ sol (sou, shilling) = $1/240$ livre (pond, pound, Pfund) in most European money-of-account systems. A denier was also a measure of weight: in the livre de Paris, 1 denier = $1/24$ once, with 24 grains to the denier; in the English Troy pound, 1 pennyweight (dwt) = $1/20$ ounce (with

24 grains to the pennyweight) = $^1/_{240}$ pound. Finally, it was also a measure of silver fineness: 12 deniers argent-le-roy (qv) = commercially fine silver, 95.833 per cent pure.

DOUZAIN

Latin: duodenarius. A royal French silver coin, a transformation of the old blanc (qv) of 10d tournois, first issued with the increased value of 12d or 1 sol tournois by Louis XI on 2 November 1475, under the official name of grand blanc or blanc au soleil. The coin, stamped on the obverse with the device of three fleurs-de-lis in a trilobe surmounted by a blazing sun, was struck with a taille of 78$^1/_2$ to the marc (qv) and a fineness of 4 deniers 12 grains argent-le-roy (= 1.120 grams pure silver). By Charles VIII's debasement of April 1488 the value of this coin was raised to 13d tournois, so changing its sobriquet to treizain; and at the same time a new douzain of 12d tournois was struck with a taille of 86 to a marc of 4 deniers 12 grains argent-le-roy fineness (= 1.023 grams pure silver). This new douzain, officially the grand blanc à la couronne, stamped on the obverse with the device of three fleurs-de-lis formed in a trilobe surrounding a shield, and surmounted by a coronet, remained unaltered until Francis I next debased the silver coinage in July 1519.

DUCAT

A pure gold coin of 24 carats fineness, weighing officially 3.559 grams, first struck by the Doge of Venice in 1284 – 32 years after Florence had struck its first florin. The device stamped on the obverse was the Doge in kneeling position, receiving a banner from the hands of the patron St Mark; on the reverse, the device of Christ standing in an oval of stars, surrounded by the inscription: 'sit tibi, Christe, datus quem tu regis iste ducatus,' whence comes the name ducat. From 1517, the term 'ducat' was used to represent a money-of-account with a fixed value of 6 lire 4 soldi Venetian, while the actual coin continued under the name zecchino (sequin d'or) after the zecca, the mint where it was struck. Because the ducat-zecchino was supported by Venice's immense commercial and financial power, and especially because it retained its purity and full weight until about 1840, it served, along with the Florentine florin, as an international medium of exchange *par excellence* for most of medieval and early modern Europe. As such, it was often counterfeited or simply copied; and the accompanying appendix A on gold coinage lists one of the most famous and faithful imitations: the ducat of Hungary or florin of St Ladislas, this one probably struck by King Mathias Corvinus (1458–90).

DUODENARIUS. See DOUZAIN

ÉCU

= shield. The first, oldest French royal gold coin, issued by Louis IX as part of his great monetary reform of 15 August 1266, with 58¹/₃ struck from a marc de Troyes of 24 carats fine gold (= 4.196 grams), and accorded the nominal value of 10 sols tournois. It was stamped on the obverse with the device of the royal shield, containing fleurs-de-lis in a polylobe. Various other royal French gold coins were subsequently issued; but the next minting of a coin known as an écu was by Philip VI in January 1337: the ecu à la chaise, 54 struck from a marc of 24 carats fineness (= 4.532 grams), stamped on the obverse with the device of the king in full armour, seated on his throne, with one arm on a shield containing three fleurs-de-lis in a trilobe. A similar écu of the same weight, but of only 21 carats fineness, was struck by King John II in 1351. In the neighbouring Low Countries, various mints issued several widely circulated imitations of the current écu or 'schild' during the fourteenth and early fifteenth centuries.

ÉCU À LA COURONNE

One of the most famous of all royal French gold coins, first struck by Charles VI on 11 March 1385, at 60 to a marc of 24 carats fineness (= 4.079 grams fine gold); stamped on the obverse with the device of three fleurs-de-lis in a trilobe placed on the royal shield surmounted by the crown of France, itself also composed of fleurs-de-lis, it thus came to be known as the couronne or crown. From 1388 to 1429 this écu vieux underwent several debasements, renforcements, then more debasements to end up at just 18 carats fineness and a taille of 70 to the marc (= 2.622 grams fine gold). On 28 January 1436, Charles VII struck a new écu à la couronne – the écu neuf – at a taille of 70 to the marc of 24 carats fineness (= 3.496 grams fine gold). It, too, was subsequently debased several times: in 1445, 1447 (and then strengthened that year), 1448, 1450, 1461, and 1474, then ending its 89-year career with a taille of 72 to a marc of 23¹/₈ carats (= 3.275 grams fine gold).

ÉCU AU SOLEIL

The immediate successor to the couronne, it was first struck by Louis XI on 2 November 1475, at a taille of 70 to a marc of 23¹/₈ carats (= 3.369 grams fine gold). This écu was stamped on its obverse with the device of the royal shield, again containing three fleurs-de-lis, and surmounted directly by the royal crown, which was in turn headed by a blazing sun. Identical écus au soleil were issued by Charles VIII (1483–98) and Louis XII (1498–1515). From 1488 to 1507 its official money-of-account value was 36s 3d tournois.

EXCELENTE

Spanish royal gold coin struck from 1497 at the same fineness and weight as the Portuguese cruzado (qv): $23^3/4$ carats and 3.780 grams, for a fine gold content of 3.741 grams.

FARTHING

The smallest denomination of the English silver coins, worth one-quarter of the penny (pence sterling), first issued by Edward I. In Erasmus' day (and to 1526), it weighed 3 Troy grains (= .1944 gram), and was of the traditional 11 oz 2 dwt fineness. See appendix B on silver coinage.

FLORIN

This fiorino d'oro of Florence, stamped on the obverse with the device of one large fleur-de-lis (whence the name florin in fact) and on the reverse with that of St John standing erect, vies with the much less famous genovino of Genoa for the honour of being the first successful gold coin issued in western Europe since the reign of the Carolingian emperor Louis the Pious in the ninth century. Struck from 1252 to 1533 consistently at 24 carats fineness and a weight of 3.536 grams, it competed quite successfully with the Venetian ducat as the prime 'dollar' or international exchange medium of medieval and early modern Europe. Indeed it was by far and for long the most widely imitated gold coin in Europe – once even by England (1343); and its imitations were themselves in turn widely counterfeited. The accompanying appendix A on gold coins lists florins, or florin-type coins, struck by the four electors of the Rhineland, the dukes of Burgundy then Hapsburg archdukes in the Low Countries, the archdukes of Austria, the dukes of Bavaria, the dukes of Guelders, the bishops of Utrecht, and of Liège. (See also GULDEN.)

FLORIN OF THE RHINE (FLORIN OF THE FOUR ELECTORS, RIJNSGULDEN, MAILLES DU RHIN)

From the monetary convention of 1354, this florin was issued collectively by the four imperial electors of the Rhineland: the count palatine and the archbishops of Mainz, Trier, and Cologne. Originally struck at approximately the same weight as the Florentine florin, 66 to the mark of Cologne (= 3.543 grams) and of slightly less fineness, $23^1/2$ carats (= 3.469 grams fine gold), it had been reduced to 19 carats and 3.508 grams ($66^2/3$ to the mark) by 1419, to 3.490 grams (67 to the mark) in 1447, to 3.439 grams (68 to the mark) in 1454, to 3.406 grams ($68^2/3$ to the mark) in 1464, and finally to 3.278

grams ($71^{1}/_{3}$ to the mark) in 1490, when its fineness was also reduced to $18^{1}/_{2}$ carats (= 2.527 grams fine gold). It then retained this gold content until its last issue, in 1626. For most of the fifteenth century, it was stamped with the device of the standing figure or of the arms of the issuing elector, but from 1488 with that of Christ. This florin quickly became the chief medium for the commerce of South Germany and the Rhineland, and, by the early fifteenth century, for that of the eastern Low Countries as well. For this reason the Rijnsgulden was frequently and widely counterfeited by the bishoprics and petty principalities of this region, whose often drastic debasements had forced the Rhine electors in turn to reduce the standard of their florin.

FLORIN OF ST ANDREW (ST ANDRIES FLORIN)
The first of the gold florin coins struck in the Burgundian Low Countries by Duke Philip the Good (1419–67) from 23 May 1466, with almost exactly the same weight and fineness as specified for the current florin of the Rhine: a taille of 72 to the marc de Troyes (= 3.399 grams) and a titre of 19 carats (= 2.692 grams fine gold). It was stamped on the obverse with the device of St Andrew, facing directly, and holding his large cross before him; on the reverse, with the device of the shield of the Burgundian ducal arms on a long cross. This St Andries florin was reissued without change by Duke Philip's successors for the next thirty years: Duke Charles the Rash (1467–77), Duchess Mary of Burgundy (1477–82) and her husband Maximilian of Hapsburg, and Archduke of Austria Philip the Fair (1482–1506). In 1496, it was superseded by the considerably debased florin of St Philip (qv). That the Burgundians adopted this Rhenish-florin gold standard in place of the long predominant French standard (as exemplified by Philip the Good's own prior issues of the 1433 Philippus and the 1454 Lion) undoubtedly reflected the important change that had occurred in the economy of the Low Countries from the 1450s: the shift of the economic centre of gravity from the Flemish port of Bruges to the Brabantine port-fairs of Antwerp and Bergen-op-Zoom. The rapid rise of these Brabant fairs that led to their becoming the leading entrepôt and financial capital of northern Europe from that time was essentially the result of the current South German mining boom in both silver and copper and the resulting aggressive expansion of South German trade in those metals, fustian textiles, and Rhenish wines. At the Brabant fairs, these German goods were exchanged for English woollens and, by the end of the century, for Portugal's East Indies spices – a trade which in turn attracted merchants from all over Europe. Significantly, the dominant axis of both the commercial and the monetary flows ran from Venice through South Germany and the Rhineland to Antwerp.

FLORIN OF ST PHILIP(PE)

The considerably debased successor to the St Andries florin, first struck by Archduke Philip the Fair on 14 May 1496, with a taille of 74 to the marc de Troyes and 16 carats fineness (= 2.205 grams fine gold); in 1500, he reduced its fineness slightly more to $15^{11}/_{12}$ carats (= 2.189 grams fine gold). The device stamped on the obverse was St Philip standing, holding the cross and the bible; that on the reverse, a jewelled cross with the shield-arms of Flanders at its centre, and surrounded by the shield-arms of Austria, new and old Burgundy, and of Brabant. This florin of St Philip continued to be struck by his son and successor Charles, later the Emperor Charles v, at the same fineness and weight until 1521.

FRANC

First struck, with a taille of 63 to a marc de Troyes of 24 carats (= 3.885 grams fine gold), on 5 December 1360, in order to provide the ransom of King John II of France, according to the provisions of the recent treaty of Brétigny with England; hence the famous sobriquet 'franc,' or 'free,' in the opinion of most authorities. The original issues were known as francs à cheval because the device stamped on the obverse was the king in full armour, brandishing a sword, and riding a horse at full gallop; on the reverse was stamped the device of a jewelled cross within a quadrilobate surrounded by pointed tre-foils. In many respects, especially in terms of the device on the obverse, this gold coin was the counterpart of the English gold noble (qv); and the signifi-cation of the king as 'franc' and similarly placed at the head of his feudal nobility may offer an alternative explanation of the origin of the name. In April 1365, Charles v of France issued a new franc, also 24 carats in fineness but with a taille of 64 to the marc de Troyes (= 3.824 grams), known as the franc à pied, because the device stamped on the obverse showed the king standing under a pinnacled canopy, wearing a mailed tunic of fleurs-de-lis, and holding his sword in one hand and the instruments of justice in the other. Finally, in September 1422 and November 1423, Charles VII (as dauphin of France) issued a third franc, closely resembling the franc à cheval of John II in the obverse and reverse devices, at 24 carats fineness and a taille of 80 to the marc de Troyes (= 3.059 grams). Each of these three francs, when initially issued, was valued at 20 sols tournois or one livre – though the last was worth about £1 13s 1d in 1498–1500; and thus the word franc in common parlance came to mean simply one livre.

FREDERICUS

An imitation of the Rhenish florin of the Four Electors as struck by the bishop of Utrecht in the mid-fifteenth century.

The ryal or gold rose noble of Edward IV as struck 1465–83
obverse and reverse
diameter 3.6 cm
Royal Ontario Museum, Toronto

GENOVINO or GENOIN

Pure gold coin, theoretically 24 carats, weighing 3.560 grams, struck by Genoa from 1252, as perhaps the first gold coin issued in western Europe since the ninth century (see FLORIN). It was less successful as the 'dollar' of late-medieval and early modern European trade than the florin and ducat. But note that the weight of the genovino was very close to that of the florin (3.536 grams) and of the ducat (3.559 grams), so that these three Italian coins were commonly acceptable at the same value, quite interchangeable, and indeed were indifferently called florins or ducats.

GROAT

The largest, heaviest of the English silver coins, before the issue of the shilling or teston (tester) in 1504, worth four pence (4d) sterling. It was first struck by Edward I as part of the great recoinage of 1279, but only regularly from Edward III's recoinage of 1351, when half-groats (2d) were also first issued. The name comes from the Middle-Dutch 'groot,' meaning 'great, large, thick,' and is in fact analogous to the Flemish silver groot and the French gros tournois (qv); but on the continent this English coin was more popularly known as the stoter. From 1464 to 1526, the groat was struck at $112^{1}/_{2}$ to the Tower pound (= 48 grains Troy = 3.110 grams) and of the traditional fineness of 11 oz 2 dwt (= 2.877 grams pure silver). The device stamped on its obverse was the bust of the king, full-faced and crowned, placed within a border of eight foliated cusps; that on the reverse, a large cross, a traditional symbol on English silver coins since late Saxon times.

GROS TOURNOIS OF FRANCE (GROSSUS TURONENSIS ARGENTI)

Large silver coin first struck by Louis IX as the foundation of his great monetary reform of 15 August 1266, at a full 12 deniers argent-le-roy (qv) fineness, and a taille of 58 to the marc de Troyes (= 4.220 grams); it thus contained 4.044 grams pure silver. On the reverse was stamped the distinctive device of the 'châtel' or castle-turret of St Martin of Tours, surmounted by a cross with the inscription + TVRONVS CIVIS, and surrounded by a border of twelve fleurs-de-lis. Following the Italian precedent of the heavy silver grossi (= large) of Venice (1202), Florence (1237), and Milan (c 1250), St Louis valued his gros at one sol or shilling, equal to 12 of the current deniers tournois. Then in 1295 Philip IV, beginning his silver debasements, raised the gros' value to 15d tournois, and later even higher, but did not reduce its silver content until the debasement of 1303. Although Philip IV did restore its original standard of St Louis in 1305, his successors reduced the weight of the gros, and then from 1337, with Philip VI's minting of the gross à la couronne, its fineness as well. From 1364, it was effectively superseded by

TOP The Burgundian-Hapsburg gold florin of St Philip
as struck by Archduke Philip the Fair in 1500
obverse and reverse
Bibliothèque nationale, Paris

CENTRE The fiorino d'oro or gold florin of Florence
as struck from 1252 to 1533
obverse and reverse
British Museum, London

BOTTOM The écu d'or au soleil de Bretagne
as struck by Charles VIII from 1483–98
obverse and reverse
Bibliothèque nationale, Paris
The coins on this page are reproduced at 120 per cent of size

the blanc (qv). In Erasmus' day, the royal French silver coin having the gros tournois' initial value of 12d tournois was the quite heavily alloyed grand blanc à la couronne or douzain (qv). The direct physical descendant of St Louis' gros, the gros-de-roi, as struck by Charles VIII and Louis XII, from May 1489 to 1512, at 11 deniers 12 grains argent-le-roy and a taille of 69 to the marc (= 3.258 grams pure silver), was instead worth 3 sols or 36d tournois. Such was the extent of debasement of the silver coinage since the days of St Louis: a 73.15 per cent reduction in the quantity of silver in the sol tournois.

GROS or GROOT OF FLANDERS
The silver coin that constituted the base of, the 'link-money' for, the livre gros or pond groot money-of-account system of Flanders, and was thus always worth 1d in that system. Flanders, as a royal fief of the king of France in the Middle Ages, originally formed an integral part of the French mone-tary system, with the northern royal French denier parisis (= 5/4 denier tournois) as the local medium of exchange, supplemented from 1266 by the royal gros tournois (= 9.6d parisis). But the counts of Flanders also struck their own silver coins in that independently held stretch of land east of the Scheldt which was *de jure* an imperial fief. The first 'grosse monnoie blanche' so struck there was the double sterling (qv) or esterling, minted by Countess Marguérite of Constantinople (1244–80) from 1275, at two-thirds the weight and value of the royal gros tournois. Her son and successor Count Guy de Dampierre may have struck the first of the Flemish gros, in direct imitation of the royal gros tournois. His monetary ordinance of 2 April 1300 (ns) ordered the striking of 'gros deniers d'argent, aussi bons de poids et de loi que le gros tournois le roi,' which were to be in fact somewhat inferior: only 11 deniers 12 grains argent-le-roy fineness and struck at a taille of 56½ to the mark of Cologne (= 59.133 to the marc de Troyes = 4.139 grams), thus containing only 3.801 grams pure silver instead of the 4.044 grams in the true and as yet unaltered gros tournois of France. Philip IV the Fair's conquest of all Flanders and his imprisonment of Count Guy that very same month may have prevented the issue of this gros. But after Flanders' liberation by the battle of Courtrai in 1302, his sons and successors, counts Jean de Namur and Philippe de Thiette (1302–5), then Count Robert de Béthune (1305–22), certainly did strike Flemish gros that were close imita-tions of the royal gros tournois, with the distinctive device of the castle tur-rets surmounted by a cross, and surrounded by a border of twelve trefoils (instead of fleurs-de-lis), stamped on the obverse. From about 1318, after the French and Flemish had both halted their severe debasements and restored strong silver coinages respectively, the Flemish began asserting their monetary independence more fully by instituting their own pond

groot or livre gros money-of-account system, with 240 of the current Flemish gros to the livre; and further by permanently tying the previously current, French-based moneys-of-account directly to the Flemish gros. Henceforth they maintained the following fixed, frozen equivalences: 1 livre gros Flemish = 12 'strong' livres parisis (new) = 40 'weak' livres parisis (old, debased) or pond payemente, as it came to be called. Consequently from that date the Flemish livre parisis was a 'ghost money' that no longer had any relationship whatsoever to the French denier or livre parisis; and the French coins, parisis and tournois, were almost fully displaced in domestic circulation by the native Flemish gros and its subdivisions (down to the mite, which equalled $^1/_{24}$ gros). The Flemish gros itself, however, as struck from perhaps March 1318, remained similar in form though quite inferior in silver content to its French counterpart until April 1337: with 115 demi-gros = 57$^1/_2$ gros struck from a marc de Troyes of 10 deniers 6 grains fineness, so that each gros contained 3.484 grams pure silver compared to the 3.909 grams silver in the French gros tournois of 1329–37 (60 struck to a marc of 12 deniers). Thereafter, with the severe debasements of both King Philip VI in France and Count Louis de Crécy of Flanders (1322–46), both from 1337, the French and Flemish silver gros differed completely in their forms, values, and histories. By 1499–1500, in Erasmus' day, the Flemish silver gros (1d) contained only .474 gram pure silver (134 taille to a marc of 3 deniers 6 grains fineness): just 12.47 per cent of the silver in Count Guy de Dampierre's original gros.

GULDEN

= golden. A florin, especially the florin of the Rhine of the Four Electors (qv). In the Burgundian-Hapsburg Low Countries, from about 1460, the gulden or florin also represented a fixed money-of-account, equivalent to the livre de quarante gros: 1 gulden (f) = 20 stuivers (s) = 40 (d) gros of Flanders = 1/6 livre gros. But as notional money tied to the current silver gros, this money-of-account value bore no direct relation to that of the actual gold coin.

HARDI

French royal silver coin worth 3d tournois. Although a royal French silver coin of the same fineness and value had been struck in June 1423 (the Trésin or Trézain by the government of Henry VI in Paris), the hardi itself originally came from Gascony-Guienne, an English province until the fall of Bordeaux in 1453, where it had circulated as a petty coin worth approximately the same as the farthing. The name is derived from the device stamped on the obverse: the 'bold' or 'intrepid' prince or king, holding an unsheathed sword in one hand, and ready for battle. As an official royal coin, the hardi and its cousin the liard (qv) were first issued by Louis XI in October 1467 at 3 deniers argent-le-roy fineness and a taille of 192 to the marc de Troyes (= 0.305 gram pure silver).

HENRICUS NOBLE
English gold noble (qv) struck from 1412 to 1464

KAROLUS
Royal French silver coin worth 10d tournois, and thus also known as the dizain (and as the blanc), first struck by Charles VIII in November 1488, at 4 deniers argent-le-roy and a taille of 92^1/$_2$ to the marc de Troyes (= .845 gram pure silver). The device stamped on its obverse was a large K, with a fleur-de-lis on each side, the whole surmounted by a crown.

LIARD
French silver coin worth 3d tournois, originally from the Dauphiné, that was first issued as a royal coin by Louis XI in October 1467, at the same time as and with the same fineness and weight as the hardi (qv). The name 'liard' signifies 'grey,' thus indicating that by its alloy (with 3 deniers argent-le-roy fineness) it lay between true 'silver' coins and the monnaie noire, or billon.

LIVRE. See POUND

MAILLE TOURNOIS
Half a penny, a demi-denier of the tournois system of French silver coins, classed as billon. See also OBOLE and appendix B on silver coinage.

MAILLE DU RHIN. See FLORIN OF THE RHINE

MARC DE PARIS, or MARC DE TROYES
The unit or standard of mint-weight established in France during the reign of Philip I (1060–1108), and in the Low Countries during the early fourteenth century. Containing 8 onces de Paris, with 24 deniers to the once, and 24 grains to the denier, for a total of 4608 grains to the marc, it weighed 244.7529 grams: that equalled precisely one-half of the livre de Paris (16 onces = 489.5058 grams) – the direct descendent of the pound of Charlemagne (12 oz = 489.60 grams) – and two-thirds of the livre de Troyes (12 onces = 367.129 grams), as used at Troyes during the Champagne fairs.

MARK OF COLOGNE (KÖLN)
The standard or unit of mint-weight of the Rhineland, and parts of northern

Germany, Scandinavia, and the eastern Low Countries, weighing 233.856 grams, or .955 marc de Troyes. It had also been the Flemish mint standard, until displaced by the marc de Troyes in the early fourteenth century. The widespread influence of the Cologne mark may be seen from the fact that it weighed almost precisely one-half of the Brabant (Brussels) pound and two-thirds of the English Tower pound (qv).

MARK STERLING

An English money-of-account of Danish origin worth two-thirds a pound sterling, or 13s 4d ($= 160$ pence)

NOBLE OF ENGLAND

English gold coin first struck by Edward III in August 1344 to supersede his abortive florin of December 1343. (The very first English gold coin was, however, Henry III's unsuccessful gold penny of 1257, valued at 20d sterling). Struck initially at $39^{1}/_{2}$ to the Tower pound (136.7 Troy grains each) of $23^{7}/_{8}$ carats fineness – a gold standard which remained unaltered until 1526, it thus contained 8.812 grams of fine gold, the most then to be found in any European coin. But in 1346 its weight was reduced to 128.6 Troy grains ($= 42$ to the Tower pound); in 1351, to 120.0 Troy grains ($= 45$ to the Tower pound $= 7.733$ grams fine gold); and finally in 1412, to 108.0 Troy grains ($= 50$ to the Tower pound $= 6.962$ grams fine gold). This last issue of 1412–64, as struck by Henry IV, V, and VI, was known on the continent, and indeed into the seventeenth century, as the Henricus noble. All of the nobles, from the original 1344 issue, were valued at 6s 8d or one-third of a pound sterling. But in 1464, Edward IV raised the price of the Henricus noble to 8s 4d sterling, only to replace it the following year with his Ryal and Angel nobles (qv). On all the nobles issued from 1344 to 1464, the device stamped on the obverse was the crowned king in full armour, standing full-face in a ship (quite out of proportion), holding in his right hand a sword and on his left arm a shield emblazoned with the royal emblems of France (ancient) and of England; the device on the reverse was a figure of eight arches, with a cross in the centre, fleurs-de-lis placed at the end of each limb, and lions surmounted by crowns within the other four cusps. The significance of especially the obverse device was not lost upon Englishmen of this era; to quote the anonymous author of *Mare clausum*:

> Foure things our noble sheweth to me
> King, Ship, and Swerd, and Power of the See.

The English noble (and half- and quarter-nobles) became an important medium of exchange in North European trade, especially in the Low Countries, and as such it was also widely counterfeited.

NOBLES OF FLANDERS AND BURGUNDY

Counterfeit imitations of the English gold nobles, struck by the dukes of Burgundy in the Low Countries to profit both their own treasuries and those subjects who used these coins to purchase wools or other commodities at the English staple port of Calais. The first and most successful of these counterfeits was struck in Flanders by Duke Philip the Bold from October 1388 to June 1402, at $23^3/4$ carats and a taille of $31^2/3$ to the marc (= 7.649 grams fine gold, or .084 gram less than that in the current English noble). The counterfeits of the Henricus noble struck by Duke John the Fearless in December 1416, and those by Duke Philip the Good in June 1425 and September 1427 were evidently failures. But the noble struck by Duke Philip from November 1428 to February 1430, at $23^1/2$ carats and a taille of $35^1/4$ to the marc (= 6.799 grams fine gold), enjoyed a moderate if quite fraudulent success at Calais before the English authorities finally halted its distribution there. Even so, it long continued to circulate in the Low Countries. Finally, in April 1487, the regent Maximilian of Hapsburg struck the noble de Bourgogne, at $23^4/5$ carats and a taille of 33 to the marc (= 7.355 grams fine gold), as a quite inferior counterfeit of Edward IV's heavy 'rose' or ryal noble (qv) of 1465.

OBOLE, OBOLUM

A demi-denier, a halfpenny. Originally an obole was $1/6$ a Greek drachma, and later also $1/6$ a Roman drachma or denarius; but it also equalled one half a scruple. Consequently it came to be considered as half a denarius of the value of the scruple. In Carolingian times, the obole was a demi-denier, but later the term maille (qv) came to be more popular for such coins.

PARISIS, DENIER AND LIVRE

One of the two royal French systems of silver coinage and moneys-of-account, the denier serving as the 'link-money' for the latter, having a value of $5/4$ or 125 per cent of the tournois system (qv). Although the denier parisis was descended from the silver pennies of the Carolingian and early Capetian monarchs, it was first issued as an official royal coin with that name and the distinctive inscription FRA – NCO by Louis VII (1137–80). Philip II Augustus (1180–1223), in seeking to suppress rival feudal coinages, firmly established its circulation in all royal territories and direct royal fiefs of northern France (including Flanders and Artois); but elsewhere his newly authorized deniers tournois (qv) predominated from 1215. For the royal fiscal accounts of the Trésor and Hôtel du Roi, the livre parisis system was used, but royal monetary administration itself came to be carried out almost exclusively in the tournois system. The deniers parisis coins themselves were used by the monarchy only for alms-giving and were rarely issued after 1365. The last verifiable denier parisis was struck by Charles VIII in March 1495 (appendix B) – if not by Louis XII in December 1505. Finally, the parisis money-of-account system was itself abolished by Louis XIV in April 1667. In the Low Countries, Flanders used the denier parisis until the early fourteenth century, when it was supplanted by the independent Flemish gros (qv). The livre parisis, however, continued to be used there as a money-of-account until the Napoleonic reforms. But from about 1318 it functioned only as a 'ghost money,' permanently tied to the Flemish livre gros (qv) at the ratio of 1:12 (so that 1d gros = 1s or 12d parisis), thus forever severing any relation with the French denier and livre parisis.

PATARD

Burgundian silver coin, the double gros (2d gros of Flanders = 3d gros of Brabant), also known as the vierlander, the plaque, the griffon, the briquet, and most popularly as the stuiver. From the Burgundian monetary reform and unification of the Low Countries in October 1433 to the debasement of May 1466, it was struck at a taille of 70 to a marc de Troyes of 6 deniers argent-le-roy (= 1.675 grams pure silver); in Erasmus' day, from 1499 to 1521, at a taille of 80 to a marc of 4 deniers argent-le-roy (= .977 gram pure silver). For this latter issue, the device stamped on the obverse was the shield of Austria and Burgundy surmounted by a crown; on the reverse, an ornate cross, bearing the provincial symbols, within a quadrilobate.

PHILIPPUS

Burgundian gold coin first issued by Duke Philip the Good also as part of his great monetary reform and unification of the Low Countries in October 1433. In its weight and fineness, with a taille of $67^{1}/_{2}$ to a marc of $23^{13}/_{16}$ carats (= 3.598 grams fine gold), it closely resembled but was in fact slightly superior to the current French gold saluts, the Italian florin and ducats, as appendix A demonstrates. In its design, however, it more closely resembled the lighter weight but pure gold French franc à cheval, especially in its obverse device: the duke in full armour, on horseback, galloping to the right. For this reason it, too, was sometimes called the franc à cheval, but more commonly the cavalier (= chevalier) in French and rijder (or ryder, rider = rider) in Flemish. In January 1454, it was superseded by the lion d'or (gouden leeuw) of 23 carats, with a taille of $57^{1}/_{2}$ to the marc (= 4.079 grams fine gold); but the cavalier-philippus long continued to circulate in the Low Countries thereafter. About a half-century later, this sobriquet was also popularly applied to the Burgundian-Hapsburg gold florin of St Philip (qv) as struck by Archduke Philip the Fair from 1496.

POSTULAAT (POSTULAT)

A type of grossly inferior imitation of the Rijnsgulden (florin of the Rhine), the first of which was struck by Rudolph of Diepholt when he was postulant-bishop of Utrecht, from 1426 to 1432; and such postulats continued to be struck by Rudolph, evidently in more debased form, while he was regular bishop of Utrecht, from 1432 to 1455. The device stamped on the obverse resembled that of the current Rijnsgulden: the standing figure of the bishop St Martin, instead of that of the issuing elector. Similar counterfeits of the Rijnsgulden were struck by his successors at Utrecht, by the bishops of Liège, and even some by the archbishops of Cologne; they were all also called postulats by virtue, so to speak, of their ecclesiastical origin. At Liège, Bishop Jean de Heinsberg (1419–55) struck postulats de Lambert, as imitation Rijnsgulden, at a taille of 78 to a marc of only 12 carats (= 1.569 grams fine gold); and his successor Bishop Louis de Bourbon (1456–82) struck even more inferior postulats de Bourbon, apparently at a taille of 105 to a marc of 15 carats (= 1.457 grams fine gold), as well as somewhat better quality pieter-florins, at a taille of 70 to a marc of 16 carats 8 grains (= 2.380 grams fine gold).

POUND (LIBRA, LIVRE, LIRA, POND, PFUND)

As the standard, almost European-wide money-of-account system, having the equivalences of £ = 20s = 240d, it was established by Charlemagne (c 790–802) to equal in fact the new Carolingian pound weight of silver (12 ounces = 489.60 grams). Only deniers were then struck, 240 to the pound (each thus weighing in theory 2.040 grams). In England, also, from its inception, the pound sterling of late Saxon, certainly early Norman, times equalled precisely the Tower pound weight of silver, of 11 oz 2 dwt fineness (92.5 per cent pure), with 240 pence struck to that pound of 5400 Troy grains, each pence thus weighing ±22.5 grains. But by the time of Henry III's recoinage of 1247, the number of pence struck to the Tower pound had risen slightly to 242d; and then again to 243d to the pound with Edward I's recoinage of 1279. The penny remained stable at that weight (22.22 grains Troy) until Edward III's rather drastic debasements, beginning in 1335. On the continent even more substantial debasements from the time of Charlemagne's immediate successors had long before destroyed any direct relation between the pound as a money-of-account and the pound weight of silver.

POUND WEIGHTS

The gram equivalences of the various pound units in use in Erasmus' day are as follows: 1/ livre de Paris (16 onces) = 489.506 grams; 2/ Pond of Antwerp (16 oz) = 470.156 grams; 3/ Pond of Brussels (16 oz) = 467.670 grams; 4/ Pound Avoirdupois of England (16 oz) = 453.593 grams; 5/ Troy pound of England (12 oz) = 373.242 grams; 6/ livre de Troyes (12 onces = .75 livre de Paris) = 367.129 grams; 7/ Tower pound of England (12 oz = 11.25 Troy ounces) = 349.914 grams.

RIJDER (RYDER, RIDDER). See PHILIPPUS

RIJNSGULDEN. See FLORIN OF THE RHINE, GULDEN

RYAL, or ROYAL, or ROSE NOBLE
English gold coin first struck by Edward IV in 1465, at 45 to the Tower pound (120 Troy grains each) of the traditional 23^7/$_8$ carats fineness, thus containing 7.735 grams fine gold. Heavier than the earlier Henricus nobles and Edward's accompanying angel (qv), the Ryal in fact weighed exactly the same as the noble of 1351–1412 (qv); but it was assigned a considerably higher value: 10s or one-half of a pound sterling. In its design it partially resembled the former nobles in that the device stamped on its obverse retained the king-in-the-ship design. But on the ship's stern was placed a banner containing a large E, and on the side of the hull a large Yorkist rose; on the reverse, the traditional cross was replaced by a sun in blazing splendour, with yet another Yorkist rose at its centre. For this reason, the coin was more popularly called the 'rose noble' rather than its official designation, the Ryal – a corruption of the French 'royaux,' gold coins struck by Charles VI and VII. In 1489, Henry VII somewhat changed the design of the Ryal: on the obverse, the stern banner was replaced by one bearing the red Tudor dragon; and on the reverse the sun in splendour was replaced by a large double rose, with a shield of fleurs-de-lis at its centre. He also issued a double-ryal known as the sovereign, worth one pound sterling (until 1526). See also ANGEL, NOBLE.

ST PHILIPPE FLORIN. See FLORIN OF ST PHILIP

SEIGNORAGE
The tax imposed on minting, as a percentage of the coins so struck, the profits from which provided the prince with a very strong motive for coinage debasements

SIZAIN
French royal silver coin worth 6d tournois. See appendix B.

SOL, SOLIDUS, SOU
A shilling = 12d = ^{1}/$_{20}$ of a pound

SOVEREIGN

English gold coin, worth 20s or one pound sterling, first struck by Henry VII in October 1489 to equal two Ryals: 22^{1}/$_{2}$ cut from the Tower pound (= 240 Troy grains each) of the traditional 23^{7}/$_{8}$ carats fineness, thus containing 15.471 grams fine gold. The device stamped on its obverse was the king, full-faced, sitting on a broad, bench-like throne, wearing a high, closed crown, and holding the royal orb and sceptre; on the reverse was the double Tudor rose, with the royal shield of arms at its centre. In 1526, Henry VIII raised its value to 22s and then to 22s 6d sterling. In more modern times, from 1816 to world war I, the Royal Mint issued another sovereign also worth one pound sterling: it had a fineness of 22 carats, a weight of 122.274 Troy grains, and thus contained 7.263 grams fine gold, or 46.95 per cent of that of Henry VII's sovereign.

STERLING OF ENGLAND (PENCE AND POUND)

The term refers to both the English silver coinage and the money-of-account system, as established from at least the Norman Conquest, if not from Saxon times. William I the Conqueror is often credited with formally instituting both the Tower pound (qv) of London as the official mint-weight and the sterling standard of silver fineness at 11 oz 2 dwt to the pound (= 92.50 per cent pure). But other, numismatic evidence would indicate that such a silver standard dates from at least the reign of Aethelred, c 890 AD; and the continuous issue of the English silver penny, it should be noted, dates from the reign of the kings Heaberht and Ecgberht of Kent (c 775–90), or at least from the reign of King Offa of Mercia (c 784 AD). The first recorded references to the penny as a sterling come from a later era, the twelfth century; and the etymology remains quite obscure. The once-favoured theory that the word is derived from Easterling – Baltic German merchant – is no longer considered tenable since the omission of the strongly accented first syllable is then not explained. More likely it is derived from either 'steorra' = 'star,' since early Norman pennies contained stars in the device stamped on their obverse, or possibly from 'staer' = 'starling,' since the obverse device stamped on one of Edward the Confessor's pennies contained four small birds. See also POUND.

STERLING OF FLANDERS (ESTERLING, ESTERLIN, INGELSCHEN)

Silver coins struck in Imperial Flanders by Countess Marguérite of Constantinople (1244–80) and Count Guy de Dampierre (1280–1305) that were supposed to equal one-third of a French gros tournois (qv) in weight and value. At the same time, these Flemish sterlings also had a silver content evidently closely approximating that of the current English penny. From at least Henry III's recoinage of 1247 to Edward I's recoinage of 1279, that penny, with 242d struck from the Tower pound, contained 1.337 grams pure silver; and from 1279 to 1335, 1.332 grams. Both of these amounts, only fractionally different, equal almost precisely one-third – 33.06 and 32.94 per cent respectively – of the pure silver content of the French gros tournois (4.044 grams) from its initial issue in 1266 until the 1303 debasement. Moreover, Flemish sterlings, especially those of Count Guy, closely resemble the English penny in both the obverse device of the king's or prince's bust and the reverse device of the cross; and such counterfeiting is not surprising in view of the very close, wool-based economic ties between England and Flanders of that era. In the course of the early fourteenth century, both the Flemish esterling and the French denier parisis (qv) were displaced by the new Flemish gros (qv). But the esterlin-ingelschen was retained in Flanders as a common unit of money-of-account, into Erasmus' day and after, with the following fixed equivalences: 1d gros of Flanders = 3 esterlins =24 mites, thus retaining its original historic value of one third of the gros (tournois).

STOTER. See GROAT

STUIVER. See PATARD
The stuiver also served as the 'shilling' in the gulden (qv) or florin money-of-account system of the Burgundian-Hapsburg Low Countries: 1 f = 20s = 40d gros of Flanders = 60d gros of Brabant.

TOURNOIS, DENIER AND LIVRE
One of the two royal French systems of silver coinage and moneys-of-account. The denier tournois served as the 'link-money' for the latter, and had a value of $^4/s$ or 80 per cent of the parisis system (qv). The first royal denier tournois was struck by Philip II Augustus in 1205, probably at the town of Tours itself, just after his conquest of the surrounding La Touraine from King John (Lackland) of England. Evidently based upon the current tournoisien coinage, this denier of 1205 supposedly had a fineness of 3 deniers 18 grains argent-le-roy and a theoretical weight of 1.217 grams (= 192 taille to the marc de Tours of 233.60 grams). The obverse of this and the ensuing deniers tournois was stamped with the distinctive device of the 'châtel' or castle-turret historically associated with the patron St Martin of Tours; and it bore the inscription + TVRONVS CIVIS. As the Plantagenet holdings of Anjou-Maine and Normandy were reconquered – completely by 1215 – they received as their new royal French coinage the deniers tournois, which also spread elsewhere in France, wherever the denier parisis had not

been firmly established. Its primacy was finally established most assuredly by Louis ix's striking the heavy gros tournois (qv) in 1266. In royal monetary and fiscal administration, except for the accounts of the Trésor and the Hôtel du roi, the livre tournois came to be used almost exclusively from that time.

TOWER POUND
The standard or unit of mint-weight of England, as employed in the royal Tower Mint of London from perhaps the Norman Conquest (verifiably from 1247) until 1526. Supposedly once equal to $1^{1}/_{2}$ marks of Cologne (qv), in fact it came to weigh fractionally less: its 12 Tower ounces contained 5400 Troy grains = 11.25 Troy ounces = 349.9144 grams = 1.42967 marcs de Troyes = 1.4963 marks of Cologne.

TROY POUND of England
First mentioned in English parliamentary statutes of 1414, though not replacing the Tower pound as the official mint weight unit until 1526, it may have originally been based upon the French livre de Troyes (= 367.129 grams) of the Champagne fairs; but it weighs slightly more: 373.242 grams. It consists of 12 ounces, with 20 pennyweight (dwt) to the ounce, and 24 grains to the dwt, for a total of 5760 Troy grains; and the weight of the Troy grain thus = .0648 gram.

TROYES, LIVRE AND MARC DE. See POUND, and MARC DE TROYES

ZECCHINO. See DUCAT of Venice

SELECT BIBLIOGRAPHY

A. Blanchet and A. Dieudonné *Manuel de numismatique française* (Paris: Auguste Picard 1916) ii

Georges Bigwood *Le régime juridique et économique du commerce de l'argent dans la Belgique du moyen âge* Mémoires de l'Académie royale de Belgique 14 (Brussels 1921)

Marc Bloch *Esquisse d'une histoire monétaire de l'Europe* Cahiers des annales 9 (Paris; Armand Colin 1954)

Sir John Craig *The Mint: A History of the London Mint from AD 287 to 1948* (Cambridge: Cambridge University Press 1953)

J.A. Décourdemanche *Traité pratique des poids au moyen âge* (Paris: Leroux 1915)

Louis Deschamps de Pas *Essai sur l'histoire monétaire des comtes de Flandre de la maison de Bourgogne* (Paris 1863) from *Revue numismatique* 2nd ser, 6 (1861), 7 (1862), 11 (1866)

A. Dieudonné *Manuel des poids monétaires* (Paris 1925)

Arthur Engel and Raymond Serrure *Traité de numismatique du moyen âge* 3 vols (Paris: E. Leroux 1891–1905)

Sir Albert Feavearyear *The Pound Sterling: A History of English Money* (2nd ed, revised by E.V. Morgan, Oxford: Clarendon Press 1963)

Victor Gaillard *Recherches sur les monnaies des comtes de Flandre*, I: *Depuis les temps les plus reculés jusqu'au règne de Robert de Béthune inclusivement*; II: *Sous les règnes de Louis de Crécy et de Louis de Mâle* (Ghent: De H. Hoste 1852, 1856)

J. De Chestret de Haneffe *Numismatique de la principauté de Liège et de ses dépendances* (Brussels: Hayez 1890)

Jean Lafaurie *Les monnaies des rois de France*; I: *Hughes Capet à Louis XII*; II: *François Ier à Henri IV* (Paris: Emile Bourgey 1951, 1956)

Adolphe Landry *Essai économique sur les mutations des monnaies dans l'ancienne France de Philippe le Bel à Charles VII* (Paris: Honoré Champion 1910)

Robert S. Lopez 'Back to Gold, 1252' *Economic History Review* 2nd ser, 9 (1956) 219–40

– and I.W. Raymond (eds) *Medieval Trade in the Mediteranean World: Illustrative Documents* (New York: Columbia University Press 1955)

H.A. Miskimin *Money, Prices, and Foreign Exchange in Fourteenth-Century France* (New Haven: Yale University Press 1963)

John H. Munro *Wool, Cloth, and Gold: The Struggle for Bullion in Anglo-Burgundian Trade, c. 1340–1478* (Brussels: Editions de l'Université de Bruxelles, and Toronto: University of Toronto Press 1972)

– 'An Aspect of Medieval Public Finance: The profits of counterfeiting in the fifteenth-century Low Countries' *Revue belge de numismatique et de sigillographie* 118 (1972) 127–48

– '*Billon-billoen-billio*: From bullion to base coinage, an essay in numismatic philology' *Revue belge de philologie et d'histoire / Belgische Tijdschrift voor Filologie en Geschiedenis* 51 (1973)

Charles Oman *The Coinage of England* (Oxford: Clarendon Press 1931)

M. Prestwick 'Edward I's Monetary Policies and their Consequences' *Economic History Review* 2nd ser, 22 (1969) 406–16

G. Pusch *Staatliche Münz- und Geldpolitik in den Niederlanden unter den Burgundischen und Habsburgischen Herrschern, besonders unter Kaiser Karl V* (Munich 1932)

T.F. Reddaway 'The King's Mint and Exchange in London, 1343–1543' *English Historical Review* 82 (1967) 1–23

Rogers Ruding *Annals of the Coinage of Great Britain and its Dependencies* (London: John Hearne, 1840) I (3rd ed)

F. de Saulcey (ed) *Recueil de documents relatifs à l'histoire des monnaies frappées par les rois de France depuis Philippe II jusqu'à François Ier* (3 vols, Paris 1879–92)

Friedrich Schrötter *Wörterbuch der Münzkunde* (Berlin: Walter de Gruyter 1930)

W.A. Shaw *The History of Currency, 1252–1894* (London: Wilson and Milne 1895)

F.C. Spooner *The International Economy and Monetary Movements in France, 1493–1725* Harvard Economic Studies 138 (Cambridge, Mass. 1973)

Peter Spufford *Monetary Problems and Policies in the Burgundian Netherlands, 1433–1496* (Leiden: E.J. Brill 1970)

– 'Coinage, Taxation, and the Estates General of the Burgundian Netherlands' *Anciens pays et assemblées d'états / Standen en Landen* 40 (1966) 63–88

– 'Coinage and Currency' in M.M. Postan, E.E. Rich, and E. Miller (eds) *Cambridge*

Economic History of Europe; III: *Economic Organization and Policies in the Middle Ages* (Cambridge 1963) 576–602

J.D.A. Thompson *Inventory of British Coin Hoards, A.D. 600–1500* (Oxford: Royal Numismatic Society Publications, 1956)

– 'Continental Imitations of the Rose Noble of Edward IV' *British Numismatic Journal* 3rd ser 25 (1949) 183–208

H. Enno Van Gelder *De Nederlandse Munten* (Utrecht-Antwerp 1968)

– and Marcel Hoc *Les monnaies des Pays-Bas bourguignons et espagnols 1434–1713*: *répertoire général* (Amsterdam: J. Schulman 1960)

Herman Van der Wee *Growth of the Antwerp Market and the European Economy (fourteenth-sixteenth centuries)* (3 vols, The Hague: Martinus Nijhoff 1963)

Hans Van Werveke 'Monnaie de compte et monnaie réelle,' 'Munt en politiek: de Frans-Vlaamse verhoudingen vóór en na 1300,' 'Currency Manipulation in the Middle Ages: the Case of Louis de Mâle, Count of Flanders,' in *Miscellanea Medievalia* (Ghent: E. Storey-Scientia 1968)

F.A. Walters 'The Coinage of the Reign of Edward IV' *Numismatic Chronicle* 4th ser, 9 (1909) 132–219

MONEY AND COINAGE OF
THE AGE OF ERASMUS
APPENDIXES

A Gold coinage
B Silver coinage
C Purchasing power
D Prices of cloth
E Western European moneys-of-account

APPENDIX A

Gold Coinage

The weight, percentage fineness, and intrinsic gold contents of the gold coinages of France, the Burgundian-Hapsburg Low Countries, England, Italy, Austria, Hungary, Bavaria, the Rhineland Electors, Guelders, Utrecht, and Liège

gold coin	year first struck at given fineness and weight	weight in grams	percent fineness	grams fine gold	gold content as percent of 1496 St Philip florin
A FRANCE					
franc à cheval*	1423	3.059	100.00	3.059	139.05
salut	1433	3.496	100.00	3.496	158.91
écu à la couronne*	1461	3.447	96.35	3.321	150.95
écu à la couronne	1474	3.399	96.35	3.275	148.86
écu au soleil	1475	3.496	96.35	3.369	153.14
écus of Guienne, Brittany, & Savoy				4.298*	195.38
B ENGLAND					
Henricus noble	1412	6.998	99.48	6.962	316.45
angel	1465	5.184	99.48	5.157	234.41
angelet	1465	2.592	99.48	2.578	117.18
ryal, royal, or rose noble	1465	7.776	99.48	7.735	351.59
sovereign*	1489	15.552	99.48	15.471	703.23
C BURGUNDIAN-HAPSBURG LOW COUNTRIES					
clinquaert	1425	3.653	70.83	2.588	117.64
clinquaert	1431	3.599	62.50	2.249	102.23
noble	1428	6.943	97.92	6.798	309.00
demi-noble	1428	3.472	97.92	3.399	154.50
pieter	1433	3.600	75.00	2.700	122.73
philippus or cavalier (rijder)	1433	3.626	99.22	3.598	163.55
lion (leeuw)	1454	4.257	95.83	4.079	185.41
florin of St Andrew	1466	3.399	79.17	2.692	122.36
grand réal (royal) of Austria	1487	14.834	99.17	14.710	668.64
noble of Burgundy = demi-réal	1487	7.417	99.17	7.355	334.32
ducat of Burgundy = demi-noble = quarter-royal	1487	3.708	99.17	3.677	167.14
demi-noble	1489	3.400	95.20	3.237	147.14
florin of St Philip	1496	3.300	66.67	2.200	100.00

The values of these gold coinages in terms of silver gros of Flanders, livres tournois of France, and pence sterling of England, according to Archduke Philip the Fair's proclamation for the Low Countries of April 1493, and the English schedule of official exchange rates at the Calais staple for 1499–1500

| gold coin | value in Flemish gros | | Flemish gros | values in 1500 | |
	April 1493	1496–9		French livres tournois	English pence sterling
A FRANCE					
franc à cheval*	53	65	68	1.656	48
salut	60	73	76	1.875	54
écu à la couronne*	57	69	72	1.781	51
écu à la couronne	56	68$^{1}/_{2}$	71	1.750	50
écu au soleil	58	71	74	1.813	51
écus of Guienne,					
Brittany, & Savoy	74	90$^{1}/_{2}$	94	2.313	67
B ENGLAND					
Henricus noble	120	147	153	3.750	108
angel	91	111	116	2.844	80
angelet	45$^{1}/_{2}$	55$^{1}/_{2}$	58	1.406	40
ryal, royal, or					
rose noble	136	166	173	4.250	120
sovereign*	272	332	346	8.500	240
C BURGUNDIAN-HAPSBURG LOW COUNTRIES					
clinquaert	44	54	56	1.438	39
clinquaert	38	46$^{1}/_{2}$	48	1.250	33
noble	116	142	148	3.625	102
demi-noble	58	71	74	1.813	51
pieter	46	56	59	1.500	40
philippus or					
cavalier (rijder)	62	76	79	1.938	54
lion (leeuw)	72	88	92	2.250	63
florin of St Andrew	48	59	61	1.500	42
grand réal (royal)					
of Austria	288	352	367	9.000	260
noble of Burgundy =					
demi-réal	144	176	183	4.500	130
ducat of Burgundy = demi-noble =					
quarter-royal	72	88	92	2.250	65
demi-noble	58	71	74	1.719	51
florin of St Philip	–	48	50	1.225	36

gold coin	year first struck at given fineness and weight	weight in grams	percent fineness	grams fine gold	gold content as percent of 1496 St Philip florin
toison d'or	1496	4.490	99.17	4.453	202.41
florin of St Philip	1500	3.300	66.33	2.189	99.50
D ITALY AND THE HOLY ROMAN EMPIRE					
florin of Florence	1252	3.536	100.00	3.536	160.73
genovino of Genoa	1252	3.560	100.00	3.560	161.82
ducat of Venice	1284	3.559	100.00	3.559	161.77
ducat of Hungary	(c 1308–42)†	3.536	100.00	3.536	160.73
florin of the Rhine (of Four Electors)	1490	3.278	77.08	2.527	114.86
Johannes florin**				2.527*– 2.392*	114.86– 108.73
florin of Bavaria**				1.740*	79.09
imperial florin of Austria				2.204*	100.18
Guillermus florin**				2.784*	126.54
Fredericus florin of Utrecht**				1.914*	87.00
florin of Guelders**				2.320*	105.46
Arnoldus florin of Guelders**				1.392*	63.27
old postulaat florins of Liège	(1419–55)	3.138	50.00	1.569– 1.392*	71.32– 63.27
new postulaat florin of Liège				1.044*	47.44
postulaat de Bourbon of Liège	(1456–82)	2.331	62.50*	1.457*	66.23
pieter *forgié*				3.480*	158.18
pieter of Guelders				2.088*	94.91
pieter-florin of Liège	(1456–82)	3.496	68.06	2.380	108.18

NOTES

*estimated: 1/ The franc à cheval, the écu à la couronne of 1461, the sovereign, and the first of the old postulaat florins of Liège were not listed in either ordinance and their values have been calculated according to their relative gold contents. 2/ The gold contents of the other coins marked with a single asterisk, coins which were listed in one or both of the ordinances, have been estimated according to their relative silver prices on the assumption that they, like the other coins listed, except the very best and most recent, were priced at only 96.70% of their intrinsic gold values.

**These gold coins had evidently undergone debasement between 1493 and 1499.

†The Hungarian ducat of this fineness and weight was first struck in the reign of Charles Robert (1308–42).

| | value in Flemish gros | | Flemish gros | values in 1500 | |
gold coin	April 1493	1496–9		French livres tournois	English pence sterling
toison d'or	–	96	100	2.453	72
florin of St Philip	–	–	50	1.225	36
D ITALY AND THE HOLY ROMAN EMPIRE					
florin of Florence	62	76	79	1.938	55
genovino of Genoa	62	76	79	1.938	55
ducat of Venice	62	76	79	1.938	55
ducat of Hungary	62	76	79	1.938	55
florin of the Rhine (of Four Electors)	46	56	58	1.438	41
Johannes florin**	46	53	55	1.319–	38–
florin of Bavaria**	30	37	38	.938	28
imperial florin of Austria	38	46$^{1}/_{2}$	48	1.188	34
Guillermus florin**	48	59	61$^{1}/_{2}$	1.500	42
Fredericus florin of Utrecht**	33	40	42	1.031	29
florin of Guelders**	40	49	51	1.250	35
Arnoldus florin of Guelders**	24	25	26	.625	18
old postulaat florins of Liège	27*– 24	33*– 29	34*– 30	.845*– .750	23*– 21
new postulaat florin of Liège	18	22	23	.563	16
postulaat de Bourbon of Liège	25	31	32	.764	22
pieter *forgié*	60	73	76	1.875	53
pieter of Guelders	36	44	46	1.125	32
pieter-florin of Liège	41	49	51	1.215	35

SOURCES

Archduke Philip the Fair's coinage ordinance of April 1493, for the Burgundian-Hapsburg Low Countries, in Louis Gilliodts-van Severen (ed) *Inventaire des archives de la ville de Bruges* VI (Bruges 1878) 377, no 1246

Flemish copy of an official English schedule of exchange rates at the Calais staple, 'valuaere van den ghelde zoe men betaelen moet, naer de tafel van Calis den jaere voorscreven (1499–1500),' in Algemeen Rijksarchief (België), Rekenkamer no 1158, f 226–7

Particulars of the fineness, weights, and the years of initial striking: see the Select Bibliography, pages 332–3.)

APPENDIX B
SILVER COINAGE

The fineness, weight, intrinsic silver contents, and values in deniers
tournois, gros, and sterling of the silver coinages of France, the
Burgundian-Hapsburg Low Countries, and England in the days of Erasmus

silver coin	titre out of 12 deniers argent-le-roy	per cent pure silver	taille to the marc de Troyes	weight in grams	grams pure silver content
A FRANCE 1488–1519					
gros de roi	11d 12g	91.84	69	3.547	3.258
grand blanc au					
soleil (treizain)	4d 12g	35.94	78^{1}/$_{2}$	3.118	1.120
grand blanc à la					
couronne (douzain)	4d 12g	35.94	86	2.846	1.023
karolus = dizain	4d	31.94	92^{1}/$_{2}$	2.646	.845
demi-blanc = sizain	4d 12g	35.94	172	1.423	.511
demi-karolus	4d	31.94	185	1.323	.423
hardi, liard	3d	23.96	234	1.046	.251
double tournois	1d 12g	11.98	182	1.345	.161
denier tournois	1d	7.99	252	.971	.078
maille tournois[1]	15g	4.99	300	.816	.039
denier parisis	1d 3g	8.98	220	1.113	.100
B BURGUNDIAN-HAPSBURG LOW COUNTRIES (1496–1521)					
toison d'argent	11d	87.85	72	3.399	2.986
double patard	8d	63.89	79	3.098	1.979
patard, stuiver[2]	4d	31.94	79	3.098	.990
gros, groot	3d 6g	25.95	134	1.827	.474
demi-gros	2d 16g	21.30	224	1.093	.232
quarter-gros	1d 20g	14.64	316	.775	.113
quatre-mites	12g	3.99	162	1.511	.060
double mite	8g	2.66	227	1.078	.029
C ENGLAND[3] (1464–1526)					
groat	11d 14g	92.50	78^{1}/$_{2}$	3.110	2.877
half-groat	11d 14g	92.50	157	1.555	1.438
penny	11d 14g	92.50	315	.778	.720
halfpenny	11d 14g	92.50	630	.389	.360
farthing	11d 14g	92.50	1260	.194	.180

NOTES

1 The maille tournois was last struck in September 1483, before the debasement of 1488.

2 From May 1499 the mint masters at Bruges and Antwerp were cutting 80 instead of 79
patards (double groots) from the marc de Troyes, of the same silver fineness, thus
reducing the patard's weight to 3.059 g and its fine silver content to .977 g. But the coin's
official value remained the same, and no other coin was altered in any respect.

3 The English mint standards of fineness (11 oz 2 dwt per pound of silver) and of the Tower
pound weights have been converted to the French argent-le-roy and marc de Troyes
standards to facilitate comparison

silver coin	value in deniers		
	French tournois	Flemish gros	English sterling
A FRANCE 1488–1519			
gros de roi	36	6.19	4.22
grand blanc au soleil (treizain)	13	2.24	1.53
grand blanc à la couronne (douzain)	12	2.06	1.41
karolus = dizain	10	1.72	1.17
demi-blanc = sizain	6	1.03	.70
demi-karolus	5	.86	.59
hardi, liard	3	.52	.35
double tournois	2	.34	.23
denier tournois	1	.17	.12
maille tournois[1]	1/2	.08	.06
denier parisis	1 1/4	.20	.14
B BURGUNDIAN- HAPSBURG LOW COUNTRIES (1496–1521)			
toison d'argent	34.88	6	4.12
double patard	23.25	4	2.75
patard, stuiver[2]	11.63	2	1.38
gros, groot	5.81	1	.69
demi-gros	2.91	1/2	.34
quarter-gros	1.45	1/4	.17
quatre-mites	.97	1/6	.11
double mite	.48	1/12	.06
C ENGLAND[3] (1464–1526)			
groat	33.82	5.82	4
half-groat	16.90	2.91	2
penny	8.45	1.45	1
halfpenny	4.23	.73	1/2
farthing	2.11	.36	1/4

SOURCES

See the select Bibliography, pages 332–3.

APPENDIX C

THE PURCHASING POWER OF COINAGE IN THE DAYS OF ERASMUS

Quantities of common commodities that could be purchased by the current silver coinages of France, the Burgundian-Hapsburg Low Countries, and England, and by the chief current gold coins, according to their current prices in Flemish gros in Lier, Brussels, Malines, and Antwerp, 1498–1500

coin	nominal value in	value in Flemish gros	red Rhine wine (litres = 35 oz) Easter 1498	Easter 1499	Easter 1500	butter (pounds) May 1498–9	May 1499–1500	May 1500–1
A SILVER COINS								
France	*tournois*							
douzain	12d	2.06	.65	.65	.84	1.61	1.60	1.53
sizain	6d	1.03	.33	.33	.42	.80	.80	.76
hardi, liard	3d	.52	.16	.16	.21	.41	.40	.38
denier tournois	1d	.17	.05	.05	.07	.13	.13	.13
Burgundian-Hapsburg Low Countries	*gros*							
double patard	4d	4.00	1.26	1.26	1.62	3.13	3.10	2.97
patard, stuiver	2d	2.00	.63	.63	.81	1.56	1.55	1.48
gros, groot	1d	1.00	.32	.32	.41	.78	.78	.74
demi-gros	12m	.50	.16	.16	.20	.39	.39	.37
quarter-gros	6m	.25	.08	.08	.10	.19	.19	.18
England	*sterling*							
groat	4d	5.82	1.84	1.84	2.36	4.55	4.51	4.32
half-groat	2d	2.91	.92	.92	1.18	2.27	2.26	2.16
penny	1d	1.45	.46	.46	.59	1.13	1.12	1.08
halfpenny	1/2d	.73	.23	.23	.30	.57	.56	.54
farthing	1/4d	.36	.11	.11	.15	.28	.28	.27

coin	nominal value in	1498–9	1500	Easter 1498	Easter 1499	Easter 1500	May 1498–9	May 1499–1500	May 1500–1
B GOLD COINS									
France	*tournois*								
écu à la couronne	£1 15 0	68½	71	21.62	21.62	28.80	53.52	53.10	52.67
écu au soleil	£1 16 3	71	74	22.40	22.40	30.02	55.47	55.04	54.90
Burgundian-Hapsburg Low Countries	*gros*								
Philippus	6s 4d	76	79	23.98	23.98	32.05	59.38	58.91	58.61
florin St Philippe	4s 0d	48	50	15.15	15.15	20.28	37.50	37.21	37.09
toison d'or	8s 0d	96	100	30.29	30.29	40.57	75.00	74.42	74.18
England	*sterling*								
angel	6s 8d	111	116	35.03	35.03	47.06	86.72	86.05	86.05
ryal	10s 0d	166	173	52.38	52.38	70.18	129.69	128.68	128.34
Other									
Rhenish florin		56	58	17.67	17.67	23.53	43.75	43.41	43.03
Italian florin & ducat		76	79	24.00	24.00	32.10	59.37	58.92	58.70

salt beef (pounds)			Flemish smoked red herrings (number)			eggs (number)		
Nov. 1498	Nov. 1499	Nov. 1500	Lent 1498	Lent 1499	Lent 1500	May 1497–8	May 1498–9	May 1499–1500
2.56	2.56	2.44	10.30	8.73	10.73	22	20	21
1.28	1.28	1.22	5.15	4.36	5.36	11	10	11
.64	.64	.61	2.60	2.20	2.70	5	5	5
.21	.21	.20	.85	.72	.89	2	2	2
4.97	4.97	4.73	20.00	16.95	20.83	42	39	42
2.48	2.48	2.36	10.00	8.47	10.42	21	20	21
1.24	1.24	1.18	5.00	4.24	5.21	11	10	10
.62	.62	.59	2.50	2.12	2.60	5	5	5
.31	.31	.30	1.25	1.06	1.30	3	2	2
7.23	7.23	6.88	29.10	24.66	30.31	62	57	61
3.61	3.61	3.44	14.55	12.33	15.16	31	28	30
1.80	1.80	1.71	7.25	6.14	7.55	15	14	15
.90	.90	.86	3.65	3.09	3.80	8	7	7
.45	.45	.43	1.80	1.53	1.88	4	3	4
85.04	85.04	83.94	342.50	290.30	369.80	728	674	741
88.14	88.14	87.49	355.00	300.80	385.40	755	698	772
94.35	94.35	93.40	380.00	322.00	411.50	808	747	825
59.59	59.59	59.12	240.00	203.40	260.40	510	472	522
119.18	119.18	118.23	480.00	406.80	520.80	1020	944	1044
137.80	137.80	137.15	555.00	470.30	604.20	1180	1091	1211
206.08	206.08	204.54	830.00	703.40	901.00	1764	1632	1806
69.52	69.52	68.57	280.00	237.30	302.10	595	551	605
94.35	94.35	93.55	380.00	322.00	412.10	808	748	826

	loaf sugar (pounds)			tallow candles (pounds)		
coin	Oct. 1498	Oct. 1499	Oct. 1500	autumn 1498	autumn 1499	autumn 1500
A SILVER COINS						
France						
douzain	.40	.50	.53	1.07	1.12	1.14
sizain	.20	.25	.27	.53	.56	.57
hardi, liard	.10	.13	.13	.27	.28	.29
denier tournois	.03	.04	.04	.09	.09	.09
Burgundian-Hapsburg Low Countries						
double patard	.78	.98	1.04	2.07	2.18	2.21
patard, stuiver	.39	.49	.52	1.03	1.09	1.10
gros, groot	.19	.24	.26	.52	.55	.55
demi-gros	.10	.12	.13	.26	.27	.28
quarter-gros	.05	.06	.06	.13	.13	.14
England						
groat	1.13	1.42	1.51	3.01	3.18	3.21
half-groat	.57	.71	.75	1.50	1.59	1.61
penny	.28	.35	.38	.75	.79	.80
halfpenny	.14	.18	.19	.38	.40	.40
farthing	.07	.09	.09	.19	.20	.20
B GOLD COINS						
France						
écu à la couronne	13.32	16.70	18.39	35.42	37.37	39.16
écu au soleil	13.81	17.32	19.17	36.71	38.73	40.82
Burgundian-Hapsburg Low Countries						
Philippus	14.78	18.53	20.47	39.30	41.46	43.57
florin St Philippe	9.33	11.70	12.95	24.82	26.19	27.58
toison d'or	18.67	23.41	25.91	49.64	52.37	55.16
England						
angel	21.59	27.07	30.05	57.39	60.56	63.98
ryal	32.28	40.49	44.82	85.83	90.56	95.42
Other						
Rhenish florin	10.89	13.66	15.03	28.96	30.55	31.99
Italian florin & ducat	14.78	18.53	20.50	39.30	41.47	43.64

All the prices of the commodities were given in gros of Brabant, which have been converted into Flemish gros at the ratio of 1.5:1 (or 1d gros of Brabant = ^{2}/3d gros of Flanders). All the pound weights in the table are expressed in the English pound avoirdupois = 453.593 grams.

1   Red Rhine wine: as sold at Lier, Brabant, by the gelte = 2.840 litres. 1 litre = .88039 imperial quart, or approximately 35 oz (which today is a common-sized bottle for *vin de table*)
2   Butter: as sold in Brussels by the pond of Brussels = 467.670 grams = 1.03103 lb avoir-dupois
3   Salt Beef: as sold at Mechelen (Malines) by the pond of Mechelen = 469.247 grams = 1.03451 lb avoirdupois
4   Dry smoked Flemish red herrings: as sold at Brussels and Mechelen by the stroo of 500 herrings
5   Eggs: as sold at Brussels, by the hundred
6   Loaf-sugar: as sold at Antwerp by the pond of Antwerp = 470.156 grams = 1.03652 lb avoirdupois
7   Tallow Candles: as sold at Brussels, Lier, Antwerp, and Mechelen by the pond of each city; the pound units have been averaged at 469.02 grams for these calculations, which = 1.03402 lb avoirdupois.

SOURCES

1   Commodity prices and quantities are calculated from: Herman van der Wee *The Growth of the Antwerp Market and the European Economy, fourteenth–sixteenth centuries* I (The Hague 1963), 298, 214, 226, 285, 207, 320, and 252, respectively.
2   Coinage values: see appendices A and B.

APPENDIX D

Prices of luxury woollen cloths, 30 ells long, in the Burgundian-Hapsburg Low Countries, as purchased for the civic alderman of Mechelen, Ghent, and Ypres

type of cloth and town of manufacture	year	florins of St Philip (1496)	livres gros of Flanders	livres tournois of France	pounds sterling of England
A MECHELEN (MALINES)[1]					
black Rooslaken	1498	52.080	10.416	60.480	7.161
black Rooslaken	1499	47.105	9.421	54.703	6.477
black Rooslaken	1500	45.700	9.521	55.283	6.546
B GHENT[2]					
for civic functions					
black Dickedinnen	1498	73.335	14.667	85.163	10.084
black Dickedinnen	1499	73.335	14.667	85.163	10.084
black Dickedinnen	1500	70.402	14.667	85.163	10.084
for the festival of Onse Lieve Vrouw of Tournay					
dark-blue Dickedinnen	1498	58.250	11.650	67.645	8.009
dark-blue Dickedinnen	1499	60.000	12.000	69.677	8.250
blue Dickedinnen	1500	56.400	11.750	68.226	8.078
blue Helleman	1498	47.500	9.500	55.161	6.531
dark-green Helleman	1499	47.500	9.500	55.161	6.531
blue Helleman	1500	45.360	9.450	54.871	6.497
green Strijpte Laken	1498	57.500	11.500	66.774	7.906
dark-blue Strijpte Laken	1499	55.000	11.000	63.871	7.563
green Strijpte Laken	1500	52.800	11.000	63.871	7.563
C IEPER (YPRES)[3]					
black Dickedinnen	1498	62.000	12.400	72.000	8.525

1 Cloths of Mechelen: 30 ells long = 20.670 metres = 67.816 ft. = 22.605 yards
2 Cloths of Ghent: 30 ells long = 21.000 metres = 68.898 ft. = 22.966 yards
3 Cloths of Ieper: 30 ells long = 21.000 metres = 68.898 ft. = 22.966 yards (apparently)
The widths of these cloths, dyed and finished, averaged 2¹/₂ ells (10 quarters) = 5.742 ft. = 1.914 yds = 1.750 metres.
The cloths were all priced in terms of the silver-based livre gros of Flanders. The ratios of the monies-of-account in terms of their silver contents, as used in this table, are: £1.000 gros of Flanders = £5.80645 tournois of France = £0.68750 sterling of England.

SOURCES

Mechelen Stadsarchief Mechelen, Stadsrekeningen 1497–8 tot 1499–1500, nos 173–5; and Algemeen Rijksarchief (België), Rekenkamer nos 41, 278–80
Ghent Stadsarchief Gent, Stadsrekeningen 1497–8 tot 1499–1500, nos 400:33–4
Ieper Algemeen Rijksarchief (België), Rekenkamer, no 38,721, f 47ʳ

APPENDIX E
WESTERN EUROPEAN MONEYS-OF-ACCOUNT IN THE DAYS OF ERASMUS

A money-of-account was simply an accounting system of reckoning, of recording payments. Virtually all of the moneys-of-account used in western Europe in this era, and indeed in Great Britain until very recently, were based upon, and strictly tied to, the current silver denier or penny of the country, and had the following fixed subdivisions: £1 (livre, pond, pound, Pfund) = 20s (Sols, sous, schellingen, shillings) = 240 d (deniers, penningen, pence), with thus 12d to the shilling.

1   ENGLAND used only one money-of-account, the pound sterling, but commonly also employed the mark, which equalled 13s 4d sterling, or two-thirds of a pound, as a monetary unit.

2   FRANCE used two systems of money-of-account: 1 livre tournois = 16s or $^4/_5$ livre parisis*

3   THE BURGUNDIAN-HAPSBURG LOW COUNTRIES used several moneys-of-account which had the following fixed relations: £10s 0d gros (groot) of Flanders = £110s 0d groot of Brabant (from 1434) = £6 0s 0d Artois, or livres de quarante gros = £12 0s 0d parisis.* The Flemish gros also had the following subdivisions: 1d gros of Flanders = 3 esterlins (ingelschen) = 24 mites. In parts of Brabant and of the eastern Low Countries, the Rijnsgulden (Florin of the Four Electors of the Rhine) became the basis of a common money-of-account; and around 1460 its value as a money-of-account became strictly tied to the current silver gros of Flanders, with its relation to the true gold coin thus fully severed; and in this 'petrified' form it was precisely equal to the livre d'Artois or livre de 40 gros: 1 gulden (Guilder, f) = 20 stuivers (s) = 40 gros of Flanders ($^1/_6$ pond groot of Flanders) = 60 gros of Brabant ($^1/_4$ pond groot of Brabant). 1 stuiver or patard = 2d gros Flemish = 3d gros Brabant.

---

*   The French and Flemish livres parisis were not related to each other at this time, and had not been since the early fourteenth century. See the glossary.

TABLE OF CORRESPONDENTS

BIBLIOGRAPHY

LIST OF ABBREVIATIONS

SHORT TITLE FORMS

INDEX

TABLE OF CORRESPONDENTS

BIBLIOGRAPHY

This bibliography lists articles and books referred to in the introductions and footnotes to letters 1–141. For Erasmus' writings, see the short-title list, pages 357–60.

P.S. Allen 'Hieronymus Balbus in Paris' EHR 27 (1902) 416–28

P.S. Allen, H.M. Allen, and H.W. Garrod eds *Opus Epistolarum Des. Erasmi Roterodami* (Oxford 1906–58) [Allen]

T.C. Appelt *Studies in the Content and Sources of Erasmus's 'Adagia'* (Chicago 1942)

R.H. Bainton *Erasmus of Christendom* (New York 1969)

F. Bierlaire 'Erasme et Augustin Vincent Caminade' BHR 2(1968) 357–62

P.J. Blok *History of the People of the Netherlands* (New York 1970)

La Correspondance d'Erasme (Brussels and Québec 1967–)

P. DeBongnie 'Corneille Gérard à Saint-Victor' NAKG 17 (1923) 161ff

P. Debongnie *Jean Mombaer de Bruxelles* (Louvain 1918)

P. Debongnie *Jean Mombaer de Bruxelles, abbé de Livry, ses écrits, ses réformes* (Louvain 1927)

P.A. Duhamel 'The Oxford Lectures of John Colet' *JHI* 14 (1953) 493–510

Erasmus *Desiderii Erasmi Roterodami Opera Omnia* (Leiden 1703–6) 10 vols [LB]

Erasmus *Opera Omnia Desiderii Erasmi Roterodami* (Amsterdam 1969–) [ASD]

M. Félibien *Histoire de la ville de Paris* II (Paris 1755)

W.K. Ferguson ed *Erasmi Opuscula: A Supplement to the Opera Omnia* (The Hague 1933)

E. Garin *Giovanni Pico della Mirandola* (Florence 1937)

R. Giese 'Erasmus' Knowledge and Estimate of the Vernacular Languages' *The Romanic Review* 28 (1937) 3–18

M. Godet 'La Congrégation de Montaigu, 1490–1580' *Bibliothèque de l'Ecole des Hautes-Etudes* 198 (Paris 1912)

E.H. Harbison *The Christian Scholar in the Age of the Reformation* (New York 1956)

A. Hyma *The Christian Renaissance* (New York 1924)

A. Hyma *The Youth of Erasmus* (Ann Arbor 1930)

S. Jayne *John Colet and Marsilio Ficino* (Oxford 1963)

P.O. Kristeller 'Two Unpublished Letters to Erasmus' *Renaissance News* 14 (1961) 6–9

J.H. Lupton *Life of John Colet* (London 1887, 2nd ed 1909)

J.D. Mackie *The Earlier Tudors 1485–1538* (Oxford 1952)

P. Mestwerdt *Die Anfänge des Erasmus* (Leipzig 1917)

L. Miles *John Colet and the Platonic Tradition* (La Salle, Indiana, 1961)

P.C. Molhuysen *Cornelius Aurelius: Kort schets van zijn leven en werken* (Leiden 1902), reprinted from NAKG ns 2(1902–3) 1–15

F.M. Nichols trans *The Epistles of Erasmus* (London 1901–18) 3 vols

M.M. Phillips trans and ed *The Adages of Erasmus* (Cambridge 1964)

H.C. Porter ed and D.F.S. Thomson trans *Erasmus and Cambridge: The Cambridge Letters of Erasmus* (Toronto 1963)

C. Reedijk *Poems of Desiderius Erasmus* (Leiden 1956)

A. Renaudet *Erasme et l'Italie* (Geneva 1954)

A. Renaudet 'Jean Standonck, un réformateur catholique avant la Réforme' in his *Humanisme et Renaissance* (Geneva 1958)

A. Renaudet *Préréforme et humanisme à Paris, 1494–1517* (Paris 1953)

V. Rossi *Il Quattrocento* (Milan 1933)

G. Saitta *L'educazione dell' umanesimo in Italia* (Venice 1928)

V. Scholderer 'Rutgerus Sicamber and His Writings' *Gutenberg-Jahrbuch* (1957) 129–30

F. Simone 'Roberto Gaguin ed il suo cenacolo umanistico' *Aevum: Rassegna di scienze storiche, linguistiche e filologiche* 13 (1939) 410–75

L.W. Spitz *The Religious Renaissance of the German Humanists* (Cambridge, Mass. 1963)

C.R. Thompson *The Colloquies of Erasmus* (Chicago 1965)

D.F.S. Thomson 'Erasmus as Poet in the Context of Northern Humanism' *De Gulden Passer* 47 (1969) 187–210

D.F.S. Thomson 'The Latinity of Erasmus' in *Erasmus* ed T.A. Dorey (London 1970) 115–37

L. Thuasne ed *Roberti Gaguini epistolae et orationes* (Paris 1903)

M. van Rijn 'Engelbert van Leiden' NAKG ns 20 (1927) 289ff

E. Walser *Poggius Florentinus: Leben und Werke* (Leipzig 1914)

ABBREVIATIONS

ASD	*Opera Omnia Desiderii Erasmi Roterodami* (Amsterdam 1969–) edition in progress
Allen	P.S. Allen, H.M. Allen, and H.W. Garrod eds *Opus Epistolarum Des. Erasmi Roterodami* (Oxford 1906–58)
BHR	*Bibliothèque d'Humanisme et Renaissance*
CWE	The Collected Works of Erasmus
Correspondance	*La Correspondance d'Erasme* (Brussels and Québec 1967–) edition in progress
EHR	*English Historical Review*
E & C	H.C. Porter ed and D.F.S. Thomson trans *Erasmus and Cambridge: The Cambridge Letters of Erasmus* (Toronto 1963)
Emden BRUO	A.B. Emden *Biographical Register of the University of Oxford to 1600* (Oxford 1957–9) 3 vols
LB	J. Leclerc ed *Desiderii Erasmi Roterodami Opera Omnia* (Leiden 1703–6) 10 vols
JHI	*Journal of the History of Ideas*
NAKG	Nederlands Archief voor Kerkgeschiedenis
Nichols	F.M. Nichols trans *The Epistles of Erasmus* (London 1901–18) 3 vols
NK	Nijhoff and Kronenberg eds *Nederlandsche Bibliographie van 1500 tot 1540*
Opuscula	W.K. Ferguson ed *Erasmi Opuscula: A Supplement to the Opera Omnia* (The Hague 1933)
Reedijk	C. Reedijk ed *Poems of Desiderius Erasmus* (Leiden 1956)
STC	Pollard and Redgrave *Short title Catalogue of Books printed in England, Scotland, and Ireland and of English Books printed abroad, 1475–1640*

SHORT TITLE FORMS FOR ERASMUS' WORKS

Acta contra Lutherum: Acta academiae Lovaniensis contra Lutherum
Adagia (Adagiorum Collectanea for the primitive form, when required)
Admonitio adversus mendacium: Admonitio adversus mendacium et obtrec-
tationem
Annotationes de haereticis: Annotationes in leges pontificias et caesareas de
haereticis
Annotationes in Novum Testamentum
Antibarbari
Apologia ad Fabrum: Apologia ad Iacobum Fabrum Stapulensem
Apologia ad Carranza: Apologia ad Sanctium Carranza
Apologia adversus Petrum Sutorem: Apologia adversus debacchationes Petri
Sutoris
Apologia adversus monachos: Apologia adversus monachos quosdam hispanos
Apologia adversus rhapsodias Alberti Pii
Apologia contra Latomi dialogum: Apologia contra Iacobi Latomi dialogum de
tribus linguis
Apologia contra Stunicam:Apologia contra Lopidem Stunicam
Apologia de 'In principio erat sermo'
Apologia de laude matrimonii: Apologia pro declamatione de laude matrimonii
Apologia de loco 'omnes quidem': Apologia de loco 'Omnes quidem resurgemus'
Apologiae duae
Apologiae omnes
Apologia invectivis Lei: Apologia qua respondet duabus invectivis Eduardi Lei
Apologia monasticae religionis
Apophthegmata
Argumenta: Argumenta in omnes epistolas apostolicas nova
Axiomata pro causa Lutheri: Axiomata pro causa Martini Lutheri

Carmina
Catalogus lucubrationum
Cato
Christiani hominis institutum
Ciceronianus: Dialogus Ciceronianus
Colloquia
Compendium rhetorices
Conflictus: Conflictus Thaliae et barbariei

De bello turcico: Consultatio de bello turcico
De civilitate: De civilitate morum puerilium
De conscribendis epistolis
De constructione: De constructione octo partium orationis
De contemptu mundi
De copia: De duplici copia verborum ac rerum
Declamatio de morte
Declamationes

Declamatiuncula
Declamatiunculae
Declarationes ad censuras Lutetiae: Declarationes ad censuras Lutetiae vulgates
De concordia: De sarcienda ecclesiae concordia
De immensa Dei misericordia: Concio de immensa Dei misericordia
De libero arbitrio: De libero arbitrio diatribe
De praeparatione: De praeparatione ad mortem
De pronuntiatione: De recta latini graecique sermonis pronuntiatione
De pueris instituendis: De pueris statim ac liberaliter instituendis
De puero Iesu: Concio de puero Iesu
De puritate tabernaculi
De ratione studii
Detectio praestigiarum: Detectio praestigiarum cuiusdam libelli germanice scripti
De tedio Iesu: Disputatiuncula de tedio, pavore, tristicia Iesu
Dilutio: Dilutio eorum quae Iodocus Clichthoueus scripsit adversus declamationem
    suasoriam matrimonii

Ecclesiastes: Ecclesiastes sive de ratione concionandi
Enchiridion: Enchiridion militis christiani
Encomium matrimonii
Encomium medicinae: Declamatio in laudem artis medicae
Epigrammata
Epistola ad fratres: Epistola ad fratres Inferioris Germaniae
Epistola consolatoria: Epistola consolatoria in adversis
Epistola contra pseudevangelicos: Epistola contra quosdam qui se falso iactant
    evangelicos
Epistola de apologia Cursii: Epistola de apologia Petri Cursii
Epistola de esu carnium: Epistola apologetica ad Christophorum episcopum
    Basiliensem de interdicto esu carnium
Epistola de modestia: Epistola de modestia profitendi linguas
Exomologesis: Exomologesis sive modus confitendi
Explanatio symboli: Explanatio symboli apostolorum sive catechismus

Formulae: Conficiendarum epistolarum formulae

Hyperaspistes

Institutio christiani matrimonii
Institutio principis christiani

Julius exclusus: Dialogus Julius exclusus e coelis

Liber quo respondet annotationibus Lei: Liber quo respondet annotationibus
    Eduardi Lei
Lingua
Liturgia Virginis Matris: Virginis Matris apud Lauretum cultae liturgia
Lucubrationes
Lucubratiunculae

Methodus
Modus orandi Deum
Moria: Moriae encomium, or Moria

Novum instrumentum
Novum Testamentum

Obsecratio ad Virginem Mariam: Obsecratio sive oratio ad Virginem Mariam in
  rebus adversis
Oratio de pace: Oratio de pace et discordia
Oratio de virtute: Oratio de virtute amplectenda
Oratio funebris: Oratio funebris Berthae de Heyen

Paean Virgini Matri: Paean Virgini Matri dicendus
Panegyricus: Panegyricus ad Philippum Austriae ducem
Parabolae: Parabolae sive similia
Paraclesis
Paraphrasis in Elegantias Vallae: Paraphrasis in Elegantias Laurentii Vallae
Paraphrases in Novum Testamentum
Paraphrasis in Matthaeum: Paraphrasis in Matthaeum, etc.
Peregrinatio apostolorum: Peregrinatio apostolorum Petri et Pauli
Precatio ad Virginis filium Iesum
Precatio dominica
Precationes
Precatio pro pace ecclesiae: Precatio ad Iesum pro pace ecclesiae
Progymnasmata: Progymnasmata quaedam primae adolescentiae Erasmi
Psalmi: Psalmi (Enarrationes sive commentarii in psalmos)
Purgatio adversus epistolam Lutheri: Purgatio adversus epistolam non sobriam
  Lutheri

Querela pacis

Ratio verae theologiae
Responsio ad annotationes Lei: Responsio ad annotationes Eduardi Lei
Responsio ad annotationem Stunicae: Responsio ad annotationem Iacobi Lopis
  Stunicae
Responsio ad collationes: Responsio ad collationes cuiusdam iuvenis gerontodidas-
  cali
Responsio ad disputationem de diuortio: Responsio ad disputationem cuiusdam
  Phimostomi de diuortio
Responsio ad epistolam apologeticam: Responsio ad fratres Germaniae Inferioris ad
  epistolam apologeticam incerto autore proditam
Responsio ad epistolam Pii: Responsio ad epistolam paraeneticam Alberti Pii
Responsio adversus febricitantis libellum: Responsio adversus febricitantis cuius-
  dam libellum
Responsio contra Egranum: Responsio apologetica contra Sylvium Egranum

Spongia: Spongia adversus aspergines Hutteni

Supputatio: Supputatio calumniarum Natalis Bedae

Vidua christiana
Virginis et martyris comparatio
Vita Hieronymi: Vita diui Hieronymi Stridonensis

Index

This book

was designed by

ALLAN FLEMING

and was printed by

University of

Toronto

Press